D1479828

"Explaining CHINA"

by Steve Allen

Copyright © 1980 by Steve Allen

A Herbert Michelman Book

CROWN PUBLISHERS, INC.
NEW YORK

Inquiries should be addressed to Crown Publishers, Inc.,
One Park Avenue, New York, New York 10016

Printed in the United States of America

Published simultaneously in Canada by General Publishing Company Limited

Library of Congress Cataloging in Publication Data

Allen, Steven, 1921–
"Explaining China".

"A Herbert Michelman book".
Bibliography: p.
Includes index.
1. China—Description and travel—1976–
2. Allen, Steve, 1921– I. Title.
DS712.A44   1980   915.1'0457   80-10429
ISBN: 0-517-540622

10 9 8 7 6 5 4 3 2 1

First Edition

I am indebted to Rose Avallone, of my office staff, for her untiring efforts at transcribing my dictated copy, typing it and keeping the sprawling manuscript in order, and to Herb Michelman of Crown Publishers for his wise editorial assistance.

All photographs are taken by Steve Allen and Bill Allen except for those otherwise designated.

Book design by Shari De Miskey

Copyright © 1980 by Steve Allen

All rights reserved. No part of this book may be reproduced or utilized in any form or by any means, electronic or mechanical, including photocopying, recording, or by any information storage and retrieval system, without permission in writing from the publisher.

Inquiries should be addressed to Crown Publishers, Inc., One Park Avenue, New York, New York 10016

Printed in the United States of America

Published simultaneously in Canada by General Publishing Company Limited

Library of Congress Cataloging in Publication Data

Allen, Steven, 1921–
"Explaining China."

"A Herbert Michelman book."
Bibliography: p.
Includes index.
1. China—Description and travel—1976–
2. Allen, Steve, 1921–   I. Title.
DS712.A44   1980   915.1'0457   80-10429
ISBN: 0-517-540622

10 9 8 7 6 5 4 3 2 1

First Edition

To the Reverend and Mrs. Francis J. Cotter,
who devoted years of their life in loving
service to China

BOOKS by STEVE ALLEN

BOP FABLES	*Simon and Schuster*
FOURTEEN FOR TONIGHT	*Henry Holt & Co.*
THE FUNNY MEN	*Simon and Schuster*
WRY ON THE ROCKS	*Henry Holt & Co.*
THE GIRLS ON THE TENTH FLOOR	*Henry Holt & Co.*
THE QUESTION MAN	*Bellmeadows Press, with Bernard Geis Associates*
MARK IT AND STRIKE IT	*Holt, Rinehart & Winston*
NOT ALL OF YOUR LAUGHTER, NOT ALL OF YOUR TEARS	*Bernard Geis Associates*
LETTER TO A CONSERVATIVE	*Doubleday & Co.*
THE GROUND IS OUR TABLE	*Doubleday & Co.*
BIGGER THAN A BREADBOX	*Doubleday & Co.*
A FLASH OF SWALLOWS	*Droke House*
THE WAKE	*Doubleday & Co.*
PRINCESS SNIP-SNIP AND THE PUPPYKITTENS	*Platt & Munk*
CURSES	*J. P. Tarcher*
SCHMOCK, SCHMOCK	*Doubleday & Co.*
WHAT TO SAY WHEN IT RAINS	*Price, Stern & Sloan*
MEETING OF MINDS	*Hubris House–Crown Publishers*
RIPOFF!	*Lyle Stuart*
MEETING OF MINDS, SECOND SERIES	*Crown Publishers*
"EXPLAINING CHINA"	*Crown Publishers*

Contents

Even if I were licensed to record everything I heard from Mao it would not "explain China."

—Edgar Snow

I am one of those who are very willing to be refuted if I say anything which is not true, and very willing to refute anyone else who says what is not true, and quite as ready to be refuted as to refute; for I hold that this is the greatest gain of the two, just as the gain is greater of being cured of a very great evil than of curing another. For I imagine that there is no evil which a man can endure so great as an erroneous opinion.

—Socrates

While no one person can grasp the truth adequately, we cannot all fail in the attempt. Each thinker makes some statement about nature, and as an individual contributes little or nothing to the inquiry. But the combination of all the conjectures results in something big. . . . It is only fair to be grateful not only to those whose views we can share, but also to those who have gone pretty far wrong in their guesses. They, too, have contributed something.

—Aristotle

Introduction

THE title of this book—despite quotation marks—will perhaps strike China experts and scholars as presumptuous. But I would not presume to explain anything whatever to those better informed than I on the subject. The lamentable fact is that 99 percent of the American people have been dreadfully poorly informed about China. That being the case, almost anyone who has visited the country, who has done even a moderate amount of reading about it and who has devoted some time to speculation about what he has seen and heard is in fact qualified to enlighten those who know nothing of the subject.

The present volume naturally could not hope to explain all of China. A library of a thousand works would not be equal to that task. This necessarily sketchy outline therefore is meant primarily as an introduction for readers to whom China is foreign in every sense. Such a book might be profitably examined if it dealt with Iceland, Ecuador or Zambia. If the proper study of mankind is man, as indeed it is, then we ought to know about our brothers and sisters all over the planet. But whereas increasing one's knowledge about the three above-mentioned countries might in itself be a stimulating pursuit, it could scarcely be de-

scribed as of paramount importance in the context of today's serious international tensions. Increasing our knowledge of China, however, is literally a matter of life and death. An incredibly important social experiment has been taking place in that nation for thirty years. Its success or failure has crucial implications for every American. The importance of the present volume, then, lies totally in its subject matter: it makes no claims of a literary, journalistic or philosophical nature. The serious reader would be well advised to set this book aside at once and proceed to the writings of scholars who have devoted a lifetime to study of a land whose history—from antiquity to the present moment—comprises an almost incredible drama. Consider what happened to China in just one recent year—1976:

• The death of one of the most influential world leaders of the modern era, who as Mao Tse-tung's chief aide remade his country in his own lifetime, Chou En-lai.

• The death of the nation's most prominent military hero, a survivor of the famous Long March and founder of the Red Army, General Chu Teh.

• The brief reemergence from ill favor to supreme power of Teng Hsiao-ping, who welcomed President Gerald Ford to China and not long thereafter was, for the second time in less than ten years, consigned to darkness (only to be resurrected again in early 1977).

• The death of Mao Tse-tung, a leader almost deified by the majority of Chinese and considered, even by his enemies, a figure of heroic and decisive importance in modern history.

• A series of violent earthquakes that killed hundreds of thousands and caused untold property damage.

• The sudden fall from power of Mao's widow, Chiang Ching, and her "radical" colleagues—the so-called Gang of Four—an event that not only took even lifelong China scholars by surprise but plunged China into social unrest as the newly installed Premier Hua Kuo-feng, assisted by the military, attempted to assert the authority of the more moderate faction of the Chinese leadership.

And—among other surprising events—there have been: the cataclysmic upheaval of the late 1960s called the Great Proletarian Cultural Revolution; the unexpected opening of China's doors to the United States, confirmed by a formal diplomatic understanding on January 1, 1979; the growing nuclear strength of the ancient Middle Kingdom; increasing bitterness following the sharp break with the Soviet Union in 1960; the death of Nationalist leader Chiang Kai-shek; the breaking of our treaty with Taiwan; the radical revision of Maoist policies by the increasingly powerful Teng Hsiao-ping, and more.

Although those large, dramatic events were, of course, reported in the Western media, it is nevertheless almost impossible to exaggerate the general American ignorance about China. Having once shared that ignorance, I am familiar with the view from both sides of the issue, but I do not believe it would be an outrageous exaggeration to say that the average American knows as much about the moon as he knows about a nation with a 5,000-year history and the world's largest population.

An instructive instance is recalled by John B. Powell, in his *My 25 Years in China*. In 1920, Powell, an American journalist, traveled

from Shanghai to the United States for the purpose of establishing advertising contacts. A few days before his sailing, J. Harold Dollar, of the Dollar Steamship interests, and Carl Seitz, American lumber merchant, told Powell that they wanted him to go to Washington to "put through a China trade act, providing federal incorporation for American concerns doing business in the Far East."

Powell accepted the assignment and en route stopped over briefly in Chicago to visit Colonel Robert McCormick of the *Chicago Tribune* who, when he learned about the China trade matter, immediately set up an appointment for Powell to meet President-elect Warren Harding in Marion, Ohio. When Powell entered Harding's drawing room, he explained, as briefly as possible, the purpose of his visit. Harding, Powell reports, "listened with unexpected interest and told me he had always been curious about China because he had an aunt who had been a missionary in that country. I found out afterward his aunt had been a missionary in India, but I had become accustomed to having Americans confuse India with China, and even with Africa, when it came to the matter of missionaries."

I am grateful to my wife, Jayne, for many things, not the least of which is introducing me to the Chinese people. Because she was born in China, it was natural that she would have a number of Chinese friends. Over the twenty-five years of our marriage, therefore, I have been able to share this good fortune with her. It is unfortunate that millions of Americans will go through their lifetimes without even meeting a Chinese. A great many will come into contact with Chinese-Americans, of course, but will never encounter a citizen of mainland China.

Great numbers of Americans, to the extent that they give their fellow citizens of Chinese ancestry any thought at all, do so through the filter of racial prejudice. The average American, if he is honest on the point, would concede that he feels superior to the Chinese he meets. But this attitude, I believe, grows more out of a sense of class than racial or ethnic distinction. Because almost all emigrants from

China for the last century have been impoverished peasants from the southern provinces, it was only natural that they would take jobs as menials: hand laborers, laundry workers, servants, restaurant help. It was these groups from which Americans created their image of the Chinese-American.

Lest the Chinese feel in any way singled out in this regard, they should know that precisely the same fate befell generations of Irish, Italians, Eastern Europeans and others who came to the U.S. from the poor farms and ghettos of Europe.

Like the earlier European immigrants, the present generation of Chinese-Americans has produced its share of artists, doctors, lawyers, authors, educators, scientists, scholars, engineers and businessmen. Not only is there therefore no basis for the feeling of superiority that some of us manifest toward the Chinese, one could make out a strong case for just the reverse. Indeed, since most people base ideas of their superiority on the achievements of their group rather than themselves as individuals, it would be a rash European or American who would assert that the glories of his ethnic culture are superior to those of the Chinese.

China achieved a high degree of scholarship, technical proficiency and dazzling artistic accomplishment thousands of years ago. European man stepped out of the primitive forest, comparatively speaking, only yesterday. Even the brief glory of ancient Greece and the military grandeur of Rome were hardly representative of the general record of the barbarous tribes of Europe. These few factors suggest the difficulty of focusing on a true rather than distorted picture of China and its people.

If the informed reader will pardon the digression, a preliminary word is necessary concerning the impossibility of arriving at general agreement as to "the truth" of any large and complex social drama. As those with legal experience will be aware, it is remarkably difficult to determine the facts of even the simplest cases. In the absence of a four-camera, full-color, stereo-sound record of what transpired, those who attempt to ascertain what did occur

in any given instance must depend either upon physical evidence or the testimony of witnesses, and if there is anything less reliable than the unaided human memory, even in the presence of the most virtuous intentions, it is difficult to think what it might be.

I am not deluded, therefore, that this book is reporting "the truth" about modern China. There is disagreement among the most distinguished scholars on many particulars. The best one can hope to achieve is to give as factual and unbiased a report as possible about the small minority of people, places and events one has been privileged to regard. And even if some sort of record unprecedented in its accuracy and fairness is compiled, it can progress no further than the page in its relatively pristine form. Ten thousand readers of that record will, alas, subsequently give ten thousand separate interpretations as to what they have read. Given the depressing variety of psychological barriers to accurate communication, it is not in the least surprising that humans communicate so haltingly. The astounding thing is that we ever get anything straight at all.

There is a cliché apparently impossible to avoid when the traveler sets out to write a report on whatever part of the world he may have visited. In referring to the length of his stay in a foreign country he invariably observes, with the faintest possible touch of humor, that such a brief visit "hardly makes me an expert" on the area in question. After which he generally conducts himself very much as if he were an expert.

I stress at the outset—largely for Chinese readers—that the observations and assumptions that follow are purely personal. There is nothing the least bit official about them, nor have I any idea to what extent other American visitors to China might share them. I assume, however, that most of my comments will seem generally reasonable to the majority of American readers. For that reason only they might make for better communication between the people of China and the United States.

Communists, except Vietnamese, Soviet and certain other European Communists, will want this report to consist of unqualified praise for the modern Chinese experiment. Anti-Communists will wish to read nothing but criticism. Apparently the majority in both camps has insufficient interest in the truth. Just as all individuals are a combination of good and evil, so it is with societies. One of the many reasons for the present misery and confusion of the human predicament is that for three decades the mainland Chinese have heard little but the propaganda of praise about their own programs, whereas most Americans have heard nothing but negative criticism of the Chinese experiment. Both camps are therefore to a degree deluded.

It would be absurd to attempt to paint an accurate picture of what life is like in China if one determined, from the start, to make no critical observations whatsoever.

Turn the situation around. Imagine that a Chinese has been sent to New York and told to give his honest impressions of it. Could he possibly do so by referring only to the beauties of Manhattan's rivers, the U.N. building, the handsome skyscrapers, Central Park, Fifth Avenue, the harbor, the Statue of Liberty, the swank apartments and town houses on the East Side? Obviously not. In addition to writing of the virtues and glories of the city, he would also be obliged, by every conceivable standard, to report on the Black and Puerto Rican slums, the danger of walking the streets at night, the depredations of organized crime, the daily traffic snarls, the heroin-addiction nightmare, the paralyzing labor strikes, the general deterioration in civic services and the other ugly factors that now characterize New York City life.

Just so, it would be absurd for the Chinese to assume that visitors to their country could possibly write accounts consisting entirely of complimentary observations. One must, out of respect for truth, tell not only what is good and admirable about China but also what, to the visitor, seems unfortunate about it. Indeed, a good many Chinese concede as much. "Ours is not a perfect society," they say; "we have much to learn. Much remains to be accomplished. We welcome your criticisms so long as they are constructive and not spiteful."

One of the reasons for American ignorance about China, of course, is our general lack of knowledge about communism and socialism. Considering the incredible barrage of anti-Communist propaganda to which all living Americans have been subjected for the greater part of their lives, it is remarkable how little information we have been given about the *causes* of communism. That one fundamental error by the defenders of the capitalist system has led to widespread confusion accompanied by an enormous amount of emotion wrapped in surprisingly little factual information. Fellow ignoramuses of the world, let us unite! We have nothing to lose but our striking naïveté about everyday principles of economic philosophy. I must here beg the indulgence of the reader sophisticated about the dominant human debate of the last century. I address chiefly those to whom literacy has meant primarily a means of confirming their prejudices.

I spoofed this ignorance, too often encountered even in high places, in one of the "Senator Philip Buster" comedy sketches on my television show.

"Senator," Jayne says, "there's a great deal of concern in this country just now about Sino-Soviet relations. How do you view that problem?"

"Well," the senator responds, "I consider myself quite knowledgeable about this matter because I have made a careful study of Soviet foreign policy and in fact have just returned from a trip to the Soviet Union."

"I see."

"Of course," the senator adds, "I admit I have never been to Sino."

On another show the following exchange took place:

JAYNE: Senator, do you think the United States should defend Taiwan against attack?

SENATOR: Miss Meadows, I take a very firm stand on that particular issue. I personally would fight to the death to defend *Taiwan,* but I would not permit one American fighting man to be sent to protect *Formosa!*

You may remember that this is consistent with my stand on Quemoy and Matsu. We must continue to defend Quemoy, but the sooner we wash our hands of Matsu, the better!

I became a China watcher, as I have mentioned, through meeting Jayne. That phrase "China watcher," by the way, has an odd sound. I do not recall having heard of Japan watchers, Germany watchers or Argentina watchers. I do not recall even having heard of Russia watchers, though there are such. Apparently the term came about because there was a unique reason to observe the modern Chinese experiment. Certainly there is a peculiar fascination with its failures and successes.

I set about satisfying my own curiosity, in 1965, by doing two things: reading widely and voraciously about China, and exploring the possibility of visiting the country. It took me ten years to receive permission to enter this nation that had for so long been closed to Westerners—opened for a brief period of history—then closed again.

When I finally was permitted to make the trip I had to do so—you will laugh—as a rug dealer.

Here is how it came to pass.

One of our Chinese friends is an interesting lady named Lily Wen. She is the wife of a brilliant scientist, Wen Kwan Sun. (With Chinese names the last name is given first. Teng Hsiao-ping, for example, would be Mr. Teng, not Mr. Ping or Mr. Hsiao-ping.)

Lily's family has lived through the incredible drama of modern China. Her father, a military officer and high official of the old regime, fought the Communists and was killed by them.

Her mother, a beautiful, refined and resourceful woman, adapted to the new regime and holds a position of honor in her homeland. She has four intelligent, attractive daughters: Lily; film-worker Irene (Tung Kuo-ying), who has lived in Peking; Mary, a concert pianist, and Renata, a librarian with an M.A. degree from Columbia University.

It was this family that, after three years of effort, was able to help in arranging for Jayne and me to visit a carpet and rug exhibition scheduled for March, 1975, in Tientsin, a city on the northeast coast of China that a year later would be struck by a devastating earthquake. But to qualify, it was necessary, of course, that we actually be in the importing business. Lily and Jayne therefore finally formed the East-West Carpet Company, which they had discussed a couple of years earlier. I joined them, and in we went, for an unforgettable experience.

My fondness for the Chinese people increased. I was fascinated by all that I saw. The fact that I personally would still rather live in, say, Seattle than Shanghai would be meaningless to the Chinese. Many individual Chinese, if they understood totally the specifics of the choice, might prefer Seattle themselves. But that is speculation. As regards reality, they have no opportunity to appreciate the comparative factors involved, nor do they have freedom to act upon such a choice if they knew how to make it. Life, for all of us, is a daily matter of selecting among available alternatives. If a man was faced with only two possibilities, being hit on the head with a lead pipe or a wooden stick, he would choose to be hit with the stick. A passerby, not knowing of the narrowness of choice, would of course be puzzled by the spectacle.

So, after ten years of intermittent effort, I was accepted. Subsequently—again through the good offices of the Tung family—we were invited for a second visit, in July, 1975. In February, 1979, I returned again. This book is a report of our travels and adventures. I am grateful to my Chinese hosts for permitting me to enter their country three times when thousands of Americans, many highly placed, have not succeeded in getting a visa.

It will occur to many Americans to wonder why travel to China is presently still so restricted. Practically all other countries, so the thinking goes, are anxious to increase their tourist trade. Many, in fact, depend so heavily on tourism that they carry on powerful advertising campaigns in more affluent parts of the world, encouraging vast armies of tourists to invade the host territory. The point is that the same considerations do not yet apply in China, though they may soon. There are not enough hotels, for one thing, and even if there were, the Chinese would have a serious shortage of translators. Americans tend to think of this as being nothing more than a matter of training a few thousand more young Chinese to speak English. But of course they must also be taught to speak French, German, Italian, Japanese, Spanish, Russian, Arabic and other languages as well. The Chinese have made remarkable strides in this very area; any perceptive visitor will be impressed by the variety of languages spoken by his Chinese hosts. We Americans are, of course, the worst linguists in the world, largely because of our geographical and psychological insularity. The Chinese, over the centuries, have been even more isolationist than ourselves and until quite recently in their history shared the American failing as linguists. That is all changed now, of course, but it will still be some time before any large percentage of those who wish to visit the Middle Kingdom will be allowed to do so.

One reason I consider myself fortunate in having made three separate visits to mainland China is that the second and third permitted me to correct certain errors in thinking and observation committed during the first. The total drabness of attire noted in midwinter, for example, proved to be related partly to the bitter cold of North China. And certain customs I had assumed to be common to the nation turned out to be merely regional.

It is easy for the traveler to assume that something accurately enough observed in one city, or perhaps two or three, is therefore true of a nation as a whole. A Chinese visitor to the United States, going first to a small town in Texas, might leap to the conclusion that most American men wear cowboy boots. If he visited Las Vegas he would assume that almost all Americans gamble heavily. A visit to a small Kansas community would lead him to believe that most Americans are conservative Republicans. I have tried to avoid this sort of error but would not be surprised to learn that I have not been totally successful.

These comments should lead you to question my political biases. Not my motives but my past social conditioning and the general political outlook to which it has largely given rise.

To deal with the reader's most obvious question first: I am a product of the Great American Anti-Communist Machine. From the age of six I have been preached at, lectured to and, on rare occasions, even instructed about—no, not communism, but the evils of communism. Perhaps no one not reared in the American lower-middle-class, Studs Lonigan, big-city Irish Catholic culture can adequately grasp how effective this unceasing indoctrination is —or was—for the millions who have lived with it. Communism becomes, to those so propagandized, a vast conspiratorial, monolithic, warlike, diabolical atrocity to be vigorously and, if necessary, violently opposed.

As for the crucial question: What *caused* communism?—not, I swear it, not a word.

Eventually I was able to locate published material which, though anti-Marxist, or anti-Soviet, was at least not an insult to the intelligence. Millions never press on to that stage.

In any event, though sorry to disappoint rightist readers, I am on published record as an anti-Communist since schooldays. The special fortieth-anniversary edition of *Esquire* (1973) includes a lengthy debate on the subject of communism between the late screenwriter Dalton Trumbo and me in which I said:

I concede my strong anti-Communist bias. Since there are those seriously afflicted by the Either-or disease—a malady apparently as common on the political Left as it is on the Right—I am therefore obliged to state that my opposition to political tyranny does indeed take in all 360 degrees of the circle that stretches to the political horizon, which is to say that I am also revolted by Nazism, Fascism and McCarthyism. It is all very well for Communists to resent the criticisms of Liberals and Democratic Socialists; the hard fact remains that Liberals and Democratic Socialists in power do *not* send Communists to execution chambers and political prisons; whereas Communists in power—in country after country—do indeed exercise a barbarous vengeance against those members of the non-Communist Left whom the Communists correctly identify as their true rivals for the political affections of the masses.

It would be to a degree irrelevant and presumptuous here to review the political history of the last half-century but I cannot conceive how any true Liberal, being familiar with that history, could be anything but anti-Communist. As a Liberal, I am in favor of freedom of the press, freedom of speech, and of freedom of assemblage. But I know of no Communist society in which such freedoms exist. I am also opposed to the death penalty, as are most Liberals, but it is clear that Communist societies cannot function without the threat, and frequently the reality, of state murder. As a Liberal I am suspicious of official censorship, but I observe that it is harshly dominant in all Communist cultures. . . . The civil liberties the ACLU so courageously defends are not the foundation-stones of any existing Marxist society. . . .

You delay an approach to the essence of our argument by raising the irrelevant question as to whether Mr. Schlesinger would distinguish, in his disapproval, among Communism of the Russian, Chinese, Yugoslavian, Czechoslovakian, Hungarian, Albanian, Roumanian or Cuban sort. That no two of these are precisely similar is obvious enough, but the large question is no more necessary than would be the question as to whether, in your disapproval of Fascism, you would be more or less tolerant of it in its German, Italian, Spanish, Japanese or Argentine guise.

It is irrelevant to our purposes—or to mine, at least—to waste time considering the different dictionary meanings of "Communism," the first letter capitalized or not. Obviously there is always a difference between the purely theoretical statement of a philosophy on the one hand and its flesh-and-blood embodiment on the other. In every historical case the ideal is superior to the practice. I see no purpose, therefore, in debating the abstract philosophy of socialism or Communism. What I am here interested in is the undeniably clear record of Communism-in-practice and with—more specifically—the activities of the American Communist party, a political instrument which over the years is on record as endorsing the Hitler-Stalin pact, justifying the Soviet attacks on Poland and Finland, opposing Lend-Lease aid to Europe and assistance to Great Britain before Hitler's surprise attack on Russia, attempting to sweep under the rug of history Stalin's slaughter of millions in his domain, bitter opposition to Franklin Roosevelt during the period of the Soviet-Nazi pact, opposition to the Marshall Plan (Communists wanted Western Europe to collapse, not recover), serving as apologists for the Moscow trials, the crushing of the Hungarian rebellion, the Soviet invasion of Czechoslovakia, and all the rest of the sickening list.

Liberals may or may not be opposed in principle to the *economic* theory of Communism (though they will look in vain for evidence of its concrete realization). But by the very definition of the word *liberal* they are logically obliged to oppose the omnipresent despotism of Communist *political* practice and belief. A liberal, as such, may be an atheist, or a devout religionist. But the one thing he cannot possibly be is an apologist for the ruthless imposition of Communist minority party rule that for more than half a century has characterized the exercise of Marxist authority.

That is not to say that Communists, or socialists of other kinds, are wrong in all their criticisms of capitalist practice, or of American foreign or domestic policies. For many years Western capitalism has propped itself up with a certain amount of socialist timber, and Western democracy has come to understand that—mutual annihilation by either nuclear or conventional weapons being an unacceptable alternative—it will have to come to some sort of terms with the Marxist powers. The more responsible elements in each camp, then, may hope that the other side will mellow and evolve.

The last thing I will say on this point, for the present, is that even if a liberal were unable to perceive that reason demands his opposition to all forms of tyranny, he ought to be anti-Communist simply because Communists are anti-liberal. When Stalin's armies enlarged the Soviet sphere of influence at the conclusion of the Second World War they almost ignored Conservatives, Reactionaries, Nazis, and Fascists in the areas that came under their control. These pathetic souls had already been defeated, slaughtered in great numbers by the process of war itself, or done in by their own underground movements. The few remaining were in disgrace as having sympathized with Hitler and accordingly posed no threat to Stalin's legions and indigenous Communists. The true threat came from non-Communist socialists and liberal democrats who—though anti-Nazi to the core—enjoyed a popular following and therefore were rivals for the affections of the liberated masses. It was these unfortunates who suffered most tragically at the hands of the Soviet "liberators."

Well, these are certainly hard words and their meaning is plain enough. Moreover, they are consistent with everything I have written on the subject since at the age of seventeen I had a letter published in that bastion of reaction, the *Chicago Tribune,* concerning what I viewed as Communist infiltration of youth groups in that city's Hyde Park High School, which I then attended.

Nevertheless, though the reader may now find it hard to believe, I have been for the last twenty-five years regularly attacked by the kind of political dunces who, sad to say, comprise a remarkably large percentage of the American right-wing movement. I naturally do not refer to conservative intellectuals who, being by and large educated and respectful of evidence, are practiced at making those political distinctions which both common sense and morality require. But conservative intellectuals in the United States are sadly few in number. I wish there were a great many more of them and have, toward that end, attempted for years to convert John Birch-type American reactionaries to the true conservative movement—although my own position on most significant issues can be described as progressive—primarily by urging them to stop reading the paranoid trash by which they have been victimized and subscribe instead to periodicals such as *National Review,* which, though it has often made me grit my teeth, nevertheless generally presents a rational rendering of the American conservative philosophy. Actually I know the American reactionaries better than I know conservatives since I come from among them, being a product of that portion of the American sector that was, in the 1930s, totally under the influence of the anti-Semite Father Coughlin.

One regrets having to take up several pages in clarifying this point, but it is necessary to do so because millions of Americans are incapable of accepting the assurance that two and two equal four unless they have run a security check on the mathematics instructor. Now on to more important matters.

I visited China—despite my social conditioning—with as open a mind as possible. One prejudice I succeeded in divesting myself of was that unfortunately common one among my fellow Christians, the assumption that, in some never-quite-defined way, God himself takes such a personal interest in our economic survival that he practically flies the American flag outside the pearly gates. There have been frequent examples in history of individual Frenchmen, Germans, Americans, Jews, Italians or whatever actually suggesting that God was with them, to the exclusion of other nations, in an armed conflict. If God has any daily personal interest whatever in human military conflict his reaction can only be one of horror. The same kind of absurd thinking has in recent years been advocated by conservatives who apparently assume that the deity has some special interest in the preservation of the free enterprise or capitalist system. To begin with, the proper attitude of capitalists toward God Almighty would be one of abject humility and shame for the countless economic atrocities perpetrated for purely selfish rather than moral motives. But the worldwide economic debate is confusing enough on its own merits. It is quite nonsensical to presume to speak for God by attempting to drag Him into the issue.

The only practical standard of judgment for an economic system is precisely the one commonly used to evaluate any system: the factor of practicality. We must be pragmatists rather than moralists when it comes to economics. If a system works, it is good. If it does not work, it is not good.

I prefer the free enterprise system to that of the totalitarian version of socialism because it has produced—in our own country, at least, if not in a great many others—a remarkably high standard of living for the majority. Second, I have the personal peculiarity of not wishing to be dictated to, by anyone. I enjoy being debated with and am perfectly willing to listen to attempts to persuade me to one course of action or another. But as for orders issued with a no-back-talk clause, I have rebelled against them since early childhood.

The more or less capitalist structure of the American economy seems to work reasonably well for us, despite its creakings and groanings in the late 1970s. It cannot simply be plugged in and turned on, however, like some sort of magical prosperity machine, in primitive, poverty-stricken and underdeveloped societies. The capitalists of pre-1949 China have little to be proud of and an enormous collection of acts and policies for which they should be ashamed.

Nothing I have said to this point may be taken as suggesting that Chinese-U.S. tensions for the last thirty years have been solely or largely the fault of capitalists, Christians or other anti-Communists. The Chinese have been party to the general breakdown of accord. But now that the "thaw" has begun, each side is obliged to renew efforts to understand the other. If we make the attempt we will come to understand some of the reasons for Chinese wariness toward pale-faced visitors.

It is extremely difficult for Americans—and some Europeans as well—to think rationally about China. The primary reason, of course, is that we carry into the moment of thought a heavy burden of prejudice, bias, distortion and ignorance.

Consider, by way of clarification, the concept of an occupied nation. Recall the French resentment at the German occupation during World War II. Well, for a great many years China was an occupied nation, in which the British, French, Portuguese, Germans, Russians, Dutch, Italians, Japanese and Americans occupied territory, did whatever business they wished to and generally had their way, simply because the Chinese rulers were too weak to risk military retaliation by foreign intruders. Somehow, from our utterly biased point of view, all of this may not seem an especially terrible thing. It is true that a good many warm-hearted individuals—missionaries, doctors and educators, for example—were part of this European and American cultural invasion. Jayne's father and mother spent thirteen years in China, working hard in often painful and dangerous conditions, to bring the message of Christianity to the Chinese. If all visiting Westerners had been like the Reverend and Mrs. Cotter the modern world would no doubt have been spared at least some of its present difficulties. The fact is that only a small percentage of the Western invaders were so high-minded.

But suppose that the invaded territory had not been that of China but of the United States, that around the year 1800 Chinese and Japanese gunboats had begun to sail into the harbors of Seattle, San Francisco, Los Angeles and San Diego, to put military officers and troops ashore, to take over sizable areas of real estate, and to open up powerful corporate business enterprises. Suppose further that they employed poverty-stricken American workers at very low wages, treated them with contempt, sold them massive amounts of narcotics, and forced the terms of this shocking social experiment on weak rulers in Washington.

It would be absolutely inevitable that patriotic bands of Americans would spring up around the country with no motive more sinister than the wish to throw the foreign invaders out, including their minority of well-intentioned missionaries who had opened, let us assume, Buddhist, Taoist and Confucianist schools that were converting many heretofore Christian children and adults to Oriental philosophies.

Perhaps by concentrating for a few minutes on such a fantasy we can begin to understand modern Chinese attitudes toward certain questions.

It has been clear for some time that perhaps the paramount internal question facing Western man is: Are we civilized enough, compassionate enough, to continue to live in freedom? At some point will we come to assume that the price of freedom has become too high? Naturally one hopes not. But could we eventually believe that there is too much crime, too much corruption, too much poverty, pollution, drug-trafficking, pornography, inefficiency, selfishness, ignorance, delinquency and social chaos of all kinds to continue with a system that was effective enough in simpler times? If we do come to that point there will be no shortage of voices—on Left and Right—preaching Law and Order vs. Freedom.

One of the profound differences between the United States and China, in this connection, is that in our country a great many people seem to be unaccounted for. There is much isolation, loneliness and alienation in America. Thousands of young people run away from home and wander our streets and highways. The very old may live and die alone. In every large American city one sees strange, lost souls, defeated, walking the streets, prowling the alleys, looking through garbage cans, behaving eccentrically. In modern China, on the other hand, almost everyone seems to fit into one social system or another. It is easy to dismiss this as simply a matter of being watched over by Big Brother. The state does indeed intrude into all walks of life. But it urges the Chinese, with evident success, to *care about each other.*

American reader, have you begun to feel uncomfortable?

In the analysis of any Communist-Socialist society it is evidently impossible to avoid reference to Lincoln Steffens's observation, after an early return from Russia, that "I have been over into the future and it works," sometimes rendered as "I have seen the future and it works." On the basis of my own visit to the Soviet Union I say rather that if I have seen the future it has certainly gotten all screwed up. Strangely, one did not—in the late 1970s—get that same feeling from a study of the Chinese situation. Being prejudiced by past experience, I would not wish to live permanently in either the People's Republic of China or the Soviet Union—among many other states dominated by Left or Right—but if obliged to make a choice I would select the Chinese alternative. The sense of failure, oppression and treading water that one draws from the Russian experiment does not follow a visit to China. There is not the slightest prospect, in the foreseeable future, that the Chinese prescription will be applicable to America's economic and social ills. In 1975 I noted that it was more likely that the Chinese would revert—to some extent—to capitalist practice, as the Maoist leaders themselves daily warned, but that is only speculation. As regards the present realities, there is no question but that the Chinese experiment is working, according to the sensible standard, that of *comparison*—not to a perfect ideal— *but to pre-Revolutionary conditions in China.*

Lastly, at the risk of seeming to cop out, I believe it fair to explain that this book was for the most part written during 1975 and 1976— the first draft dictated into recording equipment in China—but during a time in which I was writing an autobiography, a novel, doing

two television series, entertaining in theaters and nightclubs and composing a great deal of music. These factors, coupled with a complete absence of academic or scholarly assistance, make it inevitable that the present account can be only a personal narrative supported by factual information and interpretation derived for the most part, though by no means exclusively, from research.

Inasmuch as the early drafts of the manuscript of this report were based on perceived realities as of 1975–1976, I was originally distressed that the exacting press of numerous other professional obligations had delayed presentation of the book, in ready-to-print form, to a publisher so that it could have come out in 1977. Though attention to important news emanating from the mainland in 1977 and 1978 required updating the manuscript, I was nevertheless not happy about the delay. The remarkable restoration of the power of Teng Hsiao-ping in the latter half of 1978, however, made me realize that it was fortunate indeed that *"Explaining China"* had not been published in 1977, for the reversal of many Maoist policies, an accelerating process which began with the arrest of Chiang Ching and the Gang of Four, the whole dizzying series of changes both within China and in the larger context of China's relations with the world, meant that any generalized report that failed to take such developments into account would quickly have been seen as both out of date and unbalanced.

Another odd benefit of the delay in publication has been that the viewer may now make comparisons between China as its social affairs were conducted during the Gang of Four period and the last three years. It is important, in this connection, to grasp that much of the 1977 to 1980 Chinese criticism of the Gang of Four is actually criticism of Mao. But the Chinese are now paying a price for having deified the chairman for so many years and that is that the new rulers must be very careful about the choice of words employed when attacking Mao's programs. The Gang of Four is a convenient scapegoat and indeed deserves such criticism—at least within the context of Hua-Teng bias—but the ultimate authority for the now-criticized programs nevertheless was Mao Tse-tung himself.

At this point it wouldn't be the worst thing in the world—at least for the more scholarly reader—to turn to Chapter 12, "The Cultural Revolution," and read it first since virtually everything of a factual nature reported in this volume needs to be interpreted in the context of that great social upheaval which lasted, roughly speaking, from 1966 to 1976.

As for sources depended upon, they are, for the most part, referred to in the text. A fuller listing is given in the Selected Bibliography. Footnotes have been avoided simply because the book is intended for the general rather than scholarly reader.

The informed reader will note that I have adhered to traditional Romanized spellings of the names of places and individuals in China. The reason is that this report is intended for the general American reader who will be familiar with the old, not the new, versions. China belongs to the Chinese, who naturally may change or clarify the Western spellings of their words as they choose. But to the average resident of the U.S., China's capital city is still Peking and not Beijing. I have frequently included the Pinyin spellings in the first use of place names not listed below. Within another few years the new system will perhaps have been generally adopted all over the world. For those who care, here are a few instances of long-familiar proper names and their new equivalents.

NAMES

OLD	NEW
Chiang Ching	Jiang Qing
Chou En-lai	Zhou Enlai
Hua Kuo-feng	Hua Guofeng
Liu Shao-chi	Liu Shaoqi
Mao Tse-tung	Mao Zedong
Sun Yat-sen	Sun Zhong Shan Ling
Teng Hsiao-ping	Deng Xiaoping

PLACES

OLD	NEW
Canton	Guangzhou
Hangchow	Hangzhou
Nanking	Nanjing
Peking	Beijing
Sian	Xian
Soochow	Suzhou
Tientsin	Quingdao
Yenan	Yanan

Oh, my last preparatory note:

In China, historical time may be reckoned in the context of the various dynasties. Since they are mentioned the reader should be at least generally familiar with them.

Hsia	21st to 18th century B.C.
Shang	18th to 12th century B.C.
Chou	12th century B.C. to 221 B.C.
Chin	221–206 B.C.
Han	206 B.C.–A.D. 220
The Three Kingdoms	220–280
Chin	265–420
The Six Dynasties	420–589

Sui	589–618
Tang	618–906
The Five Dynasties	907–960
Sung	960–1279
Mongol	1279–1368
Yuan	1260–1368
Ming	1368–1644
Ching (Manchu)	1644–1912

The First Journey

February, 1975

Part 1

The First Journey

February, 1975

1. From Japan to China

TOKYO

OUR excitement mounted as the time for the trip drew near. Jayne, working through her own Meadows Travel Agency in Los Angeles, had assembled a small group of American importers, decorators and merchants since the Chinese—with few exceptions—accept only groups, not individual travelers.

We had a meeting in our home one night to get to know each other and plan details of the trip. Two members of the party were personal friends, Mrs. Marge Levy and her lovely daughter, Victoria. Marge is a gifted interior decorator who works in Beverly Hills. Then there were Jerry Fisher, an executive of an industrial rug company, and his wife, Louise, who had been a teacher. Jerry looks like Steve McQueen, is a master of judo and karate, and eventually emerged as the chief officer of our group. His wife is sweet, pretty and affable.

A friend Lily Wen had invited from her home city of Santa Barbara, journalist Beverly Jackson, also joined us. Beverly is bright, loves to laugh and proved to be a good egg. The remaining two members of the party were Mrs. Helene Pollack, an interior decorator from Los Angeles, and Herbert Cole, who works with her.

The others left Los Angeles for Hong Kong on Saturday, February 22, 1975. Due to televi-

sion obligations I could not leave till February 24. Accordingly, I flew in through Tokyo rather than via the southern route. It's quicker but one misses the drama of passing from Hong Kong through the New Territories, crossing the long-closed border and going up to Canton on the train.

Jayne was ecstatic about the prospect of returning to her birthplace. Lily had gone ahead earlier and was waiting for the main party in Hong Kong.

The flight north out of Los Angeles was pleasant, uneventful. I suppose one of the reasons travel is so popular, at least among those who can afford it, is that it is stimulating. New sights, new sounds, new people, new experiences lift us out of our habits and complacencies. Sea travel generally relaxes me so that my mental computer—which ordinarily clicks along on its own mysterious rhythm all day long, with little nudging from my conscious will—is somehow wound down and relaxed. Air travel, on the other hand, makes the internal machinery race faster than ever.

Hugh Sidey, writing in the April, 1975, issue of *Travel & Leisure,* observed:

Height lessens the scars, dims the ugliness for almost anyone who wishes to be lifted out of himself. I have seen it bring color back into the faces of this nation's Presidents, my special study, as they soared over their troubles. Scowls have turned to smiles, and once again, as the surface receded, the problems of America seemed manageable. Some day, perhaps, a scholar will write of the therapeutic effect of airplanes on men of power. It is not hard to imagine the deep religious stirrings the astronauts felt as they fled from the earth and it shrank into a blue-and-white orb in their windows.

Although I do not often give thought to either political or religious matters while airborne, I do indeed reach heights of energetic creativity almost every time I fly, which is frequently. Since I ordinarily do not look out the window, such sights as are available can have no connection with my mood. I suspect the effect is produced by the so far not clearly understood effects of cabin air pressure or some other physical factor on the total human mechanism, including the brain cells.

About five minutes before our scheduled stop in San Francisco a flight attendant advised us that there would be a plane change.

Once on the ground I was pleased to see, in the Pan Am waiting area, a section marked "Reserved for Nonsmokers." The Japanese-American attendant who kindly helped with my extra hand luggage said, after I told him how pleased I was to see that the comfort of nonsmokers was considered important by Pan Am, "Well, you know who's responsible for this, don't you?"

"No, I don't," I said.

"You are," he said, "by your letters."

I had indeed written to Pan Am—and all other American airlines—suggesting no-smoking areas in waiting rooms.

"Thank you," I said. "That is music to my ears. And to my nose."

While sitting in the Pan Am waiting room, near Gate 28, I continued to prepare for the visit to China, in this instance by reading one of those remarkable books that have the power to clarify and simplify complex issues, *The New Cold War: Moscow vs. Pekin,* by Edward Crankshaw.

Written in 1963 by the London *Observer*'s correspondent on Soviet affairs, it sets out, in superbly rational terms, the background of that astounding drama, the Chinese Revolution, and its effect on both Soviet conduct and significant world events generally in modern times.

You should never travel anywhere, by the way, even to Cleveland, without reading about your destination first, preferably well in advance. Even the most casual pass at some relevant literature will have a striking effect on what you eventually see, hear and understand.

On the long flight from San Francisco to Japan I busied myself with further reading about China and studied pocket-size flash cards of Chinese words and phrases.

TOKYO

When we landed at Tokyo airport in midafternoon, I found I had two hours to kill before a bus could take me to my hotel. Outside the terminal, at the curb, I inspected the Japanese taxis. They were remarkably shiny, well groomed, immaculate compared to any American cabs more than three days old. With their bright colors and sleek lines they looked more like medium-priced sports cars. One of the reasons for their spotless condition became clear when a driver pulled up to the curb, parked, hopped out and immediately began wiping all exterior surfaces of his car with a large feather duster.

I felt in no way different walking the soil of Japan except for one strange fact. I had observed, on a trip to the Orient several years earlier, a sense of being much taller than I would have felt in, say, Boston or Kansas City. Being six feet three inches, I am tall even by American standards, but it is by no means uncommon for me to have to look up to other men, particularly in an age when tall, husky athletes abound. Not long ago I walked through a hotel lobby in Philadelphia, moving upstream, as it were, through the members of a professional football team coming into the hotel. I felt very short indeed at that moment. But in Japan I had a sensation of looming above the crowd which made me feel oddly conspicuous, although the Japanese, being more polite than Americans, did not stare.

A baggage dispatcher approached, near the terminal's bus waiting lounge, held out a piece of paper and said, "Sir, will you give me a sign?" It took a moment to translate his remark as a request for an autograph. Although my television programs have rarely been seen in Japan, I am known in the Orient as "Benny Goodman," having appeared in the motion picture version of the famous clarinetist's life. It turned out that an old videotape of a Judy Garland show on which Jayne and I had been guests had been telecast in Tokyo the previous week.

An interesting incident: as I stood on the sidewalk enjoying the brisk February air an American approached the orange-and-white airport service bus, carrying luggage. Instantly a bus attendant ran from the curb to his cockpit, got the keys and hurried to the side of the bus to open the baggage compartment. I cannot remember how many years it has been since I have seen any American service attendant *run* to accommodate a customer.

Tokyo is a pleasant, stimulating city to visit. Although it is one of the world's largest and most overcrowded cities, it is remarkably safe. Mugging is practically unheard of, and a woman walking alone, day or night, need have no fear, something no longer true in any sizable American city.

At ten minutes to five the bus for the Keiyo Plaza Hotel finally arrived. Within sixty seconds its few passengers had boarded and we left for the hotel. The drive to the city was fascinating. The Westernization, even Americanization, of Japan was much in evidence. To call this imperialism, even cultural imperialism, seems to me nonsense. It would be as reasonable to say that because my home is full of Japanese pens, radios, flashlights, TV sets, record players and tape recorders, because I drink Japanese wine and drive a Japanese car, I am a victim of Japanese imperialism.

Directly outside the airport one comes upon a river, the banks of which are lined with decrepit-looking small boats. The area is dominated chiefly, however, by enormous factories.

The freeway traffic jam we almost immediately ran into made me feel uncomfortably at home. A combination of ignorance and American cultural bias made me see the lettering on Japanese trucks and station wagons as "colorful." Because the printing was unintelligible, the graceful Japanese letters and numbers seemed charming abstract designs rather than the commercial pitches they actually were. I was reminded of G. K. Chesterton's observation when, half a century ago, he was taken to see the lights of Times Square. "What a beautiful sight," he said, "for a man who couldn't read."

It was one in the morning back home, 5:00 P.M. Tokyo time. I decided not to change my watch so that I could instantly tell, without having to calculate, what time it was in Los Angeles.

Except for those "quaint" old boats in the river and the Japanese lettering on signs, there was nothing distinctively Oriental or Japanese observable on the way in to the city. One could have been driving through the industrial section of almost any metropolis on the planet. There was the one obvious enough difference since all visible autos were Japanese, but there are now so many Datsuns, Toyotas, Hondas and Subarus on American roads that this did not seem striking. Far more noticeable was the fact that every car was clean and dust free. Presumably the Japanese keep their cars cleaner than we do for the same reason they keep their homes so immaculate.

To the right of the freeway was the gently curving track of a raised monorail and beneath it a now wider river, or inlet from the sea, full of thousands of rough logs. It was the kind of sight one sees in the United States only in rural logging communities.

The entire industrial area, with its factories, warehouses, loading docks, storage sheds, parking lots, now seemed crisscrossed by rivers and streams. Finally, about half an hour from the airport, we began to pass dwelling places, apartment buildings, schools. But even these were surrounded by factories, factories and more factories. And then yet further stretches of river, harbor, bay. It looked as if Detroit had been superimposed over Venice. The sense of industry, prosperity, bustle, was not all that strange to anyone accustomed to New York, Philadelphia, Chicago. But what, I wondered, do the Communist Chinese think of Tokyo, and modern Japan generally? Are they envious? Contemptuous? Puzzled?

Suddenly we turned left, passed over a wide expanse of railroad tracks, and were then on an elevated roadway in Tokyo proper. More factories, side by side with small and large apartment buildings. Apparently many Japanese can walk to work.

Here and there, among the sea of modernity, I noticed small tranquil-looking islands of antiquity, garden areas, tree-shaded, with gravel walks and the curved roofs of old-style Oriental buildings. Were they private homes? Public gardens?

From our high vantage point we could now look into the third, fourth and fifth floors of office buildings.

When China's present leaders insist that the nation is not at all a superpower—that it is, in fact, a primitive, underdeveloped country—they are not indulging in false modesty but speaking the truth. China is, of course, a very powerful backward country but backward nevertheless. Such terms are, obviously enough, relative. The word is meaningless until one asks: Backward compared to what? Well, clearly enough to the Western nations, but backward also compared to its nearby Asian neighbor, capitalist Japan.

We were next down on the street level, in a neighborhood of skyscrapers of the American sort. In large U.S. cities there is a sort of automatic division of territory according to function and class. There are industrial sections, large, beautiful, suburban neighborhoods, teeming lower-class ghettos, etc. But in Tokyo I could detect no such divisions. The classes, the functions, are all together, in one enormous, fascinating jumble.

The Keiyo Plaza was a brand-new, glitteringly beautiful hotel situated in the Shinjuku section of Tokyo. The area somewhat resembles New York's Park Avenue neighborhood in the mid-fifties, with its tall, ultramodern buildings. The Shinjuku Mitsui building—at fifty-five stories the tallest in the plaza, and in Asia—opened in late 1974. Other tall structures in the area were almost completed.

The hotel's food must be described as superb. For dinner I was served a succulent ham —two generous thick slices—spinach cooked with onion, which made it interesting, an excellent tomato-vegetable soup, and a small, delicately flavored salad. When I was shown the wine list I handed it back to the waiter saying that I would prefer a small glass of Japanese plum wine. He could not have appeared more puzzled if I had requested a glass of battery acid.

"Prum wine?" he said.

"Yes," I said. "It's a very sweet wine, made of plums, and bottled here in Japan. We serve it in our home in the United States." He could only point again to the wine list, which seemed to offer the same variety of French, German, Spanish and Italian wines that one might find in any good restaurant around the world.

"I would prefer to have a Japanese wine," I said.

"Yes, sir," he said, pointing to a particular page on which the names of all the wines were given in French.

"Were these wines bottled in Japan?" I asked.

"Oh, yes, sir," he said.

"Can I order any of them by the glass?" I asked.

"Just the Bordeaux," he said.

So I had the Japanese Bordeaux, a kind of wine of which I am not particularly fond. But this was literally the best I'd ever tasted. Smooth, rich, without that wretched after-bite that makes most dry wines distasteful.

My room—1439—was somewhat small, though larger than many rooms at Washington, D.C.'s Capitol Hilton, but entirely comfortable, spotlessly clean, and attractive. A floor-to-ceiling window looked out on a vast expanse of the city. The bath mat, towels and washcloth were of that unique Japanese yellow I associate with the color of the rising sun in the national flag. It is not what Americans ordinarily think of as yellow, nor does it approach orange. Unartistic peoples, or individuals, I suppose, to the extent that they give thought to colors at all, tend to divide them into the basic large categories: red, blue, yellow, green, brown, etc. But where the artistic sensibilities are more refined, the idea of variety in color invariably is important. In the France of Louis XVI, for example, the members of the court placed enormous importance—no doubt too much—on the introduction and wearing of new and subtle variations of color.

In the kind of explanatory booklet one finds at better hotels around the world, there was a description of "New Year's at the Keiyo," in which it is explained that "past midnight guests will be invited to ring out the temple bell in the lobby, 108 peals to absolve man of his 108 passions." In the Western tradition I suppose the only equivalent would be the Seven Deadly Sins: Pride, Covetousness, Lust, Anger, Gluttony, Envy and Sloth. The Japanese, having been civilized centuries longer than we Westerners, have had time to develop a sophisticated theory of sin just as they have of color. I was reminded again of the utter importance of moral and ethical codes to the rational function of all societies, something Mao consistently stressed. Just as your neighbor's lack of honesty is annoying to you, so statistically any significant degree of thievery is importantly annoying to a society. To put the matter simply, it ends up costing everyone more money, criminals and honest people alike. It has an effect on prices, insurance rates and the general atmosphere of trust. In this connection I would shortly be struck by the remarkable degree of personal honesty in China.

When I awakened the following morning at five it was still dark out. I was greeted by the sight of an enormous full moon, for which I thanked the universe. The universe didn't hear me, I know, but I do such things for my own sake, not that of the universe.

By the time I got down to the lobby, which was abandoned, at about ten after six, I was told that the bus I had assumed was leaving at six-thirty was actually scheduled to leave at six-twenty, which gave me very few minutes to pay my bill and have a bit of breakfast. In a beautifully decorated coffee shop, in which I

was the sole customer, I was served a large glass of Mandarin orange juice, a grade-A cup of coffee and the two very best Danish pastries I have ever eaten.

A Japanese gentleman and I were the only bus passengers to the airport. Riding through the city was again a pleasure. At six-thirty there were few cars on the street, the air was clear, the sun slanting in cheerfully. I'm not sure whether we went to the airport by another route but this time, at about six-forty, we passed a sizable harbor, in which several large cargo vessels lay at anchor, the brilliant sun behind them.

Incidentally, the bus, made by the Kinsan Coach Company, was clean and—blessedly—smoothly quiet. I don't know why it is that American buses move with ear-splitting roars, but the Japanese bus was so quiet I thought perhaps it ran on electric power, although it did not.

On the left, at about 6:45, we passed a beautiful racetrack around which, in the early morning air, several jockeys with their mounts were trotting peacefully. Beside the track, the river or canal was choked with thousands of enormous logs. And—again—all around were factories, factories, factories, stretching as far as the eye could see. On most of them, it is interesting to note, the names were given in both Japanese and English. A courtesy to customers, no doubt. Everywhere the familiar brand names were in evidence: Canon, Yashica, Sony, Hitachi.

The Japan Airlines flight to Peking departed on time. We were soon above the clouds, where all parts of the planet look the same. The trip took longer than it would have on an as-the-crow-flies path because these crows are not permitted to fly over Korea. I busied myself with paperwork, studying a number of articles on China.

After a while I practiced with the Yashica camera I had bought at the hotel the night before (Jayne had mistakenly locked up my old Nikon at home, before taking off for Hong Kong) and tested the batteries in my hand-held Hitachi cassette recorder, into which I planned to talk my head off while observing life in China.

After several hours we began to descend through the clouds, approaching Peking. I could not restrain my excitement. There is a sense of emotional anticipation produced by a visit to any foreign country, but when one goes into an area in which, for whatever reason, the inhabitants have long been viewed as "the enemy," the emotional component is increased. Unease and apprehension, in my case at least, are not part of the explanation. Rather I feel a tension between the sense of opposition and disapproval one is "supposed" to feel and the sympathy and understanding I do feel toward the human beings I am meeting. Systems are one thing, humans another.

PEKING

Far below the earth was a patchwork of tan, tawny fields and farms. Because it was late winter nothing green could be seen. Nor was snow visible. Everywhere a pale brownish expanse, only lightly varied by similarly colored roofs clustered in communes—large country farms—and all seen through a faint haze that consisted of dust from the plains but was reminiscent of that sickening pall that befouls the air of most large American and European cities.

We landed smoothly on a somewhat bumpy concrete runway. The airport was enormous, as it must be to accommodate large jets, but only a dozen or so jumbo planes were visible, not the scores one sees at major European or American airports. But of course in the winter of 1975 the doors to China had been open only a comparatively short while.

I knew none of my fellow passengers, of whom there were about fifty, apparently from various parts of the world.

When we got off the plane it occurred to me to wonder what sort of reception we would have had if the weather had been bad. The walk to the terminal covered, I should guess, about 150 yards. The weather was good, the air brisk and I needed the exercise, but it was not at all clear why the planes could not move closer to the terminal, as they do in other parts of the world. Surely there must be some passengers who are crippled, very old, ill, or likely

Bill Allen in front of the large picture of Mao at the Peking air terminal.

for other reasons to be intimidated by that football-field-and-a-half walk with, needless to say, one's carry-on luggage.

Except for the enormous color portrait of Mao that dominated the airfield there was nothing whatever Oriental about the terminal building.

After the standard delay by health and customs inspectors—one of whom spoke excellent English—we passengers arrived at the luggage area and gathered our belongings. I asked one Chinese if there were porters to assist getting luggage up to the street and to the taxis or buses I assumed would be waiting.

"I am sorry," he said, "there are no porters here today."

Mao statue, Peking airport.

a passing Chinese in peaked cap and fatigue-dress to carry his luggage. Chinese military uniforms carry no insignia of rank, and he was addressing the Colonel commanding the airport guard."

The main lobby of the terminal was dominated by an enormous white stone or plaster statue of Mao Tse-tung which appeared to be about eighteen feet high.

The idolization of Mao, incidentally, was by no means something that flowed simply out of Communist philosophy and practice; the precedents for it are purely Chinese. As John C. Haughey, S.J., observed, "It is not uncharacteristic for this people to endow a man with celestial stature. They did so with their emperors, their sages and Confucius himself."

A number of visitors to the mainland since 1970 have reported that the cult of Mao, so far as visible evidence is concerned, has been deemphasized. It is said that a number of the large statues and portraits of the leader had by 1975 been removed from public exhibition in the larger Chinese cities. If this is indeed the case one can only marvel at how extensive the Maoist displays must have been before the alleged winding down started.

Visitors to China for the last thirty years have not commented on statues of Chou En-lai, Liu Shao-chi or former defense minister Lin Piao, three other important leaders. Such deference was paid only to Mao. Foreigners who have witnessed the visit of Red Guards, "the inheritors of the Revolution," to Mao's birthplace at Shaohanchung, the peasant village in Hunan Province, report an attitude on the part of the young people more solemn, more fervent than that evidenced by modern Christians who walk the streets of Jerusalem or Bethlehem.

I later learned that there are never any porters, as such, available, but he was perhaps trying to avoid stating the fact baldly. The word *porter* is no longer used because of its unpleasant associations with colonialist and upper-class abuses of the past. "Coolies" and all that. In any event the man did point out a representative of the China Travel Service, a harried young fellow named Mr. Kim, who helped by carrying some of my bags to the upper area. I carried the rest. In such Socialist societies "servants" are, of course, hard to come by.

A foreigner in any land invariably is led, totally by his own ignorance, into moments of embarrassment or confusion. Hugo de Burgh of Edinburgh University described, in *Blackwood's* magazine in 1975, an awkward moment in the company of a group of British businessmen at the Peking airport. "Another visitor, a self-important person, refused to believe that there were no porters, and ordered

After photographing the statue I walked to the front of the building and waited, with some other passengers, to be given instructions about transportation to the Peking Hotel. A number of taxis, all looking like private cars, waited in the square below. Some seemed to be of Japanese manufacture. Others that looked like small copies of 1957 Chevys were Chinese.

Country road, 1975.

Chinese autos at Peking airport.

Just as had been the case in Tokyo, every car was spotless.

To our left was a glass door on which the phrase "No Admittance" was written in English as well as Chinese. Somehow seeing this small instance of one's own language induced a feeling of gratefulness.

A clean, medium-sized robin's-egg-blue bus pulled up and parked at the foot of the steps. Since we received no instructions to board it, we did not do so. Off to the right were some massive three-story buildings which I assumed were army barracks or offices since a number of soldiers, with the modern olive-green uniforms and red star insignia, were strolling about.

After perhaps fifteen minutes, Mr. Kim appeared again and herded us into the bus, which pulled away immediately. Its engine was considerably louder than that of the Japanese buses. The ride was also quite bumpy because the concrete road leading away from the airport consisted of individual slabs, perhaps six

by nine feet in size, laid out in endless sequence. It was the joining-cracks which accounted for the unevenness of the ride.

Although there was not a leaf in evidence, it being late February, it was clear that an incredibly extensive job of tree planting had taken place, evidently in recent years. On both sides of the road there were perfectly straight lines of trees—three or four rows per side—that turned out to stretch ahead for what seemed the next fifteen miles. Many were painted white up to a height of about six feet. Beyond those were firs, pines, fruit trees and thin ones that looked rather like our birches.

At one point several miles down the road we passed a few workers repairing barbed wire. Barbed wire to keep out whom? For fear of what? Perhaps they protected the fruit trees.

Since the leafless trees had no natural beauty of color to them, the primary impression one got was of a tremendous emphasis on order, planning.

The Peking area seemed naturally dusty.

Street scene, Peking.

There was a faint haze in the air itself. The weather was overcast but not from any visible clouds. Obviously the area stood much in need of trees. So here, when the weather is more pleasant and green things are growing, all visitors, leaving the airport, must receive an immediate impression of peace, green vegetation, natural beauty.

Eventually, off to the right, I perceived through the bare trees another, more primitive road running parallel to ours, whose chief traffic was horse-drawn flatbed wagons carrying a great variety of loads.

There was mostly light foot and bicycle traffic on the main road. We passed few other buses or cars. As we came up behind each pedestrian or cyclist, the driver honked his horn—it seemed to me excessively—to warn of his coming. Later, as we moved into more crowded streets I discovered that the endless furious honking of horns was characteristic of city traffic.

As we approached the central city of Peking, we began to pass apartment buildings, some quite old, others new and modern, some under construction. They were four and five stories high and well built, not all fake and façade, as had been the case with buildings I observed in East Berlin in the 1960s.

In and around these new apartments we caught occasional glimpses of old farmers'

quarters, simple one-story structures that were little more than huts with shingled roofs. They seemed to have no color at all. Almost every one had a little courtyard area. In some cases the exterior plaster had worn completely off so that one could see that the construction was of adobe earth-bricks. Some courtyards were walled off, others had fences of cornstalks.

In some of the small country houses chickens hopped about the backyard. I saw one dog, the only one I was to note in several days in the area. With meat still in relatively short supply China cannot accommodate carnivorous pets.

After what I estimated to be about twenty-five miles, the bus turned left and briefly passed from concrete to asphalt, which made for a much smoother ride.

We passed, on the left, a wide building, of beautiful architecture, the first large Chinese-looking edifice we had seen, apparently an army headquarters. One more turn brought us to what was obviously an important city thoroughfare. It was very wide, like the streets of Moscow, wider than American streets by far. Quite a few buildings of middle height were now in evidence. In front of one of them, next to a tree, a line of laundry was drying, right on the street. In most American cities, God help us, the clothes would have been stolen within a few hours.

Air vent grating, Peking Hotel.

After a while Mr. Kim pointed to a large building two or three blocks ahead. "The Peking Hotel," he said. I was pleased that in a few minutes I would be meeting Jayne and the other members of our party there. Suddenly the bus turned left, hurried down a smaller street, clearly away from the hotel. I gestured to Mr. Kim and broke into Pidgin English.

"No," I said. "I go to Peking Hotel."

"No," he said, adding details I could not understand.

"But," I insisted, "my wife is at the Peking Hotel. I must meet her now."

He just smiled, shrugged and on we sped. In a few minutes we arrived at the Hsin Ciao (Xin Qiao) Hotel.

Eventually I was told, by another Travel Service employee—highly intelligent, quick in thought and movement—that Jayne and the others had left Peking the previous day, bound for Tientsin, and would meet me there.

I spent the next few hours exploring the hotel and the immediate neighborhood. No one objected to my strolling about the streets alone, even with camera and tape recorder in action, thus disproving one assumption common back home.

Almost everywhere that tourists are quartered in China there are tables or library racks of free political literature, which visitors are encouraged to take and study. An interesting sidelight on this custom is that—at least as of 1976—a considerable portion of this material

was still published in Russian. One can understand, inasmuch as the Chinese are not wasteful, that older books and pamphlets published in the Russian language would not be discarded. But it is not clear why new Russian material continues to be printed since there were few if any Russian tourists in China during the 1975–1976 period. In the street a truck passed, with a red flag on its right fender.

The general grayness and tan-ness of wintertime China makes the red flags, banners and posters one sees stand out more than they would in other parts of the world. Billowing red flags are sometimes planted on farm fields, and there are giant red poster signs, which look like our billboards but are usually made of brick, concrete or stone. More red flags flap in the wind on the front of locomotives, and red backgrounds are painted behind many of the statues of Mao that one sees. Though this red is political, it is one more instance of that man-made beauty, for centuries so natural, so typical of the Chinese.

To record that beauty, I started using my camera that afternoon and did not stop till I left the country. Of the perhaps 250 color slides I took on that first trip, incidentally, I find that the one most interesting to friends and audiences is a shot of nothing more photogenic than the metal screen or grating over an air-conditioning vent at the Peking Hotel. Ordinarily such an object would not attract the interest of photographers or, for that matter, even the casual observer. The reason I photographed it, nevertheless, is that the pattern of it is quite beautiful. It could be smeared with inks or paints and used to press an interesting wallpaper design. The point is that if only practical considerations were paramount, the grating would look like those in all other parts of the world in that it would be made in the familiar pattern of scores of small rectangles resulting from crisscrossing perpendicular and horizontal lines. But in the Chinese air vents the pattern of the metal is artistic as well as functional and hence pleasing to the rare eye that might encounter it.

After a few hours of strolling around the Hsin Ciao Hotel, having lunch, making small

Train station, Peking.

purchases in the lobby shop, exploring the adjacent streets and taking photographs, I joined several other foreign visitors bound for the Tientsin Carpet Fair. We were transported by bus to Peking's large, crowded rail terminal.

Grand Central station on its busiest day cannot have been so crowded. Part of the traffic was military, but most of it was just people, many thousands of them, traveling alone, in pairs, in families. Luggage was primitive, with few suitcases in evidence. Simple boxes, bags, crates or just bundles of belongings wrapped in netting, sheets or blankets were everywhere. There was the low bustle and rumble of excitement but no voices were raised. Everyone seemed calm and purposeful.

Two other Americans and several Europeans, none of us having anything in common but the color of our skin and our destination, were herded off the bus, through the crowds, up an escalator to an upper level and then into a waiting room apparently reserved for Westerners. After a few minutes in this large room with its comfortable chairs, I strolled back out to where the crowds were, partly to get away from concentrated cigarette smoke but mostly to study the people who milled about or waited patiently in small groups. I felt exhilarated, curious, aware. Everything visible held enormous interest.

A Train Ride to Tientsin

Eventually our group boarded the train to Tientsin. Five of us, all of whom spoke English, shared one compartment. One of our party was a gentleman from Paris, another a Los Angeles rug dealer. The other two were an Iranian-American from St. Louis and his wife, who laughed so readily she could easily have got a steady job attending television comedy shows.

After a few minutes we became aware of the high-level volume of what was either a radio or tape-originated sound track, played into all compartments of the train by means of squawky loudspeakers. What I assume was Revolutionary music was interrupted from time to time by a woman's voice giving announcements. Since the volume made it difficult to conduct conversation I stepped out into the passageway, located an attendant and asked if it would be possible for the volume to be lowered. The young lady nodded; within a few seconds the request was granted.

A small table at the window was provided with teacups. Hot water was brought, when requested, by attentive, competent young women wearing white jackets. We discussed general news of the day, China and the rug business, from which discussion I learned a number of facts of interest. I had had no previ-

One of China's many modern diesel engines.

ous experience with the purchase or importing of rugs but, to keep matters entirely ethical, had indeed participated in a "gentleman's agreement" with Jayne and our Chinese-American friend Lily Wen.

The countryside through which the train moved was flat, brown, dusty and somber-looking. Shortly darkness fell and there was nothing more to be seen outside.

At first I had been struck by the relative "sameness" of the Chinese I had met or seen. Now I began to observe differences. Just as we Americans know that ours is not a culturally uniform country, we should not expect China to be either. Diet, dress, manners, customs, laws may be quite different in New England from what they are in, say, Alabama or Wyoming. Just so one finds a wide variety of manners, mores and customs in China. Even within one city—from one hotel to another, in fact—there are slight differences. We were to find that the general attitude of service personnel at the Peking Hotel, for example, was more cordial and cooperative than at the Hsin Ciao Hotel.

All judgment is relative. Pound-for-pound comparisons between Americans and Chinese, however, are difficult. In a sense there is no such thing as "the American people" if by a *people* we mean the sort of entity we describe when we refer to the French people, the Italian

people or the German people. There are 57 varieties of Americans, each with its own ethnic history. Observations that might be true of a poor Alabama Black could be quite untrue of a wealthy Jewish merchant of New York, an Oklahoma cowhand, a Swedish dairyman from Minnesota, or an Irish truck driver from Chicago.

In studying the Chinese, then, I rarely thought of American equivalents. So many are nevertheless given in this report because it helps the reader to understand something he has not experienced by offering him a comparison to something with which he is familiar.

In a nation as large as China, which is much larger than the United States, there are people from various ethnic and national backgrounds, intellectuals and simple peasants, young and old, tall and short, even Communist and non-Communist.

There are even different flesh colors in China, from very pale skin in no way different from that of, say, a northern Italian, to quite brown shades such as we see on darker American Indians. Nor is it the case that all Chinese have the unindented upper eyelid, as Westerners assume. The eyes of some Chinese seem no different from those of southern Europeans. Needless to say, there is no such thing as "slanted" eyes.

TIENTSIN

It was dark, a bit windy, and quite chilly when, after a two-hour ride, our train pulled into Tientsin station. We wrestled our luggage off the train, with some help, were met by affable and courteous China Travel Service personnel, taken to a bus and thence to our hotel.

As we drove through its darkened streets we could see little of Tientsin. Thousands of bicycles glided past. The sidewalks seemed still crowded despite the late hour. I could see curious faces staring at the pale foreigners on our bus. We were taken to Tientsin Hotel No. 1, the name of which was, before 1949, the Astor House, a British establishment. In the lobby more smiling faces greeted us.

In his charming book, *A China Passage*,

John Kenneth Galbraith makes an important observation. "I think of how casually we handle visitors in the United States in contrast with the care with which we are being looked after here."

It is not possible to determine all the causes of this difference. The American reasons are obvious enough: we are simply too busy with our own affairs to give much of a damn about anyone else, granting a few happy exceptions. Politeness and hospitality are not the great American virtues they once were. Presumably a tourist would have to be either from Mars or a very important personage to merit the especially careful attention of many of us. The Chinese, on the other hand, have always been a courteous and respectful people.

As regards the care the modern Chinese give to visitors, part of the attention perhaps grows out of a simple wish to keep an eye on us. Wandering off by oneself, while by no means forbidden, is nevertheless not encouraged, but largely for the traveler's own good; he'll miss parts of the planned program.

When I arrived at our room, 522, I found Jayne sitting on one of its twin beds, surrounded by four apparently adoring Chinese teenagers, two boys and two girls. They all spoke English, though not fluently and, because she speaks Chinese, were anxious to practice their English on her. At one point one of the girls responded to an observation of Jayne's by saying, "What a drag."

Jayne laughed and said, "Where in the world did you learn *that* expression?"

"Oh," the girl said, "an American taught it to me not long ago."

The many questions the young people put to us were not merely the result of personal curiosity or government instruction. For countless centuries it has been the custom in China to put questions to visitors and strangers. "Where will you be going?" "Why are you traveling there?" "What is your honorable surname?" "How old are you?" "Are you tired?" Such questions, which in the context of American etiquette might seem too inquisitive and personal, are in China asked with the most cordial and proper of intentions.

The next day in the lunchroom Jerry Fisher said that when he had made a point to one of the boys that morning the young man responded by saying, "I'm hip." Jerry laughed heartily, asked where he had learned the expression, and was told that Jayne had taught it to him.

All the members of our party had been given rooms in the same part of the hotel so I spent the next half-hour greeting the Fishers, Beverly, Marge and Victoria Levy, Helene and Herbert. They were full of reports of what they had seen and done in Hong Kong, their adventures in crossing the border with Jayne and Lily, both of whom have the nervous system of hummingbirds, their flight to Peking and their train trip to Tientsin.

Tientsin Hotel No. 1 was, by American luxury-class standards, second-rate, though chiefly because of its age. On the other hand, American residents of a Harlem slum, an Indian hovel, an Appalachian shack, a Mexican farm-worker's hut, or a crowded Puerto Rican tenement would consider it palatial. Compared to U.S.A.-1980 living, the hotel was a step back into the 1920s. The light bulbs—in fact most of the bulbs we saw in China—were incredibly dim. Despite the exemption for hotels, no rooms at night were bright unless they had a great many bulbs burning at once. Pale neon is used in many homes. This is not a complaint, merely a report.

There is, of course, a reason for everything and the reason for the dimness of lights in China is to save electricity in dwellings and offices because it is needed in the factories. Chinese citizens generally are aware of the importance of energy conservation and willingly cooperate. Families, therefore, use bulbs of about 25 to 45 watts. When one of the bulbs burns out, incidentally, it is not simply discarded but turned into a neighborhood store where it is exchanged for a new one, with some additional payment. The used ones are collected and sent back to the factories to be rebuilt.

In some districts, at certain times, it is necessary to turn electricity off for a few hours or days and, in rare cases, weeks, in order to concentrate electric power where it is absolutely essential, in factories. In such cases people depend on candles, oil lamps and flashlights. They also adjust their sleeping schedules so that they can retire early in the evening and awaken at dawn, to take advantage of the approximately twelve hours of daylight.

Hotels for foreigners, foreign embassies and Friendship Stores (for foreigners only) are generally exempted from this national program.

The rooms were nevertheless quite comfortable, the service excellent, and food prices reasonable. With the exception of one member of our party none of us was in a mood to complain. We were very glad to be in China, in Tientsin, in our rooms and, before long that evening, in our beds.

The pillows in Tientsin, incidentally, were hard by American standards. Victoria said she had been told they were filled not with feathers but with flour. It seems a reasonable hypothesis, given their weight and the fact that once you position your head on one of them it seemed to stay in that position for much of the night. After the initial shock I found that I preferred them to the soft type. Other pillows in China may be filled with either duck feathers or *mu-mien,* a special kind of cotton. But the "bean-bag" pillows are actually filled with either rice husks, brown wheat husks or green bean husks, suitably dried.

Before we could retire, however, we were visited by an interesting fellow named Mr. Sung, who appeared to be about thirty. Everyone else we had met, the Travel Service people, the hotel personnel, had been extremely affable. Mr. Sung had the kind of personality that in the U.S. we associate, usually quite correctly, with policemen, detectives and military officers. He smiled dutifully enough and extended the requisite courtesies. But no matter how much he grinned, he radiated, to every member of our party, the same almost threatening quality.

Mr. Sung knocked at the door, did not wait to be welcomed and, although I was partly undressed, he entered, with another man. I later learned that the custom of entering without waiting for an invitation is common in Chinese hotels. I had not experienced anything like it since my high school years, when I moved from Chicago to Phoenix, Arizona. There too I had been startled when my new friends walked into the living quarters I shared with my mother with the same freedom with which they would have entered their own.

Mr. Sung introduced us to the man with him, the "Responsible Person," meaning in this case the official responsible for supervising our group's activities in Tientsin. For whatever the point is worth, we did not see him again, responsible or not. The primary object of their curiosity at the moment was Lily Wen who, Jayne had just told me, was in her room, ill.

"Why do you think she is ill?" Mr. Sung asked. "She seems very nervous. Why is she nervous?"

I have never met anyone else in my life who used the word *why* as often as Mr. Sung did, during our stay in his city.

It shortly seemed that our East-West Carpet Company was under suspicion. It was not possible to determine whether we were suspected of being casual tourists simply masquerading as rug dealers, or individuals who were politically suspect, possibly connected with the C.I.A. or some anti-Chinese entity.

When the inquisition was over I went down to the dining room. The food at the Tientsin Hotel, as in most of China, was quite good except for the chlorine problem. Some of the waiters and waitresses were inexperienced but cheerful teenagers; a few were old-timers from pre-Revolutionary days, friendly, quiet, competent.

The others' attempts to order orange juice produced only orange soda pop. All members of our party drank large amounts of it because the Tientsin water was, in a word, terrible. Apparently medical considerations required that it be heavily laced with chlorine or a similar purifying agent. Consequently the dominant flavor in any dish prepared with water— such as coffee, tea, soup, boiled rice, etc.—was not that of the natural taste itself, but chlorine. The orange soda, fortunately, was delicious. It was not served cold, however, but at room temperature.

The bread was great, sort of "health food"

style, as a result of which I began to put on extra pounds almost at once. For dinner the first night I had the common whole fish, served on a large platter swimming in a savory meat-gravy sauce. I dined with the Fishers, who told me of the welcoming banquet I had missed the night before. It had taken place in a large hall nearby. Good food, many smiles, a few speeches, toasts, and then a dazzling vaudeville show with incredibly gifted acrobats, dancers, jugglers and magicians.

It is not surprising that Chinese variety entertainment is of such a remarkable order of excellence. China has had countless centuries to perfect such arts.

In a handsome book, *The Freer Gallery of Art,* showing prize specimens from the Charles Freer Gallery in Washington, D.C., there is a picture of a small statue of a juggler, holding aloft a sturdy pole on the top of which a small bear is balanced. The work was created over five hundred years before the birth of Christ.

The same Freer collection, incidentally, features a jade covered cup, made in the same early period, that looks remarkably similar to the covered cups in which tea in China is served to this day.

It is in studying such collections that one gets a deeper sense of how very ancient the Chinese cultural tradition is. One item is a pottery urn made *some 3,000 years before Christ.* In fact, before the New Testament period, ancestors of today's Chinese had lived through the Yang-Shao culture, the Lung-Shan culture, the Shang dynasty, the Western Chou dynasty, the late Eastern Chou dynasty, and the Han dynasty. Inasmuch as we have recently celebrated only the two-hundredth year of our form of North American civilization, some of the reasons for the Chinese sense of superiority can perhaps be understood better.

After dinner I strolled outside again to get a bit of fresh winter air but even more because I wished to see the people and the nearby streets. Even though it was now perhaps nine-thirty thousands of bicycles continued to glide by in an endless flow. Since Chinese bikes are black and almost none of them carries lights,

it is difficult to see them or their dark-clad riders in the evening. For protection against cars coming from behind they carry a white patch about six inches long painted on the back fender, in the center of which, on most but not all bikes, is a red glass reflector.

As I stood in front of the hotel a few passersby slowed, stared and began to gather. Not wishing to attract attention I returned to our room.

Jayne gave me more information about what had turned out to be the near-disaster of crossing the border. Apparently Lily had brought in a great many gift items by asking the Caucasian members of the party to add them to their luggage. Jayne had the impression the customs inspectors were not fooled but reported that they had been cordial. Her excitement at returning to the country of her birth was so high, she said, that when she reached the center of the famous border bridge and realized she was actually in China, she began to cheer, an exercise in which all the other women in the party joined.

The plumbing at the hotel, as in Oriental countries generally, is not quite what Americans are used to, though the Chinese have either created or borrowed one clever detail. For those who might have trouble reading one language or another, the hot and cold water handles, in the Fishers' bath at least, carried red and blue buttons, the red naturally signifying hot and the blue the cold water control. The buttons, however, were on the wrong fixtures.

The next morning I began to explore the neighborhood.

Across the street was a Friendship Store, with much beautiful merchandise—silks, furs, clothing, works of art and household products.

The primary difference between American cans, packages, bottles, wrappers and those of China is that the Chinese versions can actually be described as artistic. A Chinese package of tea or can of vegetables could be considered esthetically attractive in a way that a can of, say, Campbell's tomato soup is not, Andy Warhol to the contrary notwithstanding. Displays of Chinese merchandise therefore may look especially attractive on shelves in shops.

The Friendship Stores are beautiful, in a clean simple way, though one of the reasons is that they are showplaces, designed for the convenience of, and to impress, foreigners. It is therefore more fun to shop at a real Chinese department store, where things are considerably more funky. The Friendship Stores are almost empty. The local stores on the other hand are crowded, bustling, much like the average American store during the last few days before Christmas. Business is always good, despite low Chinese salaries.

Although Americans assume that virtually everyone in China is poor, the word is relative. One should always inquire "Compared to what?" when considering such concepts. Suppose, for example, that your present salary is $200 a week. Now assume that our president goes on television and says, "My fellow Americans, starting tomorrow morning the salary of each of you will be cut exactly in half. Now for the *good* news. The *price* of everything in America will also be cut exactly in half."

At the first part of his announcement you would be dismayed. But a moment later you would rejoice to learn that the car you had been planning to buy for $4,000 could now be purchased for $2,000, that the $100 suit you were thinking of ordering could now be purchased for $50, etc.

Something roughly like this applies in China. Salaries are low by American standards; workers may earn only $35 or $45 a month. But food is so inexpensive, rents may run just a couple of dollars a month, clothing is so modestly priced and so many services are free, that the small salaries do stretch out till the next payday.

The Chinese pay essentially nothing for items that may cost Americans many thousands of dollars, such as education and medical care. I refer to this background by way of explaining that, although practically no one in China is well-to-do by American standards, nevertheless the shops and department stores seem always to be doing a tremendous volume of business. There are several reasons why Chinese department stores can offer good merchandise at very low prices. The stores spend no money whatever on advertising, they do not have to staff credit departments, and they are not faced with the serious shoplifting problem that troubles all American stores.

A block away from the hotel entrance was an extremely beautiful and spacious mansion, which we were told had been the pre-Revolutionary British office for liaison with the Chinese coal industry. Its formal grounds were now a public park.

We were told there was once a sign at the entrance that said "No Chinese and no dogs allowed."

One wonders if the British could ever have been actually so insensitive.

The next day I took a cab to a "downtown" section, with Mr. Moonjy, an American attending the rug display. No guide accompanied us. We shopped at a large, well-stocked department store. When we came out I suggested we walk back to the hotel, perhaps five miles away. The jaunt was exhausting but fascinating. We were greeted along the way by many warm smiles and curious stares, partly because of the small Japanese hand-held cassette tape recorder into which I constantly dictated my observations.

(If you plan to use a tape recorder, calculator or pocket radio in China, by the way, be sure to take along extra American batteries. Chinese small transistor batteries are the same size as ours, but not as powerful. Some remarks recorded in Tientsin were lost because my Chinese batteries had run down and I didn't become aware of it until too late.)

We continued to merit Mr. Sung's attention day and night during our days in Tientsin. He would appear at odd times, always unannounced, and immediately begin to question us. That same evening Jerry Fisher, Herbert Cole and I were standing in front of the hotel, wanting to clear our heads, after a heavy dinner, with a bit of frigid air and exercise. I was jogging in place, doing knee bends, when suddenly Mr. Sung approached from the lobby.

"Why are you out here?" he said, without the usual smile.

"Just getting a bit of exercise," I said, underlining the obvious.

"You do not feel well?" he said.

"Well," I said, "I'm not getting enough exercise on the trip, although earlier today I did get quite a lot when I walked from the department store all the way back here to the hotel."

"Alone?" he said.

"No," I answered.

"I know," he said quickly, "you were with Mr. Moonjy."

So deep is American ignorance about China that few of us had ever even heard of Tientsin till it was devastated by the 8.2 earthquake of July 28, 1976. In pre-1949 China the only Americans who visited the city were military people, fur traders, carpet importers and other merchants, missionaries and individuals allied with European businesses. Our hotel was on the street of main interest to these Western visitors, then called Victoria Road, although that has not always been its name, nor is it so identified today. Before 1949 only ships below three hundred tons in volume could come into Tientsin's port. The Communist regime has constructed the large artificial Hsinkang harbor at nearby Tangku, which makes it possible for cargo ships with upward of 10,000 tons capacity to dock. Tientsin is therefore a bustling trade and import city visited by ships of registries from all over the world. Situated on the northeastern coast, it is roughly comparable to the position of New York on the U.S. map.

Since there had been substantially no Americans there for almost a quarter-century, the members of our group, when we left the hotel, were stared at as if we were sideshow freaks. The staring was of a unique kind, however, not the furtive sort to which an odd-looking visitor might be subjected in the U.S.A. A Tibetan horseman, for example, walking the streets of Kansas City would certainly attract a great deal of attention, but it would be entirely individualistic. If the visitor were to glance directly at someone who had been looking at him, that someone would almost certainly turn away and pretend he had not been staring at all. This is quite different from what happened in the mid-1970s in those Chinese cities, like Tientsin, in which Eu-

ropean or American visitors were a rarity.

If you are walking, bicycling, or riding in a car, people simply observe you as you pass, as they might anywhere in the world. If you stop, however, to purchase something, to take a photograph, to study a site of interest, you are almost immediately surrounded by a crowd, sometimes quite a large crowd, numbering perhaps two or three hundred. You are not pressed or addressed directly. The members of your audience keep what might be described as a respectful distance, ten or fifteen feet away. They form a large, loose semicircle around you and then simply look at you as if you were quite the oddest thing they'd ever seen. There is not the slightest trace of antagonism or disapproval in any of the faces. They express either simple curiosity or blank stupefaction. If you smile, several people will smile back. If you address an individual in his own language, he will first appear surprised, then almost certainly return your greeting with a smile, or perhaps a laugh at your pathetic accent.

The Tientsin Carpet Fair

The morning after I arrived we were taken to a large industrial auditorium, the site of the Tientsin Carpet Fair. The Chinese are probably the world masters of rugmaking. The colors, designs, workmanship and all-round beauty of their rugs and carpets are literally breathtaking. On the basis of our group's experience, however, the mainland Chinese in 1975 may not have been exactly the world's champion businessmen, at least by American standards.

The people with whom we negotiated were by no means lacking in intelligence, intuitive understanding or general knowledge of carpet manufacture. But, even taking problems of translation into account, it seemed incredibly complicated to do business in the way that has for centuries been common in most other parts of the world.

Part of the problem was that it seemed impossible to talk business with just one authoritative representative of the carpet industry. One dealt rather with a hierarchy of staff people. There is nothing inherently wrong with that except that you may get mutually contra-

Jayne at the Carpet Fair, Tientsin, 1975.

dictory answers from different negotiators. To a question such as "Can I order just *one* of this model?" the answer from one official would be *yes* and from another *no.*

Another complicating factor is that prices on the tags attached to each rug were given in Madarin. Now that the Chinese are encouraging the sale of their carpets in other parts of the world, it would seem reasonable to have pricing and other relative information given in, say, English, French, Spanish and Japanese. The rugs and carpets, I repeat, were truly beautiful. Several were remarkably lifelike reproductions of photographs and paintings. From a distance they appeared, in fact, to be paintings or photographs. It was only as one moved closer that one could see that every detail was a matter of individual stitches by the handweavers of the area. One enormous carpet, showing a mountain scene and the Great Wall was, we were told, to be a gift to the United Nations.

Lily began placing orders for God knows how many carpets. They were all quite expensive.

A Mrs. Chen, bright, poised, articulate, was in charge of conducting business with our group. She reviewed the history of Chinese rugmaking, quoted the customary blur of statistics, and offered details of the procedure of placing orders for rugs. There is something competent, even formidable, about such modern Chinese women that I find attractive, as contrasted with the fly-me-to-Miami sort of personality.

Mrs. Chen explained that a great step forward in the making of rugs was the recent introduction of electric scissors, which look somewhat like garden shears at the business end. The new tool is important not only to efficiency but in terms of the physical well-being of the workers.

"In the old days," she said, "the workers' fingers would become distorted, crippled, from wielding scissors over the years. Now that problem had disappeared."

Mrs. Chen, by the way, had a good sense of humor. At one point, after she poured me a bit of tea, I said, *"Sye-sye"* (Thank you).

"You speak Chinese very well," she said, with a faint smile, putting me on.

"The longest journey," I replied, quoting a Chinese proverb, "starts with one step."

I have since learned that the possibility of this first visit came about because Mrs. Chen Yu-lai, chief officer of the department of carpet export, happened to see Lily Wen's magazine clippings of Chinese-design antique carpets which had been made in Europe. Mrs. Chen, herself a carpet designer, corresponded with

Lily about the reason the Chinese themselves were not making carpets of the particular sort shown. Mrs. Chen then informed Lily of the coming Tientsin Carpet Exhibition. Our invitation followed.

One morning, under Mr. Sung's guidance, we took a bus tour of the city. Victoria Road was lined with European-style buildings including several Greek and Roman temples that had been banks in the old days.

After crossing the river we came upon an enormous square or plaza, seemingly as large as a dozen football fields. To the left, strung out along the water's edge, stood giant stone panels, perhaps fifty feet high, on which were painted portraits of Marx, Lenin, Engels and Stalin.

On the opposite side was a large civic building on the front of which appeared the traditional portrait of Mao as well as the standard large red-and-white political signboards.

Despite its age and history Tientsin is in every sense a modern metropolis, boasting a large, well-equipped hospital, an imposing museum, Nankai University and the general sort of commercial busyness that one associates with large port cities around the world.

It is both a very clean and very dirty city, clean in that the kind of filth that litters some American streets and cities, even in some upper-class neighborhoods, is nowhere encountered. In other words, one does not see wastepaper, garbage, beer cans, broken bottles, and other assorted junk littering the ground. The dirtiness of Tientsin comes from the dreadful smokiness of its atmosphere. Part of the smoke comes from the area's heavy and light industry, the rest from the millions of small furnaces and chimneys in every part of the city.

In 1975 the Chinese seemed almost not to have heard of three problems which had rightly assumed importance in the American mind: air pollution, noise pollution and lung cancer. But then it took a long time to awaken the American people to these problems and many still have not gotten the message. The first wave of consumer advocates and conservationists, in the early 1960s, were called Communists, criers-of-doom, etc.

Piled bricks, Tientsin.

The dreadful dirtiness of the Chinese atmosphere is brought about chiefly by the burning of sulfurous coal. Lung cancer relates mainly to the smoking, the endless serving, the pushing of cigarettes. They are repeatedly offered to foreign guests and, among Chinese who can afford them, seem to be smoked widely. They were advertised and available in the few stores we visited.

Noise pollution comes chiefly from the horns of buses and automobiles. The drivers honk repeatedly as they move through city streets and country roads, to warn pedestrians and bicyclists of their coming. In the case of the bike riders the incessant horn-blowing seems necessary. Perhaps because there has not been a great deal of auto traffic on Chinese streets until recent years, cyclists seem not as yet fully accustomed to it. They certainly do not grant the automobile the deference it is accorded in America. Cyclists keep to the center of the streets and seem only grudgingly to give way to the buses, trucks and cars that attempt to pass them.

Everywhere we continued to notice the old European influence. Several of the public buildings were formerly Christian churches although all identifying crosses and statues have been removed. We saw a great number of handsome old mansions as well, the exterior of each as filthy from Tientsin smoke as the

Bike rack, Tientsin, February, 1975.

humblest hovel. One can appreciate architectural or sculptural beauty despite dirt. Imagine, for example, Michelangelo's *David* covered with soot and dust. It would still be a masterpiece.

One of the more fascinating discoveries was the old, pre-Revolutionary "Italian neighborhood," with many buildings in the Mediterranean architectural style. The old Italian Club is now called the Workers' Palace. It is a palace indeed.

A few minutes later we passed a very tall metal smokestack painted in patches of bright blue, green, brown, red and black. Our guides could not explain why it was painted in such a way, although an obvious theory was that it was camouflaged. If so, it seemed a poor idea inasmuch as the chimney appeared to be the only brightly painted large object in town.

We next approached the Tientsin Old City, in the center of the urban area. Once surrounded by a wall, it was, under the Europeans, the equivalent of Chinatown, a Chinese-only area. Chinese in the old days, you see, were often not allowed to enter the various European compounds without special permission. So much for "freedom."

We passed a thousand and one fascinating sights on our tour of the city, but when we asked if the bus could be stopped to enable us to take photographs, Mr. Sung's answers

became evasive and we continued to move. Finally, at Tientsin's beautiful Water Park, we were permitted to get out and take pictures to our heart's content. This would be the equivalent in New York of not permitting a foreign visitor to take pictures within the city, then driving into the heart of Central Park and allowing him to photograph anything he wanted.

The Water Park in Tientsin, with its small lake and canals, is beautifully landscaped. In the middle of the lake are two small islands, joined by a gleaming white bridge made with that delicate curve so typical of Oriental bridges. Bridges in the West are straight, flat. This is another example of the Oriental ability to combine practical function with esthetic charm. The art of building such structures can, of course, be applied only where the waterway to be spanned is narrow. One can hardly envision a gently arched Brooklyn Bridge or Golden Gate Bridge.

Oddly enough, in the park I saw the only instance of American-type littering we encountered. On and around the steps of a pagoda-tower I observed scraps of paper, containers from boxes of film, candy wrappers, orange peels, etc. In trying to determine—without putting the question directly—whether this debris had been cast about by local people or visiting tourists, I picked up a discarded film package and said to Mr. Sung, "Did this contain Japanese or Chinese film?"

"Chinese," he said.

Evidently there are slobs in every part of the world. The percentage of them in China, however, is certainly small.

Chinese Honesty

All American visitors to China are thunderstruck, and rightly so, by the honesty of the people, as well as by their neatness. In Tientsin no keys are provided for hotel rooms, although floor attendants do lock the rooms if they are to be vacant for any period of time. The purpose of this, we were told, was the danger that other foreign tourists might be tempted by valuables left in the rooms.

While standing in front of the hotel one day I reached into my overcoat pocket for a small camera and, without noticing, dropped some paper money on the sidewalk. Several teenagers standing nearby pointed this out to our guide who in turn drew my attention to it. When I thanked her she said, "It was these young men who saw the money fall." At which I turned, bowed, and thanked them profusely.

Other American travelers tell stories of the great pains to which their Chinese hosts have gone to return items that would seem to us to be of no value whatever: a small pocket comb, a hairpin, a pencil stub. Americans are now so accustomed to being ripped-off that the sudden sense of security in China is richly pleasurable. On the day I arrived in Peking, while waiting at the Hsin Ciao Hotel, I left Jayne's mink coat, valued at several thousand dollars, in our unlocked bus, along with my personal luggage, which contained several items of value. Can the reader imagine doing this in New York, Chicago or San Francisco?

Another aspect of the modern Chinese emphasis on honesty is that countless millions of tons of valuable equipment and supplies are stored out in the open, in fields, on sidewalks, in lots, piled against buildings, or at the sides of roads. Can you imagine leaving bags of cement, motor parts, automobile tires or lumber on the streets of Boston, Cleveland or Los Angeles unguarded, for weeks at a time? This is common all over China; virtually nothing is stolen.

Water park, Tientsin, 1975.

We were saddened as we made the inevitable comparisons with conditions back home.

Of course it cannot possibly be the case that there is no crime in China. It could not be so even in one small village. The statement nevertheless has a certain relative statistical truth in that street, or personal, crime in China is not a social problem as it is in the United States. By way of analogy, consider that at present some 25,000 people are killed each year in the U.S. by guns. If by some means we could reduce that number to 1,000 we could rightly proclaim that *as a social problem* the situation had been very successfully dealt with. But there would still be those 1,000 individual tragedies per year.

Offices, shops and business enterprises in the heart of Manhattan are now tightly locked in broad daylight. Proprietors will admit you only after they have determined that you do not appear threatening. In the same crowded neighborhood even pedestrians are not totally safe. My son Bill, when he was fourteen, while walking near Forty-seventh Street and Seventh Avenue at midday, was accosted by a young tough. The boy demanded money, and when it was not immediately forthcoming, threatened to beat Bill up.

One of the editors of the *Los Angeles Times,* when we discussed the possibility of contrasting this deplorable situation with the total safety with which one can walk Chinese streets, said he doubted that it was necessary to draw the readers' attention to the negative American side of the picture. "You can just say," he suggested, "that the streets of China are safe. Americans will draw the proper moral."

No doubt most will. Because others might not, however, I think it necessary to go through this admittedly painful process because I am concerned about the absurd attitude of total superiority that many Americans are guilty of. Our nation has many glories and can boast of amazing accomplishments. I am proud to call it home, but American stupidity that cannot tolerate any public self-criticism whatever is worsening our present predicament. There is no lack of reports on the tragedies and scandals that shame our nation. But incredibly enough, many people still have not been adequately informed about the facts of these cases, partly because those who attempt to enlighten their fellows are often tarred with the epithets "unpatriotic," "anti-American," "criers of doom," "confirmed pessimists," or "bleeding hearts."

A good example would be Ralph Nader. Originally he worked totally alone, against overwhelming odds and powerful corporate interests, but he nevertheless forcefully spoke out. He wasn't right in every detail—no one ever is—but he has been right a great part of the time. The American people are deeply in his debt. But witness the ferocious attacks upon him by the conservative press. I suspect that the faith of these fierce defenders of America may be brittle rather than comfortable and assured. Closer attention often reveals that they're not actually dedicated to certain constitutional ideals.

It should be important to determine to what extent the all-pervasive Chinese honesty is creditable to the new regime and to what extent it is a reflection of a general Chinese superiority to Americans and Europeans in this respect. Perhaps both elements are operative, although pre-Revolutionary China was seriously corrupt. And today in Hong Kong there is a good chance that one will be cheated by anti-Communist Chinese merchants taking advantage of the visiting tourists' eagerness for bargains. One American told me that a friend had purchased a Japanese camera recently in Hong Kong, at a fair price, but that the clerk told him he would be wise to buy an additional piece of equipment, some sort of lens attachment. The American purchased the attachment at what he was assured was a great bargain price of $40. Upon returning to Los Angeles he checked with local camera stores to find out how much of a savings he had made. He learned that the attachment could be purchased anywhere in Los Angeles for about $10.

From time to time as we explored Tientsin —and other towns—we saw walls with pieces of broken glass studded in cement at their top. Other walls were topped with barbed wire.

This suggests that while China is far more honest than the Western cultures, honesty is nonetheless not total. At the height of its moral influence, Christianity, despite widespread conviction that the commandment "Thou shalt not covet thy neighbor's goods" came directly from God Almighty, seemed nevertheless powerless to prevent a great deal of stealing. I know of no evidence, in fact, that we Christians are less inclined to steal than are non-Christian peoples. All the more reason, no doubt, why we are impressed by the honesty of modern China. We were told that much of the broken glass was set into walls during the turmoil of the Cultural Revolution, not to prevent theft but to discourage violent confrontations. In 1975 our Chinese hosts made such comments about the Cultural Revolution somewhat guardedly. By 1978 the ascendancy of Teng Hsiao-ping had brought out into the open a good deal more such frank criticism of excesses by Mao's fanatical young Red Guards.

Wall studded with broken glass, Peking, 1975.

Chinese Physical Types

On our travels about Tientsin we saw several large, attractive pictorial posters. It occurs to me there may be a strange, subtle sort of Western "imperialist" influence revealed in the faces that government-approved Chinese artists draw into street posters and the illustrations of magazines and books. Every man in these pictures is remarkably handsome, every woman beautiful. Since I did not grow up in the Chinese culture, I cannot completely grasp what standards of physical beauty are to the Chinese, but it does seem odd that the handsome and beautiful people in the pictures all appear remarkably "Western" or "American." They look like Italians or Spaniards with perhaps one Oriental grandparent, as the accompanying illustration shows.

The variety of skin colors in China also came as a surprise to this ignorant American. No one in China really has yellow skin, by the way, but for that matter the entire human language about race would seem incredibly imprecise to a visitor from a more rational planet. White people, for example, are not at all white. Snowmen are white, alabaster statues are

A pictorial poster showing "Western" faces.

Faces, Forbidden City, Peking.

ists' Commune, outside of Sian, one of the officials we met looked remarkably Irish. He had light skin, small features, Occidental eyes, and a mostly un-Oriental face.

I also saw a good many faces in China that strikingly resembled well-known Americans. I must have seen at least two dozen men who looked like actor Jack Webb, a handful who resembled Ricardo Montalban, three or four who looked like Charles Bronson, a couple who looked like comedian Buddy Hackett, several women who looked like entertainer Kay Ballard, and one who strikingly resembled Lily Tomlin.

We saw hundreds of Chinese faces that could have mingled unnoticed in any random crowd of Mexican villagers. In fact, after our visit to China the theory that the Indian inhabitants of North and South America originally came out of the Asian continent, across the Bering Straits and down through what are now Alaska and Canada, seemed far more understandable than ever before.

Friday night Jerry Fisher suggested that our group have dinner not at the hotel but at a restaurant other American visitors had recommended to him. Eight of us decided to go. Two cabs took us to a place, the name of which, I think, would be translated as "The Little Dumpling." It was in what appeared to be a downtown-type commercial district, although *downtown* doesn't mean in Tientsin what it would in Chicago or Philadelphia. Since there are few tall buildings in the city it is somewhat difficult—at least for a foreign visitor—to determine just where the dynamic center of the community is. In any event, there were many shops in the area.

We entered a very old building through a courtyard entrance which led, via a short dark alley, to what once had been a private dwelling, obviously of a well-to-do person. There is no evidence of fresh paint or new wallpaper in such structures now; consequently to American eyes they all appear run-down. But they are sturdy, serviceable and far better than what the great majority of Chinese have enjoyed in past centuries. Our group was shown to a comfortable room on the second floor in

white and Marcel Marceau is white, at least his face is, but the rest of us Caucasians are a unique color for which, as it happens, there is simply no word accurately related to the color spectrum. Consequently, we use the two unsatisfactory terms "white" or "flesh color." The same thing, of course, applies to the other races. There is no such thing as a *black* man, although some African tribesmen have extremely dark skin. But American Blacks aren't any more black than Northern Europeans are white. Nor is the American Indian red. As for the Chinese, their skins are generally one or another variety of a shade more tan than yellow. A few have skin as light as my own, and I saw a small percentage of Chinese with skin so very dark brown they could sit in with the Count Basie band and never be noticed.

That there would be a wide variety of physical types in the United States is natural since, with the exception of the Indians, there is really no such thing as "the American people." We are a nation of immigrants from all corners of the earth. But the majority of Chinese are of the Han people and therefore it is surprising to see great differences in facial types on Chinese streets. We saw in China many individuals who "looked Italian," "looked Greek," "looked Jewish" or "looked Spanish." On my second trip—in July, 1975—at the Hsien Art-

which there was one large round table. A number of old-fashioned easy chairs lined the walls. The chairs are used if visitors wish to socialize before or after dining. We ignored them and placed ourselves immediately around the table.

Dinner was excellent, starting with an antipasto tray, the most interesting item on which was old, very dark green egg slices, as well as sausage, duck and cheese.

One of the nine courses we were served was a fish cooked whole on a large platter, the same dish I had enjoyed on my first evening in town. The recipe, which I can only guess at, is one that should not prove too difficult for American chefs to duplicate. The secret of it seemed to be to cook a fish not in the traditional way but in a *meat* sauce. The juices and gravy that saturated the fish had a definite meaty flavor and there were bits of what might have been pork or chicken sprinkled through it.

The last course was apparently the specialty of the house, from which the restaurant took its name. Each of us was served a small dish on which were piled ten separate dumplings. In design they looked rather like a pasta imitation of a fig or tiny punching bag. Inside was a combination of meat and other, to me, unidentifiable substances. No one at the table was able to finish ten, although some of us approached that number. Since there is little or no waste in China I wondered what happened to all the leftover dumplings.

Before dinner a waiter brought to our table eight bottles of a superb beer, the label of which identifies it as simply Tientsin, China beer. It was smooth, had no bitter after-bite and would sell well, no doubt, if it is ever introduced into the United States. (By 1977 Chinese beer was available in the U.S.) One bottle of Mao Tai, the strongest liquor I have ever tasted, was put on the table, to be drunk out of liquor glasses so small that they hold, I would guess, about a third of the volume of an American shotglass. Even this was too much, in my opinion, considering the wallop and bitterness of the colorless liquid.

When we had finished eating we realized that our cabs would not be returning for another twenty-five minutes. Since I love to walk the streets anywhere in the world I suggested that, rather than simply stand in front of the restaurant, we take the opportunity to explore the neighborhood on foot. Lily, Beverly, Peter —a Danish gentleman—and I strolled down the street to our left, immediately attracting the attention of the usual friendly bands of children and young people. The population of China, incidentally, seems overall remarkably young. At a hasty glance one could be forgiven for thinking that almost everybody in the country is either five or twenty years old.

Red neon signs were still lighted in the otherwise quite dark streets. We strolled toward one and discovered that it identified a movie theater. An advertising poster showed a heroic figure in heavy winter clothing standing near some oil wells. Some young people kindly told us that the film was about a hero who had worked in the northern territories, distinguished himself by great service to his people, and died there.

After a while we decided to move back toward the restaurant and, amid a flurry of *sye-syes* and *szaidjans* (goodbyes) left our new friends. At the corner I noticed a handsome old house, classic European in architecture.

"I wonder," I said, "what the history of that house is. It can hardly have been built by Chinese architects." We strolled across the street and asked some young men if they could tell us about the house.

"It's a dormitory for workers," one of them said.

"No," I said. "Ask them about the history of the house. Was it in the old days an American house, or English?" A young man explained that it had once been owned by the French. The fellow who gave us this information was good-looking, very pleasant and obviously quite intelligent. As he was still speaking, smiling broadly, his body suddenly began to move backward through the crowd as if he were on roller skates. After a moment I saw that the reason he was moving away from us was that another man, with his back to us, had put a hand on his chest and was quietly urging him to retreat. At this the whole crowd melted away quickly. The pusher, who did not address us, evidently carried authority.

I have since learned that such incidents were not uncommon during the rule of the Gang of Four.

Meanwhile, back at the restaurant, I learned later, Jerry Fisher had become somewhat alarmed. By simply standing in the front entrance to the restaurant he had attracted the usual crowd. A gentleman connected with the restaurant was being particularly attentive and cordial. Suddenly a sober-faced young man, wearing what looked like army fatigues, approached and seemed to take a dim view of the presence of American foreigners. He spoke sharply to the restaurant employee, who immediately walked away from Jerry and appeared fearful. The "policeman" stepped out into the street, then curtly ordered the crowd to disperse. They left quickly and without question. One man, Jerry later reported, paused momentarily and apparently said something along the line of "What's the problem? Why can't I stand here?" The young official pointed at him, raised his voice, and said something that apparently alarmed the man, who took off fast. (Such incidents, fortunately, had become extremely rare by 1979.)

We were to observe this pattern later in China, that of unquestioning obedience to authority. This is naturally what one would expect in any totalitarian society, where the penalties for back talk to the police or military can be severe, although they are by no means necessarily so in each instance. The threat of punishment—as well, no doubt, as its occasional reality—must explain such a pattern. But it is not, I think, the total explanation. The Chinese and Japanese have generally been more respectful of authority—the authority of parents and teachers, for example—than we Americans, who are a notoriously disrespectful people across the board.

Mail Service

Jerry came to the breakfast table a bit grumpy Saturday morning saying, "If you had planned to mail anything from here, forget it."

"Why?" I asked.

"It's just too complicated," he said. "I just spent twenty minutes trying to mail some things. They got about seven or eight people into the act, and they told me they had to *read* the letters before I could mail them."

"Do you mean that literally?" I asked. "They actually read your mail?"

"That's right," he said.

We had all assumed that there was at least the possibility of mail being read, without our knowledge, should we attempt to dispatch it from within the country, but had not expected that the procedure would be conducted so openly. The desk attendants had also explained to Jerry that he could not enclose some material he had wanted to mail back to the States, that correspondence and goods, in other words, must go separately.

On the other hand, we later had no trouble at all mailing letters from Peking and Shanghai. Nor should it be assumed that our trouble with a few inexperienced young fellows at a hotel desk in Tientsin in 1975 represented national policy.

No gummed stickers or Scotch tape are used in wrapping packages in China, by the way. The papers are folded neatly and remarkable things are done with a thin twine, which is strong enough to secure the packages but weak enough to be broken, where needed, with a quick snap of the hands.

As regards the reading of mail I would not in the least be surprised to know that there was such a censorship of correspondence in mainland China though I do not have actual knowledge that this was the case. We *do* have knowledge that it is the case in the United States since recent revelations about F.B.I. and C.I.A. activities have made clear that for a good many years the United States Government has regularly violated the privacy of the mails if it thought there was some political excuse for doing so.

There continue to be puzzling instances of this sort in my personal experience at home. I had heard about a remarkable issue of the *Holy Cross Quarterly,* published by the Jesuit fathers of the College of the Holy Cross, Worcester, Massachusetts, on the subject of modern China. On two separate occasions I was sent copies of that particular issue, which is sympathetic to much if not all of what modern China has accomplished. In neither case did the issue reach me. I have also been advised, by the editor of the *Quarterly,* that a number of copies of it, sent through the Springfield, Massachusetts, post office, were received with covers either torn off or defaced. On the cover of that particular issue there is a large reproduction of Andy Warhol's portrait of Mao Tse-tung.

In another instance I engaged in a correspondence with Ben Sprunger, president of a Mennonite Christian college in Bluffton, Ohio, on the general subject of China. When he told me that he was beginning to be attacked by know-nothing right-wingers in his community I sent him some relevant literature. In the normal course of events it would have reached him in two or three days. *He did not receive it until four weeks later.* Who are the faceless dunces who read my mail to a fellow American and delude themselves that they are acting patriotically in doing so?

Chinese Clothing

As many American tourists have observed, the dress of adults in China is quite limited in color choice. It therefore seems drab and monotonous to us, particularly when during the average day one may see literally hundreds of thousands of people all wearing the same three or four basic outfits. The commonest is dark blue, though some wear khaki materials of various shades, others black, others gray. There is not a great deal of difference between the attire of the men and women, though this was true in old China as well. H. G. Wells, in his *Outline of History,* refers to "the blue uniformity of the multitudes in China."

One exception to this monotony is small children. Since they obviously do not choose their own clothes, it may be that parents take the opportunity to express through their children what they might possibly say for themselves were it possible. The little angels therefore wear bright reds, greens, purples, yellows, in a great variety of flowery prints, stripes and plaids.

An American citizen, forced to wear present-day Chinese attire, would feel restricted, limited. But it is by no means certain that the Chinese feel the same. It must be understood, of course, that fashion is a matter of psychological attitude. If it were purely a matter of common sense, the only factors important in choosing a wardrobe would be that the clothing should be well made, reasonably priced, long-wearing and well adapted to conditions of climate (not too warm for hot weather, not too light for winter conditions). These four factors are, in fact, operative but we take them for granted and instead concentrate on the ephemeral factor of *fashion,* much of which makes no sense.

It is literally the case that a dozen or so of the Western world's leading designers could—if they conspired to do so—decree that next year every American woman should wear—attached to the top of her hat—a bright green tennis-ball-like object. A visitor from another land might ask a woman why on earth she had the green tennis-ball-like object on the top of her head. She would no doubt answer, quite sincerely, "Well, it's just because I think the thing looks sort of cute up there. It *is* in style, you know."

Just so, the Chinese apparently consider their clothes "in style" and do not have the same attitude toward them that Americans would. They are pleased with their serviceability, the fact that the materials are of good quality, fairly priced and not vulgarly ostentatious.

What I have described is, of course, cold-weather attire. There is considerably more freedom in the selection of summer wardrobes though during hot weather most men wear a plain white cotton shirt which hangs outside the trousers since that is more comfortable than tucking it in. On extremely hot days young men may wear colorful "tank tops," sleeveless undershirts, or school athletic shirts. Women wear light blouses in a wide variety of patterns and colors.

When, after several days, it at last came time to say adieu to the Tientsin Hotel, at seven o'clock in the evening, our farewells were strangely emotional. Even Mr. Sung, so obviously a party member, so concerned with security, seemed suddenly more likable. We honestly all felt that we would miss him in the days to come. One young man, Wong Chin, a handsome, intelligent and friendly teenager, rather tall, extremely polite, had tears in his eyes as he said goodbye. The Fishers—politically conservative—had grown so fond of him that they embraced him and wept when they bade him farewell.

We were taken to the station in large buses and put aboard a train quite different from the comfortable compartmented one on which we had arrived. Our party shared a plain, ancient car with a sizable contingent from the People's Liberation Army including, oddly enough, one cute little fellow about four years old, who was perhaps the son or brother of one of the soldiers.

There were more warm and slightly tearful goodbyes at the station. Mr. Sung, Wong Chin and the young ladies stood on the platform, refusing to leave until the train itself started to pull away, as is the charming Chinese custom. Through the window Wong pantomimed that we should not cry.

All of us do indeed look forward to returning to Tientsin someday and our hearts went out to the good people of that city when we heard of the dreadful quakes of 1976, in which hundreds of thousands were killed. If such a disaster had occurred in Chicago or Los Angeles we would consider it the tragedy of the century. Our few days in that remarkable community were not nearly enough to learn a great deal about it. We all had the feeling that per-son-to-person contact can somehow surmount a good many, if not all, of the political and philosophical problems that now separate humanity.

On the train we were pleased to discover a young woman prepared to provide all hands with as much hot tea as we wished. American technology is, in most respects, superior to that of the Chinese; there are certain areas, however, in which the Chinese seem better, as, for example, in the making of beautiful thermos jugs. Most of those I buy in the States are fragile and don't seem to keep things hot, or cold, for more than a few hours. The Chinese serve tea in tall, beautifully designed containers, which seem to keep liquids warm for about two days. Their glass interiors don't often survive the rough trip back to the U.S., however.

The rice that had been served with our last meal at the Tientsin Hotel had not had the terrible chlorine taste that had spoiled the flavor of all other water-based dishes the three previous days, and on the train to Peking the tea was delicious, with no trace of chlorine. A Chinese gentleman whose home was in Hong Kong, riding on the train with us, explained that the Tientsin water was not ordinarily so distasteful, but that the authorities had decided to add extra chlorine to it purely for the safety of the visitors to the carpet fair. Not wishing to have any sick foreigners on their hands, they had taken extra precautions.

2. Peking

ABOUT two hours later we arrived at the Peking station in the cold and dark. It was a scene of incredible bustle and life. Hundreds of soldiers and other uniformed people —apparently coming in from communes and People's Liberation Army bases—hurried past carrying tremendous amounts of baggage in the traditional Oriental way, with the load distributed into two approximately equal halves, hanging from five- or six-feet-long pieces of bamboo balanced across the shoulders.

As they came up a steep ramp they stopped at the street level and set their weights down. When a few minutes later they lifted them, they did so by squatting down to the floor, placing their backs and shoulders under the poles and then standing up, which seemed to be quite difficult. With such heavy loads they could not walk in the normal manner but had to move forward in the kind of singsong, chop-chop fashion that Occidentals think of as characteristic of walking in ancient China.

The Chinese actually do walk somewhat

differently, it seems to me, compared with Americans. They seem to take shorter steps, to move in a somewhat smoother manner, in the way that one might move, for example, in balancing something on one's head. We Americans, I only now realize, do considerably more lunging and swooping as we walk.

I wonder if the reason for the Chinese walk is that for countless centuries the majority of Chinese had to walk while carrying heavy loads of one sort or another. It is impossible to walk in the American way while carrying anything heavy. One automatically takes shorter steps and tries to maintain equilibrium. Perhaps this social habit developed in that way.

A problem emerged at the Peking station. When we finally got up to the streel level we were asked, by China Travel personnel, to present our passports, which we did. There then ensued not the ten- or fifteen-minute delay we had anticipated but something more like an hour-and-a-half wait, during which first a discussion, then something very close to an argument developed concerning our authorization to remain in Peking for the next several days. At one point the Travel Service people said that we would be permitted to stay in the city only for twenty-four hours, after which, presumably, we would have to return to Tientsin.

Later—after we had finally been put aboard a bus to the Peking Hotel—that position was altered. The young man in charge told Lily, rather coldly, that *she* would be allowed to stay for only twenty-four hours but that the rest of us could stay longer.

While waiting in the station we saw one old peasant woman—apparently in her seventies, whose feet had obviously been bound in childhood. It is shocking to American eyes to see bound feet. They appear, and in fact are, deformed. The feet are actually about half the normal length. The old woman was leaning on the arm of a younger woman and walking along in a strange bouncing, tottering style. The foot-bound women seem rather like babies who are learning to walk. In the old days they did little walking. To Western eyes the deliberate binding of a human being's feet, to make

Except for the railroad tracks this peasant might have strolled out of the tenth century.

them very small, seems as irrational as the African Ubangi custom of enlarging the lower lip till it can encompass a saucer, and it must naturally be asked why such a harmful practice arose in the first place. The reasons behind it were purely sexual. In the ancient Chinese tradition the ideal, ultrafeminine woman was a helpless doll who, because of her weakness, had to depend on a strong man to see to her needs. It is Jayne's theory that this represented an emotional insecurity in the men of old China. Be that as it may, the men found it sexually stimulating to observe a woman who seemed a little, tottering, simpering doll. Toward this end the feet of girls were wrapped from infancy, to render them helpless. Needless to say, modern China—Communist and Nationalist—has recognized the absurdity and destructiveness of the practice; it has not been permitted for many years.

Americans should not feel too smugly superior when considering the custom of foot-binding, however. About fifty years ago something close to it prevailed in our own country. In my mother's generation it was considered important for a woman to have small feet and most unfortunate if her feet were large. So ingrained was this absurd idea that if a woman's feet were a few sizes "too large" she "solved" the problem by wearing shoes that were painfully small. All the women in my mother's family therefore had terribly deformed toes, frightful-looking bunions, and many painful corns. That women would deliberately make themselves suffer so hideously for vanity seems incredible today but, as I say, some of the same psychological factors were operative as in the case of Chinese foot-binding.

Although the alarming confusion about our travel documents was still not settled, we were allowed to proceed to the Peking Hotel. Unlike the Hsin Ciao, the hotel is strikingly beautiful. The lobby of the newest wing, with its massive open marble floor, great stretches of red carpeting, and four massive gold-trimmed pillars, seems an odd combination of Hilton-modern and old Chinese. The combination works.

The argument in the lobby was gradually transferred, along with our luggage and weary bodies, to the seventh floor where, with Lily's increasing desperation (the rest of us were merely stunned), the situation became considerably more dramatic. The two young men representing the Travel Service seemed to vacillate between two mutually contradictory positions: all of us would have to leave Peking within twenty-four hours—going God knows where—or only Lily Wen would have to leave in twenty-four hours; the rest of us could stay for an unspecified but longer period.

For all the luxury of the hotel, and the attractive decor of our room, it was even more difficult to flush the toilet in Peking than it had been in the old, somewhat run-down hotel in Tientsin. Nor did I have any better luck with the tub when I tried to fill it to take a bath.

Only a trickle of water could be drawn from either the hot or cold faucet, so I switched the flow to go through the Swedish-style hand-held shower nozzle and bathed that way, though sans shower curtain! I would suggest to the Chinese: to hell with trying to acquire the plans to the American H-bomb, the ICBM, or the space station. Steal a good American bath-tub and toilet bowl and copy them, down to the last detail. Or make a flat trade. The secret of the Chinese thermos jug in return for the secret of American toilet plumbing.

But if the plumbing in our Tientsin and Peking hotels left something to be desired, public toilets in China, Japan and other Oriental countries are generally, by American standards, a horror. The familiar toilet bowl, on which one sits, is provided in the Orient only in quarters especially planned for Westerners. The indigenous equivalent is either a recessed small open rectangle set in the ground or cement floor, or else, in slightly better water closets, a porcelain receptacle, set into the floor. One simply stands over it and hopes for the best. There is no paper unless one personally provides it.

Public toilet, Tientsin.

The view from our room at the Peking Hotel, summer, 1975.

A closer comparison for Americans would be the odiferous outhouses that were common in our country up to the 1930s and are still encountered in backward rural areas. But the worst shock—to Europeans and Americans—comes when one encounters one of these latrines in the countryside. There is no privacy. There is—well, forget it.

The heated negotiations now having been adjourned to Lily's room, I suggested that the only sensible thing to do was to make immediate phone contact with the China Travel people in Tientsin, who had assured us that there would be no problem concerning our planned itinerary. About half an hour later the call was finally put through. As I had predicted, it led to a prompt if somewhat embarrassing solution. The man in Tientsin pointed out that there was in reality no difficulty whatever and that he had personally attached the necessary document to Lily's passport. A quick search of her papers revealed the specified document. At

this, I washed my hands of the matter and went back to the room, leaving Lily wailing in embarrassment, apologizing to the two young tourist guides whose time we had taken up at such great and unnecessary length.

Before retiring I went downstairs to see a bit more of the hotel. The oldest of the three sections of the establishment, in those days known by its French name Hotel de Pekin, was managed, at the turn of the century, by M. and Mme. Auguste Chamot. Chamot was a Swiss hotelman whose name is entered in historical records for his dramatic courage during the Boxer Rebellion siege, known to most contemporary Americans chiefly either from Peter Fleming's book *Siege of Peking* or the motion picture *55 Days in Peking,* which starred Charlton Heston and Ava Gardner.

For all the spaciousness of the lobby, by the way, the Peking Hotel does not have a check-in desk, as one might expect, nor in fact does one check in. Such details have been attended to before you arrive since the Travel Service and the hotel are all part of the same large organization. Rather there are two comparatively small desks—one to the left and one to the right—which in an American hotel might be the base of operations for the bell captain. This is not as odd as it might seem, however, in that on each floor there is a separate desk with attendants who can take care of a good many, if not all, of one's needs. White-jacketed, young attendants offer prompt, cheerful service and would not dream of accepting a tip.

The rooms have a wonderfully efficient system for calling floor personnel. Two convenient buttons, one at the door, one near the bed, light up when pressed, cause a light to be turned on outside one's door, and produce a beeper signal in the attendant's area.

Jayne, not knowing they were call signals, thought the buttons were nightlights. She turned them on and naturally made no connection between this and the fact that shortly thereafter an attendant appeared at the door and rang the bell. She explained that she wanted nothing, thank you, after which the young man turned the signal light off. At which Jayne said, "Oh, darn it, these lights keep going off," and turned them on again. This comedy was repeated two or three times before she made the connection in her mind. Perhaps she seemed inscrutable to the attendants.

You are not to address them as "Waiter" (*hwoji*), incidentally, though, being chiefly in charge of room service, that's what they are. To the Chinese the word smacks of the old order, with its master-servant relationships. The word of address, to practically everybody, is *Comrade,* which after all means *friend.*

In the morning there was the almost overpowering smell of incense in the elevators and the lobby area near them. We shortly learned that the reason was a dreadful stench, apparently from a plumbing problem on the basement level, a problem, alas, that the incense could not totally disguise. One might have been forgiven the impression that National Night-Soil Week was being celebrated at the hotel. After a day or two, happily, the difficulty was resolved.

After breakfast we were taken, in clean, smoothly running taxis, a few blocks down the city's main thoroughfare, to see a true wonder of the world, the Forbidden City.

As we drove through the fairly cool early-morning streets we passed, at four separate locations, groups of people, some banging drums and cymbals, some singing, others waving red flags. The ceremonies were to give groups of young people a good send-off as they went to serve in nearby communes.

THE FORBIDDEN CITY

I do not believe there is anything on our planet that approaches the Imperial Palace in overall combination of beauty and power to impress. One naturally thinks, by way of comparison, of the Vatican, the Winter Palace in Leningrad, the Louvre, the Taj Mahal, the pyramids. But the ancient Chinese royal estate surpasses them all. Since many Americans have seen St. Peter's Basilica in Rome but few will ever view the Forbidden City, I suggest it is possible to get an idea of the impression the Chinese palace makes on the visitor by imagining that, after one has strolled through and out the back of St. Peter's, one enters upon an enormous, beautiful open plaza, at the far end of which is yet another St. Peter's. Imagine further that the process is then repeated three or four times and that each succeeding cathedral is even more beautiful than the last.

It suddenly occurred to me, after spending several hours in the Forbidden City, that I had seen no pigeons in China. If they ever were here perhaps they had been chased away, or eaten.

One eventually comes to separate museum rooms in which ceramics of the most bewitching beauty are displayed—bowls, vases, dishes, cups, teapots, pitchers—from various periods of Chinese art. It is no wonder that the Western world uses the word *china* to describe the best dishware.

So enormous and extensive are the Forbidden City plazas and byways that our group

Gate to Forbidden City, Peking.

Child, Peking's Forbidden City, 1975.

A lovely plaza in the Forbidden City.

became lost or at least disoriented—in the Orient, at that. We had expected to find our taxi waiting at the north gate, but when we finally located an exit, several hours after entering the grounds, we were unable to determine whether it was to the west or east of the area.

At this exit, simply the north gate to us, I was not at that moment aware that a fascinating Chinese custom had in times long gone been enacted on that very ground, now occupied simply by waiting taxis, buses and wandering visitors, up till the very moment the Manchu dynasty fell in 1912. Since Enid Saunders Candlin describes this colorful footnote to history so well in *The Breach in the Wall,* I shall simply quote her.

It was at this North Gate of the Forbidden City that the officials and courtiers who waited upon the Emperor used to muster, long before dawn, to await their summons of entry. In the dark, often in cold and windy weather, this was a trial to them, frequently remarked upon by writers and poets. Po Chu-i speaks of such an occasion in "An Early Levee," which was, in his day at Ch'ang-an, then the capital of the T'ang. Nothing had changed in the way of protocol and etiquette, however, right into our century in Peking. Poor Po Chu-i speaks of there being a foot of snow on the ground, and his having to attend a dawn levee to congratulate the Emperor for some reason. His horse slips on the causeway, his lantern blows out, and he has to ride facing north the whole way, his ears freezing, his hair and beard covered with icicles—how he envies his friend, who can stay warm under the covers, sleeping, at home!

We had an artistic friend, Billy Dunn, who lived in Peking quite early in the century, and in spite of bad weather, he used sometimes to go himself to that North Gate, in the dark, to watch the spectacle of the courtiers assembling, coming up in sedan chairs or on horseback, in their ceremonial clothes, their mandarin buttons and long feathers, with their files of servants, and having to wait for a long time before they were admitted. No one ever dared to be late—there was no shelter—it was an example of the imperial power, which could command even its senior administrators to undergo such an unnecessary trial. This continued right up to the fall of the dynasty;

ceremonies have such endurance. The Emperor or Empress had of course also to rise before dawn to meet the officials, but they at least did not have to endure the storms at the outer gate. However, it was a fine show, and Billy used to wonder that he never met anyone else there watching—no one ever hindered him.

On the same side of the Forbidden City lies Bei Hai Park, once the pleasure ground of the imperial family in the Ching dynasty. Like most Chinese parks, it is beautified by waterways, graceful bridges and temples. Its most imposing edifice is the famous White Pagoda, built in 1652 as a gesture of respect to the Dalai Lama, at the time a guest in the city. White pagodas, which are found at various locations in China, are generally superb specimens of Buddhist architecture.

There was no sign of our cab when we emerged from the back entrance of the palace grounds. Herbert Cole and I decided to return on foot. (On both trips to China in 1975, by the way, I walked the streets at will, without guides.) The stroll back to the hotel was fascinating. We passed through neighborhood streets then rarely, I would guess, seen by American tourists. The overall impression was gray, gray, gray. Here and there in the window of a small shop or restaurant we would see brightly colored fruit or vegetables, candy-bar wrappers, children's clothing. But otherwise the sensation of color blindness was again powerful. Not only did things seem gradually to have turned gray and colorless, as a result of countless years of smoke, dust, poverty and neglect, many actually appeared to have been painted gray to begin with.

It is not enough to observe that apparently 90 percent of things in this area of China are painted gray. One must ask, Why? Two possible explanations suggest themselves. One is that the Chinese actually admire the color. But I doubt that a people with such a distinguished artistic tradition could prefer such a dreary color. The other hypothesis is that, since almost everything in northern Chinese cities seems to end up covered with coal, soot and earth dust, it has been found that gray is the

Tien An Mien Square and the Forbidden City, Peking.

Forbidden City, Peking.

Pagoda, Soochow.

The corner of Chang An Boulevard and Wang Fu Jing Street as seen from an upper floor of the Peking Hotel. The pall of smog overhanging the city is so thick one can scarcely make out the buildings across the street.

color least likely to be significantly altered by such an onslaught.

But the sights and sounds we experienced were fascinating nevertheless. Almost everything in China seems to be surrounded by a wall. If Robert Frost was right that "something there is that doesn't like a wall" the spirit of that something must be unhappy in China. This has nothing whatever to do with communism-socialism; the importance goes back thousands of years. In addition to the world-famous Great Wall there are millions of little walls, around countless homes, compounds, factories, and public buildings of all kinds, the construction of walls being one more ancient custom today's rulers have not seen fit to revise. The walls around the buildings we passed appeared to be about ten feet high and quite thick. One enters the private dwelling areas by a gate that opens on a small courtyard. I glanced into some of the courtyards. Many angled off at once so that within one small area there might be several tiny homes, shops, repair sheds, laundry facilities or whatever.

At one point we saw, up ahead, a small crowd of perhaps forty people, roughly half of

them children. They paid no attention to us as we approached, since they were all busily engaged in some activity, which turned out to involve sorting junk that had been collected. On an open table old women were receiving and sorting into separate piles bottles, bales of newspapers, twisted pieces of metal, etc. In China nothing is wasted.

A moment later we passed a parked truck loaded with the long green cabbage that is so important a part of the Chinese diet. The taste definitely classifies it as cabbage but it more closely resembles a long, thick celery plant.

We stepped into a small neighborhood shop, purchased excellent chocolate bars, very inexpensively, and a few minutes later bought, from a street vendor, what turned out to be "popsicles," of indeterminate flavor.

Chinese chocolate is the best I've ever tasted. Another thing seemingly better in China than in the U.S.A. is coffee. When our coffee is strong enough to satisfy those who like it that way, it is often bitter. Chinese coffee, on the other hand, is full-bodied and rich with not a trace of bitterness. I do not know what part of the world it comes from.

One Chinese to whom I put the question answered "China." Another said, equally authoritatively, "South America."

THE SUMMER PALACE

Another glory of Peking—pre-Revolutionary, of course—is the special playground royalty enjoyed during warm weather, the Summer Palace.

This resort of the Chinese emperors is, to put the matter plainly, possibly the most beautiful site of its kind in the world. The combined works of nature and man are united in a physical symphony of indescribable appeal to the senses. One could sit in any part of this lovely park chosen at random and be endlessly fascinated by the impressions available to the eyes, the ears, the senses of touch and smell. Water, sky, trees, hills, architecture, sculpture, painting, ceramics, landscaping, masonry—it is all quite too much to be properly appreciated by our weak receiving mechanisms.

Curving for 1,170 feet around the shore of the adjacent lake, the Painted Gallery, a covered walkway, is such an achievement of high art that words cannot begin to do it justice; the reader is urged to seek out photographs.

In most of the beautiful palaces and museums with which Westerners are familiar, one wanders through comfortable, spacious corridors and rooms, encountering perhaps every few feet some remarkable individual work of art. But the Painted Gallery itself is one enormous work of art, with scarcely an inch of its surface that cannot be observed with esthetic enjoyment. The upper interior side panels, and all the visible surfaces on overhead beams, are hand-painted with exquisite portraits, still-lifes, scenes of nature, court life, illustrations of contemporary or historical events.

One learns with true shock that in 1860 invading French troops set fire to this temple of beauty. It is not too difficult to grasp why the Chinese long considered Europeans barbarians.

In one of the throne rooms of the Summer Palace, we saw two remarkable figures, perhaps five feet in height, colored black, made entirely out of gnarled, twisted, polished roots. In their heads were fierce, staring eyes. They bore a remarkable resemblance to Sesame Street's woolly Cookie-Monster.

THE GREAT WALL

Monday morning, as our group breakfasted in the enormous dining room in preparation for our trip to the Great Wall, I was approached by a pleasant young man who identified himself as Robert Oxnam. He explained

Baked goods truck, Peking.

Great Wall.

that he was traveling with a delegation sponsored by the U.S.-China Friendship Committee. Oxnam, who is the son of the famous bishop of the same name, teaches Chinese history at Trinity College in Connecticut.

"If you're interested," he said, "some of us are going this evening to visit a remarkable man who has lived in China since long before the Revolution. You'd be welcome to join us if you'd like."

"Certainly," I said. "Who is the man?"

"Rewi Alley," Oxnam said. "Are you familiar with him?"

"No," I said. "Is he East Indian?" In my mind I had visualized Alley's name as spelled *Ali*. Smiling, Oxnam explained that Alley was a New Zealander who had lived through much

of the drama of modern China. I told him that I would be glad to accompany him and his group that evening and thanked him for the invitation. We made an appointment to meet in the lobby at seven-fifteen.

I later realized I had read Alley's name several years earlier in one of Edgar Snow's books. He has indeed played an important role in the Chinese history of the last fifty years.

If it were possible for tourists in China to see only one site of historical interest most would elect to visit the Great Wall. The weather was quite cold and damp as we climbed aboard a small bus and took off, immediately after breakfast, for this remarkable structure, which lies north of Peking. Jayne, who was about to come down with some sort of serious viral infection that sadly would keep her bedded in the hotel for the next five days, dressed herself in thermal underwear, a woolen suit, a sweater, a camel's-hair overcoat and, if you can believe it, a mink coat as well.

She had cabled our office from Hong Kong to ask me to bring the mink along, having been told of freezing temperatures in Peking, though she had earlier decided not to take the coat because she thought it would be too ostentatious in a part of the world where almost everyone is poor. The coat, in fact, may be too ostentatious even for Beverly Hills. It's a tan-cream color, glamorous, rich, long and full. Jayne doesn't buy furs anymore, but continues to wear her old minks because the mink is not an endangered species. So now she was wearing it, with its large hood over her head, as well as a scarf. She was by this time used to being stared at but on this particular day drew a few more puzzled glances than usual.

I must say, though, that the bitter, icy winds that whipped us when we finally stood atop the wall made us agree she was not overdressed.

Leaving Peking, we moved through drab, tawny-colored countryside, seeing small farms, an occasional commune, and now and then a low industrial building. Looking at the farm fields, it suddenly occurred to me that I had not seen a single insect in China. Surely they must exist there, if only to feed the birds. On the other hand, we saw few birds. Six or seven large black crows flapped lazily about in

Near the Great Wall, Peking.

Terraced hillsides near the Great Wall.

the rocky country nearer the Great Wall, and several dozen unusually sturdy-looking chickens scratched the earth along the route. Other than that no birds were seen anywhere. It was late winter, of course. Perhaps some birds return in the spring.

As we approached the mountains we noticed that the walls around small farms now were made with heavy round stones, rather than the flat adobe bricks of the lowlands. Presumably over the course of millions of years gravity and water flow have torn boulders

loose from the high ground and strewn them over the surrounding countryside. The rugged hills we gradually moved into looked like tall mountains anywhere. They support, however, much less vegetation than do the American Rockies. Shortly after heading up into higher altitude, we observed that we were running beside a railroad track which, we learned, was the Trans-Siberian Railroad.

Then, the moment of excitement when a section of the wall first came into view! It was crumbling, broken down totally in spots (not surprising after so many centuries), standing in others, but there it was. For the next half-hour or so we were able to catch glimpses of other portions of the long, twisting, climbing, falling structure before we would approach the section of the wall that tourists are permitted to climb, the part invariably shown in photographs.

As is the case with all earthly things that are massive—the pyramids, the Grand Canyon, Niagara Falls, Yosemite—seeing them is such a dramatic experience that the senses tend to be overwhelmed, so that the natural reaction of awe and amazement is mixed with a sort of blank stupefaction. There is simply too much to take in; the human receiving mechanism is not equal to it on brief exposure. The Great Wall is an amazing achievement considering both time and space. As for time, this remarkable structure was erected more than 2,000 years ago. Compared to such an antiquity our own national history seems a very brief chapter indeed. As for space, the wall winds through some 1,500 miles of China's northern provinces and with its many twists and turns may actually be twice as long.

Building an enormous wall for well over a thousand miles would be an extraordinary achievement even on level ground. But China's Great Wall rises and drops with the outline of the Pataling Mountains north of Peking. This gigantic defensive structure, winding over valley and plain east and west through the mountains, has been likened to an immense dragon adapting itself to the earth over which it lies. It stretches from Shanhaikuan on the Pohiac in the east to Chiayukuan in Kansu (Gansu) Province in the west. It is sobering to think that much of this impressive structure was built three hundred years before Christ walked the earth. Even before that time the North China feudal states of Wen, Chao and Chin had built separate walls through the Yinshan Mountains. In the third century B.C., at which time China was unified under the rulers of Chin, the three separate walls were joined and additionally lengthened to make the Great Wall more or less as it is known today.

Portions of it have, of course, collapsed and

been rebuilt at various times over the thousands of years of its existence. Much of the most important reconstruction was done during the Ming dynasty period (1368–1644).

The sections of the wall on which today's tourists are allowed to walk has been repaired and reinforced in recent years. Metal handrails have been added for the convenience of weak-legged visitors. I can assure you, from personal experience, one is grateful for the addition on the long walk to the highest points to which visitors are allowed to climb. Oxnam had suggested that, inasmuch as American and European visitors are generally urged to ascend to the left, I might find it more of a challenge to take the wall on the right side since, because the climb is considerably steeper, few non-Chinese visitors make it to the top.

I was the only one of our group who walked in that direction and since I was alone for much of the time it would be easy to claim that I reached the highest point. The fact is I finally gave up about fifty yards short of the end. As readers who have traveled a great deal will know, a conscientious tourist spends most of his time in a state of at least moderate exhaustion. Since one naturally wants to see and do as much as possible, it seems pointless to spend long hours sleeping or socializing in one's hotel. This is fine as far as it goes but it inevitably means you get less sleep than you are accustomed to at home. All of which adds up to a physical condition in which the last eighty yards or so of the right-hand expanse of the Great Wall of China—in a stiff wind and freezing temperatures—can seem a very steep climb indeed.

Jayne and some of the others, having taken the leftward route, had had an easier time of it and a number of them made it to the uppermost point.

MING TOMBS

On the way back from the Great Wall, one may visit the famous Ming Tombs, where ancient emperors were buried.

Shortly before arriving at the tombs, we encountered a fascinating sight. On both sides of the road stand enormous stone creatures

Jayne looking down into Ming burial room, winter, 1975.

Stone elephant, Ming Tombs, winter, 1975.

Jayne and I descending into Ming Tombs.

Jayne at Ming Tombs park, winter, 1975.

which the Ming emperors must have assumed guarded the access to their holy ground. Pairs of stone elephants, camels, griffins, Fu dogs and fierce warriors stand in pairs, facing each other, serving now only as irresistible magnets for tourists and photographers.

One of the curious facts about the Ming Tombs is that they were discovered only a few years ago, during the Cultural Revolution, reportedly by a peasant digging in the area, for reasons that are not clear though it had long been assumed that royal tombs were somewhere about because of the enormous stone guardian warriors and animals on the approach road.

The visitor descends into the earth and eventually comes to large, well-wrought stone passageways leading to the inner sanctum where the dark red caskets of the Emperor Yung Lo and his family were found. It is said that several hundred workers who had labored on the construction of the tombs were murdered so that the emperor's secret burial place would never be known. It is interesting that

the same account is related in so many parts of the world. Whether its commonness testifies to its truthful or legendary character it is difficult to say.

Perhaps the most remarkable detail of the tomb's construction is the device used to seal the massive double doors to the inner chambers, presumably for all time. A "pole-vault" sort of base, just a few inches deep, was dug into the floor, of a size large enough to accommodate an enormous square-cut stone pillar. As the doors were closed these tipped forward and would seem to prevent the doors from ever again being opened from the outside. How the trick was turned despite this mechanism was not explained to us.

The reason for such emphasis on secrecy in the grave was that according to Chinese Buddhist belief, the entry or robbery of a family tomb was the worst possible sort of misfortune. The disturbance of the tomb was regarded as a literal disturbance of the sleeping souls by evil forces.

These particular Ming Tombs have been

referred to in China as "the 13 tombs." According to some historical records thirteen emperors were buried in the area. This means there may be twelve more lying about, an exciting prospect for archeologists the world over.

On our way out of the surrounding park I photographed a beautiful light blue and bright yellow wastepaper and refuse can, to show that even a utilitarian object can still be a work of art. I do not suppose the combination of beauty and garbage-can-ness would normally occur to American designers.

A VISIT WITH REWI ALLEY

That night Lily and I could not locate Robert Oxnam's group in the lobby at 7:00 P.M. After waiting until seven-fifteen, we assumed we had misunderstood their instructions, left a note for them at the lobby desk and walked across the street and around the corner to Rewi Alley's house.

(A fascinating sidelight on the Chinese passion for avoiding waste occurred three days later when Jerry Fisher asked at the desk for a piece of paper on which to jot something down. They gave him the note I had written to Oxnam and pointed out that the back of it could still be used.)

Alley lives in a large, comfortable compound inhabited exclusively, I believe, by resident foreigners.

We were ushered cordially, by a Chinese woman, into an old, somewhat musty, but typical writer's apartment that I later learned had been occupied for many years by the late Anna Louise Strong. It was naturally crammed with books and objects of art. The furniture was old but comfortable. Rewi Alley is a poet and political writer who has been in China constantly since 1927. Needless to say, he is a Marxist.

"What were you doing the year before it occurred to you to come here?" I asked him.

"I was a sheep farmer in New Zealand," he said. He explained that the late 1920s was a very bad time for sheep farming. The price of wool had fallen and he decided to get out of the business, selling out to a partner. Having

apparently no commitments in life at that time he more or less at random elected to go to China, without making any plans as to how long he would stay there.

"Were you politically sophisticated at that time?" I asked.

"No," he said, "I was not. But I hadn't been here very long when I found myself intrigued by the conditions here. It was impossible to observe conditions in old China without developing political reactions."

One of Alley's guests was an equally famous old China hand, a Lebanese-American, now a Chinese citizen, named Dr. George Hatem. He had come to China, I gather, at about the same time that Alley did.

Oxnam joined us a few minutes later, with four members of his party, an elderly couple from, I believe, Philadelphia, named Grimm, and two young women from New England, who were rather stern representatives of the American women's liberation movement. We asked Alley and Hatem to share with us some of their recollections of pre-Revolutionary conditions in China.

Pre-1949 Conditions in China

"In one province I visited in 1927," Alley said, "one hundred thousand people died from famine. In another part of the country, in the northwest, eight *million* died. These incredible facts were not even *mentioned* in the Shanghai newspapers at that time!"

It is too easy for a relatively disinterested foreign reader—American or not—to reflect for half a second on such tragic raw material, and then pass along to the next bit of information, putting out of mind what one has just learned. But it is wrong to do so. I have just mentioned that *over 8 million people died in a famine* and that in the busy, prosperous, sophisticated city of Shanghai the authorities did not see fit to make reference to such a monumental tragedy. I did not point out that the Communists too have been party to this "let's not publish bad news" policy in quite a number of instances, since 1949. Two wrongs are, of course, two wrongs.

Imagine that tomorrow a series of natural

and social disasters strikes the United States. Suppose 8 million people in the American West die of hunger, their carcasses littering the roads, fields and city streets as if they were so many dead dogs. And then imagine that in the newspapers in Chicago, Philadelphia and New York there is *no mention of what has happened.* The population of Shanghai was then, Alley said, about 6 million. The city's upper class was cultivated, well educated and wealthy. They got along famously with the Westerners, with whom they often cooperated in business ventures.

Alley and Hatem explained that even in old Shanghai conditions for the working people were so atrocious that it is probably impossible for us to get a true intellectual and emotional grasp of them, even when we hear them described in detail. It was possible to buy and sell children, in pre-1949 China, as Americans today might buy and sell household pets. Our pets, in fact, can count on a better fate to that of many children in old China. A girl of eight or ten might be sold into prostitution. A girl in those days cost half as much as a donkey. Since in such depressing conditions the natural physical beauty of a young woman would fade quickly, the prostitutes were therefore very young. Dr. Hatem reported that they lasted an average of two years after leaving the houses of prostitution, then were usually mercifully relieved by death.

Even for young girls fortunate enough not to be drawn into prostitution, city life held dangers for the daughters of the poor. A contract labor foreman, Alley explained, might say to an impoverished man, "I have a nice job for your daughter and I'll give you sixteen silver dollars for her." Such prices tempted many a poverty-stricken laborer. In any event, children were actually sold in this way. The girl would then be taken to a factory, which ran twenty-four hours a day. Half the force would sleep while the other worked. The girls were obligated to three years of indentured slavery. The prettiest among them would still be urged to enter houses of prostitution. They would be wined and dined, as the Western saying has it, taken to visit the houses, which would be cleaned up for the occasion, excellent food would be served, and the best possible

clothing given to them, the object being to make the physical surroundings more attractive than anything they had ever known. Those who succumbed to temptation would, of course, shortly discover their mistake but by then they were trapped. When the girls had finally been used up by the prostitution mills they would literally be thrown out on Fuchow Road. Many of them were so ill, Dr. Hatem explained, that he had seen cases of girls suffering from eight separate diseases at the same time. *The whole hideous practice was stopped instantly in 1949 after the Communist takeover.* Special attention, in fact, was given to the unfortunate young women who survived. They were first given medical treatment, then offered an education or trained for decent work.

There was literally slave labor in China in those days. Alley described one moderate-sized room he visited that had been partitioned halfway up so as to make two stories out of it. About fifty children labored on each level, in cramped, dreadfully unhealthy conditions. Naturally they did not live very long in such a situation. As they died their bodies were simply tossed over a nearby fence into the riverbed where, over the following days, they would be eaten by roving bands of hungry dogs. Imagine the questions that might eventually form in your mind about an economic system in which such atrocities were common.

Among other problems of that time were the widespread use of opium and the utterly intolerable taxation, which could run as high as 60 percent of the income of poor people. After the Revolution, taxes were drastically cut, thus automatically greatly increasing the purchasing power of the poor. Inflation was so severe that paper money in the ordinary denominations was literally worthless.

Alley described the hundreds of poor in the late 1920s pathetically trying to move away from the various areas hit by famine, all their worldly possessions piled in a wheelbarrow or on their shoulders. "Thousands of them," he said, "died along the roads."

When the twin factors of China's alleged 800-million-plus population and the population explosion were introduced into the conversation, Dr. Hatem observed that there is really no way of knowing how many people live in China.

"We don't know how many people were here in the old days," he said, "because the country was so disorganized then that any sort of census was extremely unreliable." He felt that because figures seem always to be rounded off to the nearest hundred million this indicates that all census numbers, even now, are partly guesswork. Philosophically, of course, it does not make an enormous difference whether the correct figure in 1975 was closer to 700 million or, for that matter, 900 million. The important thing is that the population is the largest in the world and still growing fast, despite the government's encouragement of birth-control programs.

In speaking to Alley and Hatem, as well as to native-born Chinese citizens, I remembered that many American conservatives feel that Communists are evil monsters and murderers. This is an incredibly foolish attitude. There are indeed some Communists who are murderers, just as there are more than enough murderers on our side of the fence. But when you meet a Communist, you may discover that he is a person remarkably like yourself. He is usually an individual whose intentions are good and whose activities grow out of revulsion at the undeniable shortcomings of the capitalist system and the injustice, poverty and oppression under which so many millions languish around the world. Unfortunately, when Communists take power in a country, though it is true that a majority may be given more food and better clothing than they had before, inevitably many have to give up a certain amount of their liberty. They then have little or no freedom to protest against the unjust acts of their government.

But in some parts of the world, such as China, the average man never did have a great deal of political or economic freedom, so the Chinese and others do not consider communism as oppressive as we would in this country. To people who have not been taught to read, freedom of the press has no meaning.

We asked Alley to comment on the new administration's methods of putting an end to the narcotics traffic. He explained that at the

first stage orders simply went out, publicly and to the opium dealers themselves, that the traffic was to stop immediately. Some obeyed the orders, others persisted in the criminal traffic. A number of these were shot, after which, apparently, the opium trade ended. As for the addicts, some died, others eventually recovered.

The Communist authorities confiscated enough opium in those days to provide for all conceivable medical needs for at least a hundred years.

"Why wasn't the Kuomintang administration able to stop the opium traffic?" one of our party asked. "They were obviously as prepared to resort to capital punishment as were the new rulers."

"The problem was," Alley explained, "under the old regime the police and government officials had no serious interest in stopping the traffic since some of them were part of it."

No doubt a number of the Americans in the room thought how similar this was to the present situation in large American cities where some policemen and corrupt officials are in league with narcotics dealers rather than opposed to them. None of us brought up the point, however.

Since Alley and Hatem are Communists, and we were their guests, there would have been no point in putting sharp questions to them or engaging in heated debate. What we wanted to hear, after all, were *their* views on various important matters.

I did, however, bring up the touchy question of what happens to those Chinese who want to leave the country. Alley seemed not at all disturbed by the question. His silver hair, blue eyes, and manner remind me of Americans like Robert Frost or Carl Sandburg. He seems a rural, grandfatherly type. Hatem, however (who reportedly wiped out venereal disease in China, an astounding achievement), seemed almost to take the question as provocative.

"If people want to leave," he said, "they can, although there are difficulties and it takes time. It takes time in any country. But most of the Hong Kong refugees are people who are looking out for themselves, not for their country. They want more money or they can't accept the life that others lead."

It must not be thought in executing some opium-traffickers that the Communists were introducing a practice in the least novel. General Joseph Stilwell had recommended, in the early 1920s, that opium dealers be shot. A number of the warlords and Kuomintang leaders would have heartily endorsed such a program, but under the old regime it was never practical; the Chinese peasants whose lives were so miserable that they willingly became addicted to the pain-killing drug would have raised a great popular outcry. And, of course, there was the problem that some provincial rulers derived a sizable revenue from the tax they placed on opium.

Chinese Emigration

There is no question but that in 1975 the Chinese regime discouraged emigration. It would appear to have been extremely difficult to leave the country, though not impossible. It should not be thought, however, that this is a Maoist innovation totally unprecedented in Chinese experience. The Manchu rulers, who reigned in China for 268 years, from 1644 to 1912, took a dim view of emigration. The basic Chinese laws touching on the subject until 1860 prohibited emigration and viewed those who attempted it as guilty of something very close to treason. The first poor Chinese laborers who did leave their homeland, when doing so was no longer legally impossible, were scorned as stupid, unpatriotic and hence not worthy of the sympathetic concern of their government.

According to C. H. Lowe, author of *The Chinese in Hawaii: A Bibliographic Survey,* "It had remained for an American lawyer, diplomat and friend of the Chinese to help set up the diplomatic and legal green light in favor of free and open Chinese emigration. Anson Burlingame ... about to retire as United States Minister in Peking after six years of service, was ... appointed in November, 1867, by the Imperial Government of China as ... envoy to America and Europe. While in Washington, D.C., Burlingame negotiated ... on behalf of the Chinese Government a treaty of trade, consuls and emigration with Secretary of State William H. Seward."

The agreement, signed July 28, 1868, stipulated that "the United States of America and the Empire of China cordially recognize the inherent, inalienable right of man to change his home and allegiance, and also the advantages of free migration and emigration of the citizens and subjects respectively, from one country to the other, for purpose of curiosity, of trade, or as permanent residents." (This would have been an interesting treaty for those Americans to bring up who were denied permission by their own government to visit China during the years of the Cold War.)

There was, of course, nothing particularly generous in the hearts of American participants to the treaty. Cheap and docile labor was urgently needed in the United States for building railroads, opening mines and winning the West generally.

Since the Chinese were in extremely impoverished circumstances and were known as an energetic people, they became a natural target for American business interests who preferred not to have to pay the higher wages which would have been demanded by American workingmen, unionized or not!

Speaking of the welcoming of Chinese to the U.S., it is not generally realized here how recent have been the changes in the immigration restrictions. Before 1965 we legally permitted the entry of only 105 Chinese immigrants each year! The 1965 immigration law liberalized restrictions and placed all nations on a first-come, first-served basis. That meant that the Chinese now had the same opportunity as other Asians, Africans and Europeans competing for the 170,000 visas issued annually to people desiring to enter the United States permanently.

The U.S. Immigration and Naturalization Service, no doubt recognizing that the restrictive number of 105 was unrealistic, had permitted so many exceptions, in what were considered special circumstances, that in 1965 a total of 4,769 Chinese were granted permission to enter. In 1966 the figure jumped to 17,608. In 1967, over 25,000 Chinese entered the U.S.

By the late 1970s about 2,500 Chinese, the majority ship jumpers, were entering the country *illegally* each year. A surprisingly small percentage of immigrants in recent years have given political reasons for leaving their homeland. The majority either wish to be reunited with family members or come for the same reason that brought earlier generations of Irish, Italians, Poles, Czechs, and other Europeans—an awareness that the American standard of living was higher than their own.

David Ho, executive director of the Chinese Youth Council of New York City—an anti-Communist, is it necessary to say?—told Edmund Newton of the *New York Post* in March, 1972: "People have the illusion that everybody here is rich. Of course they're usually forced to say that they want to come for 'freedom and democracy' but it's really the money. If there were a bad economic crisis here you'd see a lot going back to China."

According to a member of New York's Chinatown Planning Council, "There are some people who detest the Communist government, but I don't think that's the major reason for coming here. Money and family ties seem to be more important. Also a number of college-educated people have come because the government assigned them to do manual labor. It was difficult for them to adapt."

We thanked Alley and Hatem, two world-famous participants in the drama of modern China, for their time and attention and prepared to resume our travels.

As I was leaving Alley's apartment, his housekeeper approached holding a woolen scarf. I explained that it was not mine but that I would take it back to the hotel and try to locate the member of the party who had forgotten it.

Once in the hotel I walked into the enormous dining room, since it was dinnertime, where I found the U.S.-China Friendship Association people at their usual large table. I walked the length of the room, approached the table, held the scarf aloft and said, "In the United States this probably would have been stolen by now, but here in China we return such things to the owner." They all dutifully laughed; the woman who owned the scarf thanked me.

NURSERY SCHOOL NO. 2

The next afternoon we visited Nursery School No. 2, in what was once the poorest section of Peking. As our group entered the building about twenty adorable, tiny children waved brightly colored paper banners and sang in English, with a marvelous rhythm, "You are *welcome*, uncles and *aunts!*" They were about three and four years old, dressed in vivid reds, greens, yellows, blues—beautiful children waving colored streamers and jumping up and down in something close to unison.

We were greeted by school officials, all women, and taken to the usual table provided with hot tea and the open saucers of cigarettes. I suggested we visitors and our Chinese friends should not sit on opposite sides of the tables so that the conversations would not look too much like negotiations. Our hosts dutifully smiled.

The nursery section of the school, we were told, opens at six o'clock in the morning. The schools close at 7:00 P.M.

The children are left at the kindergarten in the morning and picked up in the late afternoon, after their parents finish work. A staff of 20 takes care of 140 boys and girls. There is a clinic in the school.

The little ones are taught from the very beginning to serve society. The dignity of labor is strongly stressed. The children consequently soon wish to serve not only the Chinese people but the people of all the world.

In order to help the parents even more, the teachers will cut the children's hair, trim their nails, and do minor repairs on their clothing. Parents pay about $6.50 per month to enter a child in the school. There is a separate fee of about $5.00 per month, paid by the factories where the parents work.

The children's drawings in the six-year-old class were remarkably good, much more advanced than sketches by American youngsters of the same age. One little girl drew a realistic bright blue truck, the back of which was loaded with bags of grain.

At one table eight small boys were working

with green or yellow clay. One had made a little teapot and teacup. I'm sure I could not do nearly as well. One eager boy gave me a remarkably beautiful paper flower he had made. Another presented me with a clay pistol. Another child gave me a very well made yellow elephant. A boy who couldn't have been more than five had made an amazingly realistic military tank.

A beautiful child with red paper flowers in her hair gave me a handsome braided belt she had fashioned, and insisted on draping it around my neck. At one table children were making what we think of as Japanese paper origami birds. In the Orient it is not easy to know whether a particular custom originated in Japan or China, since there has been cultural interchange between the nations over the centuries. The Japanese, we were told, learned the art of origami from the Chinese, presumably centuries ago.

As the children presented us with the various objects, they would speak up remarkably forthrightly in a forceful, almost adult manner, not with the shy, withdrawn attitude common to children at such moments. The boys and girls were composed, confident, obviously enjoying themselves. When the teacher asked for volunteers in the four-year-old class, every hand went up.

Some of the recitations they did for us, in Chinese of course, had the rhythm of "Pease porridge hot."

The teacher explained, to the four-year-olds, why it was necessary to criticize Confucius and Mienkiow! The song they then sang said if anything is wrong in our society according to Confucius and Mienkiow, we would never correct it, but we *do* want to correct things.

A small boy recited a poem called "One Grain," carrying a moral remotely resembling that of the parable of the mustard seed. "I am just one grain of rice, but don't drop me on the ground and forget about me. I can be used. I can grow. If you'll let me grow, that will feed people and the worker will be able to work with that food. So appreciate one-grain-of-rice."

The teacher used rather modern "Sesame Street"–style instructions, putting the number

three on a cloth board along with three cutouts of radishes, and so on.

On top of a bookshelf I noticed a little fluffy pink doll, the face of which was Western.

In doing arithmetic the children did not work simply with numbers on the blackboard, in the old-fashioned American way, but with objects on a table, all of them toys. One duck, two panda bears, three dolls. The children would not only give the number of objects referred to but also identify the objects. "I pick one elephant. I pick two ducks," etc. The teacher picked up a well-made little ambulance-truck, with siren, rolled it across the floor to one child or another, and then asked questions about the truck. "How many trucks is this? Does one man drive the truck, or two?"

There were many songs, all of which teach a social moral. Until Mao there had evidently not been such concentrated use of music to inculcate morals and ethics since the old common use by Christian churches. Nor is this teaching device totally foreign even to nonreligious America. All of us were taught as children, "My country, 'tis of thee," "The Star-Spangled Banner," "Oh, Beautiful for Spacious Skies," etc. Many of the children's songs were accompanied by a truly charming head movement where, for two beats, the head is turned to the left and then, in rather doll-like fashion, swung to the right for the next two beats of the measure. It is rather like the head movements we associate with the dancing of Thailand. It was explained that the movement is indeed characteristic of "minority group" dances encountered most commonly among the herdsmen of Mongolia. The reason the dance movement is taught is that it is a strong philosophy of the modern Chinese leaders that the minorities are to be encouraged to consider themselves equal with the otherwise more dominant Han majority.

One of the songs we heard sounded remarkably like "Jingle Bells," particularly the portion of the melody that goes with the words "dashing through the snow."

When Jerry Fisher told our hosts that I was a pianist, the teachers asked if I would play for the children. The program finished with myself as the last act. I played three selections, one an extemporaneous comedy American impression of Chinese music, consisting of sing-song chop-chop fragments, the humor of which, I quickly concluded, was not at all apparent to my audience. The second was Jerome Kern's "The Song Is You," and the third a quick boogie-woogie jazz number which—to my surprise—the children seemed particularly to enjoy, at one point clapping their hands in rhythm.

The school's playground was well equipped, the ground immaculately swept, although it must be impossible to use in wet weather.

In the playground about thirty children were gathered in a large circle, keeping time in the same hand-clapping rhythm. They sang about friendship. They would skip from one side to the other, greet a member of the circle, singing, "I Found Another New Friend." In a sense there's nothing specifically "political" about this, though it is obviously of political benefit to a culture if its members regard each other as friends rather than competitors or enemies.

One game the children played is known in America under the title "Cut the Cake." It involves two children racing, one clockwise, the other counterclockwise, around a large circle to see who can get back to his position first. The child who loses must run around inside the circle and "Cut the Cake" at another point. The game in China is called "A General Line," meaning a telephone line.

We noticed in one or two of the groups individual children whose interest in the proceedings did not seem to be as enthusiastic as that of the others. It would be interesting to know the reasons behind their lack of concentration and interest. Perhaps it was caused by difficulties within their families or because they were new to the school.

Not all the playground activities are organized by groups. About twenty children were playing freely, some with toys, some leading little wooden duck-trucks, others climbing on a sort of jungle-gym, some using slides, swings, tricycles.

In China there are very few disciplinary problems of the sort that Americans refer to under the term "juvenile delinquency" and those emerge at the high-school level.

The American theory that much misbehavior and crime grows out of sordid conditions, poverty and consequent collapse of the family would be consistent with the Chinese experience. Since almost everyone in China now is well fed and well cared for there is not that sense of aimlessness and frustration that leads to juvenile crime.

The schoolchildren are taught to have great respect for workers, soldiers and peasants. In other words, the poor of China are being taught *self*-respect, which was rarely the case in the old culture, where the young were led to respect success, money, prestige, scholarship, and so on.

It is interesting to see how present Chinese attitudes toward life are reflected in the emotional coloration of certain words. In pre-Communist China it was no compliment to a man to identify him as a "farmer" or "peasant." The word *peasant* in fact could be used as an insult, as if accompanied by the unspoken but implied adjectives *dumb* and *poor.* Today those who are peasants are proud to be so called. Since they do, after all, constitute over 80 percent of the Chinese population, it obviously makes for a happier society if the inherent dignity of physical labor, such as that performed on farms, can be successfully inculcated. For centuries Christian theologians have written extensively, even profoundly, on the dignity of labor. The lesson, unfortunately, was never successfully communicated to the actual laborers who were supposed to sense their dignity.

For the rare disciplinary cases in Chinese schools there is no harsh punishment, no physical abuse, no isolation, no expulsion. The individual is *persuaded,* by argumentation and encouragement, to behave as a more responsible citizen.

The discipline problem is, of course, greatly simplified by the ancient Chinese tradition of respect for authority, starting within the family.

The educational program is planned so that there is never a dull moment. The wisdom in the old Christian saying, "The devil finds work for idle hands to do" would seem to be operative. To make them feel a part of the larger adult society, the children are taken on tours of communes, farms, factories and museums.

Special training to encourage individuals with remarkable gifts does not take place until the high-school level.

I had the opportunity while in China to meet a few children who had *not* been conditioned in such neighborhood schools. Although the matter would naturally have to be researched carefully before any hypothesis, much less a conclusion, could be drawn, I did have the impression that the children raised more or less in the old-fashioned way, which is to say with a great deal of personal family influence and apparently a minimum of collective school influence, were different. The family - oriented children seemed more "American," shyer, less socially confident. A handful of examples do not a nationwide survey make, but because the question is of such importance one would think it might be of great benefit to our nation to conduct appropriate investigations of the phenomenon. There may be some relevance here to the precedent of the kibbutzim in Israel. Evidently children in the kibbutzim too were more self-reliant, more confident than children reared in the traditional manner.

I have heard reports that one result of early conditioning in a kibbutz was an almost total absence of homosexuality. Since it would appear that something in the present American social experience is producing a higher percentage of homosexuals than was formerly the case, and clearly a much higher percentage of homosexuals than exist in China, it would certainly be to our interest to isolate the contributing factors.

Dr. Theodore B. Cohen, a prominent child psychiatrist in Philadelphia, who has made a study of the treatment of small children in China, reports that the nation cares for its children "with warm, consistent gentleness," an approach, he suggests, the United States might do well to adopt. Cohen and his medical colleagues concluded, on the basis of their research, that modern China has created and is sustaining an environment in which the physical abuse of children (a tragic and growing problem in the United States) is totally unheard of, in which children are well fed and

clothed, are obviously smiling and happy, and in which they do not have to look forward to drug abuse and delinquency—problems that worry so many American parents.

Although the reality is painful to contemplate, we must nevertheless give careful consideration to the fact that in contrast to the apparently happy nurture accorded small children in China, the situation in the United States is not nearly so appealing. In 1975 a national study to determine the extent of child abuse was conducted under the auspices of the Health, Education and Welfare Department which described the crime as "a social problem of epidemic proportions." More than a million American children each year suffer neglect, malnutrition and physical or sexual abuse! An incredible *3,000 a year* are presently *killed* by their own parents, and approximately 15,000 are being permanently *brain-damaged* as the result of physical attacks!

Cohen also mentions another problem that does not perplex the young of China—venereal disease.

"Is it actually possible," he asks, "that there is no VD in a country of eight hundred million people? All the evidence seems to say it is." By 1980, in the southern city of Guangzhou (Canton) there was some slight evidence of such disease, perhaps because of contacts with nearby Hong Kong.

Parenthetically, it is the famous Dr. Ma, Dr. George Hatem, the Lebanese-American mentioned earlier, who became a Chinese citizen and who is given credit for this marvelous medical achievement. It might well be that if there were 800 million Americans, the problem could never be wiped out. The reason is that Chinese and American attitudes toward sex are remarkably different. The modern Chinese attitude, in fact, being puritanical, is consistent with that generally advocated if not always practiced by American conservatives. Dr. Cohen reports that there seemed to be little or no premarital sex in the China of the 1970s.

It came as a surprise to most Americans to learn that in Chinese schools—as of 1975—academic instruction took second place to political indoctrination. Our automatically negative response to this intelligence arises chiefly out of the fact that the political indoctrination is Marxist-Leninist. I do not believe that most Americans object to this on principle, though I do. I suspect the majority would enthusiastically endorse such a program if the political instruction inculcated "Americanism."

I *don't* think such popular endorsement would follow if the primary moral preached were that of freedom. The staunch defenders of freedom in our society are generally talking about freedom from Communism and freedom from "government interference." But this is a strange state of affairs since our nation is not in the slightest danger of being dominated by any Communist force on the planet. As for the federal intervention that displeases some of us, it often involves an attempt on the part of Congress, the judiciary, or the president to enlarge the freedoms of the disadvantaged and protect the freedom of the American consumer.

It is obvious that there would be certain similarities between Chinese and Western education at the nursery school level; what is more important is the difference between the two approaches, which occurs in the area of moral teaching. A certain amount of political indoctrination takes place in American schools, of course, and the children at least hear such words as *democracy, freedom* and *Americanism,* although their understanding of them must range from very hazy to nonexistent. The kind of attitudinal instruction dominant now in Chinese schools has its precedent in American experience only in a religious context. Children exposed to American Catholic parochial education, to Protestant Sunday school instruction, or the equivalent instruction in the schools of Jewish synagogues, are indoctrinated with the moral verities. In China this sort of instruction starts almost as soon as an infant has learned to walk.

By 1980 it was clear that despite the admirable side of Chinese education the nation had nevertheless paid a price for the degree to which its schools concentrated on ethical and political factors. That price, of course, was a measurable deterioration in academic achievement. It is interesting that something like the same problem has presented itself in the United States as a result of the perfectly virtuous desire to do something to improve the deplorable conditions facing black, Latin and other poor minority children. The much-maligned busing program represented nothing more than an attempt to upgrade poverty-area schools by introducing some white students to them and by bringing some blacks into the much better schools in white neighborhoods.

In both nations such edifying hopes have been dashed on some hard rocks. Both the very poor children of the United States and the very poor peasants' and lower-class urban workers' children of China have been benefited somewhat. Unfortunately other problems have emerged as it became clear that the poor children of largely ignorant parents start school so far behind their more socially fortunate peers that it is almost impossible for them to catch up. In China, the decade of the Cultural Revolution eventually ran counter to the Chinese wish to modernize in the areas of science, technology and industry.

As mentioned earlier, I had the pleasure of meeting, while in China, a Christian named Ben Sprunger, president of Bluffton College in Bluffton, Ohio. After returning home he was kind enough to provide me with copies of a number of papers he prepared summing up the experiences of his twenty-five days in China. In commenting on the development of political consciousness in Chinese schools Sprunger wrote: "Political consciousness to the Chinese is what the Christian ethic was to us years ago —that is, *practicing self-denial, putting others first, serving the state, [living a] simple life, wasting nothing, honesty, sexual morality, hard work, non-violence except against enemies of the state, and self-sufficiency both personally and in community.*" (Italics added.)

Not only is such training important within the Chinese educational context—which is obvious enough—but it is *more* important than training in the traditional intellectual disciplines. This, too, would be consistent with the history of Christian education in which context it was always argued that a man might eventually forget some of the facts and theories he was taught but that he could not possibly forget his moral training.

Oddly enough, Sprunger, while conceding that "babies and primary children appear happy and joyous in their environment," nevertheless reports being "alarmed at how efficient two-year-olds had become robot-like as they sat for periods of time on their benches without moving . . . and then how they all performed neatly and precisely the exercises asked by the teachers."

His observation about the joyous and cheerful attitude of children in Chinese kindergartens is consistent with reports by every visitor to the nation's day-care and nursery schools. Because of our conditioning, many of us can conceive of two-, three- and four-year-old children sitting quietly and well behaved only if they have somehow been terrorized and forbidden to move about. Perhaps such a result could be achieved but it could not possibly result in children that appear relaxed, happy and well adjusted. I had what I must describe as the misfortune to reside in certain boarding schools when I was quite young. Although I appreciated then, and still do, the selfless dedication of the kindly nuns who staffed such institutions, I regarded the schools, as I do now, as essentially prisons for small children. In this regard they were much like orphanages in that the children involved had no control whatever over their fates. Because these early recollections are still so vivid, I can offer both personal experience and common sense as support of the argument that Chinese children appear happy because they *are* happy.

A VISIT TO THE U.S. LEGATION

Jayne and I had met former Ambassador to the United Nations George Bush and his wife in New York at an embassy party at the Waldorf given by then-U.N. Ambassador John Scali, who followed Bush in that office. The Bushes were about to leave for China. When we explained that we had applied for permission to visit the country, they told us to be sure to let them know when we arrived in Peking. (In case the reader has had the pleasure of meeting Mr. Bush during his years of service to the Republican Party, or later as head of the

C.I.A. or presidential hopeful, I am sure he would appreciate my mentioning that it is not possible for him or his successors to be of the slightest help in your visit to China. He was not in a position to do anything of the sort, even during his tenure as liaison officer.)

By the time we did get to Peking, Jayne was unfortunately suffering severely from the flu and was in bed for five days, so we did not at first call on the Bushes at the legation. I was so busy with tour activities, plus reporting these to Jayne that the matter possibly would have slipped my mind except that some other members of our party, who wanted very much to visit the legation, repeatedly brought the subject up.

Several of us therefore called on George and Barbara, who provided a most cordial reception. The number one subject of conversation, obviously, was China. Some of our party, concerned about the huge duties on the import of rugs purchased in Tientsin, asked if there was any prospect of improvement in regard to the tariff problem.

We were told that Senator Henry Jackson's attempt to handicap the Soviets in trade with the United States, out of consideration for Israel, had also had an effect on the problem of Chinese tariffs, though Jackson had not intended that resutlt. But there had to be an overall U.S.-China trade agreement, we were told, before any significant improvement in the tariff problem could take place. As of 1975 the U.S. held about $80 million in frozen assets belonging to the mainland Chinese. They had about $190 million in frozen assets that formerly belonged to American interests. In general, the trade agreement as it stood would have to be seriously amended. This was not expected in the absence of full diplomatic relations. Nevertheless, in 1975 we imported goods worth $115 million from China and exported about $350 million to her, much of that being American cotton. Our Southern and Californian agribusiness tycoons are furiously anti-Communist till personal financial factors are introduced. The dollar is a great civilizer —or is it compromiser? In 1979, when full diplomatic relations between China and the U.S. were achieved, the American business community prepared to take immediate advantage of the situation.

A few days later George and Barbara took a number of our group to dinner at the Hong Bin Lou restaurant, which specializes in Mongolian-style food. Part of the evening's ritual involved the diner's cooking his own main course over a flat-topped ridged Mongolian barbecue-stove. Fragments of meat, small onions, other vegetables, oil and soy sauce are mixed together in a small bowl and then simply dumped on the hot stove-top surface. White-aproned attendants stand by to help the clumsy foreigner with the chore, but you may perform the operation entirely on your own if you wish.

The whole fish that is apparently served at all Chinese restaurants was one of the courses, but in this instance was cooked in the Szechwan style, which means with a spicier sauce. For dessert we were served deep-fried candied apples, which I had eaten before only at the excellent Shanghai restaurant on Hollywood Boulevard in Los Angeles. Small slices of apple are dipped in a batter, then cooked in a sugar syrup. You are expected to plunge each sizzling-hot apple slice into ice water before eating it. This turns the syrup glaze to a candy hardness and also lowers the temperature of the dessert, which might otherwise take a long time to cool.

The one dinner in Peking that I was not enormously impressed by—at least on our first visit—was that which is supposed to be the best of all, served at the world-famous Peking Duck (Beijing Kao Ya Dian) restaurant. The main course is, of course, the roast duck, prepared in a unique way. The skin is glazed quite thickly and served in small, delicately carved slices. The slices of browned, skinned duck are either inserted into a sesame-seed bun or rolled in a crêpe that looks exactly like a Mexican tortilla. The accompanying sauce is a spicy plum mixture that I unfortunately used too much of since I mistook it for the delicious sweet plum jam served in other Chinese restaurants. It was quite bitter and therefore overpowered the delicate flavor of the duck. For some reason not clear to any of us, this was the one expensive meal we were able to order in China, costing the equivalent of almost $10. It is not unusual to pay that for a meal in an American restaurant, but by Chinese standards the price is exorbitant. Some workers earn only $20 a month.

In some Chinese restaurants, by the way, tablecloths are not changed simply because they have become stained. Consequently, if during breakfast you spill, say, a bit of egg yolk, perhaps a few drops of coffee and a certain amount of bacon grease, you may find the stains still there when you report for lunch.

And for dinner.

And the next day.

And longer than that.

I have a theory that I will refer to later that may explain the overall excellence of Chinese cooking. I believe that if a culture is highly artistic, the creative tendency will manifest itself not only in the formal arts but in other aspects of life as well. France, Italy and China, therefore, offer the best cuisines in the world because they are three highly artistic cultures.

Jayne, unfortunately, was deprived of the pleasure of some of our sightseeing tours and visits to restaurants because of her virus infection.

Tuesday afternoon, about five o'clock, Jayne finally went to an old hospital near the hotel, originally built with Rockefeller money. She was given an X-ray: cost, 30 cents! A complete and competent medical examination: also 30 cents. The hospital staff prescribed five separate medicines, in generous quantities, which cost a total of $1.30. The bill back home would have come to $100. (Jayne was X-rayed with all her clothes on. I told her they had probably found out that she was in good health but her jacket was seriously in need of attention.)

It is interesting to contrast this with the situation that prevailed in the United States for many years, whereby pharmacists were actually legally prevented from substituting less expensive drugs in prescriptions, even though they were just as effective as the more costly ones.

In June, 1975, the California State Board of medicine worthy of the name. Housing was primitive, hygienic practices almost unknown.

Goods are carried thus all over China.

Bus, Peking.

Pharmacy finally changed its regulations to allow the substitution, which it was estimated would save California consumers up to $45 million a year! While making an item for a penny and selling it for a dollar has always been considered "good business," there was always something vaguely unethical about making a *pill* for a cent and then selling it for

a dollar, when questions of health, and in some cases life and death, were involved.

Jayne, during her enforced stay in bed, had written a couple of dozen postcards to friends in the States. When I took them down to the mail desk in the lobby of the older section of the hotel, I discovered that Chinese stamps, in Peking at least—and other cities as well—have no glue. You purchase the stamps and then apply the stickum by hand, from a small pot of it provided for the purpose. Since the stamps in Tientsin had had glue this came as a surprise.

Lily's sister Irene loaned me one of her family's bicycles and, with her pretty teenage daughter, Shao Chi, as guide on her own bike, I took off one afternoon for a tour of the neighborhood.

Peking must be the world's greatest city for bicycle riding. The streets are broad and well paved and the city is flat as a pool table so one doesn't have to worry about pumping uphill. There are few automobiles. The average twelve-year-old American with a new bike would be delirious at the prospect of those wide-open spaces.

While one sees thousands of trucks on the streets, some of them late models, a great percentage of the goods moved from one place to another about the city are carried on very primitive vehicles, either old three-wheel bicycles with flatbed backs, donkey carts or horse-drawn wagons.

Bike riding in Peking is a bit of an adventure, of course, in that one moves in a lively stream of other cyclists as well as vehicles of freight. I would not relish driving a car in the city, what with the endless honking and swerving to avoid cyclists.

An additional complication is that any foreigner who kills a Chinese citizen while driving must leave the country at once. It is considered irrelevant that the driver may have been totally innocent; he must leave nevertheless. In 1974, in fact, one of the most important members of the American liaison staff in Peking was involved in such an accident. The liaison office lost his services as a result.

We looked forward to the following day

when we would visit our first commune, one of the chief building blocks of modern Chinese society.

THE EVERGREEN COMMUNE

The morning dawned cold and hazy. Several of us piled into a small bus. China wakes very early. As the bus moved through the streets of the gray city and the country roads I began to observe a still wider variety in the types of Oriental faces.

In the mixture of drizzling rain and light snow we saw various groups of young people out doing morning calisthenics. No one was wearing a raincoat or using an umbrella, though they are obviously used in a heavy downpour since they are available in the department stores. The emphasis on exercise, "staying in shape," as Americans would put it, was to come to our attention frequently in China. Until the jogging craze of the late 1970s in our own country, only young people in school or in the military were seen exercising publicly. In China people of all ages do calisthenics.

When I was sixteen I left Chicago and bummed around the country for a few weeks. One day while hitchhiking through East Texas I was given a ride by two kindly Black drivers who stopped their truck after I had walked the roads for hours unable to get a lift. When they spoke to me I made the unnerving discovery that I was literally unable to understand a single word they were saying, so different were our regional dialects, mine Midwest Chicago, lower-middle-class Irish, theirs rural Southern Black. Matters are even worse in this regard in China. The various languages spoken in the country are generally similar but any pair of them may be no more alike than, say, Italian and Spanish. The present government has been conducting a vigorous campaign since 1949 to teach everyone the dominant national tongue, Kuoyu or Mandarin.

Although one constantly hears statements to the effect that minority peoples in China— the Mongols, Tibetans, Uighurs, Eyi, Miao, Kazakhs and others—have full equality with the dominant Han Chinese, I get the impression that such statements represent an ideal rather than an accomplished fact. We, after all, insist that American Blacks have equal rights, but our practice belies the claim.

This particular morning, while touring the Evergreen Commune, I was introduced to a foreman in charge of an extensive area in which various plants were raised in long earth, log and glass hothouses. Physically he looked quite different from my hosts. His features were not gently rounded but sharp and angular. His skin was darker and all in all he looked ethnically quite unlike the average Chinese. Speaking in English, which the man could not understand, I asked our guide, "Is he a member of one of the national minorities?" At which the eyes of all present who could speak English went up, as if in shock.

"What a question," my guide said, chuckling as if to relieve embarrassment. It was precisely the sort of reaction one might expect here if one asked an anti-Semite, "Is your friend Jewish?"

The man, whatever his ethnic background —perhaps Manchu—showed us with justifiable pride the hothouses which, however primitive their construction, make it possible to grow large quantities of cucumbers and other vegetables for the Peking area during the cold months of winter.

After inspecting the hothouses we were taken to the commune's own clinic and introduced to several pleasant young women, "barefoot doctors" (actually medical assistants).

Chinese Medicine

Another striking contrast between the China of today and that of the pre-Communist period occurs in the field of medicine.

Before 1949 the Chinese death rate was one of the highest in the world. The infant mortality rate was so high as to be incalculable. Life expectancy was less than thirty years. Natural disasters were, of course, part of the reason, but even in areas where famine and flood were not wiping people out by the thousands at any given moment, the conditions of life were so hard for the poor that there was scarcely any

Entrance to hothouse, Evergreen Commune, Peking.

Barefoot doctors, Evergreen Commune.

Human waste and garbage rotted in the open, attracting rats and insects.

Today—for the first time in the thousands of years of Chinese history—there is an organized medical program available to the masses.

At the initial stages of improvement primary emphasis was placed on preventive medicine. A national program of public health education was developed, emphasizing the importance of rational disposal of wastes.

Rats, mosquitoes, flies and other insect pests and disease carriers have been almost totally eliminated. Starting with a National Health Congress in 1950, the Communists developed wide-ranging programs to train doctors, medical assistants, barefoot doctors and nurses. Hospitals, clinics and simple rural medical facilities have been built all over the nation.

The clinic we visited was simple, even primitive, by American standards, but impressive. The rural medicine practiced is a combination of Western and Chinese traditional methods, including acupuncture.

Jayne's mother, who died in December, 1978, recalled an incident, from the mid-1920s, which says something of medical care in old China:

"I remember one time when I had been out in the countryside I hired a rickshaw to take me back into the city. As we were traveling along the road I suddenly saw a woman lying in the weeds by the side of the road groaning, obviously quite ill. I called for the rickshaw runner to stop and told him to put the woman in the rickshaw since she was unable to walk. I got out and walked and we proceeded to the city. We took her to the mission hospital. As it happened the doctor was conducting a clinic elsewhere at the time and was not present. When we left the woman there I also left instructions that I was responsible for her in case anyone wished to discuss the case with me.

"That night the doctor called me and said, 'You brought me a case of bubonic plague. We could not take the woman in because the hospital was filled with patients. The only thing we could do was send her back to the countryside, to die.' "

We were taken to a small shop on an open square. In the old days there were few such stores in small rural villages, so they are much appreciated. The merchandise was a combination of what might be found in a little American grocery store and a five and ten. I bought

Peasant family, Evergreen Commune, near Peking, 1975.

Evergreen Commune electric pump.

a charming white teapot, shaped like a sitting cat with one paw raised. The tea pours out of the paw.

But what was chiefly impressive about this commune was its efficiency and size.

The Chinese communes are as self-sufficient as the old villages they replaced and in some respects considerably more so. Under the former competitive system devil-take-the-hindmost was naturally inevitable, which led to unhappiness when resources were in short supply. But now, in a spirit of cooperation, every individual part of the commune opera-

tion can depend on the assistance of all the others.

It may come as a surprise to Americans but the U.S., too, has large communal farms. The days of thousands of small spreads, each worked by a Farmer Brown, his sons and perhaps a hired hand or two, are long gone. Such rustic retreats survive now only in scattered instances and in popular mythology. In their place are enormous growing combines owned by distant agribusiness corporations. The Depression wiped out thousands of small farms; harsh economic realities have forced many other farmers to sell out in the intervening years. So what we increasingly see in both China and the U.S. are vast farms, worked by large numbers of people. The primary difference is that in China they are owned by the people and in the United States they are owned by such companies as Union Oil, the Irvine Company, Del Monte, the Green Giant, etc.

Thrown Out of a Meeting

A visiting American, whose name I did not quite catch, told me that since I had gotten a great deal out of my visit with Rewi Alley he thought I would be equally interested to hear a talk that evening by an important Chinese official who would meet informally with the U.S.-China travel group in the oldest wing of the Peking Hotel. I thanked him for the suggestion and after dinner showed up at the appointed meeting room, arriving a few minutes late since I had some difficulty locating the room.

As I entered I saw a group of about thirty Americans gathered around a large collection of tables. A heavy-faced Chinese, in his late fifties, was addressing the group, smiling broadly. Since all the seats around the table were taken, I seated myself in a chair by the wall. I had not been in the room for more than a minute when a thin, unsmiling Chinese in a trimly cut gray suit seated himself next to me. "Who are you?" he said, speaking softly. "Are you with this group?"

"Not officially," I whispered. "I'm here because a member of the group invited me to the meeting."

"What is your name?"

"Allen."

The man stood, walked away, approached two Americans at the table and motioned that he would like to speak to them in the hall, obviously by way of checking on me.

I assume that the two Americans had not been told that I was to be present since they did not look in my direction when they entered the room a moment later but simply resumed their seats.

Mr. Graysuit seated himself beside me again.

"I'm sorry," he said, "you will have to leave."

"I will be happy to," I said.

For the next hour or so I felt annoyed at the treatment I had received. The speaker, whoever he was, had obviously not been about to share either state or military secrets with a casual group of visitors. What harm, I thought, if one more American sat in on the meeting?

I returned to our suite, did a bit of grumbling to Jayne about police states, paranoia and all that, and eventually calmed down enough to try to see the incident as it might have been viewed by my hosts. It's quite possible that if the American government made arrangements for a briefing for a group of, say, twenty-five visiting Chinese they might indeed be curious if a twenty-sixth showed up.

I do, nevertheless, make a respectful suggestion to my hosts. Assuming they are perfectly in the right in asking a visitor to leave a meeting, they might, I feel, do it with at least a minimum of good grace, including a polite, apologetic smile. I could of course make exactly the same suggestion to thousands of American policemen, by no means all of whom remember to speak politely when asking citizens to move from one point to another.

One of the things that distinguished the mind of modern China—at least as of 1975—was its difficulty in making exceptions. In almost all other cultures, whether ethnic, national, religious or political, there is a small area where officials will, in rare instances, see the wisdom of slightly modifying a rule to accommodate special and unusual cases, which need not involve showing unique favors to individuals. But in China there seemed to be room for practically no exceptions at all; things were done very much by the book.

This certainly cannot be because of a weakness of creativity or inventiveness on the part of the Chinese, whose whole history testifies to the contrary. Rather I suspect that it grows out of an unwillingness to take chances. One will usually not be blamed for following instructions precisely even if doing so leads to disastrous results. The responsibility, after all, will lie with the issuer of the instructions. But to arbitrarily step outside the rules, even if common sense suggests such a course, can lay one open to the risk of future criticism. This touches upon one of the weaknesses of the Chinese system. Fear can be an effective deterrent to evil or antisocial acts. But it ought not prevent the performance of acts which can be expected to produce beneficial results.

Chinese Humor

One thing I had the impression was in short supply in China—indeed I wasn't able to locate any of it till my second trip—was humor. This is by no means to say that the Chinese are a sour or solemn race. They obviously laugh as readily as any other people, certainly more than the Russians. Indeed, I have the impression that Orientals generally engage in somewhat more chuckling and giggling than do Western Europeans and Americans. But I also have the impression that they indulge in hearty, guffawing laughter less frequently than Westerners do.

I mentioned the subject to a number of Chinese I met in Tientsin and Peking and drew a blank. When I asked if there were any specific forms of Chinese humor, any jokes, any theatrical comedies that I might be enlightened about, my hosts seemed not to know what I was talking about.

Our guide on a bus trip one afternoon could not understand, for example, what the English word *joke* meant.

"It's a little story or play on words," I explained, "that makes people laugh, something that they consider funny."

His face remained blank.

"But what *is* a joke?" he said.

"Well," I said, "I will tell you a joke and perhaps that will illustrate the point. This is a story that was told to me by a famous American author named Norman Cousins, who reported that he had heard it while in the Soviet Union. It seems that an American and Russian were discussing political philosophy. The Russian said, 'You know, under capitalism man exploits man. But under communism . . . it's the other way around.' "

The Americans seated nearby laughed at the story. My Chinese friend's expression never changed.

Professor Thomas Katen, who teaches philosophy at the Community College of Philadelphia, knowing of my interest in the subject, later sent me a book from his library titled *Traditional Chinese Humor: A Study of Art and Literature,* by Henry W. Wells.

I regret to report that, while Dr. Wells has produced a comprehensive and scholarly work, it is certainly devoid of the very kind of illustrations the book's title would lead the reader to expect. What Dr. Wells means by "Chinese humor" seems to consist solely of faintly playful instances in sculpture, pictorial art and ancient poetry. It is certainly not humor of the sort that a generation exposed to Robert Benchley, S. J. Perelman, Groucho Marx, W. C. Fields, Charlie Chaplin, Woody Allen and Mel Brooks would expect.

Speaking of Chaplin, whose most important work was physical and did not depend on the spoken word, there are Chinese entertainers who might best be described as clowns. They do funny things with their faces and the rest of their bodies, in Chinese vaudeville shows, but so far as I was aware, when Jayne and I left China after our first visit, there is no precise Chinese equivalent of a Bob Hope or a Fred Allen.

On my second trip, however, I was to learn that my initial assumptions were groundless. Just because you can't find a thing does not mean it is nonexistent.

I have since learned that the Chinese, too, have their jokes about stupidity. Old American joke books of the 1920s often present the unintelligent person as Irish, a dumb Irish cop or laborer, sometimes also intoxicated. In the late 1930s dumb jokes were told about "The Little Moron." The "Polack" joke craze of the early 1970s was merely a continuation of the theme. Here is precisely such a story from Chinese folklore.

There was once a fool whose wife had taken a lover. The husband happened to return home one evening unexpectedly and the lover had to run for his life. But as he was climbing out a window he lost one of his shoes. Close on the intruder's heels, the husband picked up the shoe and put it under his pillow, planning that on the following day he would use it as evidence and present it against his wife at court.

His wife, however, had observed the proceedings and during his sleep exchanged the shoe for one of her husband's own. When he woke up in the morning the husband looked carefully at the shoe and, recognizing that it was his own, offered an apology to his wife. "I'm sorry about last night," he said. "I hadn't realized that it was me who jumped out of the window."

We were now nearing the end of our first trip. Jayne naturally wished to visit her home city of Wuchang (part of Wuhan, on the Yangtze [Chang Jiang] River), but we were not given permission to do so.

It was never made clear to us why we could not go to Wuchang. One Chinese friend suggested that it was for our own safety. But it was never explained why we would be in danger in that city. One theory was that a few of the more fanatical, anti-American Red Guards might still be active there and that there might be a street incident. Another excuse was that "Lin Piao Revisionist elements," who would have who knows what reason for being beastly to Americans, might foment some sort of an incident. As I say, there was considerable speculation—all sounding totally unlikely—but no hard information whatever.

Obviously it is naïve to hope that an essentially closed society can possibly be as open about things as countries of the West normally are, but one cannot resist feeling annoyed, anywhere in the world, when faced by instances of bureaucratic inscrutability. One cannot hope for the moon; there is no culture on earth in which all cards are on the table. There are perfectly understandable personal family concerns, private business matters, confidential military proceedings, industrial and state secrets, etc. But there is a degree to which this sort of thing is reasonable and a degree beyond which it seems absurd. I would quite understand if any official had said, "I'm sorry, but two weeks ago in Wuchang there was a scuffle on the street in which an American was spat upon and a stone thrown at his taxi. We don't

know exactly who was behind it but we wouldn't want to have that sort of thing happen to you. Regretfully, therefore, permission for your trip cannot be granted." Or, "We are sorry but the one foreign hotel in Wuhan is overcrowded just now." This sort of thing is par for the course all over the world. What is by no means as readily acceptable is the turndown wrapped in layers of vagueness and evasion.

If indeed there was real fear on the part of Chinese authorities of anti-American incidents—which I strongly doubt—the long-run remedy is simple. They need only place more emphasis in their internal propaganda on the crucial distinction between the American people on the one hand and their "capitalist oppressors" on the other. They may continue to attack the Pentagon, American warmongers, Wall Street, Madison Avenue, Fascist millionaires, and so on, to their ideological heart's content, but such propaganda ought not to stand in the way of rational conduct toward visiting American tourists, the overwhelming majority of whom, I am sure, harbor nothing but the most charitable wishes toward the Chinese people, and a few of whom will even be cordially disposed to Marxist philosophy.

I eventually assumed that the real reason we could not revise our travel plans on relatively short notice is that it would have run counter to the Chinese system, which involves making arrangements in advance, involving many people, hotels, planes and cars. Our son Bill and I went to Wuhan later in the year and had a marvelous time.

That evening Jayne was restless, naturally disappointed by her illness, and seemed to want to be alone. I went out for a walk—no guide required—and strolled about the nearby Tien An Men area, outside the Imperial Palace. As I walked the long boulevard in the dark I passed the walled compound in which Chairman Mao, Premier Chou and other government dignitaries lived at the time. At that moment a woman walked in front of me heading toward the gate of the compound. When she reached the entrance a brilliant floodlight from the top of the wall illuminated the area. An armed guard stepped into view briefly, the woman paused and then was given permission to enter.

The street lamps on Chang An Boulevard, beautiful clusters of round globes, gleamed romantically in the dark. A few young couples strolled past in the chilly darkness, walking close, speaking softly, some no doubt romantically interested in each other, and equally probably politically compatible.

The modern Chinese emphasis on political compatibility between two people who are considering marriage falls strangely on our ears, but if the reader will attempt to set aside his biases for the moment it might be possible to perceive that a commonality of interest on *any* subject—and particularly on important matters—is undeniably beneficial to a marriage.

The old, no longer powerful, Western strictures about marrying in one's own faith, while it had its narrow-minded side, also had a sensible, practical aspect. As all married people are aware, the married state, despite its blessings and pleasures, is far more difficult than we imagine when we are young. Every individual brings to a marriage his imperfections and weaknesses; when these come into conflict with those of the partner a degree of unhappiness is inevitable. Therefore, if any important questions can be lifted out of the area of possible controversy it can scarcely be argued that this is not a good thing.

This is not to say that "mixed marriages" always fail. Catholics may be happily married to Jews, or to Protestants, Democrats may remain married to Republicans, liberals to conservatives. But in most such cases, in marriages that persist, it may be observed that at least one partner is less than devout and committed.

A few days later, exhausted but greatly stimulated, we bid a sincere thanks and farewell to our generous hosts and returned home.

At that time I did not know that within a few months I would be back in China again.

In the States there was great curiosity among friends concerning our trip. We showed slides, gave press and TV interviews, and continued to study China.

Part II

The Second Journey

July, 1975

3. To Japan with Bill

 JAYNE and I returned home to Los Angeles exhausted but greatly stimulated by our all-too-brief visit to her birthplace.

Lily Wen's sister Irene (Tung Kuo-ying) had told us she thought it might be possible to arrange a longer trip for us, one that would permit us to learn, see and experience more than is usually possible for the purely commercial visitor. After several weeks came the good news in the document shown on the next page from Luxingshe, the China travel agency.

When the time came for the trip—one of four full weeks—a tour that would have permitted Jayne to visit her father's church and family's old home in the industrial city of Wuchang, she was most unfortunately unable to go. Her mother was quite ill at the time so Jayne accepted a role in a Los Angeles production of Kaufman and Hart's comedy *Once in a Lifetime* and our seventeen-year-old son Bill and I prepared to make the trip together.

On July 2, 1975, Bill and I left Los Angeles.

Thursday, July 3

This time, when we arrived in Tokyo, we were met by Mr. Sigeru Mizuno, for whom I would be performing from August 8 to 11 at the Hotel Chateau-Tel Akanezaki in Atami,

Japan. A Cornell University graduate in hotel management, he had lived in the United States for five years and, of course, spoke fluent English.

After a quick cab ride to the Imperial Hotel in the Ginza section, we sat in the spacious and beautiful lobby and enjoyed 7-Ups with a slice of lemon. Mizuno and I answered each other's questions, mine about the resort, his about the kind of show I planned to do. Since I had learned that virtually no one in our audiences would be able to understand English, I had to plan an exclusively musical program.

After a while, exhaustion from our long cross-Pacific flight hit us and we retired. It was then about 3:00 A.M. Los Angeles time but early evening in Tokyo. We slept, thank goodness, for thirteen hours.

The next morning after breakfast in the coffee shop, we went out to walk the streets of the Ginza section. The neighborhood is somewhat like the Times Square area of New York but cleaner and more attractive. Not an inch of its space is wasted. Passing beneath elevated train tracks we discovered that the area under them housed a long, narrow, and remarkably beautiful shopping arcade. Each shop used just a few feet of space but managed to display an astonishing variety of goods. Everything one

---

LÜXINGSHE
China International Travel Service
Head Office: 6 Changan Avenue (East), Peking.
Cable: LUXINGSHE

Ref. AM(75)/370
Date March 14, 1975

LETTER OF CONFIRMATION

Re: Your letter dated March 11, 1975

To Mrs. Allen

According to our booking on tour in China, we would like to confirm the arrangements listed hereinafter. Kindly please send the duplicate copy of this confirmation letter by return air mail before April 14, 1975 . In case of urgency, kindly please confirm by cable and then return the duplicate to us at an early date. Without receipt of any confirmation ~~10 days prior to the entry in China,~~ before April 14, 1975 we shall deem the booking cancelled automatically.

1. Name of Tourist or/conductor:
2. Number of Tourists: 3
3. Name of the tour: Allen's Family
4. Date of tour in China: From July 4, 1975 to August 1, 1975, totalling 29 days
5. Itinerary: Shanghai, Soochow, Nanking, Wuhan, Anyang(Linshien)
   Sian, Yenan and Peking.
6. Point & date of entry: Arriving Shanghai at 19.25 by CAAC Flight CA 924
   Means of transport to China: on July 4, 1975
7. Point & date of exit: Leaving Peking at 7.15 by CAAC Flight CA 923
   Means of transport from China: on August 1, 1975
8. Rooming requirements:
   Single rooms with private bath:
   Double rooms with private bath:
9. Estimated tour expenses payable to LÜXINGSHE: about 9500 JMP yuan
   ~~(commission already deducted) equivalent to~~ (the whole family)
10. Visa: Please obtain same at our ~~Embassy~~ Liaison Office in Washington, D.C.
    ~~China Travel Service Ltd., Hongkong.~~
11. Remarks: see the attached sheet

Yours truly,
LÜXINGSHE,
Liaison Department.

NOTE:
This confirmation letter is made in duplicate. The original is to be kept by the tourist or the tour conductor and the duplicate to be posted to LÜXINGSHE.

The undersigned would confirm hereby the above reservations made by LÜXINGSHE. Conductor's/Tourist's seal or signature

---

saw was attractively papered, painted, lighted and displayed.

On the second floor of the arcade Bill and I noticed with amusement that had we wished to use the men's room we would have had to duck low to enter it. Bill is a fraction of an inch taller than I am. The top of the doorway was about five feet ten inches.

After dinner we walked through some of the fascinating little alleys in the immediate neighborhood. Again we were struck by the brilliant and creative use of space. The Japanese can put three and four small shops in an area where we would accommodate one coffeehouse or shoe store.

Hong Kong, too, has its fascinating little

alleyways with crowded shops but there one encounters scenes of steamy, unclean poverty. In Tokyo the streets, buildings and shops are spotless.

I measured one of the establishments from side to side. It was exactly ten feet in width, apparently common for the neighborhood. We were on Suzuran Street. As we passed dozens of restaurants we saw groups of men in business suits, some remarkably tipsy, being bid a seemingly fond adieu by women of what I eventually concluded were a very specific type. They all were clad in the traditional Japanese kimono and wore their hair in the old-fashioned style. They seemed to be in their middle thirties, were quite pretty, and had a confident, sophisticated air. Imagine in America a hostess coming down from, say, a fourth-floor restaurant and walking out into the street to say goodnight to her customers. Well, such a thing is common in Tokyo.

Imitation food, Tokyo restaurant.

Friday, July 4

At about nine o'clock in the morning we presented ourselves at the Japan Airlines office in the hotel, as a result of having received an invitation from a Miss Shoho stating that she would be happy to advise us concerning travel plans.

Within five minutes she shared with us the unnerving information that China Airlines had no record of our reservations on their Flight 924 to Shanghai, leaving Tokyo at 2:55 that afternoon!

A few minutes later I conferred by phone with a Mr. Ching, a very helpful English-speaking representative of Luxingshe in Tokyo, who reported that it was indeed the case that there were no more seats available on the flight we had expected to leave on. The next JAL flight to Peking would not leave until Monday, three days later! Mr. Ching promised to phone back if he could improve the situation.

At ten o'clock Bill and I—upset and frustrated because we could do nothing to control the situation—went upstairs to await developments.

We turned on the television set and watched a Japanese daytime comedy-variety show, which consisted in large part of American-style rock music and comedy sketches, all of which were excessively physical.

At about 10:45 Mr. Ching phoned to tell us —thank goodness—that our problem had been solved. He had checked with Luxingshe in Peking and had been told to make every possible effort to accommodate us. The solution had been found in the willingness of two other passengers to give up seats and travel to Shanghai by Iran Air on Sunday.

I told him that if there were any possible way I could thank the two passengers personally I would certainly be willing to do so, but in lieu of that we were extremely indebted to him personally for his help.

When we went downstairs to lunch we could see through the giant floor-to-ceiling windows that a violent windswept rain was falling outside. Despite the exterior gloom our spirits were much higher because of the happy resolution of our problem.

The hotel coffee shop has a wonderfully efficient method of handling meal checks that totally does away with that annoying "Waiter, may I have my check?" business so common to American restaurants. They make up the check in duplicate as your order is given and then place it at once—at the beginning of the meal—on your table, where it is ready and waiting when the time comes to go to the cashier's desk.

At the airport China Airlines did not then have its own desk so Japan Airlines personnel attended to the formalities of receiving our luggage. Mr. Ching, who had been so kind on the phone, appeared in person to welcome us. When he began to explain that all seats on the plane were taken, for a moment we thought he was telling us that something had again gone wrong and we would not be permitted to board Flight 924 after all.

It turned out that he was merely going through the original explanation again, stressing the kindness of the two passengers who had been willing to travel two days later. I assume now they might have been Chinese returning home and thus willing to spend two more days in Tokyo if asked—or ordered—to do so by an agency of the state. Ching introduced us to another gentleman who was described as the head of his department. Although Mr. Ching was all smiles, the other man was quite the opposite. At no time during the few minutes we conversed did any expression whatever cross his face.

Later, in flying over Osaka, Bill and I were struck by how remarkably American it looked. There were quite a few tall buildings and in general the city looked like Los Angeles, including freeways and riverbeds. Bill pointed out one primary difference: no swimming pools were visible.

After we landed at Osaka it was explained that we would not be permitted to leave the plane even though it would be on the ground for about an hour. Nobody said why.

There had been, to this point, less than a dozen passengers, but we soon saw, by the pick-up of enormous quantities of luggage, that a large group was to board.

On the roof of the terminal building we noticed a crowd of perhaps five hundred people, waving and holding aloft brightly colored banners and posters. Bill took several photographs of the "demonstrators" from the back door of the plane, which had been opened to admit the newcomers. Directly behind the banners and flags, at a distance of perhaps three hundred yards, was an enormous Pepsi sign.

As the first of the passengers, all seemingly Japanese businessmen, burst out of the airport, many holding flowers, waving back to the crowd, a movie cameraman with tripod raced ahead to photograph the departing delegation, all or some of whom were perhaps persons of special stature.

4. Shanghai

WHEN we landed in Shanghai we were asked not to leave the plane until the entire party from Osaka had gotten off. This took some doing since they were such an army. They disembarked in just as high spirits as when they had entered, however, still waving flags, hoisting banners, laughing and scratching.

En route to the initial Chinese passport and health-document inspection, we were greeted by three friendly representatives of the China Travel Service, two young men and a woman who appeared to be in her thirties. They helped us through the customs inspection, which was conducted by several young fellows who did not appear to be older than twenty and were extremely cordial. It is difficult to define the atmosphere of the Shanghai airport as contrasted with that at Peking. The attendants were younger in Shanghai, somewhat friendlier and more personal in their questioning of us. This may simply have been because in 1975 so many more people traveled through Peking; the officials in the capital, after the first few weeks on the job, must have been bored with the endless repetition of the same questions and proceedings.

At last our bags and papers had been inspected, we were cleared and taken out into the steamy, tropical summer air to two waiting cabs. Bill was put in one and I in the other. The two young fellows rode with me, the woman with Bill. Once again, as during the preceding winter's visit, it was a matter of racing at high speed through darkening streets using the horn instead of lights. As we sped along through swarms of pedestrians I asked what the population of greater Shanghai was.

"Over ten million," one of the guides said.

"I think I have seen one million of them already," I said.

The two young men, from the Shanghai branch of the China Travel Service, were Shu Wu-an and Yuan Ping. The young lady was Yeh Sing-ru, of the main Peking branch. Bill told me that she would be with us for the entire tour.

Shu and Yuan later raised the possibility of our meeting some actors or directors of Chinese films while we were in Shanghai. I told them we would be very interested in doing so. Shu suggested that I prepare some written questions that he could present to the authorities, indicating the areas of my interest.

PEACE HOTEL

We had no idea where we were being taken. It turned out to be a famous old English hotel —once called the Cathay—on the bustling waterfront. Now the Peace Hotel, its address is 20 Nanking Road East. The lobby is large, spacious, European, with the addition of the literature racks and glass sales counters common to Chinese hotels.

The daily charge for our two-room suite: 38 yuan, although all costs of our trip had been paid in advance. If you ask for the air-conditioning equipment to be turned on you pay an additional 25 percent of the rate. Extra charge for heating is 15 percent. The Chinese name for the hotel on some documents is spelled *Huping,* on others *Hoping.* It is spelled two ways, that is, in the European alphabet. If there is anything in the history of human communication more screwed up than the business of trying to make the Chinese language— which in print looks like thousands of melted television aerials—more accessible to Western eyes and minds I cannot imagine what it is. There are countless variations of "correct spelling" for Westerners. The original confusion, I believe, comes from the efforts of various missionaries who, with the best of intentions, nevertheless adopted rather peculiar, not quite phonetic forms for Chinese words. Since each man is a law unto himself in new territory, there was no overreaching authority to determine that one spelling was right and another wrong. Confusion was therefore inevitable. Of course there is quite enough variation in the separate Chinese languages themselves. When ordering breakfast one morning I asked, in Chinese, for two orange juices, emphasizing the word *er,* which means two.

"Liange," the waiter corrected me, "is two in Shanghai."

Neither of us was quite right. *Er* is indeed the word for two, but only when counting. *Liange* is used as an adjective.

On our first night together in China—July Fourth, Independence Day—Bill and I unpacked, explored the hotel, had dinner and retired early, which turned out to be a fortunate move.

Saturday, July 5

According to Kipling, on the road to Mandalay "the dawn comes up like thunder out of China across the bay." Well, by God, the dawn certainly comes up like thunder in Shanghai. Now, however, the thunder is caused by automobile horns, bicycle bells, ships' whistles, foghorns, shouting voices and God knows what else.

Traffic jam, Shanghai.

At about 4:30 A.M. the noises from the street and river outside begin to intrude upon our sleep. The sound effect was remarkably similar to that of midtown Manhattan during a particularly hectic rush hour. In American cities, of course, horns are honked repeatedly only when drivers lose their temper. In China, I shudder to think what the drivers would do if they lost their temper; in their cheeriest moments their palms seem rarely to leave the horn button. It can be interesting at midday; at four-thirty in the morning it's quite another matter.

I had the impression, half-awake, that dawn came at about five. So, too, did a further increase in the volume of ships, boats, horns and bells which, added to the cacophony from the autos, made quite a symphony. Bill, I was glad to see, was sleeping soundly.

I got up about a quarter to six and while shaving looked out the bathroom window. Down to the left, in a small plaza at the edge of the broad Whangpoo (Huangpu) River, a group of about a hundred young men in light shirts was doing graceful *tai chi chuan* exercises.

Off to the right in the distance one could see buildings that almost qualified as skyscrapers. And if I ever saw a sky that needed scraping there it was. Shanghai suffered from the same air pollution we had noted in Tientsin and Peking. In fact, it was considerably worse be-cause Shanghai is an even greater industrial city.

When, a few minutes later, Bill leaned out the window to take some pictures of the *tai chi chuan* group, he called back to me excitedly, "Hey, those are the guys in Shirley Mac-Laine's movie! She showed them doing the same exercises right there in front of that big sign."

On the way to breakfast we discovered, outside our room, a charming balcony with a marvelous view of the river and the waterfront plaza. Another pleasant discovery on the terrace was a small rectangular pool that contained several lively goldfish.

We were gratified to observe, while standing on the balcony, that in contrast to the steamy, junglelike temperature of the previous evening, the morning air was cool and refreshing.

At certain moments now the traffic sounds rose to such a pitch that they reminded me not only of Times Square at rush hour but during the few minutes before and after New Year's Eve.

When, at about six-thirty, Bill and I entered the eighth-floor dining room, we were pleased to see that it commanded a superb view of several exercise groups in the plaza. The majority were doing the traditional slow-motion exercises but some, more advanced, were making remarkably proficient acrobatic flips, handsprings, cartwheels and leaps. An oval

Above and below :
Waterfront, Shanghai.

Whangpoo River, Shanghai.

ring of about a hundred spectators in the left foreground of the square was watching a group of seven young girls, performing moves and exercises we describe as kung fu.

One interesting thing about the *tai chi chuan* group was that we could not identify its leader. The experience reminded me of the question that occurs when one watches a large flock of birds in flight. They all fly in the same directions, now swooping left, now right, now up, now down. But one can never identify a particular bird as the leader or decision-maker. In the case of the Chinese in the plaza, too, I had no way of knowing which, if any, of those gathered was controlling the pace of the movements.

At exactly seven minutes to seven, responding to God knows what signal, about half of the people suddenly dispersed.

For breakfast we were served basic American fare: Spanish omelet or scrambled eggs with bacon, buttered toast, jam, coffee and orange juice that was absolutely class-A. As for the eggs, I don't know what the Chinese feed their chickens but whatever it is our poultry farmers should get with it at once. Chinese scrambled eggs have a rich yellow color and a hearty, almost meaty taste, quite different from American eggs. The bacon, too, was much higher protein than ours, with more meat and less fat and salt. The bread, I was

glad to discover, was just as good as that which we had eaten in Tientsin and Peking. White, but with a rich, chunky consistency, most of it actual bread, not air. Bill reported that his hot cocoa was superb. I reminded him that almost anything made of chocolate in China would be better than what we were familiar with.

Add to the list of things that taste better in China than the U.S.: ketchup. Sorry there, Mr. Heinz; I don't know what the difference is—perhaps the Chinese use less vinegar—but their ketchup is excellent, at least in Shanghai. There is a more tomato-ish taste to it.

The cream served in much of China has the color of our condensed milk, a shade that almost approaches beige. Its quality and taste are excellent.

There is something mysterious about Chinese coffee that I would like to have explained, perhaps by an American chemist who works for one of our coffee companies. Though Jayne and I have done commercials for Hills Brothers, an excellent brand, I drink coffee at home only about three days a week, for the common reason: too much of it late in the day can keep me awake. Because of this common reaction, American food companies have created Sanka, Brim, Decaf and other coffees with the caffeine removed. In China, for several weeks, I drank five or six cups of coffee each day, plus much tea, never felt the slightest nervousness, and

View from train of typical small bridge and canal, Shanghai, 1975.

Jayne with model of St. Andrews.

slept like a baby. I'm aware that one example can never be used as scientific proof of any proposition but, as I say, I welcome the comments of readers who might have something significant to add to the observation. Perhaps I was so exhausted at the end of each busy day that even torture would not have kept me awake.

The view from our table-for-two at the corner of the dining room was dramatic in that we could see along the Whangpoo River for miles. Compared with the Mississippi, Missouri and other American equivalents, the Whangpoo, like all rivers in China, is incessantly busy. Everything from large oceangoing vessels to small junks ply the waters, some taking the course of the river itself, others—ferryboats mostly—moving from one bank to the other.

One of the interesting aspects of the heavy river traffic was that much of it traveled in trainlike formations, with seven or eight small craft in single file propelled by the power of the front tuglike sampan.

Observing the river and its traffic from our high vantage point was such a pleasurable exercise that I wished I could have given long hours over to it. While looking at the large brown ribbed sails on the junks that drifted across the river's murky waters, the possibility occurred to me that whoever designed the first one, thousands of years ago, may have simply copied the pattern of the fins of a sailfish.

A few days later I had the same sort of insight about the uniquely beautiful Chinese roofs with their four points gracefully curved upward. The first man who created this architectural form may have gotten the idea from observing the outline of a pitched tent with the

Bicycles everywhere. Street scene, Shanghai.

sides up. Unfortunately, I know of no way of either validating or invalidating such hypotheses.

In the dining room we met members of an American tour group that included a young lady who had shared a class with my oldest son, Steve, a doctor then on the staff of New York State University at Stony Brook, Long Island.

After breakfast, Yeh Sing-ru and one of our Shanghai shepherds, the thin cheerful young fellow named Yuan Ping, greeted us in the lobby, shortly after eight, helped with some minor purchases at the hotel shop counters, and ushered us to the usual two autos. We would go, they explained, to a typical workers' residential area.

We left the hotel at eight-thirty and, driving for several miles along Nanking Road, must have passed well over a million people within the first few minutes, the overwhelming majority men. Shanghai has a remarkably European, somewhat French look, as it is a city with a long history of foreign concessions and settlements. At first I saw no buildings at all constructed in the traditional Chinese architectural style. We passed hundreds of thousands of bicycles, swerved in and around hundreds of trucks and cars, all honking furiously.

The streets were hung with large banners in many colors, decorations that had been put up to honor the prime minister of Thailand, who had just paid a formal visit in connection with his country's recognition of the People's Republic of China.

There is only one situation in which, in the United States, one sees such crowds on the streets. That is at an important public event— Pasadena's Rose Parade, New York's Thanksgiving Parade or something of the sort. In the large cities of China it is as if crowds are out to see a parade every day. Oddly enough, in spite of the crowds, one does not feel boxed in or suffocated as in the basement of, say, Macy's in New York City, perhaps because there seems no pushing or shoving in Chinese crowds.

As we drove through a narrow street we suddenly encountered a traffic jam. The drivers of our two cars crossed over on the wrong side of the road and moved up until we found the explanation for the blockage. A long train was about to pull through, as a result of which, after a few more minutes, traffic was held up for several blocks back. Bill and I got out, photographed the train and greeted a few curious young Chinese who had gathered, after which our cars backed up and took an alternate route.

The attitude of Chinese pedestrians and cyclists toward motor traffic is unlike anything we had seen anywhere else in the world. I was not able to learn whether it comes from day-

School, Shanghai.

dreaming and absentmindedness or the age-old resentment of the foot soldier toward the cavalry.

Everywhere else in the world, if a motor vehicle bearing down on you honks a warning, you hop out of the way and are well advised to do so. Nobody hops in China. The pedestrian, threatened by a car, suddenly adopts the attitude of a matador before a rushing bull. He seems to consider it a loss of face to give so much as an inch of ground. Inches are given when absolutely necessary, of course. No one seems willing to die for this peculiar principle.

Most of the young men on the street wore lightweight white summer shirts, hanging outside the belts. The young women, however, wore skirts and blouses with more variety, in various pastel shades and prints. So much for the Blue Ants theory.

As we drove through the city I noticed several women, obviously quite poor, wearing two-piece suits that consisted entirely of what looked like denim patches, some dark blue, some light blue, some gray, some almost white. While it was poverty that led to the fashioning of such attire, they bore a striking resemblance to the ultrachic multipatch Levi's jeans' outfits then being worn in the States.

As we drove along I recalled that in Tientsin and Peking enormous piles of bricks awaiting use had been stacked in artistic forms. On the streets of Shanghai they were simply piled up American style.

Shanghai is considerably funkier than Tientsin or Peking. This impression, of course, may have come from nothing more than the fact that it was now summertime, early July, with the result that the town was green, warm, moist, earthy. Odors were common, some pleasant but most not, and many impossible for Occidental noses to identify.

CHAO WAN WORKERS' RESIDENTIAL AREA

The Chao Wan workers' new residential area—green, quiet, attractive—naturally boasted its own nursery school, where we were greeted by scores of smiling, adorable two- and three-year-old infants jumping and clapping in welcome. A few were as young as one and a half but all were remarkably cheerful, composed and well behaved.

In one of the classes at the nursery our guide said, "The children are listening to a story about class struggle."

"I'm glad to observe," I said, "that this particular class is not struggling."

The little show the tiny people presented was of course charming. One of the songs performed was titled "We Love Labor." The dance that accompanied the number was, oddly enough, about doing laundry, the first laundry reference we'd heard in China.

In this modern residential area, peaceful, with a great many trees, we were taken to the apartment of Mr. Pan, an elderly gentleman, formerly employed in a foodstuff factory, who had retired in 1971. His small apartment is clean and comfortable. Four people live in the suite, Pan, his wife, son and daughter-in-law.

"In the old days," he said, "with my one salary, I had to support eight people. Now everyone in my family is working."

Before Liberation the entire family lived in one room, cooking, washing and sleeping in that limited space. Now there are two rooms for four people, plus a kitchen and toilet shared with two other families. "Before 1949," Pan said, "I had to get up at three in the morning to be on the job at four. I worked until four o'clock the following afternoon, seven days a week." Today the factory people work three shifts, each only an eight-hour workday.

"In the old days," Pan explained, "I made forty yuan a month and had to pay twenty-five of it for rent, for one small room. Three-fourths of my salary went for rent. Now we pay only five yuan [about $2.25] per month for rent. My pension is seventy-four yuan per month. Electricity costs us one yuan [about 50 cents], gas is three and a half yuan, and water, for four people, two and a half yuan per month." This must be interpreted, too, in the general context of stability of living costs, free medical care and almost no inflation.

The shared kitchen was, by Western standards, very primitive. A cement sink, two small "stoves"—gas hot plates, really—and a couple of cupboards, with screens, in which fresh food is stored. There being no refrigeration, food must be eaten shortly after it is prepared or, for that matter, shortly after it is brought into the house. Certainly neither meat, fish nor milk could be stored for long. Nevertheless, the dramatic contrast between the living quarters we saw and those that the same people had suffered in before 1949 suffices to make them not only content with their lot but rather fiercely proud of it.

Outside the open windows, laundry was drying not on rope lines but on bamboo poles that stretched from window ledges to the nearest tree, telephone pole or angle of the building.

Later we visited the area's clinic—each neighborhood has one—and strolled past its savings bank, where money earns interest just as in the capitalist world, though one cannot borrow money. Outside the small bank a group of people were congratulating one of their members who had just retired.

For lunch we were driven back to the hotel, one of the many surviving monuments of British imperialism.

A MIDDLE SCHOOL

Before 1949 the illiteracy rate in China was 95 percent. Today the rate of *literacy* is something like 90 percent. That is a remarkable achievement, by any standard. It is therefore important to study China's educational system.

After a superb lunch we were driven to one of Shanghai's remarkable middle schools, the equivalent of our high schools. At each such location the traveler finds a smiling welcoming committee awaiting, usually consisting of two or three officials and, in the case of schools, a group of fresh-faced friendly children.

The chairman of the school's revolutionary committee was our chief source of information.

The first three groups he took us to visit were the physical education class, the English class—in which the students were repeating endlessly the phrase "continue the dictatorship of the proletariat"—and the music class, in which piping voices were singing—what else?—a Revolutionary song.

Outside in the hot courtyard about a hundred children were practicing a martial arts exercise using drumsticks painted red and white.

In a physics class the students were watching a demonstration in which the instructor used a large brick as study-object. The lecturer was a worker whose factory the students had earlier visited.

At this Middle School No. 1, connected with Shanghai Teachers College, the chairman of the Revolutionary Committee told us that

School class, Shanghai.

Bright young students in a chemistry class, Shanghai.

the school, built after Liberation, presently instructed 3,013 students. There are 169 staff members. In the suburbs there is an allied base area where the students learn agriculture firsthand. The campus itself boasts a library, laboratory, swimming pool and gymnasium.

Important changes had taken place at the school since the Cultural Revolution activity of the late 1960s as the result of the campaign "to criticize Lin Piao and Confucius" and also "Liu Shao-chi and his Revisionist line." In 1968 workers came in to help teachers in stimulating the students' political awareness. As of 1975 they held positions of importance in the school, chiefly leading the tasks of struggle, criticism and transformation. This was a sharp change from the former situation of "the domination of the school by bourgeois intellectuals."

"We have an open-door policy here now," the chairman explained. "When I say open-door schooling, that means sometimes taking the students out of the school and sending them to the factories, to learn how the workers live. It also means taking them to the countryside to learn agriculture, and to be educated by the peasants. This school is connected to two separate communes in the Shanghai area. All this, you see, helps students to link theory closely with practice."

"Is it your feeling," I said, "that before the Cultural Revolution there was too much student attachment to the classroom, to books and to the teachers?"

"Yes. Now they are involved much more directly with society at large."

The school has a four-year structure. From the first its students are encouraged "to make social investigations" so that they can link up what they learn from books with what actually happens in the society around them. Soldiers, workers and peasants address the young people. There are also study groups investigating astronomy, telegraphy, model airplanes, fine arts and acupuncture. This work is done after school hours.

We were told that as part of the emphasis on physical fitness the students take part in an eye exercise program designed to help prevent nearsightedness. A young woman of the Red Guards was kind enough to demonstrate the exercises for us. One involved massaging the bridge of the nose in a circular motion for a count of about twenty. In a second exercise the index fingers massage the sinus area about an inch below the eyes. Another involved pressing the thumbs into the temples while massaging under and over the eyes with the knuckles of the index fingers.

More than 3,000 of the school's graduates had settled down *permanently* in rural and mountain areas, we were told, something that was never done before the Cultural Revolution. Earlier, under the influence of the Liu Shao-chi Revisionist line, it is said, most of the graduates would have gone on to universities. Very few would be willing to go into factories or farms. It was still possible in 1975, of course, for a student to attend a university after graduating but only following a period, running for two or three years, of serving soci-ety, perhaps in factories or communes.

The chairman explained that the Cultural Revolutionary program was still in its experimental period, that it was common for mistakes to be made at such an early stage and that therefore the practitioners of the policy would welcome suggestions from others. It would have been presumptuous for us to offer comments without further study on our part, Bill and I agreed.

Now, four years later, Teng Hsiao-ping would appear to have returned to certain aspects of "the Liu Shao-chi Revisionist line," which, in any event, seems more reasonable to millions in both the Communist and anti-Communist camps.

We were welcomed to a special study class, the purpose of which was to draw a social moral from the sad story of a young girl who recently had drowned while trying to save a companion who had fallen into a river at a commune. Her example was held up as classically heroic; the young people of Shanghai were urged to be guided by her example. It was argued that in old China there would have been a much smaller chance that the girl would have risked her life for a companion but that now, when the *important lesson of modern society is to learn to serve the people,* it was only natural for her to extend herself to try to save the life of a friend.

In the next room a class of sixteen- and seventeen-year-olds was studying logarithms. In another room a language class was repeating sentences, all of them having a social point, in English. The teacher had an English accent; therefore so did the members of her class. These students, too, were, at the moment we passed, endlessly repeating the phrase, "the dictatorship of the proletariat." But the instructor was mispronouncing it so that it came out "dah dictatahship of dah pwo-lah-teddy-aht." A disk or tape recording by a well-spoken American, Australian, Canadian or English person could solve that sort of problem simply enough.

We next visited a group of young boys and girls—perhaps fifteen and sixteen—who were learning the rudiments of medical science, specializing in this instance in acupuncture. Sev-

Learning English and philosophy.

eral were practicing sticking needles into themselves and each other. Quite obviously no one was in pain. The medical skills the students learn will eventually benefit people in factories and farm areas.

Just outside the acupuncture class there was a small, lush herb garden, the most interesting feature of which was a stack of thin logs, approximately four feet in length, on which a beautiful white fungus that looked remarkably like cherry blossoms was growing. The fungus is used in a tonic medicine particularly beneficial to the respiratory system.

In another class children were filling quart-size jars with something that looked like wet sand or sawdust. It was a granular form of another fungus. In other rooms children were learning how to make radios, electrical fixtures and connections, how to weld and how to work with transistors. The students of one group were making serviceable four-transistor radios. Chinese high schools in 1975, it would seem, had become like our technical high schools.

Our hosts took us next to a neat, efficient-looking library, which housed over 60,000 Chinese volumes. In one of its sections we discovered American books translated into Chinese, including the writings of Mark Twain, who is respected in China.

In most of the classrooms there were the historically familiar portraits of Marx, Engels, Lenin and Stalin on one side and Chairman Mao on the opposite wall.

In a large, outdoor Olympic-sized swimming pool, about sixty girls, wearing bright red bathing suits and colorful caps, were splashing happily about in the manner of young swimmers anywhere. Swimming is an important part of the Chinese physical education program.

Just the other side of the school property, over a wall running alongside the pool, we could observe the roofs of tiny huts left over from pre-Revolutionary days, apparently still inhabited. Along one section of the wall broken glass had been set into cement, to prevent climbing into the school property. To do what, we wondered. Or was this another relic of the turmoil of the Cultural Revolution of the late 1960s?

Because Bill and I had asked if it would be possible to see a Ping-Pong table and equipment, our hosts had arranged to put on a brief exhibition for us. We had not wished to put them to this much trouble; Bill and I play a fairly good game and had thought it might be amusing to play for a moment on the local equipment. But we thanked our hostess profusely and went at once to an auditorium where tables had been set up and two separate exhibition games were under way.

The players, who looked about fourteen, were top drawer. One boy on each side played the aggressive game, the other made defensive saves and returns. Since a slam is a slam in almost any language, I wasn't able to observe any significant difference between the aggressive players and good men either in America or any other part of the world. One of the two defensive players, however, had a remarkable technique in that he used only backhand shots, returning all his opponent's powerful slams with a graceful slicing stroke. Although I had been good enough as a teenager to play on the Phoenix, Arizona, team, I was never at my best moment as good as any of the four boys we saw.

We entered one large building on which was written, in giant red letters, "The working class must exercise leadership over everything." It would be interesting to know if the same message was there in future years.

A machine shop and electric-motor repair shop were well provided with equipment.

In the acupuncture clinic in the school we saw several white-jacketed medical attendants checking adults for a variety of serious ailments—hypertension, arthritis, sunstroke and partial paralysis, among others.

One elderly woman suffering from arthritis had needles in her shoulder, forearm, elbow and the back of an arm. Atop each needle was a small clump of a medicinal herb. This material was lighted and permitted to burn. It is not clear how the effect of the herb, whatever it might be, takes place, unless it is by inhalation of the fumes, which smelled remarkably like marijuana.

In what was described as the model airplane class, most of the students, oddly enough, were constructing remarkably realistic-looking ocean liners and tankers, about eight feet long. The fine-arts-class students were making beautiful traditional Chinese lanterns out of paper. The intricate cutting classifies it absolutely as art, by no means just craftwork.

At one table four young men were hand-painting, with sharp-pointed brushes, professional and beautiful sketches, about one and a half by three inches, which are set into panels of the ceiling lamps.

In one room we saw on display an array of totally professional products, all made by students—pulley-transmission belts, an acetylene torch, neon lamps, fountain pens and other items—which could be sold anywhere.

At the end of the visit to the school we were treated to another show. An orchestra played for us, using Chinese instruments as well as a few European-style violins. It would be interesting to know if the Chinese violin came before the European or the other way around. Some of the Chinese violin numbers, combined with a fast hand-clapping tempo, sounded remarkably like our blue-grass music.

Then a group of eight girls in blue overalls danced and sang, accompanied by an accordion. Three young men put on a very professional magic act. By magic indeed the words "A Warm Welcome, American Friends" appeared on a dark shiny surface that had been covered only for a moment with a dark cloth.

Out in the playground, a group of boys and girls who looked about eleven put on a demonstration of kung fu. It opened with incredibly high kicks, the foot actually going back over the shoulder.

No visitor to the school could fail to be impressed. Can the American reader imagine a foreign visitor—Chinese or not—being so impressed by a visit to even one of our better high schools? The question deserves more than passing thought.

And there was no problem of delinquency or truancy at such schools. No fights, no attacks on teachers, no narcotics, no switch-blades, no venereal disease, no vandalism.

We thanked our hosts, with whom we had spent most of the afternoon, and returned to the hotel for a shower and a brief nap.

After dinner Bill and I returned again to the lobby to meet Yeh Sing-ru and the local guides. Mrs. Yeh, we had by now learned, had served as Shirley MacLaine's guide during her two-week film tour. She was curious about Shirley and when she learned that Shirley and I were neighbors and friends, asked many questions about her.

Through the still-teeming Shanghai night-time streets we were driven to a huge theater

Shanghai. Boatbuilders' testing tank, technical middle school, July, 1975.

High school students practicing martial arts.

The musical show Children of the Grasslands.

to see a film. The building itself was Spartan, as are almost all modern theaters in China. No thick carpets, no glamorous chandeliers (unless left over from the old days), no exotic wall colors, no lushly padded seats. This was in contrast to the 1930s, at which time there were a good many modern theaters in Shanghai, most notably the Cathay, the Grand, the Lyric, the Lyceum and the Metropol. Architecturally, these could have as well served the cities of New York, Chicago or Los Angeles, so spacious and well constructed were they.

The audience now was almost totally Chinese, with perhaps three dozen foreigners from various parts of the world, all shepherded by affable China Travel Service guides and interpreters.

The film turned out to be a musical, a form that, in my Occidental ignorance, I had not realized was produced in China. In color, it

was a ballet titled *Children of the Grasslands*. Its characters were North China horsemen, sheepherders and villagers. The dancers were superb, and would be able to take their place in any ballet company in the world. The film was much too long, however, though obviously that is one man's opinion; it may not seem too long to Chinese audiences. The evil character in the story was a "rich peasant" type.

I did not know then that we would sit through two more productions of *Children of the Grasslands* before leaving China!

After Bill and I were dropped off at the hotel he was so sleepy he went upstairs to bed at once. I felt the need of a bit of fresh air after the stuffiness of the theater so I strolled alone around the corner and about the neighborhood. Scores of buses, cabs and trucks glided by in the night as did thousands of white-shirted Chinese, some on bicycles, more afoot.

The night breeze off the black, mysterious river was a godsend after the hot day.

I saw no other Occidental faces during my walk.

A CHILDREN'S PALACE

Sunday, July 6

Sunday morning too the hubbub of whistles, horns and voices began before five o'clock, at about which time a solitary young man outside began shouting something I could not translate. He repeated the same sentence several times, in a loud voice, each time ending with the loud syllable "Ughh!" I assumed he was doing some sort of karate or kung fu exercise down in the plaza but since I would have been unable to see him in the dark I didn't get up to check. Fortunately after a few minutes he stopped shouting and I fell back asleep.

I got up at seven, looked out the window and discovered that despite wet streets the exercise program was in full swing down below where a group of perhaps two hundred white-shirted young men had formed a loose circle to watch a group of teenagers doing gymnastic flips.

We breakfasted at seven-thirty and promptly at eight (almost everything in post-1949 China is done promptly) left the hotel for a famed Children's Palace, one of several in the Shanghai area. It was founded by Mme.

Sun Yat-sen's China welfare organization, after the Communist victory.

The palace, formerly an enormous mansion inhabited by a five-member British family, resembles one of the great English or French baronial estates and in the context of modern China seems to have been a particularly wasteful display of luxury. We entered and were shown into a beautiful hall, somewhat resembling, but exceeding in charm, the large rooms of the White House. At either end of the massive room enormous fireplaces, no longer functional, graced the walls. On top of the mantels were giant mirror panels.

A gymnastic display by a team of young high school boys was under way. On the floor sat an audience of perhaps three hundred children. After diving over a very high "horse" without touching it the boys repeated the stunt three more times, first with one of their members lying on top of the horse, then two, then three.

Next followed an exhibition of ballet movements by seven little prospective ballerinas who appeared to be about ten years old. They wore wine-red tutus and white bows in their hair.

After a few minutes we tiptoed away from the gymnastics and dance demonstration and were shown to an adjoining room where the first thing visible was a large counter from which some forty dolls, about a foot and a half in height, dressed in the costumes of all of China's minority groups, waved to us in the

Children's Palace, Shanghai, summer, 1975.

way that little children customarily do in China.

On a table behind the doll display was something one might expect to find at Disneyland or any other American amusement park, but with a fundamental difference. A water course with tracks for four boats was prepared for a race. At the side of the course computers with scattered Arabic numbered keys from 1 to 40 operated the individual boats. Each player had to hit all forty keys in sequence to start his craft.

We next visited a chemistry class, the members of which were studying agricultural insecticides, an entirely professional machine shop making parts for pumps and a radio shop. It is important to realize that the students in these classes contribute *their after-school time.* The "model airplane shop" in an adjacent room has a misleading name. The students were not involved in making the usual toys but were learning the basics of aircraft design; their planes were flyable.

In the next workshop students were making ships of various kinds, all the way from old-fashioned sailing vessels to modern models. In the adjoining room a water tank about twenty-five feet long was used for the purpose of determining the seaworthiness of the models. A girl of about twelve launched a beautiful tanker which under its own power successfully navi-

gated the length of the tank without deviating so much as an inch to the left or right. Two parallel dark green lines about a foot apart running the length of the tank were used to evaluate the straightness of the ship's progress. Students so trained can later work in either the shipbuilding or airplane industry because the designs involved are the same regardless of the size of the craft.

Next we were taken into a room where pairs of children, from about six to ten, were busy at eight Ping-Pong tables. Bill and I were invited to play. It was an unnerving experience to be opposed by a little fellow of about nine whom I would have had considerable difficulty defeating even if my game were in shape.

A room full of framed paintings, mostly watercolors by twelve-year-old children, was most impressive. Had the pictures been painted by American students one would have said they could not possibly be younger than sixteen—and remarkably gifted at that.

In an adjacent room children created beautiful paper-cutting pictures. The teacher of the paper-cutting class was a factory worker who contributed his services part-time. In the same class the children did handsome needlepoint tapestry, in the ancient Chinese style.

We were then escorted outdoors and led through the Red Soldiers' Obstacle Course, laid out in a small forest of bamboo and other

Animated dolls, Children's Palace, Shanghai.

Above
Little dancers in a show at school, Shanghai.

Below
Radio class, Shanghai, 1975.

plants. Rock formations, ladders, slides and other impediments had been placed in a kind of Disneyland sequence which was great fun to go through. By navigating the course the children are instructed in one of the basic infantry skills—keeping out of harm's way.

When we left the Children's Palace several of the boys and girls who had been our personal guides, holding fast to us with their little hands, specifically asked us to send their affectionate greetings to the children of America and invite them too to come to visit the children of China. I explained that I would be showing pictures on American television taken this day by my son Bill and that there-

I give a strangely Japanese response to a welcome by Shanghai kindergarten kids.

fore millions of American children would see the faces of the Chinese youngsters and would get to know them in that way and, perhaps later, more personally.

LU HSUN

After lunch and a brief siesta we were driven to one of the minor cultural shrines of Communist China, the famous author Lu Hsun's (Lu Xun's) former home in the Hungkow district on Samying Road, a quiet, attractive street. After being cordially greeted by a woman in her late thirties we entered a charming, narrow courtyard. Lu, we were told, came to Shanghai in October, 1927, and subsequently had to move his residence three times to escape government police. This was the house—though largely restored—where he lived before his death, from April, 1933, to October, 1936.

Lu Hsun was one of as many as thirty-four pen names of Chou Shu-jen, all used because it was dangerous to write criticism of the status quo under one's own. To reach those who were illiterate he advocated the use of wood carvings and other forms of pictorial art.

In an upstairs room we were shown the desk —or a replica—at which he worked for several years. Though dying of tuberculosis Lu persisted in writing to the very end. On the wall a calendar marks the day of his death. An alarm clock is set at the time, 5:25 in the morning.

Lu Hsun's nearby tomb, to which we were driven, is in a beautiful area of Hungkow Park, now known as Lu Xun Memorial Park, on Baoshan Road. Beside his grave a pair of evergreen Yi trees stand, one planted by his wife, the other by his son.

Lu, though today considered a hero by the Chinese Communists, was himself a free spirit

with a strong antiauthoritarian streak. He was a slender, good-looking man, to judge by the photographs of him on the walls of his modest apartment. Unlike many heroes of modern China he was not born of peasant stock; his people were gentry of Shao Hsing in Chekiang (Zhejiang) Province. The family was nevertheless plunged into poverty when Lu was young, following his grandfather's imprisonment and his father's death. Having thus learned from personal experience that social justice was a rare commodity in nineteenth-century China, it was inevitable that Lu would use his literary gifts, when they eventually emerged, to criticize the status quo.

He was educated at Kingnan Military Academy in Nanking and took college courses in literature, philosophy and scientific medicine in Japan. Like many thoughtful young men of his day he became an active rebel against the cruelty of the Manchu administra-

tion. After the victory of the Sun Yat-sen Republican forces in 1911, Lu moved to Peking the following year and initially spent much of his time in scholarly pursuits. It was not until 1918 that he wrote the remarkable short story, "A Madman's Diary," which can be enjoyed on both the psychological and political level. There could be no doubt, however, about the political thrust of his "The True Story of Ah Q." published in 1921. In it Lu Hsun employs a mixture of comedy and tragedy in bitterly criticizing the traditional order.

Increasingly, during the 1920s, Lu dedicated his pen to Revolutionary endeavors. In political danger in 1926, he left Peking and hid out in Shanghai, living chiefly in the apartment we visited.

It is interesting to note Edgar Snow's observations on Lu in his chapter "Literature and Music" in *The Other Side of the River: Red China Today:*

Under Kuomintang society the writer of any importance was persecuted, driven underground, and sometimes killed. (A few were buried alive.) While he breathed, his work had the meaning of an individual conscience. He helped to expose and reject despotic idiocies of the old order; he served by quickening general awareness of the "becoming" beyond the "being." The present society has corrected some of the ignorance pitilessly exposed by Lu Hsun and his disciples. Yet if Lu Hsun lived with the same courage in the same frail body today he would not be able to project life beyond *the idiocies and tyrannies in the current set of value-realities*—not before the party itself begins to rectify them. He would not be buried alive; probably he would not even be imprisoned, as happens periodically to Djilas, in Yugoslavia. But he would certainly be obliged to attempt thought-remolding. The artist is thus condemned to silence or to the repetition of party truisms—until self-criticism works its way to the top and a new set of collective truisms receives official sanction. [Italics added.]

That night we went to see a charming, polished and, I assume, ancient Chinese entertainment form, a puppet show. The drama was titled *The Red Lantern,* and related, naturally,

Puppet show.

a Revolutionary story. Because the play was being televised—or videotaped—three cameras were positioned around us.

The surprise to our Occidental eyes was that the puppets were operated not by strings from above but by thin poles, from below. The sound and dialogue seemed to be tape-recorded. Bill and I enjoyed the production thoroughly, particularly its humorous moments. The figures of fun—more exactly, of ridicule—were bumbling, corrupt officers of the old Kuomintang, not all of whose leaders, alas, were as high-minded as Chiang Kai-shek.

We were driven back to the hotel after the show. Bill, exhausted, went upstairs to bed. I decided to walk around a bit. It was about nine-thirty. I walked across the street and through the plaza where the morning exercises take place. Just the other side of it was the broad river. Thousands of white-shirted young men and women strolled about, enjoying the blessed cool breeze of the water.

All harbors and rivers look romantic at night, with lights flickering on the shiny black waters, ghostly ships gliding by in the dark. What incredible history had taken place on the banks of this river, in just this spot, for better or for worse. What hatred the Europeans and

the Americans had sown here, out of a confused mixture of good will, greed and ignorance. And all the surge of popular emotion caused by the historic blunders committed in Shanghai and elsewhere is now being credited to the Communist account.

This is the city where Jayne and her family remained for a month, away from danger, in those historic days after Chiang had turned on his Communist allies in the Kuomintang, when no one knew for sure which way to go.

There had been no luxurious British hotel for the Cotters in those days. Being a missionary family they were poor; the times were chaotic. The family lived in a sort of warehouse for a full month, experiencing living conditions that, though uncomfortable, millions of Chinese would have considered themselves fortunate to enjoy, so much worse was their daily lot.

OLD SHANGHAI

At a dinner party in Beverly Hills one evening, not long after returning from our second visit to China, I happened to chat with a friend, photographer John Swope, who, in putting questions to me about our trip, mentioned that he himself had been in Peking and Shanghai in 1930, fresh out of Harvard. (John, who died in 1979, was married to actress Dorothy McGuire.) When he said that he had kept a daily diary of his experiences I asked if I could borrow it so that I might have the opportunity of seeing the China of the 1930s through the eyes, as it were, of a more or less typical upper-class young American. John was kind enough to send the original unpublished manuscript around a couple of days later. It is fascinating. In fact it reveals a sharper contrast between the misery of the poor Chinese of that day and the luxury of their Caucasian visitors than anything else I had read.

Curious to see for himself what conditions were like in some of Shanghai's least reputable dens of iniquity Swope wrote that

[rickshaw boys] took us down the smallest, darkest, dirtiest, smelliest alleys I ever hope to see and stopped before a dark door, out of which appeared a fat, squint-eyed Chinaman. We stepped into a brightly-lighted room full of awful looking girls and rotten smells. They were the most awful looking girls I've ever seen and *some of them were only about 14 years old. Others had large heads and were idiots for certain.* I thought this place was pretty bad but the next place we went to was far worse. We got to it by even smaller and dirtier alleys and the place itself was much dirtier and much more repulsive and disgusting. The girls in here looked about as much like human-beings as a cow, and I'm sure they are not as happy as most cows. The *worst part of it is the extreme adolescence of most of them, and the presence of small children, learning the trade from the cradle.* This place was so poor as to only have one room, where a couple of dirty mattresses were lying in the corners, and the girls were sitting around on tables or boxes. The atmosphere was permeated with filth, ugly smells and thick clouds of dirty smoke . . . they must die off at about 30 because all of them have diseases of one sort or another and they looked like hell. . . . These Chinese houses can remind one only of a bunch of dirty, groveling animals in total ignorance of everything except their horrible business. And when one considers that the district where we visited is absolutely crowded with these houses where

crime, disease and pernicious deeds are all that is known, it is downright awful. And it will continue and increase because *the children are brought up and trained in the atmosphere. They simply have not got a chance.* [Italics added.]

Repeatedly Swope refers to the misery, poverty, hunger and disease that were everywhere, and this in what was then China's most prosperous city. Describing the junks in Soochow Creek, near the area of luxury hotels and swank clubs, Swope wrote:

The northern end of the Bund is jammed with junks and sampans tied together so that there is only a narrow channel down the middle of the creek. Whole families live on these boats, which are quite small and seem to lack adequate cabin space for even one person. . . . They are extremely poor and most of them go about barefooted, in spite of the cold weather. They live in the dirtiest of conditions on the filthy creek . . . it is pathetic to see so many hundreds of coolies, sailors, rickshaw boys, etc. not able to clothe or feed themselves properly.

Describing a restaurant at the other end of the Bund, Swope observed:

Around these food-stands a mob of beggars, most despicable and pitiful in appearance, stand and hope to have a few coppers or bits of food thrown to them. . . .
Practically all the laborers in every factory are over their heads in debt and keep borrowing, paying back each month with their whole month's wages and then borrowing more. In not a few cases a man will have to escape from his debts, in which case he sometimes joins the Red bandits, the army, or kills his creditors.

Compare these painfully graphic descriptions by young Swope with his casual observations of the life-style of European and American visitors to China.

Mr. Page took us to tea at the French Club . . . it is enormous and contains a large ball-room, tremendous swimming pool, gymnasium, card-rooms, dining-room, a long bar,

Children still work hard in China. Normally such simple carts carry heavy loads.

and has about 30 grass tennis-courts. Mr. Page had gathered together about ten people for our benefit and we had an enjoyable time dancing on the spring floor in the ballroom.

After lunch I went horseback riding with Rose Marie . . . it was very good fun as we rode around the flat outskirts of Shanghai . . . it is all cultivated, with a few houses here and there and excellent bridle-paths with jumps. . . . After riding I had tea at the Meyers' house where Anson met us, after which we walked back to the hotel. After dinner we went to the Canidrome, which is a tremendous layout containing enormous stands about a 500-yard race-track for the dogs. Large open spaces about the betting-booths below the stands, a large ballroom with a wonderful colored orchestra, a good show with Russian girls, a few wee golf courses and Lord only knows what else.

Another interesting aspect of life in Kuomintang Shanghai was provided by a former navy officer and U.S. Treasury representative named Charles Moore, who came to my office in April, 1976, and kindly shared his recollections of Shanghai in 1936 and 1937.

"Americans and Europeans lived very well," he said. "In 1936, for example, the British harbormaster in Shanghai was paid $50,-000 a year." (Perhaps equal to $200,000 today.) There was a custom in China in those days, Moore explained, involving something called the Hong Book. Because travel arrangements had to be made well in advance by American and European visitors, the majority of whom were connected with business firms, the Chinese would have considerable advance information about the traveler before he arrived. This information was carried in the Hong Book, which was sort of a credit-rating service. It entitled the traveler to sign tabs at the hotels, clubs, restaurants and shops frequented by non-Chinese visitors. Charges could be run up for several weeks. But if there was a failure to pay, the negative information also would be entered in the book, which could lead to complications.

"At the end of the month," Charles Moore said, "all chits I had signed were sent to the Metropol Hotel. The hotel tendered me a monthly bill for my penthouse apartment and other expenses, plus all of the chits that had come in from all over Shanghai, the Hong Book having shown that I was a resident of the Metropol. The hotel would have paid all of these outside chits, then they would give me a total. At the end of the month, or two or three months, I'd give them a check for the total amount. And when I would leave my office, to go somewhere on business, or I left my hotel to go anywhere not too far away in a rickshaw, the doorman at the Metropol, knowing me as a resident there, would pay the rickshaw boy in advance. Or else they had some other arrangement, because I didn't even have to pay for a rickshaw ride to any place I wanted to go. If I had taken a rickshaw to the theater, after I came out I would take another back to the Metropol Hotel and the doorman would take care of it. Consequently, for weeks I might never have a piece of coin or paper money in my pocket, for anything. Any time I wanted to go to the movies I 'charged' it. Incidentally at this time—1936 and 1937—we had two of the finest movie houses in the world. Films were shown in Shanghai before they were seen in the United States."

"I've heard," I said, "that it was a difficult time for Russians in the area."

"Yes," Moore said, "the plight of the White Russians in Shanghai was pitiable in the cases of those whose money ran out. I remember a Russian princess was working at one time as a barmaid in the Metropol Hotel. A number of the Russian women were in such dire straits they were being kept, as mistresses, by various foreigners. The situation became so noticeable that American personnel were discouraged from associating with the Russians. The women, however, were so well educated, so sophisticated that it was a joy to spend an evening with them."

"What was social life like?"

"Well, lunch would take two hours, and promptly at three-thirty every afternoon, no matter where one was, everything stopped for tea, served in the British manner. The principal sport was bowling, with small pinball equipment. An important athletic event was the annual football game by the American marines. Perhaps the most unusual factor about the races at the world-famous track was that the predominant requirement to serve as a jockey was social standing, rather than small size.

"The foreigners dominated the economy. The only fleet of motorized taxis in town in those days was owned by an American businessman, a member of the American Club. Another member of the American Club was the sole importer of Scotch whiskey into Shanghai. This gentleman, as a courtesy to fellow members, had a special label made up. The Scotch whiskey came in five-gallon casks and was transferred into bottles in Shanghai. This fellow turned over enough of this fine Scotch whiskey to the American Club with a label on the bottle, American Club Whiskey. Any of the members could buy this, the finest Scotch, for $1.50 a quart. But each member of the American Club had to sign a chit—your word was not taken—that by reason of paying $1.50 a quart for this whiskey, on your honor you would not resell or give away an unopened bottle. But you could get as much as you wanted for your own apartment and it was damned good Scotch."

"How were living conditions?" I asked.

"My penthouse apartment at the Metropol Hotel cost $75 per month. Three servants cost $15 a month total, or an average of $5 per month."

"Was Shanghai noisy, as it is now?"

"Well, during 1936 and 1937 there must have been twenty-five or twenty-eight local radio stations, all broadcasting in Chinese, and any time you walked down the street you could get such a conglomeration of noise it was very uncomfortable. Any time you turned the radio on in your apartment they were not tuned well enough where you could tune out one station sharply enough so there was just a babble, at least to American ears."

Moore had fresh roses and other beautiful flowers in his apartment daily. The cost: 15 cents a week!

A glass of milk, he said, cost more than a glass of whiskey. The reason was that the area around Shanghai was not well suited to the growing of hay, which had to be shipped in from considerable distances for the cows.

"Did foreigners receive good medical care?"

"Yes. It was the custom to pay American and European doctors a certain monthly fee for which it was assumed they would keep you well, rather than calling in a doctor after you were taken ill. We lived well in many ways. Not only tailors would come to one's apartment or house but even shoemakers."

Edgar Snow, who knew modern China better than any other American, vividly sketched the color and pace of pre-Communist Shanghai in *The Other Side of the River.*

Goodbye to all that: the well-dressed Chinese and their chauffeured cars behind bulletproof glass; the gangsters, the shake-downs, the kidnappers; the exclusive foreign clubs . . . the white-coated "Chinese boys," obsequiously waiting to be tipped . . . the opium dens and gambling halls . . . the sailors in their smelly bars and friendly brothels on Szechwan Road; the myriad short-time whores and pimps busily darting in and out of the alleyways . . . the beggars on every downtown block and the scabby infants urinating or defecating on the curb while mendicant mothers absently scratched for lice; the "honeycarts" hauling the night-soil through the streets . . . the jungle free-for-all struggle for gold or survival and the day's toll of unwanted infants and suicides floating in the canals; the knotted rickshaws with their owners fighting each other for customers and arguing fares; the Japanese conquerors and their American Kuomintang successors; gone the wickedest and most colorful city in the Orient: Goodbye to all that.

Thinking of the turbulent sweep of history as it affected China during this century I strolled back to our hotel.

When I got to our room Bill was sound asleep.

THE HERO FOUNTAIN PEN FACTORY

Monday, July 7

Our Monday schedule called for a morning visit to a typical Shanghai factory.

After arriving at the Hero Fountain Pen Factory, located in the middle of a green farming district, we were welcomed by Mr. Hong, head of the plant's Revolutionary Committee. The project opened in 1931, he told us, and at first had been only a small back-street operation. In the old days most of the work was done by hand because so little machinery was available. The peak annual output before 1949 had been only 280,000 pens a year. The factory was moved to its present site in 1955. It now had 1,200 workers, about a third of whom were women, and turned out some 25 million pens per year! The productivity of the place was amazing. It seemed to be producing enough pens for the whole world, but of course China, with its 800 million people, requires an enormous number of everything.

We were shown machines that made pen barrels from warm liquid plastic in various colors, machines that made points, clips and other parts.

The devices that stamped out the barrels and other portions of the pens were ultramodern, but it was interesting to note that as the pens were produced they fell into simple straw baskets of a design common in China for centuries.

Outside one of the small two-story factory buildings we saw a long green hedge on the top of which, like sprouted mushrooms, about twenty-five open yellow umbrellas were displayed. They are for the use of workers who neglect to bring their own umbrellas from home and are surprised by unexpected rains. In an open field in the middle of the factory complex we saw—to our surprise—eight large antiaircraft guns, the barrels of which appeared to be about fifteen feet long. All were covered with canvas and straw. We had chanced upon one emplacement of what must be a great many such in the Shanghai area.

Around the individual buildings there were a good many graceful hedges and brilliant flower beds, above one of which unfortunately we found yet one more tall stack belching thick black smoke.

We noticed in some of the workshops a clever invention the Chinese have developed for extra comfort in excessively hot weather. They set small platforms, about two inches

Fountain pen factory near Shanghai.

Antiaircraft guns, Hero Fountain Pen Factory, Shanghai.

high, made of several lateral strips of bamboo, with air space between, on their workbenches or chairs.

At about ten o'clock loudspeaker newscasts are piped to all workers in the factory; thus while they work they also learn. This is an admirable idea, quite aside from the question as to what it is they are hearing, because the work itself is of the kind Chaplin drew our attention to in *Modern Times*. Consequently, the ability to turn the analytical part of one's mind to something more interesting than performing the same manual task a thousand times a day must be important to the workers.

Most of the factory laborers live in the city but some do not choose to return home every night. For their convenience there are dormitories on the grounds.

The factory produces pens in the cheap, medium-range and high-quality categories though all are well-made, serviceable and low-priced. There is no place in China now for shoddy, planned-obsolescence merchandise, except perhaps a bit specifically ordered by foreign importers.

The manager claimed to have no idea as to what percentage, if any, of his factory's output was for export.

Fountain pen factory.

"We are only concerned with production," he explained. "The sale and distribution of the output is decided elsewhere."

The factory has its own clinic, sanatorium and three rooms where small children can be cared for while parents work.

The making of a single fountain pen, we were told, involves more than two hundred separate processes. The plant turns out more than 80,000 pens a day, operating on a six-day week. It is closed, oddly enough, on Thursday. Off days at different factories are staggered so that the city will not be overcrowded on the weekends.

When Mr. Hong showed us the various grades of finished product, all quite handsome and serviceable, Bill expected we would be presented with souvenir pens, in keeping with factory custom in the Western world. No such luck. I later bought one of the factory's pens at a Friendship Store for about $6, a great bargain. It was my only fountain pen till it was lost or stolen in 1977.

A SHANGHAI COMMUNE

After lunch we were driven to one of the Shanghai area's supporting state farms or communes.

We entered its grounds on a dirt road—still being dug, graded and graveled by a few dozen workers—which ran beside a man-made canal, along which a number of small boats were being poled. The rivers and canals of China are used much like our roads in that they carry a great deal of freight traffic.

Our cars raised a dusty trail through stands of corn, tomatoes and cotton as we approached the headquarters buildings. These were attractive, with whitewashed walls and smart green trim on doors and window frames. We were given the usual warm Chinese greeting and taken at once to a reception room like almost all the others in China, furnished as it was with a long table with cloth, saucers of cigarettes, covered teacups and, on the walls, Karl, Friedrich, Nicolai and Joe on one side and Chairman Mao on the other.

The name of the commune, we were told, is Hung Tu. Started in September, 1958, it has made excellent progress, was manned by 133 production teams under 16 production brigades and had a population of approximately 23,000, living in 5,000 separate households.

On its 2,100 hectares of land it chiefly produces grain and vegetables but is not solely a farm since small-factory industry, education and military aspects are also stressed. In 1974 the commune raised 34,000 pigs, ten times as many as the area would have produced in 1949. The entire complex is under irrigation and supplied with electricity, something, our hosts stressed, unheard of in rural areas of old China.

"In fact," the chairman of the Revolutionary Committee said, "more than thirty man-made rivers and canals have been dug here. Also in the past there was a serious problem in this area caused by the gentle rolling of the land, with some levels too high and others too low. The high areas, of course, would not get enough water and the low areas would get too much. The land has now been leveled and straightened, to solve this problem."

Parenthetically, on December 31, 1975, while watching the "Late Late Show" on a Los Angeles television station, I happened to see an old film starring Victor Mature, which dealt with the adventures of an American bomber squadron in China during World War II. The producers of the film had obviously acquired some actual documentary footage, not only of bomb runs and parachute jumps but also of farm and construction activity in China. Although it was well worked into the fabric of the picture it is generally a simple matter to distinguish such film from its make-believe context. I mention the picture here because quite the most fascinating scene is the authentic footage showing farmland being leveled by enormous "steamrollers." The word is in quotation marks because the giant rollers, as tall as a man, were not propelled by a steam engine but were simply pulled by what appeared to be about a hundred laborers, straining forward with ropes over their shoulders, like beasts of burden. Behind each enormous roller three men holding "reins" steered the giant cylinders. Again and again one encounters these dramatic instances of the Chinese ability to use manpower in the way the West uses the "horsepower" of machines. The Communists, obviously enough, did not introduce the practice but have employed it on a more massive and organized basis in their public-works projects to improve the country.

As for education, the Hung Tu Commune had no less than thirty-two middle and primary schools!

Living quarters for the workers were, by Western standards, primitive, but clean and serviceable. The downstairs floors were simple hard clay, the steps plain concrete. Upstairs the bedroom had a cement floor but was more attractive, partly because it housed one of this commune's special old-fashioned covered beds. In a second apartment we found another beautiful covered bed with a handsome matching chest and dresser. The commune planned by 1980 to provide better housing for one-third of its members.

An old peasant joined us at a downstairs table as we sipped tea, telling us of the misery and suffering of his former existence, and gratefully comparing it with his present security and comfort. I noticed that he spoke in the same loud, gruff voice as the elderly peasant woman we had met at the Evergreen Commune near Peking the previous winter.

The information we were given was in general similar to that absorbed at the Evergreen. Before Liberation, under the old regime, one is reminded, the peasants of the area lived in misery, poverty and squalor. Most of the land was owned by either landlords or rich peasants. No peasant would be described as rich in the United States but since the word is relative it is merely intended to describe one far better off than his unfortunate fellows.

The visitor is reminded that floods, famines and droughts were all too common in pre-1949 China. At the first stage of the agricultural revolution it was obvious that the larger holdings had to be broken up and apportioned out, as fairly as possible, to the poor peasants. Many Americans will automatically approve of this; some formal capitalists will not. Whatever the merits of the philosophical argument, the fact is that the peasant's lot improved dramatically as a result of the program.

By the mid-1950s the stage of developing mutual-aid cooperatives had been reached. If one particular peasant seemed to be failing, his problem immediately became that of the cooperative as a whole. This was in marked contrast to the heartless approach of the pre-1949 system. Evolution in the late-fifties–early-sixties period to the system of common land ownership—the commune system—came next. This, despite some false starts and early partial failures, made for more rational resolution of three problems that had for centuries troubled China: the division of large fields into tiny, disorganized holdings, the presence of too many burial sites, which were not agriculturally productive and a serious lack of irrigation facilities.

All communes in China now have irrigation systems, of varying degrees of complexity. Wells, many of which boast electric pumps, have further helped with the age-old water shortage dilemma. Crop yields on many communes, one is told, have increased seven times since 1949.

The suffering peasants would have counted the three stages of the modern agricultural revolution a success if the end product, the communes, had simply been self-sustaining, since such a thing was a dramatic contrast to their previous experience. But the communes have done far more than achieve economic independence. They now sell millions of pounds of grain, vegetables, fruits, pigs and other livestock to the state yearly. As a result it was inevitable that living standards would improve. Most commune brigade families own at least one bicycle, many have sewing machines and the homes in which families live, while hardly comfortable by American standards, are vastly superior to the hovels and huts of pre-1949 rural China. They also compare favorably with the tumbledown shacks in which migrant American farm workers must live.

Medical care costs less than one American dollar for a full year; for each member of the family rent is free, and the cost of foodstuffs very low.

This is not to say that work in the fields is much less difficult, hour by hour, than it ever was. If migrant laborers in the United States do back-breaking work we may be sure the peasants of China do the same. But for the first time in their history as individuals, or as members of a now-powerful nation, the Chinese peasants understand clearly that the government *cares* about them, and that this care is not merely an expression of pious emotion but is made very real in terms of clothing on backs, food on tables, medical care provided, education for one's children and—also important—

a sense that one is personally participating in the building of one's nation, playing an active personal role in the mighty drama being enacted on the Chinese mainland. Anyone with even the slightest familiarity with Chinese history knows that except for a few scattered individuals, in a few isolated instances, this has not happened before.

Drawing back and taking the long view of what China has accomplished in the agricultural sector in just a quarter of a century makes the achievement even more impressive. Consider: China has a *population about four times that of the United States and is feeding it well with crops grown on only 11 percent of the nation's land area!* Most of China's soil is, for one reason or another, unsuitable for productive farming.

All successful cultures in history have demanded heroes, who are necessary for their ability to inspire others to greater personal effort. China has one entire commune which may rightly be considered heroic, Tachai. "In agriculture," one constantly hears the quotation from Chairman Mao, "learn from Tachai."

There is indeed much to learn. At this remarkable commune in the Taihang Mountains production brigades attacked rocky hilltops, leveled them to enlarge farming areas, painfully dug stone out of quarries to build step-terraces on previously steeply slanted hillsides, fought soil erosion, flood damage, drought and other difficulties. Perhaps the most impressive factor of Tachai's victory against crushing odds is that its residents *worked their wonders without outside help.* "Ask not what your country can do for you," Mao might have echoed, "ask rather what you can do for your country."

In addition to crops, the Shanghai area commune raises chickens, pigs, cattle and rabbits, some for fur and some for food. It should not be assumed, by the way, because of the dramatic improvements in China's agricultural system, that the nation is totally self-sufficient in food. According to official 1975 U.S. estimates, China had imported grain for the previous sixteen years and during two recent years

—1972 and 1974—imported more grain than did the Soviet Union. But through an apparently well-balanced combination of national production and imports, the 800 million Chinese are provided with adequate nutrition, something which cannot be said for millions in some other parts of the world. And we must appreciate, too, that the United States also imports vast quantities of foodstuffs, from which it follows that simple importation of food cannot be considered to support an argument that a nation has serious agricultural problems. Visitors are told that China has purposely exported rice to foreign countries because of its higher price and, in return, imported a sufficiently large quantity of relatively lower-priced grain, such as wheat, to supplement her own need in foodstuffs. And, in this process, some extra capital has been accumulated.

As the day warmed up, our hosts presented Bill and me with conical straw peasant hats, to ward off the enervating heat of midsummer. Much that we saw on our stroll about the commune might have been anticipated on a large farm anywhere in the world, but what we had not expected was encountering small factories and workshops, each a beehive of activity. One was a large warehouse of garagelike structure in which a heavy machine shop that would not seem out of place in Detroit or Gary, Indiana, was operating. Its workers create some of their own machines, repair others, work on tractors, piping, pumps, farm wagons and other equipment needed for the commune.

The warehouse machine shop not only repairs farm machinery but also manufactures it. The equipment was entirely modern and altogether impressive in size and efficiency. There was nothing whatever of the backwoods workshop about the place. One might have been visiting a portion of a General Motors plant in the 1930s and 1940s.

Next we visited a building where basket weaving was done. The baskets were beyond question works of art although their function was merely to transport watermelons and various vegetables to market. All the work was done by hand, by true craftsmen, using thin bamboo strips. As if to underline the theme of self-sufficiency, the commune also grows its own bamboo. The long strips of wood are sliced into ribbons by a simple machine which increases by six times the productivity of a worker.

We next visited the woodworking department. A tall stack of handsome "old oaken buckets" greeted us at the door. The woodworking division of the commune includes the making of furniture. A handsome dining-room table with a set of four stool-chairs cost only about $13. It was made entirely of lumber scraps. A beautiful enclosed bed of the old-fashioned type sells for 150 yuan, roughly $75. In the United States a fair price for it would be $1,000.

The clinic was not the primitive collection of barefoot doctors' huts I had seen at Peking's Evergreen Commune. It had space for dentistry, an operating room able to handle operations up to the complexity of hernias and appendicitis, a pharmacy and an acupuncture center. Here, as we walked in, an old man was receiving treatment. He had needles in his upper arm, which caused the muscles to twitch since they were attached to an electric-current device.

We were tired at the end of our long tour of this Chinese commune, but grateful for the opportunity of seeing for ourselves the functioning of what is obviously a productive and successful component of modern China's economy. There were serious difficulties—during the 1950s and 1960s—in reaching the present stage, and the communes in distant rural areas—the equivalent of our Wyoming or North Dakota—are not as efficient as the one we visited but we must understand that the commune in China now is viable. It fares little better than large American farms in times of drought or unseasonable cold spells, but such punishments by nature have nothing to do with ideology or economics.

INDUSTRIAL EXHIBITION HALL

All foreign tourists, in Shanghai, are taken to see a remarkable museum of science, the contents and displays of which come as a sur-

Industrial Exhibition Hall, Shanghai.

The building is massive, ponderous, in that strange combination of Russian-Modern-Greco-Roman so characteristic of architecture in the Soviet Union.

In the part of the exhibition that displays musical instruments I had the pleasure of playing a locally manufactured grand piano. As a piece of furniture it was the most beautiful we had seen; as a musical instrument it was not very good. The Japanese have successfully copied—or been taught—the old German secrets of piano-making. The Chinese apparently have not yet mastered the combined science and art. Neither have some American piano-makers, come to think of it.

Tuesday, July 8

Tuesday morning at seven o'clock, when we entered the dining room for breakfast, we discovered that though the sun was shining, the air pollution was worse than ever. Los Angeles smog on its blackest day was never nearly as bad. The only thing like it in the history of American pollution was old Pittsburgh, which used to be a truly filthy city because of coal smoke from its factories.

Just past the middle of the river, directly in front of our dining-room window, drifted a caravan of junks so large that it seemed to have become a floating island, moving neither up-nor downstream. It was comprised of perhaps thirty small craft. Though we watched it for about forty minutes while breakfasting, nothing about it seemed to move except the tiny ant-like figures of men hopping here and there on the surface of the island. Then at last it was possible to discern some slight movement. The island's forward progress must have been like that of a baby walking. Something about the slowness of this pace seemed to carry an important moral about China. The United States has always been a nation in a hurry. Compared with the slower 5,000-year history of China, our modest two hundred years seem like one day. Our own achievements are remarkable in that in this single day of history we have worked certain wonders far beyond the capacity of all other countries on earth. But China has performed its prodigious feats, for the

prise to those who know nothing of the level of modern China's technical sophistication. Machinery, clothing, silks, cotton and woolens, furniture and other Chinese-made products are displayed.

The Shanghai Industrial Exhibition Hall seems, to American eyes, like a permanent World's Fair exhibit. It reminded me of Chicago's wondrous Museum of Science and Industry though it's not so large. China is entitled to be proud of its dazzling display of modern mechanical wonders. Though the building was constructed with Russian help in the early 1950s, the attractive young guides, some with baby-whisper Marilyn Monroe voices, make no mention of this fact and instead concentrate, understandably enough, on the visible proofs of the impressive sophistication of China's engineering and science.

The plumbing in the men's room was Western style, no doubt because of the Russian influence.

most part, at the pace with which this constellation of freight-laden junks crept, like part of a glacier, past our window.

Sitting at separate nearby tables were two American businessmen who had never met but did so through talking to Bill and myself. One was in the women's wear field, the other in men's wear. They were importing Chinese goods, apparently in very sizable quantities. One of the men was purchasing Chinese materials and having them shipped to Hong Kong to be manufactured as garments.

These two, and an American shoe importer, traveling separately, obviously represent an invasion of American bourgeois capitalists, warmly welcomed, needless to say, by the Chinese.

CHINESE FILMMAKERS

Perhaps because the authorities were sensitive to Shirley MacLaine's published complaint that she was not allowed to visit a film studio or meet Chinese members of her profession, Yeh Sing-ru told us shortly after we arrived that the Travel Service would be happy to arrange an appointment with some film people, a suggestion I gratefully accepted.

In another suite in the Peace Hotel, we were introduced to Li Ling-chun, an actress, Lin Tze-hau, an actor and director, and Chen Yong-shuen, who was identified only as a staff member. When three times during the subsequent conversation I tried to have the matter of Chen's specific duties clarified, the only response was an increase in chuckling, smiling and giggling, accompanied by repetition of the original identification. From all this we assumed that Chen's activities were largely political rather than creative.

There are no Clark Gable, Cary Grant, Marilyn Monroe or Greta Garbo types in Chinese films. Li Ling-chun appeared to be about forty and was plainer than one might expect of a film actress. Lin Tze-hau had more the personna of a director than an actor, by which I mean that he did not have that somewhat rakish, romantic quality common to British, Italian, French and American film actors.

As was the case with most of our interviews

in China, we stated our questions in English, they were translated, and the answers came in Chinese, translated for our convenience. One rule of this particular game is that both questions and answers must be kept reasonably short, otherwise long periods of translation can seem interminable. Everyone in the room abided by the rules except Li Ling-chun, who in responding to a number of questions became so animated that she spoke at considerable length. At one point, hoping gently to bring her attention to the problem, I apologized for the length of one of my own questions. The ploy didn't work.

Li Ling-chun had appeared, before the Cultural Revolution, in a popular film titled *Reconnaissance Across the Yangtze River*. Recently she had been seen in *The Fiery Year*.

"My first question," I said, "concerns acting style. Most cultures around the world have a more or less identifiable theatrical style. I have not seen any plays in China but I understand that actors in the old theater worked in what, to outsiders, seemed a rather formal, unnatural manner. I've also noticed that the young ladies who introduce performers in your vaudeville shows speak in what strikes our ears as an odd style of speech. It is not conversational at all, as I'm sure you are aware. Now as regards your modern films, is the style of acting ultranaturalistic or still somewhat formal?"

For what reason I do not know it seemed difficult for our Chinese friends to understand this question. Later, in seeing local films, I learned that the acting is generally done in a combination of naturalistic and heroic styles, at least for heroic characters.

Li and Lin seemed more interested in stressing political rather than purely artistic factors. In 1975, of course, Mao was still alive and his wife, former actress Chiang Ching and the Gang of Four were firmly in control of cultural matters.

"In other parts of the world," I said, "fans and special admirers write letters to film actors and actresses, requesting autographs, photographs or letters. Does this sort of thing happen in China at present?"

"There is a certain amount of fan mail written," the translator reported, "but not much. There is not so much glorification of the individual here as there is in the non-Socialist countries. It is the success of the picture itself that is considered important."

"Is there much humor in modern Chinese films?" I asked.

After discussing this point among themselves the group conceded that there was not a great deal of humor in Chinese cinema. Oddly enough, the weapon of humor was employed in stage presentations, usually by buffoonish characterizations of Kuomintang or Japanese villains, which must have been of particular interest to the Japanese businessmen and other recent visitors to China.

"In American and European films," I said, "when there's a scene with really dangerous action, stuntmen, stand-ins or replacements are used so that the actors will not be injured. Do the Chinese also employ stuntmen?"

"Only in very rare instances. For the most part the actors themselves perform their entire roles."

Bill and I were told that in China a film actor may appear in only one or two pictures a year but that he is not idle the rest of the time. He will also work in the theater and travel to distant army camps, communes and factories to put on shows. Before the Cultural Revolution, it was stressed, this sort of thing never happened. And the actors of pre-Communist China were more like American performers in that they had virtually no personal contact with the common people.

"How is new talent unearthed and encouraged?" I asked.

"Professionals," we were told, "keep their eyes open for talented amateurs to add to their ranks. For example, a recent film was titled *A Pair of Safety Belts*. A previously inexperienced girl was chosen for the lead role."

"Is there any difference," I asked, "between the salary of the older established actor and that of a newcomer?"

The answer to this struck us as odd. Indeed, we were told, the older actors receive higher pay but after a hasty conference the consensus was that this was a somewhat faulty practice

attributable to the ever-popular "Liu Shao-chi and his Revisionist line." One fascinating aspect of the salary ratio in films is that if someone who has been employed as a factory worker becomes an actor his salary is not increased as a result.

"About how many motion pictures are produced in China each year?"

No one in the room was sure of the answer to this question but we were told that about half a dozen pictures are made each year in Shanghai alone and that there are several studios also producing feature films in other parts of the country. Our host told me there are sixty-five motion picture theaters in Shanghai, a fact that demonstrates the importance of the cinema in present-day China.

As for the primary differences between films of 1975–1976 and those made prior to the Cultural Revolution, it was explained that before the Cultural Revolution a high percentage of films dealt with well-known personages, figures from the ancient past, emperors, kings and matters of interest to foreigners. The subject matter of films in 1975, by contrast, was clearly of the people, by the people and for the people.

One especially interesting aspect of the interview was that while the three actors continued to answer questions at considerable length the translators' responses were greatly shortened and, one assumes, addressed directly to the point. One of these answers suggested that all three actors felt guilty about having made "bad films" in the past. In this connection I inquired how Liu Shao-chi could be blamed for a film made as long ago as the 1950s. It developed that he was now blamed for things that happened in the 1940s and 1930s as well.

The average shooting schedule of a film is about a hundred days.

Probably nothing in American history ever made so many rural people dissatisfied with their lives as the glamorous Hollywood motion pictures from the 1920s to the 1940s. Endless goddesses in silks and furs, men in top hats, white ties and tails, sumptuous swimming pools, nightclubs, resorts, all taught a generation of bumpkins what they were missing. It was how-you-gonna-keep-'em-down-on-the-farm-after-they've-seen-Paree with a vengeance. As long as their films deal with the lives of peasants, workers and soldiers, presumably the Chinese will avoid this problem.

What is one to say about the official Maoist doctrine on the artist's obligations to the people, which by the mid-1970s—thanks to Mao's wife and her colleagues—had led to an almost total emphasis on plays, songs, novels, stories, poems and paintings that endorsed administrative policies? If the philosophy was seen as a relatively short-term measure covering, say, the next twenty-five years, it is apparent that, *within the context of Communist-Socialist biases,* the policy had its practical and demonstrably effective side.

If every carpenter, farmer, plumber, electrician, scholar and scientist must work for the benefit of the Chinese people, rather than out of purely selfish motives, and if their doing so has produced beneficial results, why should artists be excluded from this overall program? So goes the argument.

The arts have a powerful effect upon the human mind. Once one assumes the state's programs to be essentially benevolent and productive, it is inevitable that the state will encourage, persuade or force the artist to participate in the national rebuilding effort with all his creative energy. In my notes made the day of our visit I said, "If, on the other hand, China's present rulers see this policy as one that must persist either throughout all predictable time or until that Communist millennium known as the Withering-Away of the State, then surely not only Western observers but even neutralists, if there really are any, must consider the policy at least partly absurd and counterproductive."

To understand the reasons—to the extent that they are not obvious—one must ask the question, What makes art occur and flourish in all recorded human cultures? Part of the answer is relatively simple, part is rooted in mystery. The simple element relates to the evident enrichment of a society by the addition of beautiful things to it. Paintings, sculpture, ar-

chitectural forms, literature, music bring a sense of enlightenment, pleasure and beauty to the human spirit. There is, after all, a perfectly reasonable place for pleasure in human experience; nature herself provides for it. And who, if given a choice between observing either a dungheap or Michelangelo's *Pietà* would not prefer to study the sculpture? It will be interesting to learn the long-term results of the Chinese attitude in the early seventies toward unusually gifted young people, particularly those with artistic ability.

The mysterious part of the equation relates to the quality of genius. What on earth is the explanation for a Michelangelo, a Shakespeare, a Beethoven or any other master of the arts? The truth is we do not know. In my play *Shakespeare on Love* I had Hamlet and Othello comment on the mystery of their maker's creativity:

OTHELLO

What mystery *genius,* the magic flower
That grows without warm sun, rich soil or shower,
That's not dependent on a mother's grace,
That need not come from father's honored place,
That flashes like a meteor by night
From darkness come, to realms beyond our sight.

HAMLET

It is not any other God's reward.
Where virtue need not dwell its wings have soared.
Not solely to the just, nor to the meek;
Where we would predict silence, it may speak.
No, not in any simple sense deserved,
Nor even understood, merely observed.

We were told, while in China, that the very word and concept of genius was out of favor. Mao himself, it was said, did not wish to be called a genius. It was felt that those commonly referred to as geniuses are rather pampered, selfish, headstrong individuals who, though they have remarkable gifts, nevertheless would better occupy themselves in turning those gifts to the service of the people. It is conceded that their symphonies, paintings and poems might not be so highly praised by traditional standards but, the argument continues, they would certainly do far better work for the world at large if they so busied themselves.

But the Mao–Chiang Ching philosophy in 1975, at least insofar as it was explained to us in China, went even further in saying that genius is *entirely* a matter of environmental influence, rather than the freak of genetics that I consider it.

If those to whom I spoke did indeed accurately reflect the then dominant Chinese view on this question, they are simply mistaken. Mozart's genius had nothing whatever to do with the fact that he had the benefit of superior musical instruction in his early years. I know this perfectly well, as both a pianist and composer. The best piano instructor on our planet could be given a thousand students starting with a clean slate, and at the end of a ten-year period a good many of those students would have lost interest in the subject and drifted away. Another sizable percentage would be proficient enough on the instrument to take up the art professionally, though no two would be equal in ability and, at one end of the scale, there would be a small handful, probably not more than a dozen, who could be described as remarkably gifted pianists. If the teacher, and mankind, were extremely fortunate, there might possibly be *one* pianist of dazzling artistry out of the original thousand. And this is assuming that each receives the same instruction and practices precisely the same number of hours each day.

So, China's rulers as of 1975 were saying in effect, "We know perfectly well that artists generally are naturally disposed to do their best work in a climate combining creative freedom and financial security. No doubt our culture would be enriched by a good many beautiful poems, paintings and symphonies having no political or social content whatever if we granted our artists unlimited freedom.

But the fact is we cannot—for the present—permit ourselves that luxury. The artistic community must join the rest of the Chinese people in working to build a viable and rational state free of the evils and miseries that have troubled China for thousands of years. The fact that a few individual artists will be unhappy about this means nothing if the results of our program bring increased benefits to millions."

My own assumption was that the rich artistic history and tradition of the Chinese people would in the long run burst forth in some way that would enlarge the boundaries of creative freedom for a new generation of China's composers, musicians, painters, poets, sculptors. The Chinese, again, were a highly artistic and advanced nation when Western Europeans were still barbarians.

But if I may be presumptuous enough to suggest yet another thought for the consideration of our kind Chinese hosts, it would be that in the realm of art social content can never be a totally adequate criterion. This is not to argue that there is no place for social philosophy in art. There is nothing whatever wrong, esthetically, morally or politically, with instructing and edifying simultaneously. But there must be more to art than social content.

By early 1977, there were clear indications that Premier Hua Kuo-feng and his moderate faction were slowly beginning to "reverse the verdict" imposed on the arts in China by Chiang Ching and her radical associates. It was not, of course, contemplated that any political philosophy perfectly harmonious with Taiwan or U.S. views would now be transmitted by Chinese operas and plays, but in invoking the Hundred Flowers theme, which meant at least one small step in the direction of greater artistic freedom, there was no question but that the moderates wished to relax the narrow emphasis specified by Chiang Ching.

One production which could, therefore, be seen as a result of the moderate thaw was the film *Pioneers,* about the development of Taching, the nation's largest oil field. After their downfall, the Gang of Four were charged with having suppressed the film because, in their view, it included complimentary references to Liu Shao-chi, purged during the Cultural Revolution phase of the late 1960s.

By 1977 the reemergent Teng Hsiao-ping had moved even further than Hua Kuo-feng toward liberalization.

A VARIETY SHOW

That night we were taken to see a variety show at a nearby theater, a large building with a cement floor and wooden folding seats, smelling heavily of disinfectant. Inside it was much like the auditorium of an American high school except that it had a balcony. A large red-and-white poster over the proscenium read: "We give thanks to the guidance of Chairman Mao's revolutionary line in literature and art for performance for workers, peasants and soldiers."

The program was fascinating. One of its songs was titled "I Love the Oil Fields of the Motherland." A singer with an Irish-tenor sort of voice and his pianist wore dark gray Mao suits. The piano, a small concert grand, was manufactured in China. Next we saw *The Dance of the Red Lantern.* The performers, by the way, do not formally accept applause, and in fact receive surprisingly little. When they conclude their numbers they immediately are either enclosed by a curtain or else walk briskly offstage.

Next a group of five textile workers played woodwind instruments. The name of their song: "Textile Workers Learn from Tachai." The following number was "Advance Along the Broad Road of Socialism." The Chinese voice is particularly well suited to group singing. Something about its singsong nasality permits enormous volume and great expression of spirit.

One of the most interesting forms of Chinese entertainment is that offered by storytellers of the ancient type. Formerly they told tales of the past; now their stories have a modern moral. But to keep their audience's attention they continue to hold in each hand ancient wooden clacking devices, something like castanets. The clackers also emphasize their stories, which are recited in a somewhat

rhythmic pattern. In a playful moment Bill whispered that he wished he knew Morse code since he thought some storytellers with capitalist sympathies might be clicking out the secret message, "Please get me out of this country."

The last number before intermission was a charming ballet about a simple country girl—recently a mother—who, while out gathering herbs and other plants in the mountains, discovers drops of blood shed by a wounded guerrilla soldier. She finds him half-dead of thirst, pain and exhaustion. Unable to locate any source of water in the immediate neighborhood she finally saves his life by the ingenious device of filling his canteen with her own mother's milk, discreetly offstage, needless to say.

One ballet number was called *Ode to Li Yimen,* another ballet was based on life in a mountain logging camp. At last one performer, the final soprano soloist, accepted her applause in the Western manner.

There was a feeling of great exhilaration when we finally saw, in this vaudeville show, two actual Chinese comedians. And I don't mean actors who could make only Chinese audiences laugh. The two fellows we saw could have done equally well on one of my TV shows, the old Ed Sullivan show, or any other American comedy or variety program. The lead comic was also a juggler, the other a magician. But it was as comics that they won the hearts of the audience at once. Each had a perfect face for a comedian. The first fellow had a marvelous gimmick of looking straight at the audience as if in profound shock, eyes and mouth wide open when something seemed to go wrong with one of his tricks. Then, as quickly as an eye-blink, his mask of tragedy would change to one of comedy with the broadest, most winning smile I've ever seen. Facially he reminded me somewhat of two American comedians with particularly funny faces, Buster Keaton and Louie Nye. The second fellow had one of those faces that women usually describe as cute. A crew haircut, a roguish glint in the eye and a sly smile that would have gotten him a job in any television situation comedy in the world.

AN ACROBATIC TRAINING SCHOOL

Bill particularly enjoyed our visit to the Shanghai Acrobatic Training School, built on the grounds of an old estate. Opened in November, 1972, the academy trains children chosen from primary schools in nearby districts and counties. Their ages are nine to fourteen.

In the United States most people have had little interest in either taking part in or watching acrobatics, except for TV coverage of Olympic events. In China, however, the skill has a known history of over 2,000 years and is an organic folk art, of interest and importance to all the people. In old China, our host told us, acrobats were persecuted and treated rudely by the ruling class. Along with a thousand and one other social abuses, that sort of treatment has now been stopped. New trainees in the old days were always children of the poor, some of whom would be sold by impoverished parents to the bosses of acrobatic troupes. The bosses, predictably enough, treated the children as if they were nothing more than trained animals.

"One little girl, when she was only eight years old," a spokesman explained, "had to carry the weight of two adults. She was forced to perform in the streets, for little or no pay, and suffered many hardships and even injuries. Today, we are proud to say, she is a teacher in this school." A bit later in the morning we met the woman.

Despite the name of the school, we found it fascinating that it also offers instruction in Chinese literature, mathematics, history, music and political philosophy as part of the standard curriculum. The children, therefore, are not allowed to become narrow specialists as they would have done in pre-1949 China, but are trained to be well-rounded citizens. Toward that end they are taken on regular visits to farms, factories and civic buildings, to keep them in touch with their society. They devote at least a month each year to going to the countryside to learn firsthand what life is like for peasants. The children spend five hours each day, however, in practicing and developing their acrobatic skills.

As we entered the demonstration hall, which looked like an American dance studio, we were greeted with applause by about a hundred youngsters, the girls wearing wine-red shirts and black shorts, the boys dark blue shirts and black shorts.

A girl of about ten did the familiar high-pitched toylike-voice introduction, after which a boy in the background gave a verbal signal. The company did a smart left-face and marched off in military precision. About ten youngsters ran in carrying beautifully designed little benches about a foot and a half high. First the students did smart, professional handstands on the benches, remaining absolutely motionless for well over a minute with not the slightest teetering or unsteadiness! They are actually required to be able to hold that position for ten minutes. Some can do it for as long as fifteen minutes. A wristwatch had been positioned on a front bench. A little girl in the middle—on her hands—stared at the watch and called out the passage of the minutes.

Next a group of six little girls ran in, assumed ballet poses, then got up into the handstand position, on the benches, from which they did several pushups, bringing the face down to bench level and up again.

Then there were some graceful upside-down splits and other ballerina poses, all done atop the tiny benches, followed by an incredible one-handed handstand with the body in a sideways position.

Two of the children worked on the benches with three wooden blocks on each side. Moving the blocks one at a time into separate piles, they did one-handed handstands on first one set of the blocks, then the other. Then other children, in groups of twos and threes, did balancing positions good enough to have qualified them for the old Ed Sullivan show. Next the whole troop, moving across a thick, wide, red Chinese rug, performed an incredible series of lightning-speed cartwheels. Some of the students had more natural grace than others, but all performed with striking energy and vitality.

After the cartwheels they did springs which might be described as cartwheels without the hands touching the floor. Again, all the moves and contortions were astoundingly professional. Perhaps the most impressive was a series of back flips so fast that the children's bodies became a blur.

Ballet exercises at the barre were also completely professional and very beautiful. It is sad to think that in old China beautiful little angels of this age were often sold into houses of prostitution.

The parade of talent went on for hours. A group of ten little darlings in bright pink pants suits and white aprons, using two long snare-drumsticks, juggled a third, heavier stick with blue tassels at both ends, even doing acrobatic stunts while the heavy stick was aloft. The girls, in their attractive little costumes, makeup and hair ribbons, were ultrafeminine and doll-like. It was a fascinating contrast with the no-makeup, no-nonsense 1975 attitude of young modern Chinese women in general.

One little child—she looked about ten—lay on her back on a red-velvet padded stand and with her feet juggled first an enormous heavy vase and after that a large, even heavier wooden table.

A young boy of about fourteen walked to the middle of the room carrying a bamboo pole perhaps twenty feet in length. He positioned it on his shoulder and a boy of nine or ten at once shinnied to the top of it. As a safety precaution the youngster wore a belt with a rope attached. The rope did not support him; it was there merely to break a possible fall.

He performed some remarkable balancing stunts, after which the little doll who had been making the squeaky-voiced announcements was brought out and joined him aloft on the pole. As he held her by her wrists she did some fantastic stunts high over our heads.

The acrobatic arts are, of course, just as highly developed among the Chinese of Taiwan, as was dramatically proved on October 18, 1975, when ABC-TV's "Wide World of Sports" featured an incredible demonstration of hand balancing and kung fu exercises by young Nationalists.

I mentioned earlier that although the Chinese are not as interested in jokes and funny stories as Americans, they appreciate a humorous conversational point as well as anyone else. The day we visited the acrobats and jugglers school, I asked during lunch, "Who trains the magicians?" and was told that they too were trained at the same school. I told them that in Tientsin Jayne had enjoyed seeing a vaudeville show with a very good magician who produced fish from here, there and everywhere, even from nowhere. "If ever there is a serious food problem in your country, involving a shortage of fish," I said, "the government could let this man take over and feed the people." All present around the table laughed heartily.

After dinner that evening we bade warm farewells to our friendly and helpful Shanghai guides, then boarded the night train to our next scheduled stop, the city of Soochow.

River traffic, Soochow area.

Garden estate, Soochow.

5. Soochow

AT 7:40 P.M. the train to Soochow left, getting off to such a smooth start that at first we were scarcely aware we were moving except for the flurry of *dzijians* and *sye-syes* hurriedly exchanged.

The compartment was perfectly comfortable. The usual little table against the window held three teacups and a small reading lamp. As we rode along through the cool night air we took the occasion to ask Yeh Sing-ru a good many questions about recent Chinese history.

When we left the train about nine, the usual cordial welcoming ceremony was staged. Since we were tired, we were taken directly to our hotel. One of the pleasant things about Chinese hotels is you may be taken at once to your rooms, without the usual registration procedure.

Soochow—fifty-three miles from Shanghai in southern Kiangsu (Jiangsu) Province—is one of the world's most beautiful cities, known for its picturesque gardens and parks nestled among low hills and tranquil lakes. Its canals gave it the name "The Venice of the Far East" in pre-Revolutionary China. Founded some five hundred years B.C., the city developed, during the Sung, Yuan, Ming and Ching dynasties, an amazing array of beauty spots for which the name "garden" is an understatement suggesting, as it does, a chiefly botanical display.

Flowers, shrubs and trees there are in abundance—the city is strikingly green—but Soochow's gardens are actually grand, aristocratic estates in which the glories of growing nature have been lovingly set into magical, fairyland frames: walls, picture windows, gazebos, bridges, covered walkways and rock grottoes.

The area, south of the Yangtze, has always been blessed by sufficient rainfall and good soil so the architects, gardeners, landscapers and laborers who contrived its wonders over the centuries were, from the first, encouraged by nature.

The little streetside houses of Soochow are almost all painted white. With their tiled roofs they give the streets an appearance remarkably similar to those of a small Mexican town. The bridges over Soochow's creeks and canals have a beauty that arrests the eye. In most other parts of the world bridges are purely functional. There is no such thing as an ugly Chinese bridge.

And of course the name Soochow is one more of the seemingly thousands of European mistakes in pronouncing Chinese words. The correct Romanized spelling used by the Chinese—at least in 1975—was Suzhou, which would be pronounced something like "Soo-jo."

Wednesday, July 9

The Suzhou Hotel, built in 1958, was a clean, comfortable, fairly modern two-story building. Most other residents of the moment were overseas Chinese, though not from the U.S. Our two-room suite on the second floor was neat and spotlessly clean though the furniture was Spartan. In the morning we discovered that, as I had earlier noted in other Chinese hotels, the shower had been invented but not the shower curtain. This, of course, means it has been necessary to invent the mop because the floor of the bathroom is very shortly covered with water when one takes a shower, even in the recommended sitting position. A floor drain solves the problem of flooding.

The dining room was in a separate building at the far end of a spacious, beautiful garden. The entire hotel, in fact, was surrounded by

Limousine.

Pagoda, Soochow.

lush green gardens. When Bill and I went down for breakfast the following morning, overseas Chinese families were eating at nearby tables. Positioned in several locations in the restaurant were odd-looking low tables, about three feet high. The tops had circular depressions large enough to accommodate what looked like one of our old-fashioned washbasins. Filled with rice, the pot is placed into the opening in the table. The diners walk to it, set their rice bowls on an outer rim and help themselves. All other dishes are served personally.

We were driven around Soochow in a large black Russian car, the brand name of which was Gif. It was in perfect condition though it had obviously been purchased—or abandoned—no later than 1960, the year the Russians pulled out of China. It was much like an old Dodge, large, a bit ponderous, but quite comfortable. The paint was in perfect condition.

The most notable landmark of Soochow is the Pau-en Sz Pagoda, nine stories high.

We were told that the ancient leader King Wu is buried in the area of the Sword Pond, a small narrow pool at the bottom of two low facing rock cliffs. After the king was interred, the architects and laborers who knew of the spot, it is said, were killed so that no living man would know the secret of the burial place.

The ancient pagoda in Tiger Hall Park leans at rather a sharp angle, like the famous Tower of Pisa. Yeh Sing-ru asked if I had ever seen the leaning "pagoda" of Pisa. She seemed surprised that I had, perhaps because foreign travel is still rare in China.

It occurred to me that the reason they might call this Soochow tower the Whistling Pagoda is that it provides a nesting place for thousands of birds, the constant twittering of which surrounds the spire in magical music.

The possibility occurred to Bill that Marco Polo might have seen the Tiger Hill tower and described or sketched it when he returned to Italy, thus giving Italian architects the idea for the tower at Pisa. I explained that while Polo did visit Soochow, and did bring spaghetti and other Chinese wonders to Europe, Pisa's ar-

chitects had not planned the leaning of their
tower.

The pagoda, first built about A.D. 200 and
later rebuilt during the northern Sung
dynasty, is unusual in that it is made entirely
of bricks. The leaning did not start until the
Ming dynasty period, about four hundred
years ago. In 1956 the local authorities spent
150,000 yuan on repairs of the tower, chiefly
to shore it up on its weak side. At that time
priceless archeological treasures were discovered, such as thousand-year-old antique porcelain pieces, Buddhist scriptures written on
silk and other beautiful artifacts created in the
Soochow area.

I asked Chinese acquaintances in Soochow
if they could explain the mystery of the ceramic little-boy-on-the-chicken that I had noticed on the corners of ancient palace roofs in
Peking. They had no idea what the explanation was and incredibly seemed not to remember ever having seen such a thing. The only
advantage the foreign traveler has is the fresh-
ness of his vision.

For miles around Tiger Hill there are green
fields, each filled with thousands of pots in
which jasmine plants are growing. During
cold weather the hundreds of thousands of
pots are carried into hothouses. The plants are
used in the making of jasmine tea, which in my
Occidental ignorance I had assumed was made
of a separate type of tea leaf whose aroma
resembled that of jasmine blossoms. Our
guides explained that the jasmine petals are
simply mingled with the tea leaves, which then
take on a faint perfume, giving the tea its distinctive flavor.

A side temple is the House of 500 Buddhas,
some enormous in size, some only two or three
feet high but all among the world's most imposing works of art. The most impressive figure in this wing is another representation of
the Goddess of Mercy. She has a "thousand"
arms and a thousand eyes. Each of the smaller
arms, as distinguished from the eight large
ones, is carved of a separate piece of wood. The
entire figure, in fact, is made of camphor
wood.

Incredibly, no two of the five hundred statues have the same facial expression. One large

Warrior figure, Soochow temple, 1975.

Golden idol, Soochow temple.

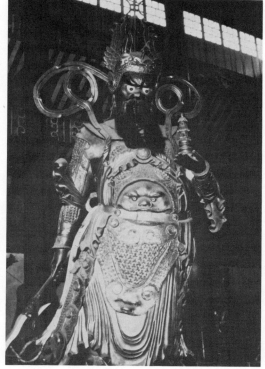

Temple of Golden Buddhas.

figure actually has three different expressions —smiling, sad and angry—depending on the position one takes in looking at its face.

Our friend Lily Wen, we have since learned, used to wander about this temple when she was a small child.

It might be thought that the modern Chinese, being officially atheistic, would close such ancient monuments to superstition. They do not, of course, despite some Red Guards nonsense of the late 1960s. As Chinese they are proud of their culture's architectural achievements and have repaired many such edifices, though they denounce superstition as such.

While I have mentioned it elsewhere, I stress again that in their vigorous campaign to combat the superstitions that have for thousands of years burdened China, the Communists have said very little new, and have in fact echoed criticisms made by generations of American and European capitalists and Christians. In *That Untravell'd World,* jointly authored by a number of scholars connected with the Groton School, published in 1928, the authors refer to superstition as one of the "two

great evils" troubling China, the other being natural calamities.

While many good practices in agriculture and economy are dictated by *tradition, a sort of dignified superstition,* yet I believe it does more harm than good. *The continual bother and expense of ceremonial . . . reverence of the dead is one of the greatest burdens that the Chinese farmer has to bear.* His house is built according to tradition, rather than according to the laws of practicability, his earnings go to the maintenance of temples and saintly beggars. All over his scanty fields are scattered grave-mounds which tradition decrees must intrude their unwelcome presence, to the lessening of crops and the poverty of the owner. And woe betide the hapless Chinaman who deserts his family's graves or fails to maintain them . . . there are a thousand curses, each worse than the one before, which would fall on his impious head. Thus it is that a large amount of fertile soil is given over to the dead and rendered useless as anything but pastureland. [Italics added.]

The authors also place at the feet of the

Chinese custom of ancestor worship part of the blame for the combined problems of over-population and intermittent starvation.

The religious custom of ancestor worship makes it desirable for one to have as many children to revere one's memory in time to come as possible . . . therefore the chief ambition of nearly every Chinaman is to have as many children as possible . . . a condition is created where the family is so large and the land so small that great effort is needed even to supply enough food.

WEST GARDEN TEMPLE

We next visited the West Garden Temple, surrounded by ancient, thick, tan-yellow walls. The upward points of one of its roofs curved at the sharpest angle we had seen in China. The main building of the temple houses several enormous statues of Buddha and, I presume, his disciples. Although the statues are painted in copper-gold, they are made of clay. Along the two side walls are ten striking figures, each perhaps fifteen feet high. They all lean forward at a surprisingly sharp angle but of course do not fall.

The back wall is a rock grotto, designed to imitate nature. It houses perhaps thirty figures, the central one about twenty feet high, many of the others life-size. The large one in the middle is the Goddess of Mercy. This temple, like most others, was closed for over a year during the Cultural Revolution. An extreme wing of the Red Guards, arguing that such places were representative of nothing more than ancient and harmful superstition, actually recommended that they and their ir-replaceable art treasures be destroyed! Fortunately theirs was a minority view. The majority of Revolutionary students agreed with the criticism of superstition but intelligently explained to their hotheaded and—one must speak frankly—stupid fellows that the shrines and their works should be preserved as art, as representative of China's ancient and unique cultural heritage. I actually winced when contemplating the possibility of such objects being destroyed.

A Chinese citizen who was living on the mainland at the time has said to me, "We must be very grateful to the late Premier Chou En-lai who was the only one in power with enough courage to stand up against the Red Guards during their most triumphant year, which was in 1966–1967. He debated with these young people day and night to convince them to be reasonable and leave the ancient cultural art objects alone. Without his efforts at the time we today might have little to show of our glorious history and art. Even with his efforts many precious objects were destroyed during those two turbulent years."

EMBROIDERY RESEARCH INSTITUTE

The Soochow Embroidery Research Institute was our next stop. It is located in an old estate and opened in 1957. Its atmosphere is quiet, tranquil, creative. In the first room visited, several gifted young artists were copying on large pieces of paper paintings and sketches originally done in smaller form. Some of the artists worked with watercolors, others oils. On a wall there were what looked like several pieces of wallpaper but were actually hand-painted sketches—remarkably beautiful—of bamboo plants and trees. If any creative souls feel inhibited by the new Chinese ideology it can hardly be the pictorial artists, who continue to paint the ancient, traditional bamboo plants, fish, birds, mountains, rivers, valleys and streams, though not to the exclusion of Revolutionary themes.

The second stage of the process involves tracing the handmade paintings or drawings. This is done on a basic cloth, pure white silk. The third stage is completed by the embroiderers, mostly teenagers and young women in their twenties, who work with the silk paintings, painstakingly reproducing, by endless thousands of individual stitches, the marks that have been made by the artists. It may take as long as eight months to complete the handstitching on one of the embroideries. One young lady we met was embroidering a beautiful picture of a pure white, blue-eyed Angora cat. The fur at the edges looked so lifelike that

I wished to touch it since, though my eyes were only about two feet from the surface of the embroidery, I was not sure that some of the individual thread-hairs did not stick up off the silk. They did not.

It takes about eight years of training before a young woman can do double-sided embroidery. As the name implies, the picture can be looked at from both sides of the cloth even though only one side is turned up while the stitching is being done.

There are four such embroidery factories in Soochow. The works of art, when finished, are presented to the state. At present they go to decorate the walls of government buildings or are presented, as gifts, to foreign visitors. A small percentage of the total output is put up for sale at the Canton Trade Fair and similar commercial exhibitions.

In another of the airy, pleasant workrooms, each of which housed perhaps a dozen workers, men were busy at looms that have probably not changed for centuries.

Apprentices, as is often the case in China, received no formal wage though all their needs were provided for. When they completed their apprenticeship period, lasting about three years, they then went on salary.

Before Liberation, when the workers were disorganized and not in touch with each other, there were only about a dozen kinds of stitches used in embroidery. But since 1949, in Soochow, Hunan, Szechwan and Canton, the entire art has been organized in such a way as to bring workers together in larger institutes. The craftsmen and women, therefore, learn from each other, as a result of which the horizons of their art have expanded and all have become much more creative.

The point is well dramatized in that the double-sided embroidery—the highest form attained by the art—was relatively unknown in pre-Revolutionary twentieth-century China. The technique of working on both sides of the pieces of silk was known well before 1949, we were told, but at a low level, involving work on clothing, blouses and scarves. It is only since 1949 that it has been widely developed to the level of art and officially encouraged.

Before the Cultural Revolution the painters of the institute, though gifted, worked only as copyists, reproducing photographs and paintings. Today, however, while still making a number of copies of other works, they are also encouraged to go out into the field and paint from nature or do portraits, by direct observation, as do artists anywhere in the world.

It is not true that the painters and embroiderers may create only pictures that carry a Socialist message. But it is considered helpful to the total society to show not only China's natural beauty, not only its traditional art forms, but also to represent its modern-day heroes, material prosperity and industrial progress.

As we wandered from room to room I noticed on low tables some lovely miniature trees in delicate pots. Wang-wei, a painter and poet of the Tang dynasty, we were told, was the one who originated what most Americans think is the Japanese art of bonsai, growing beautiful stunted plants in small containers. Most artistic developments in Japanese cultural history, in fact, had Chinese origins. The Chinese name for bonsai translates as scenery-in-a-pot.

In another work area exquisite silk screens are created. The art of woven tapestry, of the kind used in the large, six-panel screens, had gone into sharp decline before Liberation. The old artists were dying out and few young people were following in their footsteps. The art has now, fortunately for the world, been vigorously revived, for which the craftsmen give credit to encouragement by the party.

The embroidery factory also produces a certain number of portraits of non-Chinese dignitaries or honored persons, among them Dr. Norman Bethune. Although his name is unknown to the great majority of Americans he is of heroic stature in modern China. Bethune, born in 1878, was a graduate of McGill University Medical College, a member of the Canadian Communist Party and a surgeon. He went to China in 1938 and organized a medical team to assist the Chinese people in the War of Resistance against Japan. This was not his first tour of duty as a Marxist doctor, however. He had also served as a medical officer in Spain with Loyalist armies fighting Franco and his

German and Italian Fascist allies. Regardless of what one might think of his political beliefs, there is no question but that Bethune became a selfless, dedicated and courageous servant of the Chinese people. He traveled with the 8th Route Army, lived the simple life of the poor people of the countryside, and always refused to accept any special treatment or honors.

With scarcely ever a thought for his personal welfare, Bethune sometimes performed as many as twenty-five operations a day, trained Chinese doctors and nurses in surgical techniques, prepared texts for them to study, and established hospitals.

The blockade imposed in the Hopei (Hobei) area in 1939 prevented the penicillin that might have saved Bethune's life from reaching him. Serving the poor to the last, he died in Tangshan on November 12, 1939. In a memorial for Bethune written by Chairman Mao, he said, "We must all learn the spirit of absolute selflessness from him. With this spirit everyone can be very useful to the people. A man's ability may be great or small, but if he has this spirit he is already noble-minded and pure, a man of moral integrity and above vulgar interests, a man who is of value to the people."

PLAIN MAN'S POLITICS GARDEN

We next visited another estate owned by one of the privileged gentry of ancient China. Now called the Plain Man's Politics Garden, an official national monument of eleven acres, it was first constructed in the Ming dynasty, about four hundred years ago. The walls of Soochow's gardens are pure white and the curved tile roofs are black, a setting that provides a perfect frame for the vivid greens of nature. The crushing heat of July, however, slightly diminished our physical appreciation of this particular fairyland. Although the gardens of Soochow are justly world-famed for their beauty, I recommend that you do not visit them during midsummer, unless there is no possible alternative schedule.

The garden was designed by a famous painter of the Ming dynasty, Wen Chen-ming.

In one garden house on the estate we found an art form we had never heard of before. Flat marble tables, which hold about a one-inch pool of water, form the base for miniatures of mountains, moss-covered rocks that do look remarkably like the mountains of Kweiling.

There is a great, mysterious emphasis, in such areas of artistic treasure, to behindness, around-the-next-cornerness, which excites the sense of curiosity as to what beauty may lie just beyond the next bend, the next door, the next angle in a walkway, the next mountain path.

As we strolled through this maze of beauty, jet planes from a nearby military airfield flew over the gardens every few minutes, reminding one again of the long chain of connection between ancient and modern China.

The Chinese concept of the picture window —of which the estate boasted many—is particularly endearing. A frame is set on a wall, the same sort one might see around a painting. But what it surrounds is not a painted scene but an opening so that the view of whatever is outside the wall becomes a picture. Nothing viewed within that rectangle or circle is one bit different but somehow the frame concentrates and heightens one's sense of appreciation, as it does for a canvas.

The temperature in Soochow—I repeat— was extremely hot. In the afternoon it was close to a hundred in our rooms, which were livable only because an electric fan had been provided. But on each bed there was a thick woolen blanket, in addition to sheets and counterpanes. No matter how repeatedly we removed the blankets the attendants would always tuck them back into the bed while we were away. In wonder why. It would seem simpler to have stored them in the closet during the summer season.

After lunch we were taken to visit a small beauty spot called Garden of the Fishing Nets, about half a mile from the hotel. All the gardens in Soochow at one time belonged to rich people. This particular house and garden are about nine hundred years old. Of its over three hundred windows, each with its own screen design, no two are alike!

6. Nanking

THE countryside from Soochow to Nanking was the most luscious, the greenest, most fertile we have ever seen. Surely there can be no more fruitful soil than this on our planet. A wide variety of crops were growing in patches and rectangles of various sizes, all laid out as neatly as patterns on a quilt. Not only do the Chinese waste not a square foot of land, they are also growing things in the *water*. They raise peanuts, for example, by planting them on large floating rush mats, adding about two inches of soil and burying the seeds in the soil. The roots then spread out into the water below. Our train rolled through endless miles of rice, tomatoes, corn, beans, cabbage, sunflowers and other plants as well.

If we start from the assumption that it is more important that people be fed—which is to say kept alive—than to decide the economic system by means of which this end is achieved, the conclusion is inescapable that the modern Chinese method of feeding over 800 million people is far more efficient than anything the Chinese have known in the past.

The Nanking region is not merely a farming area, however. We passed many factories, some close to the tracks, most off at some distance. They appeared to involve medium and heavy industry. Since 1950, in fact, the city has grown so that as of 1979 it could boast some 1,500 industrial and mining installations. Mao's plan to disperse China's industry has certainly been well carried out.

A group of Albanian tourists was aboard our train. At one stop they burst into song. Except for their interpreters, neither the Chinese nor the Americans had any idea what they were singing. The song was not in the vigorous style of most Chinese music but sounded like a somber Russian ballad. The train stopped after a while and Yeh Sing-ru asked the Albanian's Chinese travel guide what they were singing. We were told their songs were in praise of the friendship between China and Albania, in praise of the Chinese and Albanian Communist parties, and of their respective leaders Hoxha and Mao. After about half an hour of the chorale Bill began to get a bit irked by the Albanian voices.

"In America," he said, "people on trains sing like that only when they're drunk."

"Bill," I said, "when in Rome you do as the Romans do." At which he began to sing an Italian song.

The Chinese railroad beds are smooth—I noted again—well laid out, and make for a comfortable ride. Many of the ties, interestingly enough, are made of concrete, at least in the particular track over which we passed, presumably because cement is in more plentiful supply than lumber. It may also have been determined that it does not require as much maintenance attention.

The countryside as we neared Nanking became hillier but all the way into the station there were still watery areas where crops grew. The soil was very red now, which explained why most of the houses and factory buildings we saw were of red brick. Much of the construction was new and attractive. The living quarters—we could tell what they were by laundry hanging on balconies and from windows—were well constructed.

Our rooms in Nanking had evidently been recently painted and were quite comfortable, at least after we turned on the electric fan. No shower over the tub so no need for a shower curtain. We were, however, unable to locate bath towels. The bath was provided with two towels of the sort that in the United States are used to dry dishes. There certainly was no local shortage of toweling material. The bedspreads were made of terry cloth.

If there are any "national brands" of soap in China we were not able to identify them. Each province, indeed each city, seemed to have its own soap.

Throwing oneself down on a bed in Nanking was a bit of a shock; the beds are almost as hard as card tables. Sleeping on a surface this firm makes you turn over a great deal more during the night than you ordinarily would. Perhaps some ancient sage of Nanking decided it would be a good idea to get a good night's sleep and plenty of exercise at the same time.

At precisely five o'clock the following morning a nearby trumpeter played something almost identical to our "Taps." At that moment I felt ready for it. Perhaps we should have been grateful he wasn't playing "Reveille."

At about six a group of overseas Chinese started loud and vigorous conversation, about Mao knows what, right outside our door, which had been left open to pick up a slight breeze from the garden outside.

The city of Nanking is in Kiangsu, a small maritime province of eastern China. It is part of the great plains area of China and has no tall mountains and few hills. Fortunately it is well watered. The Grand Canal runs through it on a south-north axis, the Yangtze River crosses southern Kiangsu from west to east, and there are a number of lakes and streams.

Nanking is one of those cities in which Chiang Kai-shek's Nationalist government was able to bring about considerable modern improvement; many of the imposing former Nationalist buildings such as the central Kuomintang office, the Judicial Yuan, the Supervisory Yuan, the Legislative Yuan, the Examination Yuan and the headquarters of the National government of China, still stand, as do the Central Athletic Stadium and the handsome buildings of the former National Central University, sometimes called Nanking University, which in the 1930s was the highest seat of learning in China.

Although we, in our ignorance, might assume that if you've seen one Chinese city you've seen them all, the fact is that each urban community in China has its own distinctive appearance and spirit, just as is the case with American cities. San Francisco, after all, is quite different from Coral Gables, New York is very little like Denver, Phoenix is not like Chicago and Boston bears little resemblance to San Diego. As for Nanking, we noticed at once that walls were not as much in evidence as in the other cities we visited. They surround large estates and important buildings, of course, and are often a dusty yellow, but on many of the streets the doors and shops of dwelling places open directly on the sidewalk, with no intervening walls or courtyards.

Many of the city's sights are beautiful, all are fascinating. A good many Nanking streets are lined with sycamore trees which arch out over the road and meet in the center, forming a leafy green canopy stretching ahead for miles.

Since 1949 millions of trees have been added to the area. Near one intersection we saw a motion picture theater preparing to open at eight-thirty in the morning. Several hundred young people, mostly men, were waiting to get in.

Bill and I were the only Americans in the dining room at lunch. The majority of the hotel's guests were overseas Chinese, though some were Japanese. Since the Japanese gentlemen were apparently over fifty I found myself wondering where they had been during the years of the Japanese occupation of China. If anyone had then told the Chinese that a short time into the future they would be welcoming Japanese as their guests, and glad to have them, it would have seemed an insane prediction.

What will happen in 1990, I wonder, that if predicted now would seem equally preposterous?

The paper napkins at the Nanking Hotel were of a strange waxy consistency which made them of dubious value so far as absorbing grease and moisture was concerned. It occurred to us that at every Chinese hotel we had visited the napkins, soap and towels had been different. Perhaps it is because of Mao's insistence on self-sufficiency for the individual provinces that each manufactures its own odds and ends. In America we're accustomed to finding the same soaps, toothpastes, combs and other household products the country over so the concentration on local kinds of merchandise in China seems odd to us. If I were a Chinese efficiency expert I would at the first stage of development agree with Mao and encourage each province to create its own, let's say, paper napkins. But at the second stage I would send for a napkin from each province and conduct comparison tests. If it turned out that the napkins of Kiangsu were much better than any of the others I would send out a directive that the other provinces had two alternatives available to them: either to simply reproduce Kiangsu-type napkins or, if they felt equal to the task, creating an even better product.

NANKING BRIDGE

Thursday, July 10

The world-famous Nanking Bridge—an awe-inspiring structure—was begun in 1960 and completed in 1968. Visitors are taken to a waiting room where there is displayed a model of the span, about one hundred feet long, in itself an impressive achievement. Five thousand men worked on the bridge's construction. Additional thousands of local people volunteered their services on their days off.

When the Soviets walked out of China in a huff in 1960, this created a great many problems, particularly with the construction of the Nanking Bridge since the U.S.S.R. had earlier agreed to provide the special sort of steel needed for bridge construction.

Trains can now cross the bridge in two minutes. One can imagine the difficulty of transporting freight cars by ferryboat before the bridge was constructed.

The four towers—two on each side of the river—that sustain the bridge are individually twenty-three stories high! The nine underwater pilings that support the span as it crosses the water seem almost as tall. Each is as large as a basketball court at the base. About one-third of their straight-down length is in water, below that in earth and at the bottom grounded in stone.

Quite aside from the enormous difficulty of sinking the enormous pilings down through deep water, silt, mud and rock—which both Western and Russian engineers had said couldn't be done—there is one obstacle that I still have no idea how the workers overcame. The Yangtze River, as it flows through Nanking, is the color of café au lait. Imagine a small backyard swimming pool filled not with pure clear water but rich brown coffee. Now suppose that a couple of large milk cans of cream are added to the dark brown liquid. Then picture yourself putting on eye goggles and sinking beneath the surface of that water. Obviously you would be able to see nothing whatever. How then did the divers—many of them inexperienced in such work—see more than one inch in front of their pressure helmets when they submerged to work on the underpinnings of the Nanking Bridge? We must admire the modern Chinese for their achievements.

Large characters on the side of the bridge spell "Long live the great Chairman Mao." Each character is printed on an enormous steel plate weighing five tons.

The view from the top of one of the four towers is, not to coin a phrase, breathtaking. One can see for countless miles, one way to distant mountain ranges, and across the river to other mountains. Below us a Chinese junk of the style that might have made its way up this ancient river five hundred years ago was passing under this wonder of modern engineering. Between us and the junk at that moment a modern freight train thundered across the bridge at high speed.

Through his telescopic camera lens Bill noted that uniformed P.L.A. guards carried on a foot patrol, walking between the train tracks. The fear of sabotage by enemies of the state is still very real in China. But quite aside from ideological loyalties, there is something in even the most fervent anti-Communist, I believe, that would make him shrink at even the passing contemplation of the destruction

Nanking Bridge showing twenty-three-story tower.

of what is surely one of the most remarkable architectural and engineering feats in the history of mankind.

We were next taken down to the level of the railroad crossing. Somehow one does not fully intellectually grasp the massiveness of this structure until one sets foot on it. From where we entered the train level we could hardly see the end of the "tunnel" far across the river, which is almost a mile across at this point. The sidewalk for pedestrians, which runs on both sides of the two lanes of tracks, is about six and a half feet wide but can seem rather narrow as a train roars down upon you.

After walking around the base of the bridge we were next taken to its upper, highway section. As our party strolled across the span we passed a number of young P.L.A. guards, all

of whom looked about eighteen or nineteen. I smiled at one and said, *"Ni hau,"* a greeting he returned with a broad smile and a snappy salute. I replied in kind, my old infantry conditioning producing the automatic response.

For some of the older street laborers, I have the impression that certain details of their daily lives have not changed dramatically from the old China to the new. They will now get good medical attention if they fall ill, of course, and they no longer have to worry about such scourges as floods and starvation.

But pulling tremendously heavy loads in ancient two-wheeled carts is clearly as painfully difficult today as it was under Chiang Kai-shek. As we drove through the streets of Nanking we saw hundreds, thousands of these

A Chinese junk passing under the Nanking Bridge; a simultaneous glimpse of modern and ancient China.

workers, literally straining like beasts of burden to pull enormous loads of sand, cement, bricks, metal, sacks of grain and other freight. At one place we saw an old man pulling a rather small cart on which had been placed an enormous metal boiler that must have taken twenty men or a large crane to put into position. The old fellow himself would have been unequal to the task of even budging the cart with such a giant load and so he had a younger helper walking about six feet in front of him. The helper had a strap around his shoulders and chest, from which a rope was attached to the cart, much the same sort of strap used by

the laborers who pull boats along Chinese canals.

The men's bodies were tilted forward at a sharp angle. Except that the monstrous weight behind them was a modern device, they looked like the weary laborers of China five hundred or, for that matter, five thousand years ago, bathed in sweat, wearing tattered clothes, straining—no doubt day after day—to keep themselves alive. I doubt that any American, however poor, however desperate, has ever had to perform lifetime labor that difficult.

That evening, in enjoying one more excellent vaudeville program, Bill and I finally realized that by Western standards Chinese audiences are very strange. They are fortunate enough to witness some truly thrilling entertainment but respond to it like yahoos. First of all they talk all the way through the show. At no time did total silence reign at any of the productions we saw. Second, they applaud hardly at all, even after the most incredible tricks, stunts and turns. I was born into a vaudeville family and have spent half a century in and around show business; and yet the hundreds of Chinese around us seemed not terribly impressed with the remarkable performances taking place on stage.

After the show, when I discussed this with Yeh Sing-ru, she said, smiling, "Yes, I know what you mean. I, too, do not like to applaud. I guess I'm too lazy to."

Bill noted something else about the audience response that had escaped my attention. He said, "When someone on stage makes a mistake, does something wrong, the audience makes a terrible noise. They don't quite boo but they burst into what sounds like a harsh, cruel, jeering laughter, the way a bunch of country bumpkins might."

THE TAIPING REBELLION MEMORIAL

The Taiping Rebellion, one of the most dramatic chapters in the history of China, is commemorated by the Kiangsu Museum, which is housed in a six-hundred-year-old Ming dynasty government building. It looks to

American eyes like an old temple, with its outer gate, front courtyard entrance house and spacious garden.

The museum also instructs the visitor about the Opium War, which the British launched in 1840—the first of the European wars against China. We were shown copies of the actual treaties concluded with China and France, England and the United States after China's defeat. Our hosts also drew our attention to a drawing of one of the warehouses in India where the British stored a massive amount of opium, which was then exported to China. Much of the shipping of the narcotic was handled by American three-masted schooners of the old Yankee Clipper type. The opium traffic was disastrous to China in two basic ways: first, in the harmful effects of the drug and addiction to it, and because second, the Chinese had to pay for the opium in silver. From 1800 to 1855 this severely depleted the nation's silver reserves.

The visit to the Taiping Rebellion Memorial was fascinating in all possible respects. After a few minutes it occurred to me that our guide had said nothing about the Taiping movement being essentially religious. Without addressing the point directly, I asked several questions which, had I been communicating with Westerners, would immediately have brought the point out in conversation, quite aside from the question as to opinions our hosts might have expressed about the facts. But my efforts were to no avail. The rebel leader is shown burning and personally standing atop Confucian religious texts and tablets. Admittedly disingenuously I inquired whether this fact would justify the assumption that the Taiping movement was *anti*religious. The most reasonable answer to this question, of course, would have been "Oh, no. The leader himself was a convert to Christianity and his movement was entirely based on his interpretation of Christian principles."

But no answer remotely resembling this one could be drawn from our hosts.

I had earlier learned that there are few lawyers in China. After several weeks in the country a hypothesis presented itself to me as to why this might be. The courtroom testimony that lawyers draw forth is supposed to be factual. But the Chinese—of the Right and Left —are masters at the art of avoiding discussion of facts when doing so suits their purposes. I do not suggest that they have a monopoly on this peculiar practice; it is common to every human, in some degree. But it does seem that the Chinese have developed the practice to a degree of sophistication unprecedented elsewhere.

That the Taiping Rebellion, which lasted from 1850 to 1864, succeeded at all was due more to the intolerable conditions under which the masses in China lived during the last century than wise leadership, for certainly the revolution itself was of a very peculiar order. Its leader, Hung Hsiu-chuan, had had a serious illness as a young man during which he believed he saw visions. Christian missionary literature inspired him not only to conversion but to fanatical fervor. After becoming a preacher, he took the leadership of a group of Christians in the Kwangtung (Guangdong) and Kwangsi (Guangxi Zhuang) provinces and convinced them that he was literally the brother of Jesus Christ. He had a vision of heavenly peace on earth called Tai Ping Kwoh or Heavenly Dynasty of Perfect Peace. His Christian disciples sincerely believed that his mission on earth was to lead the Chinese people out of the error of worshiping Buddhist, Confucianist and Taoist idols. That alone would have led to angry confrontations with adherents of Oriental religions, but what turned Hung Hsiu-chuan's movement into a full-scale rebellion was his belief that his heavenly kingdom could be established in China only by overthrowing the Manchu dynasty.

Starting with an uprising in Kwangsi Province in July, 1850—the year after our California gold rush started—Hung led his rapidly increasing forces into Yunan, Hunan and Hupeh provinces. Nanking, on the Yangtze, was captured in March, 1853, after which he dispatched armies to the Peking-Tientsin area while other forces moved south into Honan, Anhwei (Anhui), Hupeh and Kiangsu provinces. Hung's more rabid followers were inspired by religious conviction, but part of the appeal of the movement to millions of poor peasants lay in the socialistic features of the Taiping philosophy, with particular emphasis on land reform.

Eventually fanaticism and iconoclasm proved insufficient to the task of organizing and administering the conquered provinces and the movement began to fall into disarray.

The European nations became seriously concerned when Taiping forces threatened Shanghai, the chief treaty city. General Tseng Kuo-fan, a scholar from Hunan, was assigned the task of suppressing the Taiping rebels in 1857, although it took him seven years to do it. European and American mercenaries were allied with Chinese imperial troops in the anti-Taiping campaign. In July, 1864, during our Civil War period, Nanking fell to Manchu government forces. By the time the drama was concluded at least 20 million Chinese had been killed—Edgar Snow puts the figure at 40 million—and essentially nothing lasting had been done to improve the lot of the Chinese masses. It is interesting that today's Marxist regime pays official honor to a Christian, perhaps a madman, whose visions, despite his admirable intentions, brought about few practical results other than widespread destruction and slaughter.

The Communists assert, incidentally, that the term "Taiping Rebellion" was originated by the landlords. They have therefore "corrected" the designation to the "Taiping Peasants' Movement."

SUN YAT-SEN'S MAUSOLEUM

When, in early 1979, Sun Yat-sen "appeared" as a guest on my "Meeting of Minds" television show, we showed him slide pictures, taken by my son Bill and myself, of his famous mausoleum, the strikingly beautiful resting place of the revered Chinese revolutionary leader. A monument of dignity and beauty, it is situated east of the city of Nanking on the sloping side of Chunchan (Zi Jin) Mountain. It was designed by the famous architect Lui Yen-chi in 1926 and completed under Chiang Kai-shek in 1929. The basic structure is of colorless concrete, gracefully arched and topped with royal-blue tile roofs. The visitor approaches the shrine by a long, slanting walkway which leads to hundreds of granite steps that ascend the mountain. On the walls of the mausoleum there is the inscription of the famous "Three Fundamental Principles of the People" authored by Dr. Sun.

One naturally assumes that the imposing building at what appears to be the end of the journey is the tomb, but it turns out that it is merely a stopping place about a third of the way up the hill. The architect designed this monument in the traditional Chinese style of the ancient palaces and temples so that forward progress leads to repeated visual surprises.

We discovered a large colorful floral wreath presented by the Japanese contingent from Osaka before an enormous white marble statue of Sun Yat-sen, reminiscent of the figure of Abraham Lincoln in the Lincoln Memorial in Washington, D.C., although not as large.

The body reposes in a beautiful crypt set into a well-like circle in the last inner sanctum. The mausoleum is so imposing, so beautiful, of such stately dignity, that if Donald Duck were buried there one would feel humble and respectful within its walls. But Dr. Sun, of course, played a crucial role in modern Chinese history.

It is impossible to understand modern China without knowing something of Sun. He had the good fortune, in the context of present-day Chinese bias, to be born of peasant parentage, in Kwangtung Province near Macao in southern China in 1866. His family had already acquired a revolutionary tradition —some of its members had been involved in the Taiping Rebellion of 1850–1864. As a teenager, living with one of his brothers in Honolulu, Sun became a devout Christian. He was not a convert to Christianity but had been raised in the faith by his father, who had been influenced by the London Missionary Society. A few years later he began medical studies in Hong Kong under Sir James Cantlie, noted primarily for his studies of bubonic plague. So sincere was Sun Yat-sen about his religious philosophy that for a time he considered entering the ministry. Although from the first he saw the necessity of freeing the Chinese people

Sun Yat-sen's Mausoleum, Nanking.

from the terrible burden of imperial despotism, warlordism, banditry and exploitation by the wealthy, he nevertheless combined this patriotic fervor with a religious sense of moral mission. It was clear to him before the turn of the century that China, because of its size and population, ought to take its place among the powerful nations of the world. He perceived what was obvious enough, that it could do this only by adopting the modern technology and methods that had brought such dramatic benefits to the Western nations.

Sun Yat-sen's philosophical and political message found millions of ready ears because of conditions virtually all Chinese regarded as intolerable. Young students and professionals of that day were aware that the people of China had been shamelessly exploited by foreign powers and brutalized by the imperial government and its minions. Ignorance and illiteracy were common, even slavery was practiced. Tragic centuries of tradition permitted parents to sell their sons into bondage and their daughters into prostitution. Although there had been peasant uprisings for literally thousands of years there had never been any serious prospect that they could right the ancient wrongs.

Finally, near the end of the last century, it became clear that at last there was a reasonable prospect for successful revolution. Although the foreign invaders with their special privileges and one-sided treaties took shameful advantage of the Chinese people, there were nevertheless many Europeans and Americans of good will who felt sincere affection for the Chinese. First, they brought new ideas and stirred popular ambitions by their example. Second, the success of the Western visitors reduced the authority of the emperor's forces. Chinese armies had little will or ability for fighting. Then, too, a revolutionary leadership could arise in China at this moment of history because at the turn of the century the revolutionary spirit was gathering strength in Russia, Mexico, Turkey and other parts of the world. The spread of literacy, modern means of transportation and communication, contact among peoples, all were ingredients in the explosive new social chemistry. In 1898 Sun announced the Three Fundamental Principles of his political philosophy, *nationalism, democracy* and *socialism* or "people's livelihood." These three Principles of the People, as they were subsequently called by Sun's Kuomintang Party, were later honored by both Nationalists and Communists.

Sun was aware, of course, that he could not make a revolution with only a handful of sympathetic young intellectuals. He therefore solicited the help of the Chinese secret societies, knowing that they too were strongly opposed to the Manchu emperors, established contact with overseas Chinese groups in the United States, France, Japan and elsewhere, and began to promote "revolutionary incidents" which, it was hoped, would prove to be the spark to set off the larger conflagration for which China was clearly ready. But Sun Yat-sen's revolutionary party was not successful in its first attempt to overturn the government, or in its eighth or ninth for that matter. Between 1906 and 1911 the revolutionaries attempted ten separate campaigns. Each failed, principally because the rebels were militarily unequal to the task of confronting the larger and better supplied imperial army. Sun continued to travel about the world, raising badly needed funds.

The Collapse of the Manchus

Although "emperor" suggests a virile, ruthless adult ruler, the Chinese throne was, in its last years, occupied by children. Real power was wielded by a former concubine who had risen, by a long series of palace intrigues, to become the Empress Dowager Tz'u-hsi. The splendor of the Forbidden City, the size of the Chinese population and the geographical panorama of the empire combined to give an aura of power and glamour to the throne and those who occupied it, but the fact was that history was about to see the end of the long reign of the Manchu rulers, who had occupied the Imperial Palace for two and a half centuries. Tartar invaders from beyond the Great Wall had toppled the weakened Ming dynasty and dominated the empire, but for all their adoption of Chinese customs and beliefs they were still regarded as alien invaders.

In 1850 Manchu Emperor Hsien-feng was seriously concerned that he had not fathered a son. To solve the problem, his advisers selected seventeen virginal young women, at least one of whom, it was assumed, could produce an heir by the emperor. In 1852 one of these comely prospects, a Manchurian girl named Yehnola, became one of the specially chosen concubines and shortly thereafter bore a son by the emperor. This distinction, plus her charm and intelligence, won her the emperor's special confidence, as a result of which she was named Empress of the Western Palace and, emboldened by her new eminence, began to give the emperor the benefit of her speculations on official matters.

When her husband died at thirty-four, Yehnola, now called Tz'u-hsi, made a bold and successful bid for power. As a young girl she had been enamored of Jung-lu, who had subsequently become an important Manchu general. With his military help she defeated her enemies at court and, to secure her victory, had them all beheaded. Such was the state of civilization of the Chinese monarchy in that day.

Her son became nominal emperor, as subsequently did her nephew and grandnephew, China's last emperor, Pu-yi, but Tz'u-hsi controlled the regents who presumably officiated in the name of the boy-kings. It was Tz'u-hsi's fortune, however, to achieve control of a soon-to-be worthless prize. Daily palace affairs were in the hands of the armies of eunuchs who had served for centuries at the court. Decadence and corruption were the order of the day; Tz'u-hsi herself frivolously spent millions on entertainment, works of art, jewelry and unnecessary palace construction. For centuries to come visitors to Peking will be able to see the incredible stationary marble boat at the Summer Palace, an imperial toy the empress ordered built with funds that had been designated for construction of navy battleships. Renovation of much of the Summer Palace itself, in fact, was paid for with these funds.

Perhaps Tz'u-hsi and her associates thought the empire would persist because in her lifetime it had survived the Taiping and Boxer rebellions, the latter of which the empress had cleverly changed from a popular anti-Manchu revolution into an antiforeign war. But the outer world was finally closing in on China. A strong czarist Russia had wrested from the Middle Kingdom all territory north of the Amur River and eventually the land east of the Ussuri. Japan, in 1895, declared war and took what is now Taiwan and Korea from the weakened Manchus. France, Germany and England also sat in at the carving table, though they had no grand territorial designs and were concerned chiefly with controlling parts of treaty ports or "concession" cities for purposes of trade.

The revolution against the Manchus started in 1911 on October 10, the tenth day of the tenth month, and reportedly at 10:00 P.M. (although the last factor is open to historical question), when the officers and men of the military garrison at Wuchang had decided they could no longer justify their loyalty to the throne. Rather tentatively the commander proclaimed a republic. At once the revolt spread across the rivers to Hanyang and Hankow, the other two Wuhan cities. So ripe was China for republican revolution that in less than eight weeks thirteen of the eighteen provinces had joined the movement, chiefly by simple declaration by military units that their allegiance was to new rather than to old China.

At this point General Yuan Shih-kai was commissioned to put down the rebellion. After a show of military power at Wuhan to intimidate the revolutionaries, Yuan returned to Peking and explained to the child-emperor Pu-yi's father, Prince Chun, that the days of the Manchu monarchy were over. With Yuan serving as bridge between the revolutionaries and the monarchists the centuries of Manchu domination ended officially on February 12, 1912.

Dr. Sun was lecturing in Denver (some historians say London, others St. Louis, others Honolulu) when he received the exhilarating news of the Wuchang rebellion. Shortly afterward he arrived in China to accept his role as provisional president. From the first, however, he encountered disappointment and frustration.

The selfless Sun Yat-sen, whose passionate ambitions were for China rather than for himself, gave up the presidency to General Yuan Shih-kai, not knowing that Yuan was already considering a restoration of the throne with himself as emperor of a new dynasty.

It is perhaps unfair to assume that Yuan was an evil conniver from the first. He may have honestly doubted that the Chinese people were capable of or ready for self-government. Authoritarian rule had been the norm through thousands of years of Chinese history, and indeed subsequently persisted under both Nationalists and Communists.

After he resigned the presidency, Sun accepted appointment in the provisional government as director-general of Transportation and Trade. While China desperately needed a transportation and communications system if it was to develop an industry free of foreign domination, the primary reason for Sun's resignation was the general agreement among party officials that the nation needed a leader who could command the widest possible support rather than one who would appeal merely to Sun's limited constituency. Leadership was therefore turned over to Yuan. Shortly, however, there was dissension among Revolutionary party leaders as to how the nation's reconstruction was to proceed. Sun Yat-sen's own plans, formulated after thirty years of contemplation and research, were termed Utopian and impractical.

Yuan agreed that reforms were urgently needed. Even old Tz'u-hsi, in her last years, had made peace with the inevitable to that extent. But whether Yuan Shih-kai was always unprincipled or merely corrupted by his new power, the tragic result was the same. Within less than twelve months after becoming president he dissolved Sun Yat-sen's party, the Kuomintang, and, when Sun protested, drove him into exile. Yuan died in 1916, not missed by either monarchists or republicans.

In 1923, after Sun had been stupidly rebuffed by the United States and the European powers in his appeals for aid, he turned to the new Socialist state of Russia, which immediately offered him support. The Kremlin dispatched Michael Borodin and General Galen (Vassily Blucher) to bring structure to the somewhat disorganized Kuomintang Party and to the Nationalist armies. It was Borodin who convinced Sun and his associates that the Communist Party should rightly participate in the Revolutionary movement. Although at first this seemed a reasonable proposal, Chiang Kai-shek eventually disagreed, deported Borodin and slaughtered thousands of Communists.

To say that the Chinese Revolution of 1911 succeeded is misleading. A strong undercurrent of sentiment to restore imperial authority persisted for several years, and the republican revolutionaries, sad to say, proved unequal to the task of administering the affairs of the vast Chinese nation. A number of important generals and warlords, it became clear, had supported the anti-Manchu Revolution chiefly to enhance their personal power, and not at all out of admiration for republican ideals of freedom, democracy and land reform. Corruption, illiteracy, famine, banditry, sickness, ignorance, the ancient scourges of China, persisted in the new regime, with the result that there was widespread disillusionment about its ability to restore order and peace. Among those most profoundly disappointed was Sun Yat-sen himself, who spent eleven years, after the happy moment in 1911, trying to pick up the pieces of his shattered dream. Ill and deeply depressed, he died in 1925. Sun was a Christian all his life and left final instructions that his burial ceremonies should be conducted according to Christian custom.

Our tour of his mausoleum—with its long uphill climb—was exhausting but fascinating. Upon reaching the bottom of the grounds we went to a dining area in a large public building and enjoyed two glasses of delicious cold plum juice, and one not at all delicious "popsicle," the unsweet flavor of which was "red bean."

Ling Ku Park was our next stop, not far from Dr. Sun's mausoleum. I climbed only as far as the first gate house—itself a near palace though slightly run-down—but when Bill caught sight of the famous White Goose Pagoda itself, at the end of a long, narrow, tree-lined walk, he could not resist the challenge of climbing to the top. The handsome temple in its present nine-level form is only about a hundred years old, practically new construction in China, although it was originally built in 1381.

RAIN FLOWER TERRACE

Friday, July 11

In the late morning we visited the Rain Flower Terrace, another of the beautiful, centuries-old estates which, for all its appeal to the senses, has bitter significance for today's Chinese. For twenty-two years before 1949 it was a place where the Kuomintang military police interrogated and executed a great many Communist Party members, some authorities say as many as 100,000. Dozens of framed enlargements of small photographs of the dead hang on the walls, along with information about their individual lives and the circumstance of their deaths. Such stories sound much the same the world over and in any period of history; a minority rebel group fallen into the hands of the dominant power. The tragic and dramatic elements of such histories seem essentially the same whether the power is that of the Right or the Left; desperate rebels, many young, subjected to the most horrendous beatings and tortures, many offering brave resistance, leaving behind defiant statements from the scaffold, the swordsman's block or the firing-squad wall.

It was hard to grasp that this beautiful, out-of-the-way rural retreat, with its stately mansion walls, its ancient, graceful tiled roofs, its delicately beautiful gardens and pools, had once been the scene of brutal assaults and killings.

The Communists were, understandably enough, never able to forget, or forgive, what Chiang Kai-shek did to them in 1927, and later. At that time Communists, suspected Communists and Communist sympathizers were hunted down in a totally unexpected outburst of fury, brutalized, tortured, shot in the street like dogs. Although subsequent events would bring the Communists and Nationalists into an uneasy alliance, such events as the 1927 massacre were recalled by both sides.

When the Communists finally assumed control of China in 1949 they had a particular interest in tracking down and bringing to punishment the Kuomintang leaders and police who had taken a personal hand in that slaughter twenty-two years earlier. This is all horrible enough but no one can seriously argue that the Kuomintang would not have done exactly the same thing had the roles been reversed.

In this connection I recommend again Enid Saunders Candlin's fascinating and informative *The Breach in the Wall.* Ms. Candlin grew up in China and knows it far better than most Americans will ever know the United States. Her book contains numerous stern criticisms of Communist theory and practice. Clearly she fervently hoped that Chiang Kai-shek's Nationalists would be victorious. But Ms. Candlin is one of those rare individuals with a glowing respect for truth. In giving an account of some of the Kuomintang's sincere and admirable efforts to improve the hygiene, morale, morals and general living conditions of the Chinese, she draws particular attention to the "New Life Movement," with its giant wall posters exhorting people to improve themselves in every way possible. She also credits the Kuomintang's efforts to eradicate illiteracy, under the leadership of James Yen, who devised the Thousand-Character plan. But then the author points to those important reasons leading to the ultimate defeat of Chiang's forces.

But there was one terrible flaw the government failed to attack—the old, fatal weakness for corruption of most officials, indeed of most Chinese who had authority, position, and education. It was a legacy of the custom that an administrator was only paid a pittance with the understanding that he would make it up with perquisites. This venal trait was to be their undoing. Even during the Japanese war, when morale was for so long so high, this dreadful weakness in the national character lost the country and the government much of the respect it had earned in other directions. Many were honest, but the others attracted attention.

Minority People's sign, Nanking.

Another disastrous mistake on the part of the Kuomintang lay in their reluctance seriously to undertake the issue of land reform. Basically a soldier, Chiang Kai-shek saw his struggle with the Communists in martial terms, neglecting to probe the underlying causes on which his enemies built. The Kuomintang did not face up to the first overwhelming necessity of any government in power in China: [doing something about] poverty, and particularly rural poverty. Efforts were made to ameliorate the situation, but only in a limited way: rural cooperatives were set up, agricultural banks established, and a few areas in the country reorganized, but all this was only a drop in the bucket.

The Communists had attempted, and were still attempting, to gain the cities, but their efforts among the urban proletariat were not as rewarding or decisive as they had hoped. Recognizing this, they turned to their advantage the undeniably terrible condition of the farmer, who passed his whole life in crushing debt, over half his crop (or more) pledged to the moneylender or to an absentee landlord before it was even sown. *Had Chiang from the first recognized that the question of land-distribution, of putting the farmers in a position where they could be free of debt, keep their own crops, borrow at equitable rates of interest, was paramount, it is very possible that the Communists would hardly have had a hearing in the countryside, except through the tactics of fear and terrorization.*

But Chiang delayed. Neither he nor the Party saw how vitally important this was, and *as most of his support came from moneyed interests, to espouse such a cause would not have been easy.* Vast sums were expended on the anti-Communist campaigns—that seemed to the government justifiable—but *part of those funds should have been dispersed in another way. How sorely the farmers needed rural credit! Where were they to turn?* [Italics added.]

That, reader, explains Chiang's eventual defeat far more realistically than American right-wing nonsense about "Communists in the State Department."

We climbed a hill behind the Rain Flower Terrace where in 1950 the present government erected an imposing monument to commemorate Revolutionary martyrs. Several attractive paper-flower memorial wreaths that had just been placed by the Japanese visitors from Osaka were displayed in the sultry, sunless midday air.

Later we noticed with surprise that one of the shiny black limousines parked at the hotel was an old Plymouth. No one was able to explain how it happened to be there. The car was almost as spotless as if it had just left the showroom floor. This is explained by the fact that each driver in China is not only responsible for keeping his vehicle in good condition but himself must serve as its mechanic.

On the back fenders of the Plymouth the word *Savoi* was printed. Perhaps it was a model of English manufacture under a license from Chrysler-Plymouth.

The car arrived in Nanking in the 1950s but nothing is known of it before it arrived except that it came from Peking.

Chinese-made automobiles are quite well engineered and obviously durable. Only once during the month and a half we spent in China in 1975 did I see a car that had stalled or broken down. And I noticed only two trucks pulled over to the side of the road with the drivers working on the engines, a very small number considering that there are more trucks on Chinese streets than on American. Too, the overwhelming majority of Chinese trucks are very old. Nevertheless, they keep rolling. Planned obsolescence is obviously totally foreign to the Chinese engineering philosophy.

NANKING HISTORICAL MUSEUM

A visit to a Nanking historical museum proved most instructive. There we learned that Christian influence increased in China during the period of the Mongol dynasty, A.D. 1279 to 1368, during which time Nestorian Christians enlarged their modest colonies. The Nestorians were an interesting sect. Their name comes from the Syrian patriarch of Constantinople, Nestorius, consecrated in that office in 428. His primary activity seems to have been the

Wall display at monument of martyrs, Nanking.

Old Plymouth still in tiptop condition, Nanking.

hounding of heretics. Nestorius himself, however, fell victim to the same charge when his colleague Anastasius criticized those who referred to Jesus' mother Mary as "the Mother of God." In 435 Nestorius was banished. He is thought to have died around the year 450. His influence was far-reaching, and remains to the present day in that Nestorian Christians can still be found in Kurdistan and in the essentially Nestorian theology of the Syriac Church. When Marco Polo returned from his long tenure of service to Kublai Khan the church in Europe responded by dispatching clergy to the Middle Kingdom. When the Mongol dynasty finally collapsed, however, one of China's periodic waves of antiforeign sentiment swept over the land causing the Nestorian Catholic colonies in China to disappear in the mists of time.

A RADIO PARTS FACTORY

Even those ancient Chinese cities with a rich cultural heritage now have their factories, including both light and heavy industries. In Nanking we were driven to a typical smaller plant, the Nanking No. 4 Radio Parts Factory. Madame Chu-li, director of the Revolutionary Committee, and a group of her colleagues, all women, greeted us, in the usual gracious manner.

Of the factory's 380 workers and staff about 70 percent were women. The plant is fairly new, having been founded in 1958. That year the state made an investment in the project equaling $25,000. The operation prospered so that the loan was repaid within five years.

Much of the plant's progress, we were told, comes from the freedom that employees feel to develop creative ideas. Something like our American suggestion-box arrangement prevails, by means of which any worker, no matter how humble his position, may offer a suggestion he thinks of value. The ideas are always judged on their merits, with never any prejudice against them on the basis of their source. That would be out of keeping with modern China's philosophy anyway with its strong emphasis on the dignity of all laborers.

Since 1974 the factory had been turning out over 10 million items per year. Its new target level was 20 million, which it expected to achieve shortly.

Our stroll through the plant revealed it to be modest in size but clean, quiet and as efficient as a beehive.

One of the most striking features of Chinese factories, by the way, is that they all seem to have a separate department for making their own machinery; not just repairing it, mind you, but creating it. This is another instance of following Mao's ideal of self-sufficiency. Not only must China itself be self-sufficient because it does not know whom it can count on in today's dangerous world, but each individual province, each city, each village, each factory, each school—in fact, each social organization of any kind, right down to the individual himself—must develop the habit of summoning up internal strengths.

This is obviously an admirable idea in that it lessens dependence on outside technical specialists while simultaneously developing creativity. Combined with the abhorrence of waste, it is one of the reasons for modern China's strength and confidence. This thought was brought to mind when outside a doorway of one of the factory's buildings I saw a mop drying in the sun and noticed that Chinese mops are not made of the two hundred or so special strands of twine that ours are but consist of clusters of separate strips of waste cloth that would in other countries simply be discarded.

A number of China travelers I have talked to, some of whom have subsequently published accounts of their adventures in American newspapers and magazines, have reported that in China they wept at certain moments of deep feeling. I found such reports puzzling until, in one quick moment in Nanking, I had just such an experience.

It happened partly because when Bill and I were leaving the Nanking Radio Parts Factory our local guide, Mr. Lo, could not be found. This resulted in our standing about for several minutes while a search was conducted. There was, therefore, a bit more than usual of the mutually complimentary farewell exchanges between guests and hosts. But something about Madame Chu's attitude, as she bid us adieu, was especially fervent and warm. Bill and I strongly felt that she was not indulging in cliché pleasantries merely to be polite. Because she was an open, almost gruff peasant type, her words carried additional emotional weight as she grasped my right hand in her two, and asked me to please convey to the American people the deep affection felt for them not only by the employees of her factory but by the people of China.

"Well," I said to our interpreter, "please tell Madame that ever since the very first American entry into China the people of the United States have themselves felt a warm and sincere affection for the Chinese people. Whatever philosophical differences separate our governments, I am sure that direct communication between the Chinese and American people can do much to resolve our present difficulties and misunderstandings."

Madame Chu smiled warmly.

"The ladies might be interested in knowing," I said, "that my wife was born in China, that our family has many Chinese friends and we have always therefore had a particularly warm regard for China and its people."

Something about the expression in Madame Chu's eyes, as she listened to the translation of this remark, suddenly filled my own with tears. While I succeeded in mastering the surge of emotion, I'm sure the depth of my feelings was evident to the three women standing in the hot sunwashed courtyard before me. I felt strongly that the three, and all the women, and men, in their factory—indeed all the people of China—have every reason to be tremendously proud of the economic wonders they have worked. Combined with my emotion, of course, was sympathy not only for our three kind hostesses but, again, for the citizens of China who, despite improvements in their condition, are still living in relative poverty and working extremely hard, by no means totally free of abuses emerging from China's long, troubled history.

Women's Liberation

As we left these three factory executives it occurred to me that in some ways the liberation of women seems to have fared somewhat better in China than in the United States. One reason, of course, is that women in China started from a much lower position on the social scale. A woman was far more a humble house servant than American women have ever been and was looked upon in every way as an inferior person.

A husband's word was law in old China; if the point needed further emphasis, beating was readily and commonly resorted to. A father was something of a tyrant in his own home. All that is now a thing of the past. The Chinese women give credit for their progress to Mao, who had the simple common sense to observe that not only were 85 percent of the Chinese people peasants, who would no doubt respond favorably to courteous and considerate treatment—something they had never previously enjoyed—but 50 percent of China's population was female, which suggested the same sort of improved and compassionate treatment.

Speaking of *liberation,* by the way, it takes American ears at least several days to become accustomed to the endless repetition of the word in China. Events are dated from "before Liberation" or "after Liberation." One constantly hears "When we were liberated . . ." or "After Mao liberated us . . ." It would be a mistake to think of this as merely bearing out Orwell's prediction about the appropriation of important and attractive words by the totalitarian state. The Chinese people actually *mean* to say that they have been liberated. The more important fact is that they have, in certain specific ways. Women were liberated from the tyranny of men. Peasants were liberated from the tyranny of landlords, warlords and tax collectors, and poor students liberated from the tyranny of the old educational program, which kept education in the hands of the upper crust.

As one who supports the women's liberation movement in the U.S. I find it a bit awkward to say that some—though a minority—of its leaders are strident and sometimes unfeminine types who seem motivated largely by a terrible anger, perhaps originally aimed at their fathers, rather than out of a simple, fair demand for social justice—not that the two are mutually exclusive. They're right about the majority of their demands but a good many men and women, rightly or wrongly, are put off by some of their methods. In China, on the other hand, leaders of the movement for women's liberation seem eminently womanly and feminine. They have the enormous advantage, of course, in that the government is 100 percent behind them and indeed encouraged them to activity in the first place. Chinese women are now given good health care; nurseries and kindergartens are provided for their children if they wish to work; they attend universities and occupy important positions in society.

7. Sian

OUR next stop was the ancient Shensi (Shaanxi) Province city of Sian, once called Changan, and visited, in August, 1979, by Vice President Walter Mondale. Well, since almost all cities in China are ancient, this is perhaps a meaningless observation but the antiquity of the Chinese culture constantly impresses itself upon the Western traveler.

The trip by rail—Sian is almost a thousand miles from Shanghai—was, again, fascinating. At one stop the members of what turned out to be an Egyptian volleyball team boarded the train. They were extremely tall, muscular, good-looking young fellows, clad in sharp, decidedly Western attire, tailored slacks and expensive-looking sports shirts. We learned that they too were on their way to Sian, to compete against a Chinese volleyball team. Later we all ended up at the same hotel in the middle of the night.

Getting to the area, however, turned out to be a bit uncomfortable. Because of the extremely high temperature and soggy humidity, it was really murder on that Orient express. There was a revolving electric fan high on the outer wall of our compartment but it merely rearranged the heat; there could be no question of getting a cool breeze from it. Since dying of heat prostration seemed an unattractive prospect, the only alternative was to open our window. This indeed created a breeze but also let in a hell of a lot of smoke and soot. Oddly enough, this was not the minor disaster it would seem in the United States; after a few weeks in summertime in China one gradually adopts a whole new philosophy about dirt. You resign yourself to being dusty, sooty, sweaty and uncomfortable. Part of your mind looks forward to the next shower or tub bath, but in the meantime you concentrate on more important things.

I quote here from my notes, since they give an insight into my mood of the moment:

We are now on the train rolling through countryside as beautiful as any I have ever seen. Strange low hills that look almost like toy mountains have been formed by the yellow-tan earth's erosion, over countless millions of years. Miniature Grand Canyons pass beneath our window, every few seconds, as we glide across bridges and trestles, the floor of each depression marked with neat rows of one green crop or another. Hundreds of caves are dug into these magical, ancient hillsides. Only their black mouths are visible; it is not possible to tell what lies within.

Sharp goat paths lead up the sides of some of the loess cliffs. Now and then we see a child, a goat, an old woman, a solitary peasant pulling a cart, moving along slowly, silently, like a vision out of the China of 10,000 years ago.

We have just passed another small canyon, perhaps five hundred yards long, at its base not more than thirty feet wide. Even this narrow, Godforsaken ribbon of land has been planted!

It is now a quarter to seven. The setting sun casts a wondrous rosy-golden light over everything, making shadows sharp and dark.

Bill and I read, talked, laughed a lot, drank countless bottles of *chi swei,* a soft drink like 7-Up, had an excellent dinner in the diner and, when it finally got dark out, prepared to turn in.

When you get off the train in Sian the first thing that meets your view is a beautiful "temple" in the ancient tile-roof style, bright red pillars gleaming. This, it happily turns out, is the station waiting room itself, which sets the tone for one's visit to this attractive city.

We arrived in Sian about three-fifteen in the morning. After the usual introductions to Responsible Persons and Travel Service personnel, we were comfortably whisked through quiet, ghostly streets to our hotel. Here and there we could see people sleeping on the sidewalk—on mats—but not for the same reasons they do so in India. In that unfortunate country some of the poorest of the poor live their whole lives on the sidewalk. But in Chinese cities, on hot summer nights, people lie on neat straw mats and wooden mat cots to enjoy a few hours of cool comfort before the burning sun comes up.

Sian's streets are spotlessly clean; the town did not have the endless miles of piled-up construction materials one saw in other Chinese cities.

Weyang Road, one of the main thoroughfares, is actually two parallel streets with a literal narrow forest or parkway between the two lanes. The swath of trees runs almost half a block from side to side and straight ahead for quite a few miles.

After a brief ride through the dark streets we arrived at the town's main hotel, one of the most luxurious in China, because it was built by the Russians for their own comfort, during the 1950s. It is constructed not at all in the Chinese style and is, in fact, more attractive than many hotels in Moscow—or in the U.S., for that matter.

When Bill and I were shown to our quarters we were surprised to discover that each of us was provided with a separate three-room suite, with large comfortable furniture, plenty of electric fans, better lighting than one finds in most Chinese hotels, good beds and all in all everything that the weary traveler could hope for.

History of Sian

The Tang dynasty emperor who ruled a vast, united China from Changan from 713 to 756 was Hsuan-tsung, one of the most impressive rulers in the history not only of China but of the whole planet. Under his intelligent and determined command the Middle Kingdom reached its greatest heights of power and cultural achievement. Painters, sculptors, poets, historians, jewelers and other creative souls flourished.

Though the city was then enormous—probably the largest in the world—it was scientifically planned, lined up with points of the compass, and boasted eleven main thoroughfares, on a north-south axis, each some 482 feet across. East-west streets were at least 226 feet wide. The thoroughfares in major American cities today are not nearly so spacious.

One reason for the effectiveness of Chinese administration in such ancient times was the civil service system, by which officers were installed on the basis of proficiency at passing examinations. This was a thousand years before the idea occurred to our European ancestors.

It is difficult for Western minds to appreciate that the city was even then ancient. Changan was the capital of China 1,100 years before Christ.

One of the many incredible chapters of the history of the Sian region concerns the construction of the Grand Canal, which—like the Great Wall—still exists. Sui Wen-ti in A.D. 589 captured the throne and founded the Sui dynasty. He commissioned the construction of a canal, a hundred feet wide, and extending hundreds of miles across country, which eventually reached one thousand miles in length. Twenty-six hundred lives per mile was the gruesome cost in human suffering of such a feat. Two-and-a-half-million workers are said to have died during the construction of the waterway, some from exhaustion, others from illness and others by execution, the penalty for attempting to escape from work crews being decapitation. As an engineering achievement the canal was eminently successful and brought great financial profit to the empire. Although the sumptuous palaces that graced its banks are long gone, most of the canal is as serviceable today as it was 1,400 years ago.

The city is now the cultural, economic and political center of the province of Shensi. Although it is unfamiliar to the average American, it is no obscure rural outpost; its population is two and a half million.

Sian pagoda.

We were taken to an enormous structure, sixty-four meters high, built during the Tang dynasty in A.D. 652. The Ta Yen Ta—rendered in some translations as Big Swan Pagoda and others as Big Wild Goose Pagoda—was, we were told, used in pre-Liberation days as a barracks by Kuomintang soldiers. The Communist government was not able to turn its attention to repair and reconstruction of the edifice until 1954.

As we climbed to its upper levels and looked out, we noticed some black stone tablets on the wall marked with the Ming-dynasty equivalent of "Kilroy was here" graffiti.

The pagoda was originally built to house scriptures of the Buddhist religion, introduced to China by the famed scholar Hiueng-tsiang (Xuan Zang), who traveled to India between A.D. 629 and 645. At the request of the emperor he wrote a remarkable work called *Record of the Western Regions,* which revealed to the Chinese much of the history, culture and philosophy of their Indian neighbors.

After his long and marvelous journey he returned to Changan, or Sian-fu, in triumph. It is said that twenty horses were required to carry the souvenirs and wonders he traveled with, including hundreds of Sanskrit Buddhist volumes.

Under the Tang dynasty, approximately from the seventh to the tenth century, Sian was one of the great cities of the Orient, with perhaps as many as two million inhabitants. To this mecca of culture, in ancient times called Perennial Peace, there came, in 635, a band of twenty-one Christians, of the Nestorian sect, mentioned earlier. Their leader was Alopan. Although they had been rudely persecuted by their Christian brothers—in accord with long centuries of Christian custom —they were welcomed by the Chinese. The imperial court not only received them but provided them with land and the wherewithal to build a monastery, the first Christian enterprise in Chinese history. Eventually they fell out with their hosts, however, and over the course of the centuries disappeared, leaving practically no trace.

But in the year 1625 an enormous ten-foot-high smooth, black rectangular stone, three feet across and one foot thick—like the mysterious stone in the film *2001*—was discovered buried near Sian. Its inscription, when translated, told the story of the "Spread of Ta Chin Luminous Religion in China." Jesuit missionaries then serving in the country concluded that the table had been inscribed by their Nestorian predecessors. One sees this historically important monolith in the Sian Museum, along with other incredible artifacts and sculptures. There were moments during our tour when I had an impression of China itself as one vast museum. And, at that, Chiang's associates took enormous quantities of art treasure with them to Taiwan.

Although we imagine that it was not until after the time of Marco Polo, or after the Crusades, that China traded with her neighbors to the west, caravan routes westward were open during the Han dynasty—which runs roughly from 200 B.C. to A.D. 200—at which time the Chinese were trading with the Persians and the Romans.

When we use the word *China* historically, of course, we are not speaking of a nation with clearly defined boundaries in the modern sense, but of constantly changing boundaries and many separate tribes, some the Han people of the Middle Kingdom, others Tibetans, some Mongols, some Manchurians. What defined China through the centuries was a vague sort of cultural unity, the culture created by great numbers of intellectuals, painters, sculptors, poets, architects, philosophers, physicians, kings and teachers. It is important for us in the West today, with our dreadful habit of considering almost all other peoples on the planet as somehow inferior, to realize that, historically speaking, it is we who have been inferior to the Chinese.

One of the first sciences to be highly developed in China was astronomy. Four centuries before Christ Chinese astronomers had decided that the year was 365¼ days long!

Two hundred forty years before Christ the Chinese observed Halley's Comet.

Chinese physicians were centuries ahead of those in Europe, particularly as regards internal medicine. Many centuries before Christ the Chinese doctors knew that ephedra (known to us as *ephedrine*), a vegetable compound, was effective for treating asthma, and that iodine helped to relieve goiter.

A VOLLEYBALL GAME

The next evening Bill and I went to a local gymnasium to see our hotel neighbors, the Egyptian volleyball team, play their Chinese opponents representing Shensi Province. On the way to the auditorium we considered the question as to which team to applaud for. I told Bill that since I didn't give an Aswan Dam which side won we therefore ought to applaud vigorously for both.

While driving to the game it occurred to me that our driver in Sian wore white gloves at all times, possibly to prevent leaving fingerprints on the smog when he made a hand signal. Air pollution seems to be as widespread in China as it is in the United States.

The game was played in a large modern basketball gymnasium. The Shensi team, it developed, was sort of a regional all-star group. After the capacity audience was seated, the teams marched in, to the accompaniment of martial music. Each Chinese player held his left hand high, against the right hand of his Egyptian counterpart. Reaching the floor area they went to their separate sides, marched around the outside of the floor and then joined in the center.

Bill and I recalled our earlier surprise that Chinese audiences did not applaud much at theatrical shows. Even in this sports context the opening applause seemed very light. Since there was no air conditioning, hundreds of fans fluttered in the audience gathered around the playing floor, making it seem as if the whole room was vibrating or shimmering.

During the warmup the Egyptian players seemed considerably sharper than the Chinese. Their appearance was that of a group of tall, handsome sons of rich Beverly Hills clothiers. The Chinese team, though less colorful, was almost as tall and once the game started they trounced the Egyptians in the first two games, by five- or six-point margins. The Egyptians, surprisingly, perhaps overcoming early nervousness, won the next two games by even larger margins, which perfectly set the stage for the decisive fifth game, which was neck-and-neck all the way, the Chinese finally winning 15 to 13. Again we were impressed by what—by American standards—seemed a surprising lack of enthusiasm on the part of the audience. This is a mistaken impression, of course, in that my one criterion was lack of applause. Actually the crowd was intensely involved with the game and naturally pleased by the outcome. Nevertheless, they rarely applauded their own team and seemed to clap for the Egyptians merely to express good sportsmanship.

In a way that is difficult to explain, Sian seemed a more sensual town than the others we had visited. The people there seem gentle, soft-spoken, somewhat genteel. The young lady who showed us about the city's most famous temple was wearing a black lace skirt, through which her legs were visible. I can't imagine seeing such feminine attire in any other mainland Chinese city under mid-1970s conditions.

A smaller temple near the street housed the largest bell we'd ever seen. Its metal appeared to be about eight inches thick and the bell itself perhaps eighteen feet high. It weighed fifteen tons and was cast in the Ming dynasty. In a matching building on the other side of the court an enormous drum, similar in size to the bell, was formerly displayed. It has disappeared and is now replaced by a small reproduction.

The food at the Sian hotel was excellent, with the exception of the duck served one evening, which was so tough it literally could not be cut with a knife. Nor did trying to manhandle it help. I finally decided it was a hockey puck with legs and gave up.

One of the pleasant oddities about the Sian dining room, however, is that for every lunch and dinner we were served *two* main courses, one of which Bill ordered, the other I ordered. I don't mean an extra side dish, I mean two complete dinners, on two separate plates. One plate, for example, might hold half a duck, mushrooms and peas, and fried potatoes. On the other plate were two slices of roast pork, a large helping of mashed potatoes and gravy, and string beans and carrots. Maybe the theory was that if you didn't like one you might have better luck with the other.

AN INSULATOR FACTORY

One of our more interesting visits took us to the Sian high-voltage insulator factory, construction on which started in 1953 and was completed in 1959. The "Soviet Revisionists,"

our hosts explained, had helped with the founding of the plant, which as of 1975 had about 400 workers and staff, 170 of whom were women.

"When Khrushchev came to power," said an executive officer, "he betrayed the agreement that had already been signed, which caused a lot of difficulties to our production. One of the important raw materials was quartz. Due to poor Russian advice the quartz was produced by an open-air process, which meant that quartz particles mixed with the air and caused great harm to the workers' health. They used three-layer masks but even this did not completely solve the problem."

The Russians had also agreed to supply large machinery and stone used in the clay-making process. They shipped machinery and stone, however, at oddly inflated prices. The Chinese said, "We have plenty of stone in our own mountains, why should we import yours?"

"If you don't take our stone," the Russians reportedly replied, "then we won't supply you with the equipment."

The Russians at that time bought some grinding machines from East Germany for 153,000 rubles and in turn sold them to the Chinese for 218,000 rubles, making a profit of 65,000 rubles on the transaction. Some of the Soviet charges were 10 to 20 percent higher than they should have been.

"We discovered, quite by accident, that we were being badly overcharged because when the machines were delivered there were papers attached to them, one set referring to the price the Russians charged us, but another set, attached to the bottom parts of the machines, revealing the price that the Soviet Union had *paid*. This was the first time we realized we were being cheated. We were also, by the way, sold out-of-date equipment! They also had the nerve to sell us a kiln that did not work properly. For over nine months we complained to them that the temperatures in the kiln were not right, to no avail. Over 360,000 yuan were wasted through use of this equipment."

"How did you feel when the Russians left in 1960?" I asked.

"It was a blessing in disguise because this

forced us to depend on our own resources. We have since made over 500 technical innovations that might never have come about if the Russians were still here. We now produce over 692 varieties of products."

"How much of the factory's output is exported?"

"About 10 percent."

The Russians conceded that they owed the Chinese 1.4 million rubles in overpayment, although the Chinese say the amount was two million. The point is academic, we were told, in that none of the money has ever been paid.

Later we went for a delightful, though somewhat steamy boat ride in Hsing Ching (Xingqing) Park, in a boat with a roof supported by red columns, patterned after one used by Chinese royalty of centuries ago. Removing my slippers, I dangled my feet in what I had assumed would be the cooling waters of the park's lake. The effect was rather like plunging them into an enormous bowl of vegetable soup.

After this dubious refreshment, our party repaired to a pavilion for *chi swei* and/or hot tea. It was here we saw our first sexy-looking Chinese woman. While her face was pleasant enough, she would have given no serious competition to Sophia Loren or, for that matter, Jayne Meadows, but the rest of her was strictly Las Vegas showgirl, tall, with long legs, and the rest of the set to match. She wore her hair in a sort of provocative little bun, with a white bow. Whether she would be similarly rated by the local gentry I have no idea inasmuch as there is no such thing as a universal standard of physical beauty. In my six weeks in China, for whatever the point is worth, I saw only three large-breasted women. The modern Chinese woman, of course, wears no makeup and no provocative attire. Gone, presumably forever, is the form-fitting silk *changsam,* with the slit up the side. The whole modern Chinese concept of sex, love and marriage is so remarkably unlike our own that it seems almost representative of another planet, rather than another country populated by a species of the same human race. Chinese young people in the 1950s were provided with a handbook titled

Love, Marriage and the Family. They learned that for countless centuries marriages in China were arranged by parents. This state of affairs persisted up until recent years and probably still occurs, but now young people are taught that they have a right to make their own decisions in selecting a mate.

"The Sian Incident"

Hua Qing hot springs is about an hour's ride out of Sian. In the small village of Lintung one suddenly turns through beautiful iron gates and at once moves from rural poverty into imperial splendor. All the buildings here, including the welcoming room, are in the breathtakingly beautiful red-columned, curved tiled-roof style of architecture.

Situated at the foot of Linshen Mountain, about twenty-four kilometers out of Sian, the place has been a famous watering spot since the Western Chou dynasty. Some of the present buildings are original, others are reproductions, made after Liberation, but totally faithful to the ancient style. In the last three hundred years, we were told, "This place has been used by emperors, generals and their pampered sons and daughters." Needless to say, the common people were never permitted to enter such a resort in the old days, except as servants, concubines, laborers and slaves.

Over seven hundred years before Columbus's voyage to the North American continent —according to at least one version of an ancient story—the Tang Emperor Minhuang built the Palace of Floating Snow at the site of the hot sulfur spring which flows from the foot of the mountain. At the end of winter, melting snow from this towering steep green peak cascaded down into the pool, which the emperor further beautified for his favorite concubine, Yang Kwei-fei, who—one is told—never smiled. Even such imperial generosity brought no smile to Yang Kwei-fei's lovely face. So the emperor conceived a remarkable idea which, he thought, would cheer his loved one. He predicted she would be amused if local villagers pretended to attack the palace. He was correct in his prediction but shortly thereafter the residents of the area staged a real assault on the country palace which the guards, assuming another jest was being staged, did not take seriously. The emperor's troops were overwhelmed and he and his cheerless love were beheaded.

The chief reason that the China Travel Service directs visitors to the village where all this took place, however, is that it was the site of "The Sian Incident," the remarkable drama which led to Chiang Kai-shek's capture, and might have caused his execution, in December, 1936. The catalyst of this strange turn of events was Chang Hsueh-liang, called the "young marshal," a son of one of China's bandit-warlords, Chang Tso-lin. Though an opium addict, Chang Hsueh-liang was a competent military strategist who in 1930 had importantly aided Chiang Kai-shek in his battle against Feng Yu-hsiang, the "Christian general."

Parenthetically, in the late 1940s, Feng made a speech at the Columbia University Faculty Club in New York City in which he openly discussed the corruption of Chiang Kai-shek's regime. While returning to China by way of the Soviet Union Feng was burned to death in the projection room of a Russian ship. The official explanation was that an accident had occurred although doubts about the incident have persisted. It is a pity that Feng did not live longer; it would have been interesting to see what position he would have taken after Chiang's defeat. He was a colorful character who at one time was in the habit of baptizing his soldiers into the Christian faith en masse by use of a garden hose.

In 1936 Chiang assigned the young marshal Chang Hsueh-liang to exterminate the Communist armies, but Chang Hsueh-liang saw things differently. He was more fiercely anti-Japanese than was Chiang Kai-shek; consequently, he could not see the point of liquidating the Communists since they were more willing to attack the Japanese than were the Nationalist forces.

Disturbed by reports that the marshal was secretly giving asylum to Communist leaders, Chiang hurried to Sian to take personal charge of the situation. He ordered the leading officers of the young marshal's Tungpei army to state their total opposition to Chang, a demand that

was given a lukewarm welcome. A few nights later Chang's Tungpei troops quietly infiltrated the Sian area, blocked out Chiang Kai-shek's private commandos, and headed straight for Lintung, to capture Chiang. His personal bodyguard put up a fight and bullets flew for several hours.

We were taken to visit room 503, where Chiang stayed at the time. The suite consists of two rooms, with a floor of small tiles. The straw mat double bed against one window is where Chiang was lying when he heard gunfire. A picture frame is placed around two panes of glass shattered by bullets in the gunfight.

The Nationalist leader, not even stopping for his false teeth, ran into the night, climbed over a wall and ascended the mountain behind the compound. He eluded capture for several hours by hiding in a fox's hole high on the mountainside. Since it was midwinter, Chiang was seriously chilled when captured the following day.

There were young officers in the Tungpei army who wanted to assassinate him on the spot but an intervention was made on his behalf by an odd assortment of forces including Chou En-lai and the Chinese Communists, the Kremlin, the United States and the European allies. Each naturally had separate motives for wanting Chiang alive rather than dead, but all agreed that at that point his leadership, despite its inadequacies, was essential as a rallying point for a large percentage of the Chinese population.

Inasmuch as by that time Chiang had conducted five vigorous extermination campaigns against the Communists—slaughtering them by the thousands—it must naturally be assumed that there were those in both the Communist Party and the Red Army who were tempted by the emotional satisfaction his execution might have provided.

It was explained to Chiang Kai-shek that he could be released if he simply agreed to a united front, however imperfect, against the Japanese. Since he had no cards to play, he lost the hand and, much against his personal wishes, agreed to a face-saving announcement that seemed to suggest he had played a forceful role in the origination of the national unity campaign.

General Joseph Stilwell, among others, took a dim view of the pretense of friendship between the Kuomintang and the Communists. Incidentally, I recommend to any even moderately serious student of China, historian Barbara Tuchman's study, *Stilwell and the American Experience in China, 1911–1945.* Not only is the book fascinating and enlightening but it should put an end to the right-wing "how *we* lost China" nonsense. It was Chiang Kai-shek who lost China; Barbara Tuchman explains step by step and in painful detail exactly how he did it.

There is a certain kind of mind that derives a peculiar pleasure from having its most far-fetched hypotheses confirmed; if available evidence does not substantiate a theory, the trick is turned anyway by nothing more than a determination to believe, which even in ordinarily well-ordered minds can cloud rational judgment. As regards Chiang Kai-shek's unhappy loss of the Chinese Civil War the unvarnished reality was simply too painful for many of us to accommodate at the time. Rightists therefore shoved the pieces of the puzzle around on the playing board until they seemed to offer an "explanation" of the Kuomintang loss: Communists and their sympathizers in the China branch of the U.S. State Department. The truth was that Chiang's defeat, given the realities in China in the 1940s, was inevitable. The United States had the power only to delay the outcome, not prevent it. It consistently supported Chiang with participation in the Security Council of the United Nations, military supplies, vast sums of money and advisers. *But none of these advisers believed the Nationalists could defeat the Communists.* They readily perceived what almost any mere tourist of the time, had there been any, would have noted: whatever their other faults, Mao and the Communists were in no way corrupt. They were, in fact, self-sacrificing and idealistic. Chiang himself was not corrupt. That made him an exception in his own camp. The Kuomintang leadership generally was too incompetent to elicit wide or fervent support among the Chinese masses.

As of 1947, only two years before his defeat, Chiang's forces were vastly superior to the Communists in arms and men. The U.S. could provide billions of dollars in military and economic aid to Chiang and give him propaganda support as well. Unfortunately this last factor, designed to inflate Chiang's greatness and prestige, had the effect of covering the degree of his personal unpopularity and incompetence and the rampant corruption of his colleagues. Since military machines generally crank out optimistic reports, whether justified or not, the American people acquired the impression that Chiang was powerful. His defeat, therefore, came not merely as bad news; it came as a shock.

It is simple enough now, with the hindsight afforded by the last thirty years, to perceive the reasons for Chiang's defeat and Mao's victory, but there is one underlying cause which, in my view, is not only frequently overlooked but so far as I know has not been publicly referred to at all, and that is that Mao's side had the motivating force of a large idea while Chiang's did not. Chiang was somewhat like the Mexican establishment "revolutionaries" of our century, who are generally rather conservative and moderate, although for political purposes they still mouth the rhetoric of the earlier actual Mexican Revolution. Just so, Chiang and the Nationalists appealed to sentiments related to Sun Yat-sen's revolution against the Manchu Empire of 1911. But the reality was that within the larger context of world events of the mid-twentieth century the Kuomintang was a generally reactionary and unpopular force.

After a simple box lunch at the hot spring resort we took a casual siesta, with all of our party stretched out on sofas or in easy-chairs in the reception room. Lulled by the extreme heat, high humidity and the comforting whisper of electric fans, we were soon dead to the world. The nap was followed by a refreshing swim in an enormous pool already crowded with children and young adults. As I prepared to ease myself down into the water from the top rung of a poolside ladder my trunks suddenly became caught on a large hook and I hung half-suspended, half-perched on one foot on the ladder's bottom rung. My plight immediately was noticed by the entire population of the pool, several hundred, who having already been attracted by the two pale-skinned invaders, now greeted my predicament with peals of what I hope was good-natured laughter.

After Bill rescued me, we splashed and swam for about an hour in water that was a bit too warm and quite murky, but welcome nevertheless. Bill, who is a good swimmer, attracted additional attention by diving off the side of the pool several times, something we saw no one else doing. On two sides of the pool very old people sat, fanning themselves, in the shade, staring with blank faces that must have witnessed more suffering in their individual lifetimes than ten average Americans will ever know.

After we toweled off and dressed, the local guides continued the tour of the premises and showed us the individual rooms in which hot mineral spring water gushes into large, double-tiered stone tubs.

"These are the tubs that the emperors and members of their courts used," we were told. "Since the Revolution of 1911, dignitaries and foreign visitors have been permitted to use the quarters. Which of the three would you like to bathe in?" I selected one bathhouse at random. It consisted of a small changing room, equipped with a bed on which a bather could rest or nap after his hot dip. The pool tubs are empty. You fill them by turning a faucet which lets a fire-hydrant-size stream of hot water in. I let the water rise to the first ledge and stretched out. If Bill and the other members of our party had not been waiting outside, I would have enjoyed lolling there for the remainder of the afternoon, but I contented myself with just a few minutes in the warm water. The only thing lacking to render the experience perfect was a cold shower. As I toweled off I idly wondered which emperors, empresses, chairmen, presidents and warlords had used the same tub before me.

PANPO VILLAGE MUSEUM
Our visit to Sian's Panpo Village Museum

was particularly fascinating. The site was discovered in 1953 and unearthed in 1964. It is hard to grasp that it is 6,000 years old. Axes with stone and wooden handles are displayed, along with agricultural instruments and some weapons that look remarkably like American Indian tomahawks, arrows and bows. The people of the village culture also used a weapon consisting of a round rock tied at the end of a string. It is theorized that they used it to fling around the legs of animals and thus capture them. Fishing-net equipment and fish hooks were also found at the site and the villagers were evidently quite gifted at making pottery, more than a thousand pieces of which were found. The subject matter chosen by the artists whose clay pots survived shows that they took their themes chiefly from nature. Some quite realistic deer, trees and fish are displayed on fragments. Eventually the villagers reached a sophisticated level of art in which they were drawing stylized fish and incorporating them into abstract designs.

A small model of the village reveals that the inhabitants lived in round houses with mushroom-shaped thatched roofs. Spinning and weaving had been introduced; sewing needles were located. The inhabitants also evidently wore ornamental necklaces and pins to keep their hair in order. Apparently their arithmetical and geometrical knowledge was quite advanced for such an early period, to judge by many of the abstract designs and measurements of pots and other artifacts. The villagers had also learned to produce steam by building fires under water pots.

The excavation site of the village itself is housed in two large buildings constructed rather like an American basketball auditorium. Carbon-dating tests reveal the village existed as long as 6,080 years ago. All the doors of the village huts faced south, suggesting that the inhabitants wished to admit light but not suffer the direct heat of the sun. The communal grain-storage pits had fire-baked walls, showing that the villagers knew how to protect the contents against moisture.

8. Wuhan

Saturday, July 12

UNTIL I happened to see the Fall 1978 edition of *New China* I had not been aware that Hankow was "a city previously closed to tourism." The fact that my son and I were permitted to go to that community three years before it was "opened up" therefore casts a different light on our visit there. Many years earlier Wuchang—part of Wuhan—had been closed after sundown to all foreigners but missionaries as a result of the dangers of the Boxer Rebellion.

We made the flight from Nanking in a fast, reliable two-engine airship of Soviet manufacture, which means it must have been built in the late 1950s.

Before taking off, the plane turned into an instant sauna in that there was no air conditioning and, once the back-hatch door had been closed, no new air. The little remaining oxygen was at a premium since every seat was filled. Once aloft, however, air conditioning was provided. The plane carried about forty-five passengers. The hour-and-a-half flight itself was uneventful. I read and Bill wrote letters home.

There were only two other planes of the same style visible at the airport when we arrived in Wuhan.

For over a week Bill and I had been warned that Wuhan was "one of the furnaces of China," an extremely hot city during the summer months, which indeed it is. When we arrived, however, the weather could not have been more pleasant. The sky was almost, but not quite, blue, the temperature in the mid-seventies and the air not in the least humid. It was a great relief after the steamy Nanking atmosphere.

At the other side of the airport a few military jets were hustling in and out.

We were greeted by a top executive of the Wuhan branch of the China Travel Service, who bore a striking resemblance to the American comedian Jonathan Winters, a fact it would have been meaningless to bring to his attention because not only have the mainland Chinese never heard of Jonathan, or your obedient servant, they had not—as of 1975—heard of *any* then popular American entertainers, not Bob Hope, not John Wayne, not Elvis Presley, not Marlon Brando, not Barbra Streisand. Needless to say, the Chinese after 1949 saw no American films or TV shows and heard practically no American music, though by late 1978 there had come to be a few exceptions. Personally I found it refreshing to be treated simply as a human being in China, and not as a celebrity, although I wouldn't want this idea to get around back home.

As we pulled away from the small airport, Wuhan appeared to be a bustling, crowded city with one foot in the eighteenth century, the other in the twentieth.

Jayne's father and mother—Francis J. Meadows Cotter and Ida Taylor—after a four-year engagement bid each other a temporary farewell when the young Episcopal minister went to China.

Ida's family—the Taylors and the Hollisters—were aristocrats of Scottish descent. Her mother, a Hollister, was half-Hollister, half-Williams. The Williamses, her mother's family, gave Union Square to New York City as a permanent park for the people. By Ida's

153

time, however, the family had lost its money. Of the four young sisters—all beautiful—she was the only one who elected to go to work. She became engaged to an equally poor young clergyman, Francis Cotter, and in time talked him into going into the mission field, specifically to China.

After spending a year in Hankow alone, learning the Chinese language, he made arrangements to meet his fiancée in Yokohama, Japan, to which city the beautiful young New York society woman had traveled, chaperoned by a vice-president of Standard Oil and his wife. Because of the coincidence that an Episcopal Church Mission convention was taking place in Yokohama at the time, four bishops participated in Francis and Ida's wedding ceremony. The newlyweds proceeded on to Hankow where, a year later, their first child, Frank, was born.

Shortly thereafter, while stationed at Boone University, Frank, Sr., began making plans to open a mission at Wuchang. A few years later Jayne's brother Edward was born.

The Cotters' first mission, St. Hilda's, was a very modest affair: a small building not designed for church purposes, with a few folding chairs and a tiny table altar. Eventually, when Ida was about seven months pregnant with Audrey, they returned to the United States to raise money for the long-planned St. Andrews. Ida had been bitten by a mosquito while still in China and after arriving in New York she came down with malaria. Her doctors at Columbia University announced that she was severely ill and might not survive the pregnancy.

"She must be given more quinine," the Reverend Mr. Cotter said. For some reason the doctors resisted this suggestion but finally agreed on the condition that Dr. Cotter sign a paper relieving them of any responsibility since they expected serious effects from such a large dose of the drug, with which they were not intimately familiar, malaria being rare in the U.S. Fortunately, both mother and Audrey survived. When she was able, Ida herself gave some fund-raising talks. In due course a total of $30,000 was accumulated and the family returned to Hankow.

One sees such coal-smoke pollution in all of China's industrial cities. Wuchang.

On February 7, 1923, the Chinese Communist Party led the workers of the Peking-Hankow Railway on strike. Violence escalated; life began to be more dangerous for foreigners during this period; within another three years the stream of Europeans and Americans began to flow back to their homes. The Cotters nevertheless at first remained.

Despite its heavy industry, Wuhan was the poorest-looking city we had seen. Its old buildings were in the worst state of disrepair, its electric buses most dilapidated (they are manufactured locally), and its streets most clogged with piles of sand, stone, coal, rusted metal, dirt, bricks, logs, lumber and what-have-you, all of which seemed to have been piled up for a long time. In other cities the stacks of building materials seem to have been dropped off a truck only yesterday.

The people of Wuhan, too, looked poorer, though it may have been the summer heat of the next few days which gave them such an air. Laundered clothing dries on bamboo poles in Wuhan, as it does all over China, but in that city the garments were more patched and worn. We saw there, hung out to dry or air, several cotton quilts so incredibly frayed and tattered I was surprised that even the thrifty Chinese could still find a use for them.

Waterfront structure—perhaps once a small temple. Wuchang, 1975.

Street scene, Wuchang, 1975.

One of the reasons for the success of the Chinese Communist Party in lifting the nation up by its bootstraps in so short a time has been the essential unity of the overwhelming majority of the Chinese people. In most parts of the world there is a marked difference between peasants and workers. A peasant, being a country person, is more likely to be illiterate, crushingly poor, socially backward, able to derive satisfaction from the simpler things in life so long as his basic physical needs are met. The urban worker, on the other hand, is a sharper fellow, more worldly-wise, more prosperous and generally inclined to look down at his country cousin. In China, however, the distance between peasants and city workers is short indeed. Millions of laborers in Peking, Shanghai, Tientsin, Wuhan and other urban centers wear the same poor clothes as the peasant, engage in the same back-breaking labor, eat the same food, suffer from the same discomforts of climate. There is a higher echelon of city workers whose tasks are lighter but they are still economically of the lower class, all of which now makes for more cohesiveness and unity among the people.

Our hotel—the Wuhan—situated in the heart of Hankow, appeared to be a relic of the days of British imperialism, which meant it was quite comfortable with a spacious, attractive dining room.

All large chairs and sofas in Wuhan are covered with straw-matting slipcovers during the summer months. In America this matting appears to be used only by motorists who employ portable straw-mat seats and seat-backs to avoid sticking to leather or cloth upholstery. Our beds in Wuhan, too, were covered with matting, as were the pillows. This makes for a cooler, more comfortable night's sleep than one gets from lying on a sheet in sultry weather.

Next morning we were picked up at the hotel at eight-twenty by a truly luxurious limousine called a Red Flag. Of Chinese manufacture, made in Changsun, it had two extra fold-out jump-seats in the back and a dashboard of handsome wood with the natural grain lightly varnished.

We were told that limousines of the sort are reserved for important visitors specially recognized by the state, at which I responded that Bill and I felt appropriately honored.

"The car is given special treatment on the streets," Yeh Sing-ru said. "It receives the green light, wherever it goes." Other drivers are not supposed to pass such vehicles.

Many of the autos we saw in Wuhan were Warsaws, made in Poland. Small, mostly gray, they were obviously serviceable.

License plates on Chinese cars and trucks are the same color all over the nation. The equivalent of a Zip Code at the beginning of the number tells what part of the country the vehicle is from. If the first two numbers are 29

that means the car is from the Tientsin area; 02 means the car is from Hopei Province. The license plate is not changed every year.

One of the thousand and one interesting things about Wuhan is the custom—which we did not encounter in any other large city—of drying at least some things by simply laying them out flat on the street. I do not mean that clothes are dried in this way, but we saw several streets, full from one end of the block to the other, with rush mats drying in the sun.

Wuhan has been called the Chicago of China. Having spent most of my childhood in that Midwestern American city I see the reasons for the comparison. The Chinese metropolis has the same big, tough, sleeves-rolled-up air about it that has characterized Chicago for over a century. It is no refined world capital like Peking, no quiet repository of ancient culture or power like Nanking but, like Chicago, does have extremely beautiful lakeside parks.

In the early morning, along the curbs, in such Chinese cities, it is not unusual to see men brushing their teeth. A colored tin cup is held in one hand, the brush in the other, and spitting is done into the street.

Bags of grain, bales of grass, piles of manure or baskets of tomatoes are carried about on the small wagons that are dragged through the streets by hand, the produce of old China transported in the old way. But it is surprising that this ancient method of transport is also used to haul steel pipe, fresh lumber, modern machinery and other building blocks of the China of tomorrow.

COTTON MILL NO. 1

One of our more interesting tours took us through Wuhan Cotton Mill No. 1, in the Hanyang section, where we were greeted by the mill's director, a Mr. Chao. The plant was built, he explained, in 1951. It was now equipped with over 60,000 spinners and 1,600 weaving looms. Some 8,500 workers control the machinery. The mill was not built on open land but replaced a pre-1949 munitions plant. The staff and workers are proud that Mao personally visited the plant in 1956.

Workers who are injured or fall ill are attended to in one or another of the mill's own clinics, which have a staff of over sixty. Two thousand students continue their education within the factory grounds. Before going into the mill itself we were fitted with white face masks as a protection against the cotton dust which, I should think, would pose a health problem for the workers, some of whom wore masks and some of whom did not. Bill and I visited a number of factories during our tour of China; none seemed to hum at so frenzied a pace as the giant cotton mills. Almost every available inch of space is occupied by wondrous machinery, leaving just enough room for walkways. At the beginning of the process one sees stacks of giant bales of cotton, some of which come—the reader may be surprised to learn—from the United States. The white fluff is then fed into mysterious machines and, by what magic I do not know, converted to thread. The thread is woven into cloth of various textures and thicknesses. In several of the large rooms I had to place hands over my ears since the roar was more than my auditory mechanism could tolerate. The mill, in fact, bowled us over. I cannot imagine there being a more productive operation of its kind in the world.

It is, of course, not surprising that the Chinese are so practiced at the art of making and decorating cotton cloth. To quote Professor Tseng Wu-ho Ecke in *Chinese Folk Art in American Collections, early 15th to Early 20th Centuries:*

The skill of the Chinese in producing textiles of silk and wool is proverbial. Spindle whorls dating from the 5th millennium B.C. (Pan-p'o village) have been discovered in China and impressions of cord and hemp fabric decorating pottery of the same period have also been found. These impressions indicate that the rough hemp sacks used to carry vegetables and grain have changed very little from those used in the prehistoric period. Archaeological evidence demonstrates that by the late Chou and the Han dynasties the processes of both weaving and dyeing were highly developed and sophisticated.

According to international studies on textiles, the cotton plant was first known in regions of India, Abyssinia and the Sudan. It is believed that cotton was introduced into China around the 6th century A.D., during the Sui and T'ang periods. The plant was soon grown widely, its use spread quickly, and cotton became the most common fabric in China.

Since it was now five minutes after ten a good many workers were eating their lunch but, oddly, were not sitting at tables. They strolled about with chopsticks in one hand and large bowls of rice mixed with vegetables in the other.

An Air-Raid Shelter

The mill's air-raid shelter is under Turtle Mountain, behind the plant. Walking out the back gate, one comes upon a large open field, which looks like an abandoned lot anywhere in the world, part weeds, part stagnant ponds, part random piles of junk. A worn dirt path, about three feet wide, leads through the greenery toward the base of the mountain. Walking along this lane we came across a man tending a small farm plot no larger than ten by twenty feet. A few minutes later we passed three more plots, all approximately the same size, on which soybeans and eggplant were growing. The mountain to our left seemed to have trapped all the heat of the city; the day was extremely uncomfortable. After walking through the field for about three minutes more, we suddenly came to a small paved path, about fifteen feet wide, which led immediately to an opening in the hillside about six feet wide and just high enough to accommodate Bill's and my six feet three inches.

From this point we were in a tunnel much like those in the average mine. The ground was wet with moisture from the upper mountain; the ceiling ahead arched. We were surprised to see that the curved surface overhead was paved with bricks. It was, to our profound gratitude, cool in the tunnel, which was lighted by the usual "2-watt" bulbs about every fifteen feet.

From time to time we came to cross-tunnels branching to the right or left. After a walk of about a block we reached a dead end from which the tunnel branched off right and left farther than the eye could see. Workers in the dim, moist interior seemed to be all teenage boys and girls, laughing and talking animatedly as we passed.

In a few minutes the passage became larger, wider and higher. Since the almost-invisible light bulbs were the only source of illumination this meant that they were even less equal to the task.

After walking for a surprisingly long time—what seemed to cover the equivalent of three city blocks—we were surprised to come upon a large meeting room. Long and narrow, it could accommodate, I would guess, a convention of about two hundred people. Chairs for some seventy-five were present; several were placed around a long table covered with a slightly damp wine-red cloth. The air in the meeting room was pleasantly perfumed by incense. We were told that only during the midsummer season was the humidity that bad. On the table attendants promptly placed hot cups of tea, which in the cool atmosphere sent up wispy, flame-shaped tongues of steam. It is not necessary to mention whose large portrait was on the far wall and whose framed quotations adorned the side walls.

The construction, a guide told us, had started in 1970. The shelter has six entrances and exits. Fifteen rooms have been built, including a men's room and ladies' room. Capacity to store eight tons of water is available.

Forty-five percent of the tunnel workers are women. Incredibly enough, all the workers are laymen. There are no engineers on the staff and no one involved—we were told—had previously had the slightest experience in digging tunnels.

At the next stage of construction an auditorium large enough to seat 1,700 people was to be added. A grain-storage area and kindergarten are planned, as well as canteens, stores and a printing press. The shelter is adequate—we were told—to defend against atom bombs, chemical attacks or germ warfare. Against the last two dangers the ventilation system is equipped with filtering mechanisms, though I would question their total effectiveness.

"How long could you live in the tunnel in the event of an attack on Wuhan?" I asked.

"The authorities," said our host, "believe that those fortunate enough to get into the shelter could hold out here for three months."

It was a bit more difficult to order meals in Wuhan since most of the hotel's waiters and waitresses spoke no English. For breakfast on the second day I tried to order eggs but when it became clear that the message was not getting through took out a note pad, drew a sketch of an egg, then did an imitation of a chicken, "Ba-gack! buk-buk-buk." The waiter's eyes lit up; shortly he appeared with an order of scrambled eggs.

In Wuhan we were at least spared the daily task of trying to get either orange juice—not orange soda—or orange soda—not orange juice. Neither the juice nor the soda was available in our hotel. But one asks for *chi swei,* the drink that tastes like 7-Up, which translates literally as "gas water."

WUHAN BRIDGE

The world-famous Wuhan Bridge that makes one city of three, while not as architecturally impressive as the span at Nanking, is nevertheless a masterful achievement. Almost a mile long and 230 feet high, it was built in 1957 with help from the Russians. We stopped on the bridge for a few minutes, taking advantage of the height to peer below and off into the distance to see if we could discern either the classic yellow-tile roof of St. Andrews or any other sights familiar to us from photographs taken of the neighborhood by the Reverend Cotter in his days in China. Alas, all we could see besides the mighty river was a tree-lined shore and endless miles of large brick-red tile-roofed buildings, all apparently constructed after the Cotters left the Orient. In the distance we saw the tall, smoke-belching chimneys of cotton mills, which Rewi Alley had told us in Peking he thought had replaced most old riverside structures of the 1920s and 1930s. We did not at the moment realize that these mills, built in the 1920s and 1930s, were the very ones that Dr. Cotter had known so well. They

View from bridge at Wuchang waterfront, 1975.

were situated near St. Andrews and much of Frank Cotter's ministry was directed to their workers. He took the photographs of the neighborhood and its denizens shown in this chapter.

We explained to our Wuhan hosts that later we wished to be driven to the lower ground level so that we could explore the Wuchang area carefully for clues that might lead us to the St. Andrews compound, assuming it still existed.

The Yangtze seemed as wide as the Mississippi. God, what vast armies of Chinese, and foreigners, had moved over these waterways in centuries past. Dr. Bertha L. Selmon, in her fascinating autobiographical memoir of life in China, *They Do Meet,* describes river traffic shortly after the turn of the century.

At some of the larger towns the river steamers stopped to take on passengers. A small boat would be put out from the shore in advance of the steamer's arrival. The steamer would slow down, but not stop, and a rope thrown from the small boat would be caught expertly and towed alongside. Local Chinese passengers, perhaps making their first tour into the great world, would chatter in much excitement as they were literally dragged over a rope ladder into the larger boat. The small boat then pushed off and the steamer took on full-steam ahead.

As our car neared the Hankow side of the bridge, Bill and I observed directly ahead, on a tree-rich hillside, a white Buddhist pagoda, which turned out to be the Chih Sin Tin, Tower of Seven Stars. A famous, ancient structure, it is made mostly of white marble. Naturally, Bill brought his camera to his brow and began to prepare to take a picture of the structure.

"I'm sorry," one of our guides said. "You are not permitted to take a picture here."

"Why not?" I asked.

"Because," he said, "that is a military installation."

Bill and I looked straight ahead but could see nothing but the tower and green hillside. A

The hill we were told not to photograph. Other side of bridge, Hankow, 1975.

few minutes later when we had gotten out of our car I said to Bill, "Since whatever military installation behind that tower is totally invisible from the roadbed you're committing no moral offense in taking a picture of it. Sometime during the next few days put your long lens on and take a shot anyway." Bill subsequently did so, resulting in no breach whatever in Chinese military security.

Old Days in Wuhan

As I have mentioned, Hankow was the scene of important Revolutionary activity in the 1920s; no missionary or other Western visitor in the area at that time will ever forget the drama of it all.

Chinese Communists were admitted to the Kuomintang Party after a conference in Canton, concluded on January 20, 1924. From the first it was clear that the Communist wing of the party had certain aims and purposes not shared by the more moderate faction, although both camps naturally looked forward to the day when China would be strong, free of foreign domination, orderly and prosperous.

In late 1926 Chiang Kai-shek's antiwarlord Kuomintang army advanced into Wuhan. In a speech announcing his triumph Chiang said, "Only after imperialism was overthrown did China obtain her independence. . . . The Third International is the headquarters of the world revolution . . . we must unite with Russia to overthrow imperialism . . . the Chinese Revolution is part of the World Revolution . . . we must unite all partisans of world revolution to overthrow imperialism."

In that year, however, the fundamental

Opposite above and opposite below

Behind St. Andrews. A typical street scene, Wuchang, the late 1920s.

View from the Cotter home, Wuchang, c. 1925. It looks remarkably the same today.

Typical city gate of old China, c. 1925.

Christian church, now a storage room, Wuchang, 1975.

Cotton mill workers in winter garb, Wuchang, 1920s.

Detail of the beautiful upturned roof corners copied from the Chinese imperial architectural style. St. Andrews, Wuchang.

The Yangtze River at Wuchang. Hankow is visible in the distance. About 1930.

The ancient river junk, Wuchang, c. 1930. Such boats still transport much of China's freight.

Jayne's mother and father with staff. St. Andrews, Wuchang, c. 1925.

disagreement between the Left and Right Kuomintang divisions erupted into military confrontation. Four graduates of the Whampoa Military Academy, fearing the growing strength of the Left, had organized an anti-Communist faction. The four were Li Chi-cheng, Li Tsung-jen, Chu Peh-teh and Ho Ying-chin. Chiang Kai-shek, then head of the Central Military Academy, at first did not take sides in the controversy. He had spent some time in Russia in 1924, which caused certain conservative business groups, including Europeans, to suspect him of pro-Red sympathies. Members of Jayne's family report that it was not uncommon in missionary circles in China at that time to suspect that Chiang himself was a Communist. In fact, however, he was disappointed by much of what he saw in Russia. In 1926, responding to pressure by his strongly anti-Communist fellow officers, Chiang issued a statement that, though he intended to support firmly Dr. Sun's three Revolutionary principles, he would nevertheless cut off connections with the Communists.

Given Chiang's personal background, his choice, at this moment of decision, was inevitable. The social climate from which he emerged was conservative, industrial Chekiang Province and he had been singled out early by certain older members of the commercial and banking element as worth encouraging. Also, he was under the influence of a powerful man named Chang Chiang-hiang. Although he was strongly anti-Manchu and pro-Sun Yat-sen, Chang's massive wealth naturally made him look with small favor on the economic aspects of the Communist philosophy.

Jayne's father was in the area at the time. The following quotation is from his journal:

When asked regarding the outlook of things politically, in relation to the mission and its work, I suggested that as we were not wanted, and the Chinese desired to run their own show, it would be much wiser and better all round for us to clear out and allow them to do so. To expect the Home Church to support an educational policy that would be predominantly non-Christian and opposed to all Western influence, and meet the added costs with restricted scope, would be as unfair as it would be unwise. . . . The Church could not, in the light of political events, the temper of the Chinese, and *the policy of the Kuomintang . . . be expected to support a tendency that was not only Communist but anti-foreign as well as anti-Christian.* [Italics added.]

The events of the summer of 1926 involved Jayne's family directly. The Kuomintang, starting its antiwarlord drive north from Canton under Chiang Kai-shek and other leaders, had by the end of the summer pushed through Hunan and reached Wuchang, on the first of September. At that time Wuhan was under the control of warlord Wu Pei-fu, one of the main powers in the Northern government. Though he was allied with General Chang Tso-lin, his army had been badly defeated in late August by Chiang, at a point some forty-five miles southwest of Wuchang. A good part of the beaten Northern army retreated across the Yangtze to Hankow and Hanyang but a portion of it fell back into Wuchang, unable to cross the river. That contingent was besieged in Wuchang for forty days.

Some of its soldiers, seeing the St. Andrews compound, holed up in its buildings where, their presence having become detected, they were brought under bombardment. One projectile crashed through the family's roof and the second story and landed, unexploded, on the Cotters' dining room table. When the family returned a few weeks thereafter the adults were dismayed by the destruction, while the children gleefully pried bullets out of the walls and spat down on the large shell through the hole in the ceiling of the dining room.

Bullets had also gone through a large painting of the Last Supper and, according to Cotter family recollection, destroyed only the image of Judas Iscariot.

Chiang Kai-shek is said to have personally called off the shelling when he saw the great beauty of the buildings of St. Andrews.

During the early part of September Wu Pei-fu maintained control of Hankow and the railroad north. It was during that period that the Cotters and other Westerners came down from Chikung-shan, in the mountains, to Hankow in a converted coal car, while the Northern forces still held Hankow. By the end of September Chiang and his armies had crossed the river and taken Hankow; Wu's armies had retreated up the railroad toward the north. The city formally surrendered to Chiang's Southern army on October 10, 1926.

Because one strong component of Revolutionary propaganda was anti-imperialist sentiment, foreigners were threatened at this time and hundreds of missionaries fled to eastern cities, mostly Shanghai.

Wang Ching-wei, a leader sympathetic to the Communists, headed for Hankow, accompanied by a number of Russian and American Communist advisers. After the three cities were captured the leftists, students and other radical elements of the city staged a highly emotional celebration of what was supposedly a permanent victory over the forces of imperialism and reaction. Thousands of mine, factory and mill workers quit their jobs and took part in public demonstrations and parades. Many poor peasants from Hunan Province, already sympathetic to the Communists, came to the city to take part in the celebration. In the general confusion more missionaries were threatened and the British concession was overrun. British Consul-General O'Malley instructed all British subjects to take refuge on British ships in the harbor while he conducted negotiations with the leftist foreign minister Eugene Chen, a half-black who spoke no Chinese.

Missionary Life in the 1920s and 1930s

The Reverend Cotter's assessment of the situation in early 1927 is consistent with reports from other sources. His next observation will fall sadly on Christian ears:

From what I have seen in my few years here, we have produced no leaders. And even if we had, our peculiar contribution would be Christian and spiritual, not educational and political. The spiritual and not the educational should dictate our mission activity.

It is clear that the Americans and Western Europeans were aware of many, if not all, particulars of the peasant uprising then occurring.

Allen [a friend] reported the division of property of the large landowners, and consequent loss of life if any remonstrance was made.

Small landowners had come to blows with the Communistic element already and his impression was that it would continue.

Jayne's mother recalled:

At that time there was great unrest and antiforeign feeling in the area. The Communists were becoming quite powerful. One day I had to take Frank [Jayne's oldest brother, now a judge of the Superior Court in Los Angeles] over to Hankow to the dentist but Dad Cotter was afraid to have me go.

I said I thought it would be perfectly all right so we went over on the mill launch. When we came back later in the day the riverbank was just black with people, it was so crowded. Little Frank was afraid. He was frightened to death to go through them. I said, "Now Frank, don't be afraid. No matter what they say to us take it as a joke." So we started to get off the launch and someone said, "You cannot go through unless you pay!" So I said, "Wo sa tu men, ni bau *wo* chy'en." I went right through the crowd saying, "I'm a very poor woman; you give *me* money." Well, they laughed, the whole crowd on that riverbank! In just *peals* of laughter we went right straight through the crowd. We had to walk about a city block to get to the road. There were steps that went from the riverbank up to the street and we got rickshaws and hurried home. As soon as I got inside the gate of the compound I became hysterical. I cried and cried.

Looking back from the present vantage point of history it is possible to judge that the Communist and other leftist elements in the Kuomintang were not organizationally prepared to wield the power that fell into their hands in Hankow. Different points of view among leftist leaders emerged. Wang Ching-wei began to distrust his colleagues and Chen Tu-hsiu, according to a later analysis by Mao Tse-tung, compromised on the question of land reform. Mao was also critical, in this connection, of the Russian adviser Borodin, and Comintern delegate Roy, a native of India.

With the Left divided, the victory of Chiang Kai-shek and his more moderate Nanking faction became inevitable.

A fascinating sidelight on this chapter of Chinese history is suggested by John B. Powell in *My 25 Years in China:*

Another unexpected element in the situation was that the collapse of the radical Hankow Government had serious repercussions in Moscow and contributed considerably to the collapse of Trotsky and other advocates of world revolution. Stalin and his group seized upon the failure of the China adventure, which had cost the Soviets large sums of money and great effort, to discredit Trotsky and the whole group of advocates of "permanent world revolution." Borodin returned by a tortuous overland trip to Moscow in disgrace and became editor of the four-page English-language *Moscow Daily News.*

Sun Fo, son of Dr. Sun Yat-sen, who participated in the Hankow Government, but later withdrew, also confirmed Mao's statements, particularly the reference to the "dictatorial attitude of the Russians." Chen Kung-po, an American returned student and graduate of Columbia University, New York, who had specialized in economics and had served as secretary to Wang Ching-wei, wrote a series of articles (published in *China Weekly Review* shortly after the collapse of the Hankow Government) in which he analyzed the cause of the collapse of the Hankow Red regime. He concluded by advocating a system of state capitalism and state ownership of industries as a means of surmounting the complications which develop when privately owned industrial establishments suspend operations and throw laborers back on the Government for support. Chen argued that only through the development of state capitalism could the Chinese Government hope to cope with powerful foreign interests established in the country, which in times of crisis usually are able to marshal the support of the large native Chinese industrial and banking interest in opposition to socialistic experiments. Chen Kung-po, formerly a political associate of Wang Ching-wei, later became head of the Japanese puppet Government at Nanking, following the death of Wang Ching-wei in Tokyo in 1944. Chen Kung-po was the only Chinese student, educated in the United States, who voluntarily joined the Nanking puppet.

In January, 1976, I received an informative letter from Mrs. J. Van Wie Bergamini, who with her husband, an architect, had served in China during the 1920s and 1930s and who knew Jayne's family intimately. Mr. Bergamini designed the Cotters' summer home, at Chikung-shan; he and his family lived next door to the Cotters. Mrs. Bergamini's letter provides a vivid description of events in the troubled summer of 1926:

I am now in my 83rd year and the events of 1926 are not as clear as I would like them to be. As nearly as I can remember we spent that summer up in our summer house in Chikung-shan in Honan Province, situated about half way between Peking and Hankow. This railway starts in Peking—the terminus is in Hankow—and was known as the Peking-Hankow Railway. Mrs. Frank Cotter, and the children, had gone up to this mountain retreat at about the same time as we had. Our houses were next to each other in a somewhat isolated part of the summer community. Frank Cotter, Sr. and Van Wie Bergamini remained in Wuchang, carrying on their work there, as was customary in the summers, with occasional weekend trips to join their families in the mountains.

The journey from Wuchang meant a mile or so walk to the river, a ferry or sampan across to Hankow and then a rickshaw ride to the railway station. Then it was a seven-hour train journey. On arriving at the small station—the name of which I have forgotten—they would either walk up the mountain or take a sedan chair, carried by four coolies. It was a climb of about 2,500 feet along a narrow, uneven path which went through a small village, at the foot of the mountain. Usually the train was a night train and one arrived up on the hill in the early morning hours. In 1926 the struggle was going on between the Kuomintang forces and those of Warlord Chang Tso-lin. When Frank and Van realized what was happening, and that the city of Wuchang was coming under siege by the Southern forces, they managed to get out of the city by having someone lower them over the wall, and got up to Chikung-shan, the idea being to get their families out before they would possibly be cut off.

Ida Cotter was most anxious to get young Frank off to the Kuling American School and this involved quite a journey down the Yangtze.

In spite of Frank, Sr.'s protests she insisted that they go, which they did. Van offered to help her close the house and pack, but she would not let him help, knowing that he had to take care of his own family and house. We then proceeded to pack and secure the houses by putting shutters up on all the windows, as we did every autumn when we were leaving. Packing all the necessary belongings to take with them, all started down the mountain in sedan chairs, with cooks, amahs, and the coolies carrying the baggage on their *biendangs* (carrying poles) at a very early hour in the morning.

I cannot remember how long we had to wait at the little station but we did not leave until the next day and the train was there all night. Van selected the coal car as being the "cleanest," as far as possible—typhus, cholera, or other infectious germs were frequently carried by the troops. The servant went and bought Chinese brooms (very different from an American broom) in the village, and swept some of the coal dust out of the car. We had taken down a wicker armchair and a camp cot with us, the former for me as I was seven months pregnant, and the cot for the children.

Ida came down with a severe headache and was prostrated, so we insisted she rest on the cot. She was unable to eat the whole journey, as I remember. I sat up all night in the chair with the five children. Ida had brought along a large bottle of rubbing alcohol and a package of cotton wool, with which we tried to keep the children's hands swabbed off whenever they were going to eat anything. There were no doors to the car, or if there were we did not close them as we had to have air. We had bought sticks of joss (incense) in the village and we kept these burning all night to protect the children from the hordes of mosquitoes as we tried to sleep in the stationary train. We also used fans for this purpose. I remember that I did not sleep at all, but the children slept fairly well.

The two amahs were in the car with us, the two (or perhaps more) Chinese manservants were elsewhere on the train. It was very hot and we only had the water we took with us.

Van was terribly tired and sleepy after the strenuous trip up there and the job of packing up and closing the house. Little Edward was possessed to get out of our car on to the tracks and to go and try to find soldiers who would give him some "bullets."

Mrs. Cotter recalls the same incident slightly differently:

We'd been riding for hours and hours. Little Edward got off to get some water so we could wash our hands (he was about six at the time), and all the men—when the train started, as if it was going to leave—hurried with their pails of water, but little Edward was afraid he'd spill his so he was walking slowly. I screamed at him to hurry because if the train had gone he would have been left in that country all by himself, and we probably would never have found him again. A man reached out just as the train was starting, picked Edward up and got him on the train.

Mrs. Bergamini concludes:

When we finally got under way, some time the following day, Van took a long bamboo pole and when any child got near the door opening he would prod them to warn them away, lest they fall out of the train. Poor Ida was still hors de combat. It was all a very harrowing experience as I remember it. I think the journey took some 38 hours, counting the long time we waited for the train to leave. The soldiers on the train were Northerners going down to help bolster the defense of Hankow and, as I remember it, there were no other foreigners on the train, most of them having left Chikung-shan earlier in September or at the end of August. We were not fired upon. We had been extremely short of food all the summer—almost no meat at all except an occasional scrawny chicken, and the few canned goods that we had taken up there with us. We were unable to get back to our homes in Wuchang across the river as the siege was not yet lifted, so we went to stay in the Mission compound in Hankow. A large British gunboat was docked so near to the house that one could

Mrs. Ida Taylor Cotter and son Frank, now a judge of the U.S. Circuit Court in Los Angeles, being carried up a mountainside, late 1920s.

hear the ship's bell chime the hours. I remember that it gave me a comfortable feeling.

I do not know where the Cotter family went then as I did not see them again—

The Cotters, as it happens, returned to St. Andrews at this time, though fighting was still raging in the city. Not long thereafter, Ida Cotter remembers:

We got word from the official in charge of Americans that we must leave the Wuchang area that night, before daybreak, cross the Yangtse and get to Hankow. Our instructions were to leave at the earliest possible moment and to take nothing with us. So we did. We walked out, on all my wedding presents, all my family pictures. We left everything behind, just walked out and crossed the Yangtse River in a sampan that night. They took us in at some British missions, across the river.

We may have spent several nights there until we were able to get passage on a river boat. It held normally only twenty but there were 200 of us on board. The men all slept on the floor or deck. We traveled all the way down the Yangtse to Shanghai on the boat, which took several days. Shanghai was then very crowded, people of all nationalities flooding in from all over.

One night we decided to go out to a restaurant for dinner and when we got to the place we noticed that hanging on hooks all over the wall were the hats of the troops of different nations who had come to defend the foreign concessions in Shanghai.

Mrs. Bergamini describes more of the scene back in Wuhan:

I went in to the Roman Catholic Hospital where the Communists made the hospital staff go out on strike, but the cook got over the wall at night and came to bake bread for the Sisters. Chinese were marching around the hospital shouting "Kill all the foreigners!" My son was born on November 17th and three weeks later we sailed across the Yangtze, four Chinese and five Americans—Van, I and three children—of whom Van and I were the only ones who

could swim. It was the most frightening experience of my life because the water was rough and the large sampan with its big ragged sail keeled so far over on the flooded river waves.

Unfortunately some years later, in 1939, my diaries were lost, with everything else that we had accumulated during 25 years of married life in China, when we had to leave, bringing almost nothing out.

One of the "handbooks" on the missions of the Episcopal Church in China, published in 1932 by the National Council of the Protestant Episcopal Church in New York, refers to my father-in-law's work:

At Wuchang in 1923 the new chapel of St. Hilda's School was consecrated and the result of the enthusiasm of the Reverend F. J. M. Cotter was seen in the erection of St. Andrews Church, parish house, and school as the only Christian center in the midst of the thousands of millhands in a congested quarter of the city.

A notable event in the year 1922 was the sending of a deputation of the mission's best workers, at the request of the Christian General Feng Yu-hsiang, to conduct special services and instruction for two weeks at the General's camp in Honan, and later in Peking.

A few pages later the writer paints a quick picture of the effect in the Wuchang area of the political and military turmoil of the late 1920s:

The Church General Hospital in Wuchang was able to carry on throughout all the troubled period of the years following 1926. It was a great blessing to the city of Wuchang that this agency of the church was thus able to continue its beneficent ministration to the sick and suffering of that city, particularly during the forty days siege in 1926. During that period, with bombs bursting overhead and with such diminishing supplies that the staff was compelled to live on two scant meals a day, the American and Chinese staff courageously carried on their work. Night after night they seized what sleep they could get on the benches of the chapel, that being the part of the hospital safest from bombs.

Another indication of the scope of Christian missionary activity in the Wuhan area is given

St. Andrews Church, Wuchang, under construction in the early 1920s. It now serves as a school.

in the following comment from the same source.

In the cities of Wuchang and Hankow there are the Poor Relief Committees, under missionary auspices, which provide clothing and food in the winter to some of the desperately poor. A rickshaw coolie shelter, where hundreds of shivering men in rags may come out of the snow and sleet for warmth and hot tea, is another evidence of the interest the Christian Church has in the physical needs of mankind. A notable work is the shelter and bath house at St. Michael's Church, Wuchang, under the Reverend Robert E. Wood, which not only provides relief for men in the daytime but accommodates a few of them at night.

During the winter of 1931–1932 great suffering occurred in central China as a result of the flood in the summer of 1931. The following letter from the Reverend Y. C. Yang of St.

Andrews Church gives a vivid picture of the nature of this calamity and the way mission workers helped face it.

On the night of August 19, the Ch'in San dyke gave way to the mighty flood and our compound, which was already filled with refugees—473 of them, together with their belongings—soon found itself five feet and four inches under water, but the houses on the San Lake behind us were completely submerged. So Mr. Wang Yuen-san and Mr. Chang Hsi-san, both members of this church, and Miss Liu Chu-yin, our girl teacher and myself, besides doing our hasty jobs in water of keeping order in our compound, had to get into our newly made small boat and put out on the lake as quickly as possible to pick up those people who had crept to their housetops and were crying aloud for help. We thus saved two hundred and ten lives that night.

During the time the floodwaters were sub-

Street scene outside the Cotter compound, Wuchang, the 1920s.

siding, the Boone University campus in Wuchang took care of more than 2,000 refugees, 227 of them sleeping in the school chapel for several weeks.

The Flood Relief work gave all our workers more than enough to do. The Government undertook relief work but, as in the past, the Christians led the way in relief measures. Bishop Roots was made a member of the National Relief Committee and was in charge of much of the relief work in the great camps of 400,000 refugees outside Hankow and Wuchang. Our workers assisted in the active distribution of rice and blankets to a vast company.

The same Bishop Roots later recalled frequent friendly chats with a young Communist eager to know what Westerners thought of the tumultuous proceedings of the time. The young man's name: Chou En-lai. The two would sit on Roots's front porch and talk for hours about the meaning of life, the future of China and related subjects.

Knowing of the dramatic chapter of modern Chinese history through which the Cotter family had lived, and for personal reasons as well, Bill and I were eager to find their old church and home, if they were still findable. Setting aside a morning for the purpose we searched the waterfront area of Wuchang for about two and a half hours. Time and again we asked the driver to turn this way, now that, got out and explored certain alleys and byways on foot, but to no avail. I pointed out, during the morning, perhaps a dozen people so old that they might have lived in the area in the late 1920s and 1930s. Yeh Sing-ru questioned each but all said they had in the old days lived elsewhere, some just across the river in Hankow, others in more distant places.

The Cotter family in China, shortly before leaving for America. (Left to right) *Edward, the Reverend Francis Cotter, Jayne, Mrs. Ida Taylor Cotter, Audrey, Frank.*

THE COTTERS' OLD CHURCH AND HOME

We drove a couple of blocks farther, away from the bridge, along the waterfront. Suddenly, over the top of the riverside wall, which was about six feet high, Bill noticed what appeared to be a small, extremely ancient structure with three separate round roofs in the old pagoda style. Because I thought Jayne's family might remember it, I asked Bill to photograph it.

Its pillars and railings were of an odd, man-made marblelike stone we had not seen before. On the untended ground outside the structure, in deep weeds, were several old large jugs and pots, three or four feet high. Between the little gazebo and the river was a small roundhouse which, to judge by its visible electrical connections, had something to do with power supply. Yeh Sing-ru was able to make out on the

crumbling surface of the small building a warning, apparently to shipmasters, not to dock within a certain distance of the area, perhaps because pipes or cables entered the river at that point.

On the opposite side of the street we discovered the exterior of what appeared to be an old Christian church, although it was now totally surrounded by industrial construction as part of a giant complex called Cotton Mill No. 6, the central building of which features a large clock tower. An official at the front gate was kind enough to permit us to enter. The old buildings of the mill—which appear to have been built no later than the early 1930s—architecturally resembled the church we had just seen, although we did not know the significance of this fact.

The main building of the mill is a truly imposing edifice in the old British architectural style. After photographing it, we returned again to the road along the waterfront, walked once more to the right, and approached an extremely high smokestack belching out the thickest, blackest clouds we had ever seen.

Suddenly, as we passed a wall with an open gate, we saw several large, covered antiaircraft guns. Next door a touchy middle-aged woman refused our party entrance to what she described as "the exit of the cotton mill." She said if we wanted to go into the mill we must enter at the front. The attendant at the main gate lacked authority to permit us to enter the plant so he sent for two officials who, it turned out, could not have been more cordial. We explained to them the primary reason for our visit, at which they smiled warmly.

As we strolled about the plant the first ancient object we discovered was a tall water tower, which they told us was sixty-two years old. The offensive chimney was, they explained, part of a nearby printing-and-dyeing factory.

Exploring back streets and alleyways near the mills we suddenly came upon an old Catholic church—St. Michaels?—of sturdy brick construction. It was impossible to find the cornerstone because a small shed had been added

to the front of the church. It was strange to see the interior, still structurally in good condition, filled with thousands of gunnysacks of grain. The windows were narrow, high and arched, stained glass at the very top, although the panels were merely colored, not pictorial. The choir loft is still intact. This was not St. Andrews, however, so we pressed on.

Each time we would stop the car to ask questions a curious crowd would form, of the sort that gathers in America to view the results of an auto accident. Spying what looked like the outline of an old church, we stopped at one point, entered a small side street, and found a large open dirt lot which turned out to be a garbage dump. A number of old women, sad to say, were picking through the waste papers and other trash to see what was worth saving and reusing.

Driving farther along Chi Yu Chiao Street, we suddenly saw, over a wall on the right side, the quick flash of an old imperial yellow-tile roof. With our hearts beating with excitement, we asked the driver to stop the car, got out and walked back. A middle-aged woman permitted us to enter through the street wall. The sense of anticipation was tremendous because

Our first glimpse of St. Andrews, Wuchang, 1975.

The Reverend Francis Cotter with Boone University athletic team, Wuhan, 1918.

the church looked exactly like the five-foot model of St. Andrews that we have in our home. The first thing Bill noticed was that the pointed corners of the roof were broken off, just like those on the model. In an instant I knew our search was over! We began to take pictures and make observations. At the side of the church there was a sunken courtyard, about four feet deep. At one end of the building we discovered a couple of old exercise parallel bars.

Jayne later told me these had been installed by her father who was, as it happens, an athlete. He may, in fact, have been the first to teach American football and baseball to the Chinese. It was his custom to pitch in the annual tournaments involving missionary personnel from various parts of China.

We were told by the attendant that the church is now used as a school but that because the students were on vacation the premises were locked.

Bill pointed out that the old wide side door to the church, at the head of the stone steps, was no longer there. I showed him that the upper decorations over what had once been the doorway still remained but that bricks and newer windows had been added to the structure, probably at the time it was converted to a school. Fortunately, just as we were preparing to leave, another woman showed up with a key and we were permitted into the interior.

The old walls and floors were deep in dust and grime. A six-foot black-and-white portrait of Mao adorned a wall which had been added to the church, cutting directly across the nave from left to right. Marxist slogans were printed on wall posters.

Two pairs of old wooden tables had been shoved end to end, long ago painted dark green, to serve for Ping-Pong games. The large whitewashed pillars that supported the roof were still in sturdy condition. Through a crack in a doorway I could see that the two adjacent rooms were classrooms.

Members of the Episcopal Church will naturally be saddened that the Reverend Cotter's old parish buildings are now used to teach Marxism, but at least young Chinese are still being educated in traditional subjects within the old walls and taught ethical principles. Somehow this seems preferable to having the building serve as a grain-storage shed.

When Bill and I returned to the hotel we immediately sent Jayne a cablegram telling her we had succeeded in finding her original home and her father's church. The delivery man in Los Angeles handed her the message just as she was stepping into her car to drive to the Mark Taper theater, to appear in *Once in a Lifetime.* "I don't know what the man must have thought of me," she later said. "First I screamed 'They found it, they found it!' Then I burst into tears."

CENTRAL PEASANTS' MOVEMENT INSTITUTE

Before visiting Wuchang's historically important Central Peasants' Movement Institute we were taken to one of Mao's early dwellings, at Tu Fu Ti street, number 41, where, it is said, the chairman's now-famous *Report on the Peasant Movement in Hunan Province* was written. In the various austere rooms are displayed Mao's simple furniture, the desk at which it is said the report was composed, a large covered bed and various personal effects.

The young lady who told us of the building's history spoke in the by-now familiar hushed,

St. Andrews, Wuchang, 1975.

Interior of St. Andrews. Mao, not Christ, was exhibited in 1975. Wuchang.

St. Andrews. Only the bar of the cross removed. Wuchang, 1975.

reverential tones. On one wall was a photograph of Mao's first wife, Yung Kai-wei, killed by the Kuomintang in the slaughter of 1929. In another photograph the visitor sees one of Mao's sons, later killed in the Korean War at the age of twenty-eight. In all six members of Mao's family were sacrificed in the Revolution!

After leaving the house, we strolled two short blocks to the institute, accompanied by small children, chickens and ducks. I smiled and waved to other children watching from doorways. Each shyly grinned and waved back. They reminded me of American slum children of the 1930s, when slums were not quite the jungles they are now. Something about the combination of the children's clothing, the summer heat, the strange smells, made Wuhan seem the earthiest city we had yet visited.

A large plaque on the front wall of the institute compound carried a quotation by Chou En-lai. Incredibly, it was the first we had encountered, in several weeks in China!

Although the Cotters, who had lived not far away, were aware of its existence, they probably did not perceive the historical importance of this institute which in the 1920s was a training ground for revolution, run jointly by both the Kuomintang and the Communist Party. This, of course, was before Chiang Kai-shek had decided he could not continue to collaborate with the Communists.

Ida relates a fascinating story of getting on the Hankow-to-Wuchang launch one day, late in the afternoon and then having to sit there, for hours, because the ferry did not move. She was alone, Dr. Cotter at home ill with dysentery, and as darkness fell the American woman became alarmed.

"Why is the launch not moving?" she demanded of a crew leader.

"We must wait for some important men," he said.

Ida knew that she would have to walk alone through the dark streets of Wuchang when she did make the crossing, though foreigners were warned not to do so, anti-Western feeling running high at the time.

Finally, about eight o'clock, a group of men

Children of Wuchang, summer, 1975.

suddenly boarded and the launch pushed off. After a few minutes Ida recognized the newcomers as Communist leaders from the Peasants' Movement Institute.

Not knowing she could speak Chinese, they began to speculate about her.

"I wonder what the foreigner woman is doing out alone after dark," one said.

"Gentlemen," she said, approaching them, "I did not wish to be alone at night but the launch would not leave until you arrived. My husband is ill and he must now also be very worried because I have been delayed. My children, too, must be alarmed."

"Do not worry," one of the men said, speaking in a reassuring tone. "We will see you safely to your door."

And, as good as their word, a group of them accompanied the frightened but always courageous woman to St. Andrews. When she arrived the gateman's eyes grew wide with fear as he recognized her escorts. She thanked her new companions, entered the house and fainted dead away.

The young peasants, workers and students who attended the institute received both political and military training. We saw the old classrooms, living quarters, bunks, stacked rifles, bookshelves, a clinic. Beside the sweet voice of the pretty young lady conducting our tour we could hear the electric drone of cicadas and smell the warm, friendly aroma from a nearby brewery.

An enormous oil painting at the back of a large lecture hall shows Mao, in the long dark gown of the Chinese teacher, addressing young peasants and workers in that very room.

Would history ever accurately record, I wondered, the names of all the young men trained at the institute who later played roles, either important or unsung, in the Chinese Revolution?

The following Easter, antiforeign emotion was once again intense. Local leftist officials sent word that no public religious services were to be conducted. "I am sorry," Dr. Cotter said, "but I must do my duty to my parishioners."

"Then any who take part," he was told, "will run the risk of being beheaded. The peo-

Central Peasants' Movement Institute, Wuchang, July, 1975.

ple are very angry at the foreigners!"

Dr. Cotter reported all of this to a group of his converts and students. "Please spread the word," he said. "I will conduct services. But I will understand if no one attends."

At the appointed time on Easter morning people began filing in from all directions and the largest crowd ever to attend the church witnessed the services. Though Jayne's father was himself suffering from malaria at the moment, his heart was overjoyed.

On the way back to our hotel in Hankow we had casually discussed the subject of religion. Yeh Sing-ru wanted to know whether I was a Christian.

"I am an ethical Christian," I said, "although like many Christians who have been reasonably well educated I have reservations about literalist interpretations of Scripture, such as the theory that the world began just a few thousand years ago, that a man named Jonah actually survived being swallowed by a whale and that sort of thing."

"Do you think there is a God?" she asked.

"Actually," I said, "as regards the question of the existence of God—which is the fundamental question—it has long seemed to me that of the only two possible alternatives both are preposterous. Either there is a God, which because of a vast amount of unjust suffering it can be argued is an absurd assumption, or there is none and the world created itself. Of these two peculiar assumptions, however, it

seems to me that the latter is somewhat more difficult to believe."

Bill, knowing that communism is officially atheistic, asked, "Who do *you* believe made the world?"

"The masses created the world," Yeh Sing-ru said.

"But," Bill said, "the world existed for millions of years before any kind of man, much less the masses, existed."

Yeh Sing-ru did not answer. To relieve her discomfort I said, "What Yeh Sing-ru means, Bill, is that the masses created the modern world."

Children of the Grasslands

That evening our friend the Chinese Jonathan Winters took our party to a large open-air theater where, to our dismay, we learned that the second part of the show would consist of *Children of the Grasslands.* I leaned over to Yeh Sing-ru. "There's a bit of a problem," I whispered, "in that Bill and I have already seen *Children of the Grasslands* twice before. Although we enjoyed it I don't believe we would care to sit through another production of it."

"I see," she said, after which she conferred in Chinese with our local guide.

There was no translation of the guide's comment but his brow darkened perceptibly. The first portion of the program consisted of the usual excellent singing, dancing and acrobatics one sees in Chinese theaters. But about an hour later we began to hear the by-now quite familiar strains of the music of *Children of the Grasslands.*

"Could we leave now?" I whispered to Yeh Sing-ru.

"I'm afraid," she said, "that it would not look right because we are sitting here in the front and everyone would see us leave. They would think that we did not like the program."

"But," I persisted, "we could duck low and slip off to the side here, couldn't we, rather than walking back through the audience? I really would prefer not to sit through the same presentation again."

"I am sorry," Yeh Sing-ru said, "I don't know what we can do."

I put my head in my hands and fell partially asleep until *Children of the Grasslands* had run its course.

For the rest of our visit in Wuhan our local guide was no longer as affable as he had been. Perhaps Yeh Sing-ru had neglected to emphasize that we had seen *Grasslands* twice before. Or, inasmuch as the Chinese themselves must have seen the same few Chiang Ching operas again and again, perhaps he thought that if he could sit through one of them three hundred times I had no right to complain about having to do so only three times. I am sure that among those most grateful for the eventual overthrow of Mao's widow and the Gang of Four must have been the army of patient China Travel Service guides who had been obliged to witness so many performances of the same small number of Revolutionary dramas.

The next day, as we were driving through the streets, I said, "Yeh Sing-ru, what percentage of the young men who danced in the show we saw last night would you say were homosexuals?"

I had already concluded that there were very few homosexuals in China, but one of the dancers in the show had been decidedly effeminate, and one would have reason to question the masculinity of a couple of the others.

For a moment she simply stared at me as if I had used a word in the Martian language.

"Do you know what the English word *homosexual* means?" I asked.

"Yes."

"Well, then," I said, "what percentage of the dancers in the show would you guess are homosexuals?"

"There is no homosexual problem in China."

"I did not mean to suggest that the phenomenon had reached the proportions of a national problem," I said. "I was merely trying to find out about a particular group of young men."

"Well," she repeated, "there *is* no such problem in China."

"Does that mean," I said, "that out of the eight hundred million people in China there is not a single homosexual?"

She smiled. "That I cannot guarantee. It is social conditions that cause homosexuality," she said.

"You're quite right," I said, "if by social conditions you mean childhood experiences. But let me approach the problem from another direction. Before Liberation were there any homosexuals in China?" (There were many, of course.)

"Oh, yes," she said. "Before Liberation many people were disillusioned with society. This caused them to become homosexuals."

Out of politeness I did not respond that there was no authority on the subject who would agree. Nor did I inquire what had happened to the millions of homosexuals of pre-1949 China. Reforming prostitutes and drug addicts is one thing—and a thing of which the Maoists may rightly boast—but altering sexual patterns, which are not primarily caused by economic factors, is quite another matter. I assume that two things explain the present low incidence of mainland Chinese homosexuality: the death of many pre-1949 homosexuals and improvement in the family and other social factors presumably responsible for the condition.

EAST LAKE

For lunch we were driven to a lovely waterside park called the East Lake Scenic Spot. An interesting drink served with the meal was called Shandy, which the Chinese believe is an English rather than American word. It consists of half-beer and either 7-Up or orange pop. When our waitress in the restaurant in Nanking had started to add orange soda to our beer I had thought she was simply making a mistake. One must keep an open mind when learning about foreign customs since the moment of observation is inevitably colored by the observer's past conditioning and expectations.

What would you think of putting sliced tomatoes and cucumbers together and then sprinkling them with sugar?

It would taste terrible, right?

Wrong. We were served such a salad in the dining room of the East Lake Scenic Spot Pavilion; it was delicious.

For what reason we never learned, foods in Wuhan are served on tiny plates smaller than tea saucers. The only possible effect of this custom that I can imagine is that it makes more work for local laundries, in removing the stains from whatever inevitably spills off the edges of such little dishes.

The food served at this restaurant in Hankow, however, was the best we had found in China. We were also glad to discover that we were back in the land of absorbent napkins.

While waiting in the lounge of the East Lake Pavilion, after lunch, we met a group of about a dozen young people from West Germany—some students, some doctors, teachers. One was a policeman. Physically there was nothing to distinguish them from young Americans from any college campus. They wore the same assortment of Levi's, sports shirts with epaulets, summer shorts and T-shirts.

A Wuhan Hospital

In the company of some other German visitors we next visited the Wuhan No. 2 Hospital, affiliated with Wuhan Medical College, where we were greeted by a Dr. Guo, chief of the internal medicine department.

In the main building, constructed in 1954, the corridors have incredibly dim light bulbs so that even at midmorning on a sunny day the atmosphere was sepulchral. We passed through a clinic waiting room which looked much like those anywhere in the world. In a long, narrow room nearby, about twenty patients were lying on straw-mat cots. One woman had been hospitalized for treatment of a prolapsed uterus caused—it was said—by an abortion. Before electric acupuncture treatment, we were told, it had been very difficult for her to walk.

In the next bed a patient was suffering from a thrombosis of the blood vessels of the brain. When the man had first been admitted he could scarcely speak. He was now able to walk and talk. The woman doctor asked the man to sit up, which he did quickly and alertly, putting on his bedroom slippers. He smiled broadly, walked about the room a bit and raised his arms over his head, seemingly in good condition indeed.

He wished to show us how strongly he could grip, to demonstrate the strength in his arms. I put my hands in his. He gripped them very tightly, then showed us how he could button his shirt. The delicacy of this task made it difficult but he was able to manage it.

About 90 percent of the patients in this category, we were told, can be greatly helped by Chinese methods of treatment.

We next were shown a young man, apparently in his early twenties, who had suffered traumatic paralysis of the right arm caused by an injury sustained where he worked. Another patient, middle-aged, suffered from myelitis. Several needles were stuck in his upper arm and forearm.

At a nearby table a doctor was administering ampules containing concentrates of traditional Chinese medicines. One held ginseng extract.

"With this extract," the doctor said, "we can treat liver disease."

Another ampule contained what was identified as "musk," said to be good in treating rheumatic pains and ailments of the central nervous system. We were shown a demonstration of cupping. Small glass cups are placed on the patient's back, then by combustion the air is drawn out of them, producing a vacuum.

Our group proceeded to the top floor, where

Wuhan Hospital operation.

we seated ourselves around the viewing glass above an operating room in which a thyroid operation on a young man was taking place, using only acupuncture as anesthesia. Beneath the other overhead viewing glass a team of six white-robed specialists was operating on a woman suffering from stomach ulcers. After a few minutes I returned to watch the thyroid operation which, it developed, had now been completed. The excised tumor, a bit smaller than a golf ball, was in a small pan. A gauze pad had been put over the now-sewn wound, affixed to the man's neck by two strips of tape. He, too, was conscious, blinking in the bright surgical lights.

The tumor was shown to him. He opened his eyes wide and, in doing so, became aware of those of us watching above, at which a touching thing happened. He smiled and signaled to us that all was well. The German party and I burst into applause and waved our heartfelt good wishes back to him.

(Since acupuncture is obviously used so effectively in China as an anesthetic, why could not a Chinese infantry unit, about to be sent to battle, be anesthetized by means of acupuncture? It could increase a man's courage, or his willingness to take certain physical risks, if he were absolutely assured that he would feel no pain despite the wounds he might suffer.

As for Western military forces, drug anesthesia would not be appropriate for this pur-

pose since it makes the individual either sleepy, apathetic or unconscious.)

We were told in another briefing, conducted in a thick cloud of vile cigarette smoke, that the hospital had a staff of six hundred people. I cannot understand why the Chinese do not put the "injurious to health" warning on their cigarette packages. The only reason it took so very long to happen in the United States was that the tobacco companies fought it tooth and nail—naturally calling it "government interference" with business—but there are no independent tobacco companies in China.

The hospital, a large, busy, modern medical center with eight hundred beds and a staff of some three hundred doctors and three hundred nurses, has departments of pediatrics, gynecology, internal medicine, surgery, neurology and Chinese traditional medicine. Among its facilities are X-ray, laboratory, pharmacy and anesthetics. Besides providing medical treatment, the institution is a center for scientific research and the training of medical personnel. "It not only serves Wuhan," Dr. Guo said, "but also trains doctors, nurses and assistants who fan out into the rural areas beyond the city, ever enlarging the sphere of their service." The mobile medical teams that go out into the countryside in their teaching emphasize means of preventing once common diseases.

"How long is the period of study?"

"Before the Cultural Revolution medical

students were trained for five years. That figure has now been cut to three." (By 1980, of course, the period was again somewhat lengthened.)

Medical authorities were naturally concerned to discover whether students trained in the new shorter course would be as qualified as those trained by the older methods.

"Happily," Dr. Guo said, "the students turn out to be at the very least as well educated and often much more competent because of the experience resulting from the policy of putting them to work earlier. Only the time has been shortened. We attempt to cover substantially the same ground as formerly."

In the United States a person must study for seven years before becoming a doctor, although there are now some experimental programs that attempt to cut this to six. Here only individuals who have completed four years of college can go into medical school. In China one can begin medical training after completing high school.

"Does the hospital have a department of neuropsychiatry?" I asked.

"No," he said, "a special hospital for that one purpose has been set aside."

"How large is your student body?"

"At any one time there are about two thousand students connected with the medical university. In medicine, too, by the way, there is a concentration on training young people from worker, peasant or army families. This is in keeping with Chairman Mao's idea that the benefits of the Revolution belong to all the people, not just a privileged elite."

Students who have had particularly valuable experience—such as the barefoot doctors from the rural areas—are invited to lecture, not only to the other students but also to the teachers, who in most cases will not have had such experiences.

A crucially important point is that relations between doctors and patients are very different now from what they were before Liberation and even, to some extent, before the Cultural Revolution. In America there is a mystique about the medical profession. The doctor fills the role of Wise Man. However affable personally, he seems to most patients to move in a different world, holding himself aloof from his poorer patients, if he treats any at all. This is not at all the case in China, where a doctor may interest himself in the home life of even the poorest patient and sometimes will perform the functions of a social worker.

The present crisis in medical service in the United States caused by malpractice lawsuits is in one sense incomprehensible to the Chinese although it is consistent with their predictions about the eventual collapse of the American system. To us each additional new social problem is, of course, depressing and, if it affects us personally, perceived as tragic. But to the Chinese, while they sympathize with the individual Americans who suffer in these various problematic contexts, very little of the bad news from the U.S. comes as a surprise except for its details. Because they accept Marxian predictions of the inevitable failure of capitalism, the dark reports of present realities in our country merely confirm their expectations. There is some irony, I suppose, in the fact that they still turn to us for economic assistance.

There is not the slightest question but that Chinese medical accomplishments in the last thirty years are impressive. President Ben Sprunger of Bluffton College has shared with me his observations made at the Nashi School for the Deaf and the Mute in Shanghai. I gathered that of all the remarkable things he and his group of fellow educators saw in that nation nothing moved them quite so profoundly as this experience. The school asserts that 90 percent of its children, whose ages run from six to fourteen, learn to speak and understand voices and sounds coming from as far as forty-five feet away. This accomplishment, which will seem unbelievable to American specialists in the field, results, it is said, from a combination of repeated practice, imitation, acupuncture, tender loving care and the patience of dedicated teachers.

The instructors themselves, Sprunger reports, cannot fully explain how their method produces such remarkable results but the happy fact is that it does. "By way of explanation," Sprunger says, "we were told that the People's Liberation Army developed the method. Then they helped set up schools and

Heavy machine tools factory.

cities and for two years trained the teachers. To reduce the children's fear of acupuncture needles the army personnel put needles into their own ears, arms and neck each time they put a needle into a child. After all, in a nation where the soldier is idolized, what child won't follow the example of a brave soldier? We let slip audible ooh's and ah's as we witnessed ten-year-olds repeat numbers or words spoken to them while they had their backs to the class. At the end of our stay at the school we were brought to tears and a standing ovation as some of the older students sang, danced and played musical instruments for us."

A HEAVY MACHINE TOOLS FACTORY

The next day we were driven to the Wuhan heavy machine tools plant. Mr. Liu, the Responsible Person, and some assistants, greeted us and showed us to the usual waiting room, with cigarettes, hot tea in covered cups and comfortable chairs. The construction of the plant, he explained, started in 1956 and was completed two years later. The factory produces heavy machine tools which are, of course, intended for use in other factories. About 8,000 people work at the plant, 25 percent of whom are women.

Mr. Liu himself served in the P.L.A. for six years during the Korean War. After leaving the army in 1956 he came to the factory. He was a member of the Revolutionary Committee and did not study engineering before coming to Wuhan, but has learned a great deal about it during the years he has worked there. Some of the factory's present engineers were formally trained, others have received on-the-job training. The factory runs its own in-plant technical schools, which the workers attend in their spare time.

The products of the plant are divided into five categories: vertical lathes, planers, gear-hobbing machines, boring machines and horizontal lathes.

Mao himself visited the area on September 15, 1958. Since the chairman could not possibly visit all the thousands of factories in China, it is reasonable to assume that he meant to give particular encouragement to this sort of plant since it in turn provides the technical means required by so many other factories.

An unidentified "capitalist country," Mr. Liu said, agreed in 1960 to sell a vertical lathe to China but only on three conditions—that the lathe not be delivered for three years, that the purchasers reveal the purpose to which the lathe was to be put, and that the Chinese pay roughly $5 million for the lathe. The Chinese, knowing that the country had the lathe in storage, refused these terms and did not buy the equipment. Peking therefore appealed to the

Wuhan factory and asked them to create such a lathe from scratch. Reference was made to Mao's dictum that the things that other countries have China should have and even things other countries have not as yet achieved China would nevertheless one day have.

A number of staff people at that time said that despite the best of intentions it would simply be impossible to fulfill this task; that both materials and technical know-how were lacking.

A second group of workers did not know whether the task could be accomplished but at least were in favor of making the attempt.

But a third group, which became dominant, was determined and confident from the first.

Not only was the lathe, an enormous machine as large as a house, produced but the task was completed in just seven months! Perhaps only if the reader is an engineer will he appreciate the incredible nature of this accomplishment. The cost of producing the machine was about one million yuan, a fraction of the price the foreign nation had demanded.

Until recently everything produced at the plant had been for China's own use but by 1975 the stage had been reached where some of the equipment was being exported. Pakistan, Vietnam and North Korea were among the early customers. Rumania and Albania had also recently placed orders. It would be interesting to know if delivery to Vietnam had ever actually been made, considering that by the close of the 1970s the two nations were mortal enemies.

The giant machines the factory makes are so enormous that there is no possible way of transporting them when they have been finally assembled. They stand in that form only long enough to pass inspection, after which they are totally dismantled and shipped to their purchasers in pieces. Chinese engineers supervise installation at the end of the line.

Having heard the story of the at-first unidentified nation—which I was able to learn was West Germany—I was surprised to see one enormous machine clearly identified with the brand name Wagner.

"Was this purchased from East or West Germany?" I asked.

Our host was not in the least caught off guard.

"The machine comes from West Germany," he said, "but we did not buy it from them directly. It was purchased through an intermediary in Hong Kong."

As we strolled about the vast plant, Bill and I were surprised to see a railroad steam engine suddenly drive into the far end of the building. The factory sheds are actually large enough, I would guess, to accommodate at least two hundred such steam engines simultaneously. The buildings appear to be over a block long and perhaps the equivalent of ten stories high.

A university graduate who works in such a factory received 50 yuan a month before the Cultural Revolution. In 1975 he received only 40 yuan. The lowest wage scale is paid to apprentices, who in a certain sense receive no salary at all, but whose basic expenses are covered. These payments are called "subsidies." After two or three years the apprentice graduated to the first worker's stage at which time he was paid 25 or 30 yuan a month. Besides the obvious requirement of performing work tasks competently one can also increase one's salary by being politically virtuous and conscientious. A veteran (1975) worker might be rewarded by a salary as high as 150 to 170 yuan a month.

The average monthly wage at the factory was 60 yuan. Special residential areas for the workers have been constructed near the plant. A total of approximately fifteen three-story buildings had been erected for this purpose. Rent for a family-unit is about 3 yuan per month, *about a dollar and a half.* Workers never pay more than 3 or 4 percent of their wages for rent.

There is no charge to the workers for medical treatment. If they are on sick leave they receive full pay for the first six months. After the six-month period they will receive 70 percent or 80 percent of their regular wage, depending on how long they have worked at the factory. Other services are also free, such as attendance at motion picture theaters. If they attend films at some of the open-air theaters, employees pay 5 fen, a little over 2 cents in American money. For a haircut, which they require about once a month, they pay less than a nickel.

As for meals, the workers may either eat in the factory canteen or at home, as they wish. Of those who eat in the factory dining room in no case will they pay more than 13 yuan per month for doing so. If they eat at the canteen, by the way, they can choose from among a good variety of dishes.

Retirement age for the workers is sixty for men, fifty-five for women. After retirement they continue to receive 70 or 80 percent of their wages, depending on how long they have worked at the factory. They continue to enjoy free medical treatment and other services. The factory itself provides a special staff to look after the welfare of old people and to make sure that their needs are met. After retirement the workers may decide whether they will stay in their factory living quarters or move back to their hometowns, in which case the factory will provide moving expenses.

Almost all the workers own their own sewing machines, bicycles, radios and wristwatches. There are not a great many television sets among the workers but about forty-five employees do own sets. If all members of a family of, say, four or five are working, it is not difficult to purchase such expensive items.

It is hardly necessary to observe that the workers much prefer their present economic level of security to that of pre-1949 days. A few might have earned more money in the old days but the great majority would have earned less, if they worked at all. Today no one can go hungry, no one can go without a roof over his head, without clothing or medical attention. Who would not be grateful for such an increase in security?

At least for a while. But individuals are born who did not suffer under the old regime, and that can lead to new problems for Marxist states.

The situation, in some ways, is like that of the children of now well-off American adults who appreciate what they have because, as children, they suffered through the Depression of the 1930s. The younger generation, having known no such suffering, feels no gratitude.

The factory administration gives special ex-

tra care to the needs of women, who are permitted to take time off during their menstrual period if they feel the need to do so. Women may continue their factory work up to the sixth month of pregnancy, if they wish. After that they are assigned to easy tasks requiring no special exertion. Pregnant women are also released from work one hour early during the last few months.

After her baby is born the mother is given fifty-six days maternity leave, with full pay. To anyone familiar with the treatment of women in old China, changes of this particular sort are dazzling. The mothers will generally breast-feed the babies for their first year and a half and are given time off from their work to attend to this. Needless to say, any especially heavy physical labor is assigned to men, although women do work right on the machine-shop floor, side by side with men. Specific party officials within the factory hierarchy are charged with personally overseeing the treatment of women in the plant.

As we strolled about I noticed a little boy of perhaps four or five and inquired about his presence since children are never seen in American factories. The Wuhan machine tools plant, it develops, has its own nursery, kindergarten and clinic, among other services for the workers and their families.

A large poster or signboard—perhaps sixty feet long—inside the entrance to the factory on the right side, displayed twenty-four highly competent posters and cartoon sketches done not by professional artists but by workers in the factory. Every one of them was of absolutely top quality.

Moving from one large building to another, Bill and I were surprised to see, in several green-planted areas, palm trees and California-type cactus, which testify to the partially desert air of the region.

WUHAN UNIVERSITY

One of the charming things about China and other Asian lands is that farm animals, which elsewhere in the world might be found only on back roads and in small towns, seem equally at home in some large cities.

At one point, as we were on our way to Wuhan University, driving along a busy, wide main thoroughfare, our two cars briefly slowed so as not to hit an enormous hog, strolling contentedly in the middle of a busy intersection, apparently in the charge of no one at all. A few minutes later a flock of geese again forced us to detour slightly, helping themselves to the middle of the road and in no danger of doing so.

The funniest instance of this sort occurred a few days later when we were driving through a congested commercial area with narrow streets with the usual Chinese urban hustle and bustle. Three dusty-white chickens came hurrying along the sidewalk, suddenly hopped up the three stone steps of an office building and passed through its front doors for all the world as if they were late for an urgent appointment. It looked exactly like one of those bits of business in a Walt Disney movie where human behavior is attributed to animals.

We were naturally eager to visit Wuhan University, which was a flourishing institution long before the Communists took control of China in 1949.

The first form of the school—then named Boone University—was established in 1911, with U.S. aid, part of the returned indemnity payment connected with the Boxer Rebellion. Jayne and her brother Edward were born on its grounds.

We passed through the sixty-two-year-old gates of the university, in green countryside. What at any other major university would be the campus is at Wuhan almost entirely planted with crops. For the first five minutes or so you are simply driving through a rural village, with peasants tilling the fields, water buffalo grazing, small country huts, little shops, and dozens of women and children selling glasses of tea at roadside stands. Then suddenly there is another formal gate, large red political posters, and you are on the campus proper.

As we stepped out of our car we were welcomed by a heavyset, jovial gentleman apparently in his sixties—named Dr. Gau, vice-chairman of Wuhan University's Revolutionary Committee and professor of biology.

Professor Gau had one of those genial, fatherly and somehow non-Communist personalities, plus what seemed a practiced and conscious ability to ingratiate himself with a natural warmth and charm. Having studied biology in American universities, he spoke of our home city of Los Angeles quite knowledgeably and recalled with particular vividness his visit to Forest Lawn Mortuary.

Professor Gau also attended Rollins College in Florida, and the Rockefeller Institute in New York City. He worked with Wendell Stanley, who won the Nobel Prize in Chemistry in 1946.

It was pleasant to speak to Dr. Gau about American universities, Forest Lawn, Grauman's Chinese Theater and other recollections from his youth. It is hard to say which is greater: American ignorance about China or Chinese ignorance about the United States. If I had to make a choice I would think that, as profound as our lack of knowledge about the Middle Kingdom is, the Chinese know even less about us. American education over, say, the last century, while far from perfect, has nevertheless included geographical information about other parts of the world, and China has always held more fascination for us than many regions closer to home. But up until 1949 there was practically no education at all for 80 percent of the people of China. The merchants, conservatives and Christians who came into contact with the imperialists naturally acquired knowledge of the United States but unless they were sent to the U.S. to be educated, such information must have been rudimentary.

Since 1949 Chinese education had made almost no reference whatever to the United States except in terms of political invective. As for simple factual knowledge, I found practically none of it among the Chinese I spoke to, except for those who had studied in the U.S. This was, of course, equally true of old China.

Hundreds of thousands of Americans who lived and worked in China, or served there during World War II, eventually returned home and brought their knowledge with them. But the even larger number of illiterate Chinese who migrated to America for the most part settled here so there was no important flow of information about the U.S. back into China.

We have had a number of motion pictures with Chinese themes: *Dragon Seed, The Sand Pebbles, 55 Days in Peking, Keys of the Kingdom, The Good Earth,* and others. But who can even imagine what a Chinese film about life in Chicago or New York would be like? The mere idea sounds like the premise of a movie by Woody Allen or Mel Brooks.

Our host naturally stressed changes in China's education resulting from the Cultural Revolution. His remarks, therefore—as viewed from 1980—reveal a good deal of the state of Chinese education under the influence of Mao, and the Cultural Revolution.

"The new approach," Dr. Gau said, "required the reeducation, not so much of the students but of the teachers. To make quite sure that teachers, professors understood the real meaning of the new state of affairs it was considered necessary that they should take part in physical labor, spend some time in the countryside. This had a number of beneficial effects. Not only did it teach them the reality of life for the average man, but it brought them closer to their students. As regards the students, it is a crucially important part of the process that after a young man graduates he is encouraged to go back to his original unit, his farm, his factory, his neighborhood, and improve it by applying the education he has been given. In other countries, you know, a university graduate expects to be promoted to a high station in society. But the opposite is now [in 1975] true of China. The university graduate expects to serve the people, to serve the nation, and is quite willing to go back to the streets, factories and farms to do so. This rule applies to virtually all graduates. After a few years back on his home ground, however, if a man distinguishes himself, he may be promoted to a higher station in the party hierarchy, the army, the factory, or an official agency. We do not claim that this program is absolutely perfect. In any event, it is still in such an early stage that there will inevitably be certain mistakes. But the important thing is that we are all quite certain that we are moving in the right direction in the field of education."

The question naturally occurs: How do the various scholars and intellectuals feel at having to spend time doing menial tasks in factories and on farms? I would guess that—though a good many were displeased—they did not feel as resentful as Americans would were such a system to be imposed in our country. It is not simply that China has never been as free as the United States. A more important factor, I think, is that the majority of today's Chinese, including intellectuals, do feel a sense of commitment to their country and its modern improvements that makes them willing to make sacrifices. We must remember that millions of Americans have given up their freedom, in many cases voluntarily, and thought it reasonable to do so. Soldiers, sailors, marines, priests, nuns, ministers, members of fundamentalist religious communes, missionaries and others have sacrificed self for the benefit of the commonweal.

Undoubtedly another factor that makes present Chinese sacrifices more palatable is that the rules apply to everyone. People will not complain about hard times nearly as bitterly if they realize that everyone is in the same boat. What is galling is when some individuals suffer while others blithely exempt themselves from the rules.

No doubt there has been some percentage of urban Chinese—perhaps gifted or highly intelligent—who felt imposed upon at having to live the life of a simple farmer for a while. Some young people slipped out of camps and sneaked back to their home cities, but again such individuals apparently constitute a minority, though one that was still growing by 1980. The Hua Kuo-feng and Teng Hsiao-ping government slowly began to modify this program because of the demands of their accelerated modernization program; time will tell if they abandon it completely.

Again I return to the device of making a comparison with something in either actual or theoretical American experience by way of bringing something that has happened in China into sharper focus. To appreciate the profound and radical nature of the change brought about by the Cultural Revolution in

Chinese education, it will help to picture the presidents, professors, scholars and graduate scientists of our American universities leaving the cloistered seclusion of Harvard, Yale, Berkeley, Princeton, Notre Dame, Stanford, U.S.C., etc., and spending months on backwoods farms planting corn, digging ditches, spreading manure, driving tractors, milking cows and feeding hogs. This is precisely what happened to large numbers of educators during the Cultural Revolution. A good many also were required—or "persuaded"—to do simple factory labor in conditions and for salaries no better than those of ordinary working people.

Though one may either defend or attack such a program it is not possible to differ with the proposition that the scholars so employed would, after such experience, have a very clear understanding indeed of what life was like for the average laborer or farm worker.

Because of our American bias we could easily make the mistake of thinking that the purpose of such a program was simply vindictive, to plunge the distinguished scholar down to a lower, more demeaning depth in the structure of his society. That was not the case, though it may have been in some instances. The moral of the experiment was to show that *the worker deserves as much honor and respect as the scholar.* Artists in the service of the Cultural Revolution demonstrated the same point by including few professors or scholars in their propaganda sketches. Instead the heroic figures they portrayed were peasants, laborers with sledgehammers or hard hats, backwoods horsemen, barefoot doctors and other simple folk.

Before the Cultural Revolution, Liu Shaochi, we were told, pushed the "Revisionist line" in education and copied the Soviet educational system. Under the system of "bourgois rights," the professors at the university had special privileges; administrative department heads were all professors. The students, in the 1950s and early 1960s, were barred from having any influence on the administration of the school. They were encouraged to seek fame, position and personal profit. The university was said to be "a cradle that cultivated engineers." Graduates became professors, scientists or engineers but were—allegedly—divorced from the laboring man and his world. Unwilling to go to the factories or countryside, they wished to stay in the city and do research work.

"Our task," said a young, intense Mr. Ma, of the local Revolutionary Committee, "was to transform the university into an institution that served the people, to educate the students to combine theory with actual *practice* in society. We wanted to make our students engineers, of course, but not only engineers. We believed they should also be workers with a Socialist consciousness and culture. The university therefore should be under the leadership of the workers, under the management of the broad masses, not controlled by old school professors."

This was not just a matter of a change of emphasis. It was deep, radical transformation of the very idea of the university, under the guidance of Mao and the now discredited radicals.

"The university," Mr. Ma continued, "cannot do this alone. Consequently even the enrollment of students should be under the supervision of workers, peasants and soldiers. Naturally there must be other specifications and requirements for enrollment as well. The applicant must have Socialist consciousness and be willing to serve the people with his whole heart and soul. Secondly, he should have at least three years of practical experience *before* he applies to the university. Thirdly, he must be a middle school graduate and in good health. Since the Cultural Revolution we have realized that priority must be given to political education. Failure to do this could lead to the workers, peasants and soldiers developing bourgeois ideas of their own. But in addition to studying political philosophy the students must also go to the factory and the countryside to actually experience life with the workers, peasants and soldiers. They must see to it that they will not forget where they came from.

"Our three-in-one system combines teaching, scientific research and production work. In our school, therefore, we have established twenty-five small-sized factories, with fifty-four varieties of products, and we carry on more than eighty acres of scientific research. In the past the university merely passed on knowledge and was itself a consumer unit. We are trying to change this state of affairs. So now we also produce. We wish to create a self-sufficient institution, without necessarily depending on the support of the state and people. In the past it was all theory and then—at the very end of the last school year—perhaps a bit of practical work. We argue that the students will actually learn *theory* more effectively if right from the *start* they have to combine it with practical research. As regards computers, for example, we put the students to work right away, not only in studying this equipment but in manufacturing component parts for it themselves. It is the best way for them to learn the fundamental principles and construction of the computer. By such practical methods they get a much better grasp of theory than when they deal with it only in the abstract as a paper exercise."

In the senior year, we learned, more emphasis was put on scientific research, in which the students' individual creativity is encouraged so that they might advance the state of the art. At this stage they are encouraged to analyze problems and solve them.

"We also have established here a school of agriculture," Mr. Ma said, "so that the results of our scientific knowledge might benefit that area of society as well.

"A part-time school is presently training over seventeen hundred technicians for work in the many factories in the Peking area. We also run some correspondence schools and special-situation classes, where teachers and students meet at off-campus locations to attack and study particular problems. We wish to make the largest possible number of points of contact with the surrounding community.

"By reaching out in this way we feel we can be of direct help to perhaps as many as 500,000 individuals each year, a number far higher than that of the student body. We follow, in all of these activities, Chairman Mao's advice that intellectuals should be laborized, while laborers should be given as many intellectual advantages as possible. The desired end of this, obviously, is the elimination of separate castes and classes, which have obviously caused such difficulties in other societies, in *both* the Socialist and capitalist camps."

All too often, the university's new leaders believed, the weak point of the intellectual has been his arrogance. Because of his natural gifts and social advantages he has in many cases looked down on the workingman. Therefore, the intellectual's selfish monopoly on knowledge had to be broken. Knowledge is not a special treasure to be apportioned to a very few. Common sense dictates that it must be shared with the widest possible number. "We do not wish thereby to lower the level of knowledge and competence among intellectuals but rather to raise that level among the people."

Bill and I were taken to the acoustics laboratory, which was presently being used to test the reverberation rates of building materials. In its largest room, a white-tiled chamber in which three of the surfaces consist of curved sections, large double swinging-door panels were open, showing various attractively designed rectangular boards with punched holes to absorb sound. Originally small holes were emphasized; now it was felt that a combination of smaller and larger holes was more effective. Such soundproofing panels are being used in the ceiling of the new Peking subway to diminish the loud noise of the trains.

A smaller domed room is a center for testing lighting patterns and methods in manufacturing plants. The dome represents an artificial sky and therefore provides uniform illumination. Small-scale models, of both actual plant buildings and those scheduled for construction, are tested under various light conditions in the laboratory to determine which provides most effective illumination.

The Chinese universities were, as of 1975–1976, not just partly but totally politicized. Professor Gau said the primary purpose of schools was to turn out good citizens. The rule was, "Put politics in command. In the past students were locked in ivory towers in acquiring their book knowledge."

The acoustics laboratory, Wuhan University.

Special emphasis in instruction was put on class struggle, the struggle for production, and scientific experiment. The Department of Liberal Arts, Dr. Gau explained, should take society for its basic subject matter. After all, "the proper study of mankind is man."

Education in China in the mid-1970s was certainly a more exciting process than in the old days. The schools literally reached out into the countryside and factories, bringing education to the workers in a way totally unknown in the past.

Americans might react to this in at least two ways. They might say it's totally abhorrent or conclude that it sounds like a rather marvelous idea except that everything is put in the context of communism. Perhaps, one might say, we should try the same methods ourselves, but teach "Americanism."

As for combining education, production and scientific research, one interesting response is that superior workers are invited to the university to give lectures to the students about matters in which the workers are expert and experienced and the students are not.

The afternoon wore on as we sat in our comfortable chairs discussing education in modern China. A Professor Guo had joined us. He was tall, thin, perhaps in his late sixties. Checking my watch, I was surprised to see

that it was a quarter to six. Rain began to fall and the light of day became dimmer but our hosts seemed willing—even eager—to continue the discussion.

Having for several years been concerned with the bitter, denunciatory tone of much Chinese political rhetoric, I thought that this might be a propitious moment to bring the subject up.

"I quite understand," I said, "that critical articles published in the popular press must speak the language of the man in the street. On that level there may be justification for the studied use of insults and name calling. But although I've read quite a bit of your political literature I haven't yet been able to find any polemical material that *doesn't* have that tone. Are there critical scholarly political articles, on a high intellectual plane, that are *not* so full of pejoratives and name calling?"

Either my question was not properly translated or Dr. Gau and Professor Guo misunderstood it, for we were now faced with yet one more of those instances, perhaps more common in China than in any other country, where the answer, while interesting, does not relate directly to the question.

"Oh, yes," Dr. Gau said, "we have our intellectual journals in which a good many important questions are considered and debated. For

Dr. Gau, Professor Guo, Wuhan University, 1975.

example, there is a famous novel called *Water Margin.* Sung Ching, the protagonist in the novel, should he be regarded as a hero or a traitor? This is one question presently being discussed. And of course, these questions are also referred to in the average man's daily newspapers."

I did not pursue the point.

"I wonder," I said, launching on what was, in 1975, a rather daring question, "is a historian, or student of history, here at Wuhan University, able to conduct his research with complete freedom, or are barriers placed in his path? In other words, are there certain questions he is not encouraged to seek the answers to?"

This led to a flurry of conversation in Chinese among the others in the room, which for quite a few minutes was not translated.

Professor Guo, oddly, chose to interpret my question as, "Is there freedom in China itself?" He said that he thought not only that China was free but that Chinese freedom was the greatest in all the world.

"In the past," he said, "millions of oppressed peasants had no rights. They had only the freedom to be oppressed and exploited, but no real freedom. No freedom to resist, no freedom to master their own lives. Since Liberation, however, the poor masses in China have gained the freedom to be masters of their own destiny. Now at long last they can speak out in their own defense and display their own abilities."

Very well, but as regards academic freedom? "As for academic research, we have a directive personally from Chairman Mao that a Hundred Flowers may bloom, that a hundred schools of thought may contend. Fragrant flowers should indeed be encouraged to bloom but of course poisonous weeds should not."

But had not the party itself canceled the policy in the late fifties? "The Hundred Flowers policy," Dr. Gau answered, "was disturbed by the Liu Shao-chi reactionary line. Chairman Mao has said that we should not be afraid of the poisonous weeds. They can be turned into fertilizer. Poisonous weeds, so called, could then be published in the newspapers, you may recall. Even the writings of Confucius, and the books of the legalist school—although they are being criticized—have been published, along with the party's comments on them. People who were called 'nobodies in the country' have been able to express their point of view on *The Dream of the Red Chamber,* a novel. These two nobodies had an argument about this book with some bourgeois writers. At that time, however, the two nobodies could not fully express their opinion, because of Liu Shao-chi. But when Chairman Mao heard of this he said that the two nobodies' statements should be published, and they were."

"You see," added Professor Guo, "in China all opinions that are fully in conformity with the truth can be fully supported. Such freedom as exists in China today, therefore, has never before been seen in the world! We are *not* opposed to freedom. What we are opposed to is the *distortion* of history. This reversal of history must *itself* be reversed!"

It would have been quite simple to say, "But why must it be the case that only the momentarily dominant faction in the government must judge which reports of history are accurate? If one does not agree with the dominant line, as of a given moment, his freedom to promulgate his views is considerably restricted."

But I said no such thing since such arguments could have done nothing to change the views of our hosts. And the point, in any event, was so obvious that there can be no literate adult in China to whom it had not already occurred. The Cultural Revolution leaders knew perfectly well that they were limiting academic freedom. No doubt they considered they were justified in doing so—as the Christian churches did in Europe for long centuries and, for that matter, still do in Ireland—but I do not see how they can possibly deny the reality of the situation.

Professor Guo seemed far more emotional about his answers in defense of China's climate of freedom than did Dr. Gau. Gau, educated, as I have said, in the United States, was far more a man of the world. Although he had apparently made his peace with the dominant powers (one may assume sincerely), he struck us as an eminently civilized and humane person. Professor Guo was more intense. There was so much emotion in his voice and eyes when he spoke, in fact, that the thought passed through my mind that he might have been putting on a performance for our benefit, deliberately overstating the case, hoping we would interpret his true meaning as the opposite of what he said. Nothing can be proved on the basis of such conjectures; I merely report

that the thought crossed my mind. Jayne, in reading this portion of the manuscript, commented, "Perhaps he was trying to impress Dr. Gau and the others, or tying to convince himself."

I should very much like to speak to Professor Guo today, now that the storms of the Cultural Revolution have abated. Perhaps the future will afford me that pleasure.

Song About Liu Shao-chi

Later that day Bill and I began to wonder if there were any calamity, policy mistake or accident in modern China that would *not* be blamed on Liu Shao-chi. I started creating a comedy song on the theme, to which Bill contributed several good lines.

Liu Shao-chi and His Revisionist Line

What makes the crops go bad?
What makes the people sad?
Who makes you hate your Dad?
    Liu Shao-chi and his Revisionist Line.

Who made the Great Leap fail?
Who likes to read your mail?
Who ought to stay in jail?
    Liu Shao-chi and his Revisionist Line.

    Khrushchev blew it,
    Brezhnev knew it,
        Puttin' Mao in the shade.
    There's nothing to it
    So don't you do it.
        Liu Shao-chi almost had it made.

Who's out of favor now?
Who's bad as Lin Piao?
Who's on the skids and how?
    He and his clique
    Tried to make us weak;
    You can bet your Mommie
    He's no Commie.
Who's workin' on a farm
Or down in a mine?
    Liu Shao-chi and his Revisionist Line.

Swimmers for Mao, Wuhan.

WUHAN LAKE

Next came a pleasant outing on a large Wuhan lake where in a lovely park we were put aboard a comfortable excursion boat. We were accompanied on the launch by a group of middle-aged visitors from one or the other Germany. Make of it what you will but almost every member of the German party was decidedly overweight. I might not have noticed this at home but in China almost everyone is trim and athletic.

It was in 1966 in Wuhan that Mao made his now-famous swim of about nine miles in the Yangtze. Until one sees the filthiness of the water and the width and power of the river, one does not get this remarkable feat entirely in focus. The lake water, however, was clean.

"People who weren't raised in China don't realize what this means," Jayne has said. "In the old days very few Chinese knew how to swim. The rivers were so polluted that if you fell in and survived you probably got some disease. And nobody would jump in to save you, as a rule."

Every year since 1966 the Wuhan authorities encouraged the imitation of Mao's accomplishment, with the result that about 10,000 people swim across the broad Yangtze where

Mao did. Some of the swimmers are as young as seven, others as old as sixty. Those who are not excellent swimmers make the crossing with the aid of a life preserver or inner tube.

Out in the middle of the lake we came across what first seemed, in the distance, to be only six or seven large red flags sticking up out of the water, with a few small boats floating near them. As we drew closer we began to discern a string of small objects bobbing in the water behind each flag. Within another minute we were close enough to see that the objects were human heads. One of our guides told us we had encountered a class of high school students training for the annual imitation of Mao's swim across the Yangtze. There appeared to be about eighty students in the water, each supported by a colorful lifesaver, lined up about ten abreast in surprisingly neat formation.

At last we were close enough to hear them shouting, in hearty unison, quotations by the chairman. It was another astonishing, though by now typical, China moment. Hundreds and hundreds of young people were becoming visible now, swimming, in a beautiful lake, under a clear blue and white sky, and still engaged in political exhortation!

All hands, however, interrupted their exertions to vigorously applaud the pale-skinned foreigners drifting past in the launch. We returned the salute. It was quite touching.

Because our train was scheduled to leave Wuhan for the small town of Anyang at nine-thirty that night we were instructed to be ready to leave the hotel promptly at nine. After dinner Bill and I did some packing and then—exhausted—stretched out to rest, as we thought, for the next hour. By seven-thirty both of us were fast asleep. We were awakened at nine by a sharp pounding on the door and set some sort of world's record, I'm sure, for packing and evacuating a room. We were down in the car—still quite groggy—about eight minutes later and sped off. Just as we reached the corner to turn left a shout from the crowd of young people surrounding our car warned us we should wait. In China this signal almost invariably means the departing traveler has forgotten something, which is being returned to him. In a moment a breathless young fellow ran up and thrust a black "What's My Line"-type sleep-mask into my hands.

The local head of the China Travel Service awaited us at the station and showed us to a private waiting room reserved for foreigners. His attitude, we noticed, was still somewhat reserved, though he dutifully smiled through the appropriate farewells.

Bill and I took one more look at what was visible of the hot, dusty Chinese city in which his mother and my wife had been born, then climbed aboard our train.

9. Anyang and Linhsien

 IN a flurry of *sye-syes, dzijians* and tossed luggage we had arrived at Anyang, a city of which few Americans will ever hear.

The Chinese, by the way, are the best luggage handlers in the world. Only once or twice during our six weeks there did we have to concern ourselves personally with the pick-up, handling or delivery of suitcases. They were taken off trains and planes promptly, presented when needed, with never a mix-up. In the United States, as those who travel a great deal are aware, it is no longer uncommon to get off a plane in New York and have one's luggage go on to London, or to check into a hotel and have to wait some time for luggage to be delivered to one's room.

We were taken down to the depot's reception area and cordially greeted by Mr. Feng, the local Responsible Person. The waiting room was much the same as the others one sees—large sofas, comfortable chairs, coffee tables—used for tea—saucers of cigarettes and covered mugs of tea. The only difference here was that, Anyang being a poor community, the floor was made of plain cement and the chairs and couches were covered with the large, colorful terry-cloth "beach-towels" that in Wuhan and on the train had served as blankets.

The Chinese are possibly the most artistic furniture makers in history. It is therefore fascinating that when they make an easy-chair or a couch—an artifact borrowed from the West —they create a really klutzy, dull-looking object. The traveler sees hundreds of these unimaginative pieces of furniture. They are found in every reception room, with slipcovers and lace doilies. One would not criticize an underdeveloped country that could produce only miserable-looking sofas. But when that country makes furniture of every other kind in the most exquisite forms, the point, I think, bears mentioning.

Almost immediately we began to receive information about the area. Remarkably, however, our hosts at first left us entirely in the dark about the true historic importance of their city. It was only later that we realized that we had entered upon a magic, mysterious place, perhaps even the birthplace of Chinese civilization, the capital of the Shang dynasty, which extended from about 1523 B.C. to 1028 B.C., during Old Testament times.

The first great period of Chinese art is the Bronze period and it was largely from this place—Anyang—that the world had been given the striking and beautiful bronze plates, vases, bowls, weapons and other artifacts that reveal so much of a people advanced and cultured long before any other surviving civilization. Anyang, in the northern portion of Honan Province, eighty miles north of the Yellow River and three hundred miles from the China Sea, was in ancient times Shang, a truly great city.

Before the area was excavated, Sinologists had assumed that literary references to the Shang empire referred only to legend and myth. Finds at Anyang proved there had really been a Shang empire, highly sophisticated in art and written language. But of this, as I say, our hosts at first mentioned nothing. They wished to impress upon us that prior to Liberation the Anyang region was one of the poorest in China, with practically no industry.

Now there are iron and steel factories, a cotton mill, and a chemical industry. The city boasts, in fact, hundreds of factories and business enterprises, with over 280,000 workers and staff.

Before 1949 the Anyang area had a population of only 40,000. Now it is 400,000. The population of the county, we were told, is 700,000.

On the streets in the morning we saw—in greater profusion than in any other city— thousands of horses, cattle and donkeys and men pulling carts loaded with the usual bricks, stone, lumber, metal, grain, vegetables, people, machinery, fertilizer.

The busiest offices in China, literally, must be those which organize freight-transportation services. The millions of individual haulers, driving their trucks, pulling their carts, some helped by horses, some on three-wheeled bicycle bases, are not simply freelance independent operators. Yeh Sing-ru told us that each one receives his assignment from one or more central offices. If you have a load of brick, lumber, grain or merchandise you wish to have transported, you contact the central office and the appropriate transportation is dispatched to you.

In the countryside the transportation-control office is within each commune.

It might be supposed that the busy bustle of truck and cart deliveries of stone, rock, lumber, sand, cement and other building materials would be less noticeable in the countryside. Just the opposite is true. On the road out of Anyang we passed thousands of carts loaded with stone, lumber, brick, bags of cement. All of China seems one vast construction project.

On the small donkey or horse carts every inch of space must be used for the load. Consequently there is no such thing as a driver's seat; the driver simply sits on top of whatever he is hauling.

We drove on Am-ling Road. At the side we saw a dozen or so patches of wheat grain, spread right out on the asphalt and dirt "to dry."

Though Anyang is not a famous city to the modern world, we learned more of its great importance in the context of archeology and were therefore excited when we were told we would visit the actual place where important discoveries had been made. To reach the site we left paved roads and traveled into one of the most primitive areas we had yet seen. With the exception of a few walls made of red brick, obviously of recent construction, most walls in the neighborhood looked centuries old, though they were not. If their compressed dirt had ever been formed as separate adobe cubes or slats the distinction between one brick and another was now long lost.

The previous days' heavy rainfall had made the dirt road muddy and slippery. Once or twice we thought our driver was going to get stuck but he didn't. Suddenly we turned to the right, through two old gates, and entered what appeared to be the grounds of a stately mansion. The building, though constructed somewhat along traditional lines, with few modern touches, was erected only in 1959. Despite its imposing exterior, the museum inside is strangely plain, with floors of simple cement. Archeological work by scholars of the Communist regime began on the spot in 1958, though the remains had first been discovered at the turn of the century. At the same time as digging for art treasures began, ancient buffalo fossils were also discovered on the site.

Archeologist H. G. Creel, who worked on the Anyang excavations in the 1930s, has vividly described, in *The Birth of China,* the incredible difficulties that scholars, among them the famed Jesuit philosopher and archeologist Pierre Teilhard de Chardin, faced at that time:

Because of the danger of bandits the archeologists must pay a great deal of attention to guarding their finds and themselves. The Anyang region is especially bad in this respect . . . filled with poverty-stricken peasants, some of whom are ready to turn to banditry in sheer desperation . . . a few of them have made fortunes from digging up the antiquities with which the region abounds . . . soldiers and police are on hand to prevent it . . . but the area to be supervised is a very large one, since the finest bronzes and other objects were buried in graves, and these graves seem to be scattered over the whole countryside. As a result of the official ban on digging, the grave-robbers have developed a method of nocturnal operation . . . In preparation for digging they assemble fifty or sixty men, all with the greatest secrecy. After nightfall this band, all armed with guns, proceeds to the chosen spot. A few of them dig; the rest . . . form an armed ring . . . work proceeds feverishly and the entire tomb is gutted before morning . . . the people are bitter, feeling that they are being cheated of a rightful source of revenue. It is said that they have formed a defense association with the object of assassinating the director of the excavations.

In 1934 an important Kuomintang official advised the government to prohibit further excavations, reminding interested parties that the traditional Chinese punishment for disturbing the ancestral earth was executing the culprit by cutting his flesh in the thinnest possible slices.

Nevertheless, extraordinarily beautiful and valuable treasures were unearthed, important not only for their artistic beauty but because of the information they revealed about the life and customs of the long unknown people of the Shang empire.

When Chiang Kai-shek left for Taiwan in 1949 his people took a great part of the archeological treasures, from this and other sites, to Taiwan. When Taiwan is again reunited with China, our hosts said, it is planned that all such artifacts will be returned to their proper locations. At present it is not permitted to put up factories or other large construction in the immediate area because of the possibility that more important findings wait below the surface.

The tour through the museum's several rooms was fascinating. The unearthed remains reveal much about the way of life of ancient China. Some of the objects date from 1300 B.C. to 1027 B.C., a period when slaves were beheaded and buried along with their masters. The most amazing object on display, we thought, was a T-junction of underground water pipe with a diameter of about seven inches.

By far the most important discovery made at Anyang, however, was that of the world-famous "oracle bones," which a traveler could easily overlook if he moved too quickly through the museum. In ancient China, emperors were assumed to be descended from God, or the gods, in the same sense that Christians believe Jesus to be the personal Son of God. This led to the belief that emperors could communicate with heavenly spirits, through royal priests. The kings of the Shang dynasty felt that they could receive messages from the long-dead King Tang and other ancient ancestors. Messages to the beyond were scratched, printed on a flat piece of bone. The priest then heated a metal bar and when it reached the glowing point, pushed it through a hole that had been drilled in the bone. Cracks, caused by heat expansion, appeared in the bone and were "read" by the priests, as one might read tea leaves or playing cards. The Chinese *writings* on the bones—if not the "answers"—can be read by modern scholars. Some refer to eclipses of the sun and the moon, many centuries before any other culture could understand such phenomena. The bones provide the earliest surviving instances of writing in the classical Chinese language.

For the reader who would like to know more about the origins of Chinese civilization, I recommend Ping Ti-ho's *The Cradle of the East*, published by the Chinese University of Hong Kong and the University of Chicago Press. I found it particularly fascinating because from nothing more scholarly than idle speculation on the question it had long seemed to me highly unlikely that civilization, however defined, had sprung up in only one place and then gradually, over a very long period of time, been communicated outward in various directions to other places and their peoples. It seemed far more probable that of the original simple discoveries—how to produce fire, how to make spears, how to make clay pots, the invention of the wheel, etc.—a good many individual tribes were capable of making them and that, given the vastness of our planet, and the unlikelihood that distant tribal cultures would have any way of meeting, early achievements of invention and discovery were therefore generally localized and independent. Consequently Dr. Ping's argument fell easily on my ears. In his preface he says:

About this book I should like to make a confession and three apologies. I was born two years before the inception in 1919 of the so-called Chinese Renaissance. The intellectual tide unleashed by the Renaissance consisted of two complementary streams, namely, a nearly unqualified admiration for things Western and an almost exuberant iconoclasm toward China's past. The much more sober academic atmosphere of my college years in the mid-1930s was not conducive to systematic rejection of China's cultural heritage, but it certainly did nothing to dampen my unbounded enthusiasm for the West. In fact, prior to the sleepless night of 8 February 1968, when I stumbled on archaeological evidence of the much later beginnings of rice culture in India than in China, I had taken for granted that China must have owed some of her vital cultural elements to the ancient West. Should this book appear to some to smack somewhat of Chinese chauvinism, it can only be accounted for by the fact that for decades I was an unknowing victim of certain forms of Western intellectual chauvinism, of which, as I now look back, the most subtle and effective was the theory of the monogenesis of Old World civilizations.

I further have the idea that the strength of the monogenetic theory originated not so much from its own self-evident virtues but rather because it was philosophically harmonious with the religious history and/or myth that informed Western civilization, the Judaic-Christian account of the making of the world and its inhabitants. According to this theory, it is clearly conveyed that civilization, which is to say ordered human life, began in a specific place called the Garden of Eden—the location of which it is now, of course, impossible to ascertain—and which therefore emanated outward in ever-widening circles.

I do not see how an American traveler could possibly be bored on a trip to China, except possibly by seeing *Children of the Grasslands* for the third time. But our visits to every commune, museum, school and factory proved fascinating. The Anyang knitwear factory, run by some nine hundred workers and staff, 60 percent of them women, was a remarkable place. At one extreme it made stockings, towels, washcloths, etc., of cheap, dime-store quality. At the other, its top-of-the-line was identical to the best available in smart American shops and department stores. I picked and examined some towels and washcloths that were at least as good as the best of the Fieldcrest line.

It would be interesting to know to what areas of the Western world these handsome towels and washcloths are exported. I would guess a good part of the output goes to the United States. The Chinese, of course, do not employ salesmen to go about the world finding outlets for their merchandise. It is distributed to the Western world by means of visits to the Chinese mainland by Western capitalist businessmen whom one meets by the dozen seemingly in every Chinese city. Each has interesting stories to tell. Most complain about one degree of difficulty or another in doing business with the Chinese. In Nanking we

Textile mill, Anyang.

Making straw bags, Anyang, 1975.

heard one marvelous story about an American businessman reportedly willing to place a $60-million order for faded blue-jeans material. The Chinese reportedly rejected the order, saying, "China does not produce faded materials." Another merchant has told that his Chinese contacts refused to preshrink cotton cloth, apparently thinking they would lose face if it were determined that the cloth had suffered appreciable shrinkage.

Driving away from the factory I noticed an-other wall, on the top of which were pieces of broken glass set into cement.

"Why does one see such walls in modern China, where reportedly there is practically no more burglary or street crime?" I asked.

"Because," said our guide, with a smile, "even under socialism there still exists the class struggle. And no doubt there are still a few pickpockets and thieves who have not been properly reeducated."

The mainland Chinese, of course, have another explanation for the small percentage of such crime and sabotage as does take place. "Ever since Liberation," they say, "enemies from Hong Kong and Macao, sent by the Kuomintang on Taiwan, have been infiltrating to create dissension and sabotage. Some of these people are caught, some are not." By late 1979 the incidence of such crimes had increased, though to no such degree as that encountered in the U.S.

Whatever small degree of pilferage they might suffer, the modern Chinese have clearly succeeded in attaching far more importance to the admonition "Thou shalt not covet thy neighbor's goods" than we Christians or Jews ever did.

In the ancient central part of Anyang the streets are only as wide as American alleys. After our cars made a few tight twists and turns we finally passed through a gate and approached some old buildings, which it developed housed a small straw-products factory.

The factory occupies what was once a rich man's house. Therefore it has the usual beautiful open courtyard; the buildings on four sides, with their traditional Chinese roofs, have porticoes supported by pillars. We were warmly welcomed and shown into a waiting room in which beautiful objects, all made of woven straw, are displayed, including handbags, carpets, baskets, toys and framed portraits.

Founded in 1958, the plant originally made only straw hats. Thirty workers produced a modest volume. There are now 161 employees and 45 machines. Something about the beautifully decorated straw handbags sounded a familiar note. "Do they by any chance export these bags to Mexico?" I said.

"Yes."

"Well, I'll be darned," I said. "I have seen these exact bags for sale in Mexican resorts!"

Our next stop would be Linhsien.

At one point on the way to it we drove over a small bridge across a ravine at the bottom of which was a narrow concrete irrigation ditch, perhaps two feet wide, in which water was flowing. The ditch was lined with hundreds of

Irrigation, Linhsien.

young women, and a few men, doing their morning laundry.

Soon we were climbing well up into low mountains, which were extremely rocky. On the sides of the hills we could see workers digging chunks of stone out of the hillside and transferring them to small hand-pulled carts. Hundreds of pool-table-flat terraces had been erected in this hilly country, testimony again to the Chinese genius for using land wisely.

About half an hour later we entered Linhsien County, and began to notice masonry, in bridges and irrigation ditches, beautiful and professional enough to be displayed on Fifth Avenue.

A typical rural scene on one of China's many canals. Much freight is transported by such small craft.

Poster done at artists' commune. Linhsien, 1975.

During the next hour we were to see a strange sight—miles and miles of patches of grain, about six feet wide, stretched out on the right side of the road.

Suddenly we were in the county seat, a small town with a neat main street lined by well-constructed two-story buildings, almost all recently built.

We stopped at one of these, which proved to be a small museum, used to educate visitors,

and probably local schoolchildren, about the social history of the area, with particular emphasis on the remarkable progress the Communist regime has made in irrigation. The special feature of the museum was a fascinating mechanical moving model of the area, set up on large low table surfaces. Lighted wall maps also illustrated an informative lecture.

What little water was available in the old days, our new hosts explained, was controlled by the landlords. We were shown old enlarged photographs of local wells with pitiable peasants lined up under the stern eye of a landlord or overseer to secure their meager allotment of water. Many local villages had no water supply at all. Their inhabitants had to transport the water they needed in buckets, sometimes from a considerable distance.

Because formerly the area was so dreadfully short of water, our pretty young guide explained, it was therefore short of grain from time to time. Since certain death would follow during the long droughts, hundreds of thousands would flee in such troubled times. After Linhsien was occupied by Communist forces in 1944 the working people began to build irrigation canals and dams.

Three reservoirs with dams had been constructed to hold the seasonal spring flow of water from the upper mountains. In stages, additional portions of the map model were lighted up until finally we saw a network of canals, like blood vessels, giving life to the entire mapped-out area. One hundred and eighty tunnels have been dug through the mountains as part of the large network.

As a result of the waterflow many hydroelectric stations have been put up around the country, thus providing electricity to people who had never known it before. Once a plague spot, the area now produces far more than it needs and therefore exports grain. There were also now thirty-four factories, large and small, in the area. Before there were none.

At three o'clock in the afternoon we climbed into our cars and headed for the interior. For the first forty-five minutes or so the roads were paved, although the countryside became even more backward, rural and old China. But whereas once this had been a dry, dusty, Godforsaken section, the fields were now as lush as those of Hawaii. When the road was no longer paved we saw to the right a mountain that seemed a temporarily frozen mass of cascading rocks, some apparently recently fallen onto the roadbed.

And then there were more terraces, the incredible terraces. In other parts of the world—Italy, for instance—I have seen stair-step hillsides. But never anything like this. The masonry of the individual retaining walls was so well constructed it could have served as the base of a cathedral. And the leveled sections ascended high, almost to the very tops of the mountains.

THE RED FLAG CANAL

Of all the things we saw in China—and almost every one of them was remarkable—the Red Flag Canal made the strongest impression on us. The purpose of the canal is to bring water to lands formerly racked by frequent droughts. In the one preceding sentence, possible to read so casually, is concentrated thousands of years of suffering and death for countless millions of men, women and children. Famine is a monumental enough tragedy but lack of water is even worse, for it not only leads to insufficient crop yields but, so desperate is the human need for water, sometimes to panic and violence. Linhsien is an area of rugged mountains in the northwestern part of Honan Province. In the best of past times the amount of land available for farming there was very small. To make the situation worse, many fields lay along slopes, which meant that when there was sudden rainfall the soil could quickly become seriously eroded. Poor crop yields over the centuries meant poor farmers. In time this led to the takeover of a great part of the land by a few landlords and "rich peasants."

One puts the phrase in quotation marks because although it is used at face value in China one is considered rich in that country at a much lower economic level than in the United States. There were, nevertheless, landlords with substantial holdings. The exploitation and oppression in the Anyang-Linhsien area were particularly destructive in a country where such institutions were nowhere tolerable.

Before 1949, of the some 500 villages in Linhsien County, 370 had *no water resources whatever.* Under such circumstances there could be no such thing as irrigation of fields. The bare minimum of water to sustain life, used for drinking, cooking and slaking the thirst of animal stock, had to be transported

Red Flag Canal.

from wells, in some cases miles away. The poor of the area frequently prayed for rain but as often as not it would come with quick violence, causing floods and further erosion. When even wells and springs would dry up, peasants would have to travel even farther, to the distant Changho River, to fetch water in buckets, after which they had to carry their heavy loads up steep mountain trails. Making such a trip might take a poor farmer an entire day. In times of serious drought thousands would simply leave their homes and go begging on the roads, many never to return. Drought would lead to famine, famine to pestilence and disease. In 1878 the situation was so tragic that about 65 percent of the inhabitants of the area died. It is important to understand this long background of suffering to appreciate what the Red Flag Canal has meant to the Linhsien area.

During the time of the war against Japan—1937 to 1945—an underground cell of the Chinese Communist Party was formed in Linhsien. Not long afterward the 8th Route Army, later to become the People's Liberation Army, reached the Taihang Mountains area nearby. It was then, for the first time in Chinese history, that competent leadership concerned itself with the community's water shortage problem. Out of gratitude the residents of Linhsien became part of militia and self-defense units organized by the 8th Route Army.

As a result of cooperation between Red Army and local militia people, Linhsien was liberated in 1944, a year before Japan's formal surrender.

In 1958 Linhsien began to rebuild itself in earnest with the digging of the Hero Canal. Eight thousand people threw themselves into the job, blasting out rocks, filling up ravines, opening roads and constructing bridges. The canal was completed in six months. That same year—which was that of China's Big Leap Forward—more than four hundred agricultural cooperatives in the area were merged into fifteen large people's communes, which facilitated the building of three reservoirs connected to the Hero Canal.

In 1959, however, the irrigation project suffered a serious setback when a particularly acute drought hit the area. The canal dried up, the small amount of water left in the three reservoirs was not equal to the need and it became painfully clear that a good deal more work had to be done before the area could be considered lifted out of its historic misery.

There was no further water supply in the immediate area. The Changho River, some distance away, was the obvious, indeed the only choice as a water source, but between the Changho and the parched fields stood the cliffs, ravines and towering peaks of the Taihang Mountains along Linhsien's northern border.

Even if the area had been flat it would have been a remarkable accomplishment to take water from the distant river and transport it overland through canals and irrigation ditches. But with the mountains between the supply and the need there were many who said the situation was hopeless. The central government had made no financial investment in the project, no suitable machinery was available and there were no true experts in the field of water conservation. The only reason the people of Linhsien went ahead with the project was that the alternative, continued drought, poverty and misery, was unthinkable.

It took a special county party committee a full two months even to prepare the blueprints. When they were studied the task seemed more formidable than ever. How to get a large enough labor supply to work on the project? It was argued that if each of the nearly 4,000 production teams in the Linhsien area provided two or three people to work on the project that would provide a basic work force of 10,000 people. As for building materials, the situation was, for a change, fortunate. The Taihang Mountains are particularly rocky and the stonemasons of the area were already experienced. It was therefore decided to line the canals and build bridges and aqueducts with local stone blocks rather than use precious concrete. The components of the large task

were dynamiting, bridge building and tunneling. The mountaineers of the area were already knowledgeable about all three.

At last, in February, 1960, the call went out from the county party committee, "Start work on the project!" Thousands of eager workers hurried along a mountain path with which they were all sadly familiar from earlier times of suffering and famine. Roadside tea-stands sprang up along the route to offer the marching workers refreshments. Party propaganda groups and musicians cheered the workers as they headed into battle with the Taihang Mountains. Slogans and exhortations were splashed on mountainsides. In red paint on one particularly steep cliff someone had written, "Transform China into the Spirit of the Foolish Old Man Who Removed the Mountains."

One hears frequent references in modern China to this particular fable, which was popularized by Chairman Mao in 1957 in a report on the success of an agricultural cooperative. In 1945 Mao had written an article titled "The Foolish Old Man Who Removed the Mountain" in which he related the ancient story about a man who believed he could dig up two enormous mountains blocking the path beyond his doorway, with nothing more than the help of his sons.

A local elder known as the Wise Old Man pooh-poohed the effort but the Foolish Old Man continued to dig. In the end, according to the fable, God was touched by the man's faith and courage and sent down two angels who quickly carried the mountains away on their backs. Mao added, "We must persevere and work unceasingly and we, too, will touch God's heart. Our God is none other than the masses of the Chinese people. If they stand up and dig together with us, why can't these two mountains be carried away?"

It is easy enough to see why the people of Linhsien looked to this particular story for inspiration. But despite the courage and willingness of the workers the task was nevertheless formidable. The work force grew to 30,000 but of course practically no housing was available for them at or near the work sites. The builders therefore constructed simple sheds and dug caves into the hillside to live in while on the job. Some of the younger people slept at night, like mountain climbers, on narrow ledges on the cliffs.

It developed that the steep, narrow mountain paths made transport difficult so the decision was made to build a road from the base camp to the head of the canal. It was completed in seven days by working around the clock!

The workers had no large equipment or machinery whatever. Their basic tools were sledgehammers and steel drill rods. One or two peasants would hold the rods straight while another swung the heavy hammer. When a hole of sufficient size had been made in the hard rock, explosives were inserted and blasted off. Other workers, under the guidance of experienced masons, took the large rock fragments from the mountainside and chipped them into neat rectangular blocks.

Work slowed down, despite its feverish pace, when an unanticipated logistical problem came up. The party committee members had planned to organize a work force of 100,-000 but when the level reached 37,000 it was discovered that the narrow delivery road became hopelessly jammed with people, carts, mules and equipment. Because the work force was strung out over such an extended line, mistakes were made and in some instances digging was done in the wrong places. A meeting was called to discuss the problem and it was decided that work teams would be concentrated in fewer areas. Over 30,000 laborers united along the twenty-kilometer-long route of the trunk canal in Shansi Province and attacked the Taihang Mountains fiercely.

The work here was particularly difficult in that some cliffs were either virtually straight up and down or in some cases even hung out and slanted inward. Special volunteers therefore had to hang on ropes from the tops of the cliffs, swing out high above the abyss and try to pry or hammer loose dangerous rocks that could have killed workers far below. We met one of those heroic workers, a stout, modest peasant.

For weeks the work sites resembled battlegrounds. The repeated roar of explosions echoed across the valley floors, men shouted, struggled, climbed, ran, and in some cases were injured and died. Women, too, were part of the work force.

So determined were the workers to complete the project that they actually learned how to create their own explosives and cement. They wove baskets to carry the rocks. The construction of the canal involved not only endless drudgery but an incredible amount of physical danger. Imagine building a *canal* halfway up the side of Yosemite's El Capitan cliff and you begin to get an idea of the nature of the achievement!

At one place we were shown that the canal is built right under a river flowing in another direction so as to keep the channeled irrigation water separate from the fast-flowing river water. Because of the success of this vast effort the once drought-stricken, Godforsaken area is now a horn of plenty producing fruit, nuts, cotton, wool and, ultimately, armies of self-satisfied, proud, progressive people who bitterly remember that they were formerly treated like the scum of the earth.

Bill and I climbed up the mountainside, on a neat series of stone steps, and took pictures along the canal edge. Far below the valley floor, at times a riverbed, looked peaceful and dreamy in the bright sunlight.

The lunch served back at the hotel was superb, with a wide variety of dishes, but the meal did have one novel feature, a young waitress who stood about eight feet from our table and stared at us as if she were invisible. While this would be considered rude in the American social context it was certainly not so intended by our young friend. Her fascination with us was genuine and we understood that she acted in innocence.

Everywhere else here we were greeted with shy smiles and in general not stared at nearly as much as had been the case in some large city neighborhoods.

After lunch we got back into our car, which stopped at one point where water came cascading down the hillside in a series of manmade steps. Not only are the surrounding fields terraced, but each terrace is edged by

Red Flag Canal on the face of a cliff, 1975.

exquisite masonry. A wall of solid block stone strong and handsome enough to guard a medieval castle simply separates a field of corn from a field of tomatoes, one perhaps seven or eight feet higher than the other.

A few minutes later, walking down an endless procession of steps along the mountainside, we came to a sturdy two-story building that turned out to be a hydroelectric station. It is almost as if, rounding the bend of a path in a primitive African village, one suddenly discovers a building with equipment so modern and sophisticated it looks like something one would see at Houston's NASA space station. We were welcomed and given an explanatory lecture. Electric power and light are magic here; they were never known before.

After leaving the power station we drove along a winding mountain road beside another branch of the canal. Suddenly, around a bend, we saw a long line of perhaps three hundred children, walking two abreast, wearing the peasants' wide-brimmed straw hats, smiling and happy in the green coolness of the country morning. Schoolchildren from nearby areas,

Irrigation outlet, Red Flag Canal area, Linhsien.

they were being taken by their teachers to visit the Red Flag Canal. As we passed they burst into applause.

Once again we were reminded that inasmuch as almost all of China's children will grow up to be either rural or city workers, it is important to impress upon them at the earliest possible moment the dignity and importance of labor.

On this part of our trip, as in all the others, Bill and I continued to take photographs of the charming children and their smiling elders. Just about every visitor to China with whom I have discussed the subject since returning home, by the way, reports that all sorts of things he had been told by supposed "experts" on the matter turned out to be simply not true. I had been told by a number of people—and had read—that it was risky business to point a camera at any Chinese without warning. The suggestion was that the subject of any photograph would either react angrily or flee, with the latter alternative the more likely. It's a wonder that such people haven't recommended that if we ever go to war with China we depend on a new battle maneuver, the infantry charge with cameras-at-the-ready.

I pointed my camera at hundreds of Chinese during the several weeks I toured the country. Only in two instances did the subject seem shy about being photographed. In no case was there a protest or even a frown.

Next we visited a factory that made small but sturdy farm tractors. Called The-East-Is-Red Machinery Factory, it was started in Linhsien in 1948 by five peasants who organized themselves into a handicraft group and worked in three dilapidated houses which still remain on the premises.

Equipment at that time consisted of one winnower and two sledgehammers. All the men could do was repair small farm instruments. In 1954 the project advanced to the cooperative level; in 1958 it became a state-owned machinery factory; as of 1976, it employed about three hundred workers and staff.

About 70 percent of the factory machines—presses, lathes, drills, furnaces—were designed and made by the workers themselves. The plant now produces harvesters, threshers, polishing machines, crushers and pumps for drainage and irrigation. Since the Cultural Revolution of the late 1960s the factory has also made bright-red, 12-horsepower "walking tractors." Oddly enough one does not walk behind a walking tractor. It is so called because the steering mechanism is the same as that of an earlier model tractor behind which farm workers did walk. (Languages are full of such dumb instances. For many years American automobiles were called horseless carriages.) By 1977, our hosts said, the plant planned to turn out 5,000 such tractors per year.

During the construction of the Red Flag Canal the factory sent its machinists out into the field to live with the peasants and workers, to investigate on the spot what their machinery needs were. As a result of this experience special valves and pumps were designed. A vitally important aspect of the factory's function is that it serves as a teaching school, bringing peasants in from the fields to learn to work with machines and also sending men from the factory out into the fields.

On the way back to town a sudden rainstorm came up. It was refreshing after the excessive heat, but we suddenly thought of the endless miles of grain laid out on the road to dry. What had happened to it? In a few miles we found out. The first few piles we came to had been covered with plastic or canvas and were now guarded by anxious villagers.

Farther down the road we saw, happily, that hundreds had rallied to deal with the problem. Most of the wheat had already been put into long thin sacks that resembled the heavy canvas bags used by prizefighters in training.

One of the more charming experiences of our tour through this section of Shansi Province was a visit to the Gate of City Commune in Huxian County, then becoming world famous for the excellent paintings done by its resident farm workers. The commune itself is certainly no tourist showplace. When we arrived, it was hot, dusty, and the rooms to which we were shown were what one might expect in a rural section of a still-poor country.

Painters' Commune, Linhsien, 1975.

Two of the artists themselves—Chau Kwun-hau and Sz Hwei-fong—were among the welcoming committee. There was no question but that they lived the lives of peasants, not those of artists in Western nations.

After the introductory lecture, we were served lunch and then made comfortable—as comfortable as possible, anyway—to take a one-hour siesta. An artificial orange-flavored drink was served. It is made by dropping an Alka-Seltzer-like tablet, with a citric flavor, into room-temperature water. Bill and I smiled as we sipped it, pretending to enjoy it, so as not to seem unappreciative to our friendly hosts, but I'm not sure our performance was convincing since we left the glasses mostly full.

As we sat and talked through part of the drowsy afternoon the young man made a pencil sketch of me and the young woman a sketch of Bill. Later we were presented with handsome full-color bound volumes of several dozen paintings created at the commune. All were of excellent quality and in no way amateurish. The few that tended in this direction were reminiscent of the Grandma Moses style but even an art critic, I'm sure, would be favorably impressed with the works produced in this remote country outpost.

We strolled about showrooms where the paintings and prints were displayed and it was a pleasant surprise when later in the afternoon we were permitted to purchase additional large prints of the paintings we had just seen.

They are of a quality that would cost perhaps $15 or $20 in an American print shop but we purchased them for a few pennies each. I brought back about two dozen and was reluctant to order more only because I did not wish to appear greedy. Books of the paintings are available through People's Art Publishing, in Peking.

Oddly enough, the common people's costumes in many of the paintings were extremely colorful, in contrast to the actual clothing then seen in Peking, Tientsin, Wuhan and other areas visited. Does this represent a repressed striving for a wider variety of color in daily attire?

Later, back at our hotel, Bill and I concluded that Linhsien-Anyang is the hawking, spitting and nose-cleaning capital of China. Apparently not only do different provinces and cities have their own customs as regards food, furniture, decor, etc., they also seem to have their individual concepts of what is mannerly in the company of visitors. Horrendous sounds assailed our ears during all meals in the hotel dining room. It's very helpful if one is trying to diet.

It's a wise idea to check and recheck facts in China and ask to have statements clarified if you can't understand them the first time. One night one of our guides, referring to the miraculous construction of the Red Flag Canal, said that much of it was done "in the spirit of Chou-ta-po."

Since I had been reading intensively about China for several years, and learning a great deal about its people during the trip, I knew that I had heard nothing previously about Chou-ta-po and therefore wondered who he was.

For a moment I thought perhaps our guide might be talking about Chen Po-ta. But no, Chen was another of the prominent Communist Party officials who, though for many years one of Mao's closest confidants, was now on the night-soil list. So it was unlikely he would be spoken of with respect.

After a few minutes I finally had to ask, "Who is Chou-ta-po?"

"No, Dad," Bill said. "She didn't say *Chou-ta-po*. She said *shoulder-pole.*"

Even Chinese who speak English fluently mispronounce quite a few American words. For that matter, so do a lot of Americans. But often Chinese will pronounce *sh* as if it were *ch*. The second syllable of shoul-*der* can easily come out as *ta* because Orientals sometimes pronounced *d*'s as *t*'s and frequently do not pronounce *r*'s at all. *Po* is a common Chinese pronunciation of *pole*. Because of the strange Oriental treatment of the letters *l* and *r* I placed myself in a position one afternoon to be enlightened about the problem.

"Yeh Sing-ru," I said, "I wonder if you could explain something I don't understand about the Oriental treatment of the letters *l* and *r*, in pronouncing words in European languages. Now when you say Liu Shao-chi you have not the slightest trouble with the first letter, which is *l*. You pronounce it as any European would. But when the letter *l* is at the *end* of a word, as in, for example, the word *wall*, it comes out as if it were spelled *waw* or *war*. Can you tell me why that is?"

"Well," she said, "in Chinese we give the last name *first,* so Liu would be—."

"No," I said, "forgive me for not making myself clear. My question has nothing to do with Liu Shao-chi personally, or with the sequence of Chinese names. I'm speaking only about one specific matter now, the European letter *l*. I could quite understand it if, for whatever reason, Orientals simply were *unable* to pronounce the letter *l* or the letter *r*. For example, there are some Americans who have a problem that is called lisping. They are unable to make the sound of the letter *s*. Instead —even when they want very much to sound the letter *s*—what they actually produce is the sound of *th*, so that instead of saying *sweet* they would say *thweet*. That sort of thing, as I say, is quite understandable. But what I am unable to understand is why the Chinese, for example, have no trouble whatever in pronouncing the letter *l* in certain words but *do* have a problem when the letter is found in *other* words."

Believe it or not, though we discussed this matter for another quarter of an hour, not so much as a fragment of explanation was forthcoming. I may put out a record album of Chinese officials discussing religion, sex and the letters *r* and *l*. The record will consist of a thirty-minute silence.

10. Yenan

THE Chinese do not invite all of their visitors to Yenan, a distant, dusty little mountain town. One must first understand that it is, in a sense, the Jerusalem of Chinese communism, a place that echoes with political significance because it was Mao's Red Army base during the difficult years after the Communist defeats that led to the Long March in the 1930s.

As our plane came in for a landing in this mountain fastness I was surprised to see below a double-towered Gothic church. Architecturally the sight seemed odd; I had not realized that Christianity had penetrated so far into the remote interior of China.

We stepped off the plane into the greatest climate we'd encountered in years. Clear, bracing mountain air, a temperature in the seventies, the kind of atmosphere one associates with Phoenix, Tucson and Palm Springs on their best days. Medium-high green mountains surrounded the airport, dazzling in the midday sun. We were greeted by a Mr. Hsueh and ushered into a black Chinese car that turned left out of the airport, moving along a poplar-lined street that runs beside a dry riverbed.

One reaches the main-street section of Yenan in about two minutes. Perhaps because of the mountains ringing the town, it is remarkable how its atmosphere resembles that of a small community in the American West.

At once the famous Yenan live-in caves become visible.

To Americans the phrase "cave dwellings" suggests natural hollows dimly lighted by the sun by day and a small fire at night, with perhaps a few animal furs on the floor for warmth. Such an image bears no relationship to the cave houses of Yenan, all of which are greatly

A street corner at riverside in Yenan. Summer, 1975.

improved by man, adequately if simply furnished, cool in summer, warm in winter, and quite comfortable.

The first evening in town we were invited into the small Yenan hotel's dining room, which also served as auditorium and motion picture theater. The first film shown was done in a movable-puppet technique that I believe originated in the 1950s in Czechoslovakia. The Chinese version, called, *The Cock Crows at Midnight,* was quite well done. As with all modern Chinese films, its story is related in simplistic terms. In most countries there is one category of films for children and another for adults, but in China I gather there is no such sharp distinction in that even children's films carry a political point and may cover the same sort of dramatic ground. *The Cock Crows at Midnight* is the story of a despicable (naturally) landlord who, not content that his farm workers labor from dawn to dusk, wrings extra work out of them by telling them they must get up and go to work when the cock crows and subsequently arranging to have a cock crow not at dawn but in the middle of the night.

The son of one of the peasants hides in the barnyard one night to learn the explanation for this strange state of affairs. He discovers that the landlord himself gets up at midnight, tiptoes to the chicken house and imitates the rooster, who responds in kind. When this information is shared with the peasants they concoct a plan to deal with it.

The next night several of them hide in the barnyard and, when the landlord creeps up to the henhouse, pretend to mistake him for a chicken thief and beat him unmercifully, crying, "Hurry, everyone. Come help us. Someone is stealing the landlord's chickens!"

Needless to say, the villain, after a sound thrashing, for which he cannot possibly blame the peasants, never offends in the same way again.

Driving through the city the next morning I said to our local guide, "As we were landing the other day I noticed a very European-style church, formerly presumably Catholic. Do you know anything about it?"

"No," the man said, "I do not know of any such place."

"That's strange," I said. "It didn't appear to be in the heart of town but it couldn't be very far away. We saw it perhaps a minute before we landed, so it would be only a few miles back up the valley."

Again the man professed complete ignorance.

Later that day, as we were going through Yenan's Revolutionary museum, I saw a picture of the church with a number of party and military dignitaries standing in front of it.

"This is the church I was asking you about," I said.

"Oh," the guide said, "that is the site of the old Lu Hsun Center of the Arts. It was important during the 1940s but it is closed now."

After leaving Yenan I learned that the church had been built by the Portuguese.

One is given an enormous volume of information at the city's Revolutionary museum, both by pictorial displays and the spoken word.

A few examples:

On August 7, 1927, an emergency meeting of the Central Committee took place. Chen Tu-shiu was removed from his leading post at that meeting.

In 1929, Chairman Mao took the trouble to repudiate Lin Piao's capitulationist line in saying, "The enemy advances, we retreat. The enemy camps, we harass. The enemy retires, we attack. The enemy retreats, we pursue."

In 1931 Wang Ming "sneaked his way into the Central Committee." From 1931 to 1934 Chairman Mao had no right to speak in the Central Committee of the party! Wang Ming "had usurped the leadership of the party" during this period.

The Central Red Army suffered defeat in the campaign against the enemy's fifth encirclement and suppression. As a result in October, 1934, the army was compelled to embark on history's greatest retreat, the Long March. Losses during this period were extremely high. Pheng Kuo-tao was the political commissar of the Red force. In the museum one is told of his errors of "Right opportunism and warlordism."

A formal decision of the Political Bureau of the Central Committee, announced September 12, 1935—during the Long March—called upon all comrades of the 4th Red Army to rally round the Central Committee to combat Chang Kuo's errors.

The march finally ended on October 19, 1935, when a force under Mao's command wiped out pursuing enemy cavalry. Over 80,-000 Red Army men had started the march. We were told only 25,000 reached the end of the line. Other reports say 100,000 started and only 10,000 finished the march. Why such imprecision?

Mao is given 100 percent of the credit for Red Army military strategy and tactics in the literature of the museum. Chu Teh's name was not mentioned, though he was commanding general of the Red Army.

A large photograph of Mao, taken in 1925, reveals a handsome young man with a gentle, rather spiritual expression. In the next enlarged photo of him one sees, taken in 1936, he is wearing a Red Star Army cap. The picture reveals how dramatically eleven years of hardship changed the man. The eyes are now hard, the look calculating.

On the day after the July 7 incident with the Japanese at the Marco Polo Bridge in 1936 the Central Committee of the Chinese Communist Party issued a manifesto for a War of Resistance, calling on the people, the military and all anti-Japanese forces to unite to build a great solid wall of the national united front against Japanese aggression.

(It might help Americans to get a grasp of the essential drama of events in China during the 1930s and 1940s if they imagined that the United States fought the American Civil War and World War I at the same time, with the added factor of the Germans having occupied the eastern third of our nation.)

In another military confrontation, the "Southern Anhwei Incident" in 1941, about 9,000 Red Army men were killed.

In 1942 Mao wrote, "Fight party stereotypes in order to rectify the style of writing." This is still sound advice since Marxist rhetoric, Chinese or not, has long suffered from repetitiveness and jargon.

If ever there was a dictum of Mao's, in fact, with which I fervently agree, it is this one. The unfortunate thing is that, whereas Mao's other political references have become gospel, this one would appear to have been generally overlooked. It has nothing to do with the question of rightness or wrongness of views to say that Communist writing generally, and Chinese Communist literature most particularly, is the most stereotyped in the history of political rhetoric. Not even Nazi political literature, for all its evil viciousness, ever resorted so consistently to the repetition of phrases that appear to have been stamped out by some giant machine. By 1979, fortunately, there appeared to have been some progress in dealing with the problem.

In 1943 Chou En-lai said, "Comrade Mao Tse-tung's orientation is the orientation of the Chinese Communist Party, and Comrade Mao Tse-tung's line is the line of the Chinese Bolsheviks."

Chiang Kai-shek's third anti-Communist onslaught took place in 1943.

On August 9, 1945, Chairman Mao wrote an article calling on the armed forces and people throughout the country to "launch a nationwide counteroffensive and fight for the final victory in the anti-Japanese war."

Special orders were issued for large-scale offensives against the Japanese on August 14, 1945.

Before the war was over, Red Army troops recovered Yentai city and Chang Chiakou (Kalgan) city. According to one museum display there were 125,165 separate military actions against the Japanese during the war years 1937 to 1945. This seems doubtful.

Absolutely no reference was made at the museum as to the *reason* Japan suddenly surrendered. It was only with extreme difficulty, to the point of embarrassment, that I could gently draw from our hosts reference to the fuller facts of the case. This is absurd.

It is understandable that today's rulers of China—even if they were not Communists—would emphasize the Chinese participation in the Pacific war against Japan and leave the American contribution more in the shadow. History is a rummage-barrel of facts. All nations, alas, sift through information about the past, select that which is more favorable to their case and toss aside those facts which cause discomfort. But to make *no* mention of America's role in World War II at all is absurd. I am very far indeed from a my-country-right-or-wrong type. Like all nations the United States has both virtues and faults. It is not chauvinism that leads me to suggest that the Communist Party in China is misleading its people when it suggests to them that China was responsible for the defeat of Japan in World War II. There is no question but that the Communist armies did more than Chiang Kai-shek's Nationalists who, we now know, essentially stood back, after 1941, and let the United States do the job. To look at the problem from another point of view, one shudders to think what China's present predicament would be if Japan had not been so foolish as to attack Pearl Harbor, thus bringing America into the war. When the Japanese finally surrendered on August 14, 1945, they did so very largely because they knew their homeland faced destruction from American military force, by either conventional or nuclear weapons. For whatever minor interest the point has, I have long been on public record as disagreeing with President Harry Truman's decision to drop atomic bombs on Hiroshima and Nagasaki. The weapons could have been demonstrated to the Japanese without the slaughter of almost 200,000 men, women and children, mostly civilians. But the past cannot be changed. Therefore attempts by any government to alter the record of the past must be criticized. I naturally do not suggest lavish displays in China's Revolutionary museums to call attention to America's contribution in the war effort. I would not suggest so much as a single sentence. A simple portion of a sentence, a phrase, such as "After Japan's surrender in the face of impending destruction from American nuclear weapons . . ." would suffice. What one does see is photographs of Chinese troops reoccupying cities in the Japanese-occupied zones of China in most of the eastern portion of the nation—without firing a shot since the Japanese had already surrendered. But many young Chinese—looking at these

photographs—must assume they represent separate military confrontations and Communist victories, which is not at all the case.

The problem of rewriting Chinese history is in reality not one but several problems. First of all, the Communist revisionists do not have a monopoly on the relevant raw materials. There are books written before the Communists came to power, books by non-Chinese scholars, books by anti-Communist scholars, etc.

That it is impossible for historians to function totally without bias is self-evident. But this is not to say that all practitioners of the historian's trade are equally culpable.

It is one thing if Communist propagandists revise history so as to delude—for what they would say is the best of reasons—those who come to such sources for information. But the great danger all revisers of history face is that while in the process of deluding others they will almost certainly fall into the trap of deluding themselves.

The reader's wisest purpose, in any event, should be to respect neither the Communist nor anti-Communist versions of Chinese history primarily, but to be guided by respect for the ideal of truth. The best-intentioned of witnesses will often differ in attempting to report the same factual material, but nothing can be done about that. The reader simply should be aware that discerning the true record of the past, in any geographical or temporal context, is a difficult task. The task, then, being troublesome enough, even in ideal circumstances, it is absurd to further handicap oneself by determining, before the fact, that one will do everything possible either to accommodate or inconvenience one philosophical interpretation or another. There is a place for philosophical loyalty but that one should blind oneself by such lights, in the privacy of one's own study, is a remarkable, if all too common, instance of human stupidity.

In the display "On the Chungking Negotiations" Mao sounds exactly the note presently emphasized by American rightists who obstruct efforts toward gun control. "Our policy is to protect the fundamental interest of the people. . . . The arms of the people, every gun and every bullet, must all be kept, must not be handed over."

"China has now come to the new stage of peaceful democracy. . . . China's revolution could be turned from armed struggle to non-armed struggle, mass-struggle and struggle-through-negotiations." This statement by Liu Shao-chi, we were advised at the museum, proved his great error in thinking that negotiations could replace military confrontation with the Kuomintang.

On July 29, 1945, Mao sent a telegram to William Z. Foster, then head of the U.S. Communist Party, "warmly congratulating the American comrades of the Communist Party of the U.S.A. over their condemnation of Earl Browder's revisionist line." As modern China looks back it sees a similarity between Browder's "revisionist line" and Liu Shao-chi's.

The Civil War in China broke out in July, 1946. At that time the Kuomintang had 4,300,000 troops and was well supplied by the United States with airplanes, tanks, trucks, arms and other military equipment.

In March, 1947, the Nationalists dispatched 230,000 troops to attack Yenan.

We saw a picture of Mao with Chiang Ching, his last wife, whom he married in 1938. The picture was taken in September, 1947.

After we had looked for a moment at the photo I referred to the death of his second wife and then said, "Are the chairman's other two wives still living, do you know?"

Yeh Sing-ru's face could not have looked more shocked if she had been a nun who had just been asked about the pope's second or third wife.

"What?" she said.

I repeated the question.

"I don't understand," she said.

"Hasn't Chairman Mao been married four times?" I said.

"No," she said, "only twice."

"Oh," I said, "In Mr. Karol's book, *China: The Other Communism,* it is stated that he has had four wives. Thank you for correcting me on this point."

At this our three guides conferred in low tones, clearly in consternation. Whatever the result of their deliberations it was not communicated to us.

Mao's first wife was selected by his parents. He was fourteen when the arrangement was made, the girl six years older, but in 1936 he explained to sympathetic journalist Edgar Snow that he had never lived with her. In 1920 Mao, then twenty-seven, married Yang Kai-hui. This love relationship was important enough to him that in 1957 he wrote a poem in Yang's memory titled "The Immortals." Nevertheless, according to Jacques Leslie, Hong Kong correspondent of the *Los Angeles Times,* "Although Mao often has been described as having been deeply in love with Yang, two years before her death he began to live with another women, eighteen-year-old Ho Tzu-chen, and eventually married her. She bore him five children during the next nine years, one birth occurring during the arduous Long March in the mid-1930s."

In 1937 Ho Tzu-chen, seriously ill, went to the Soviet Union for medical treatment. Not long thereafter Mao met the young motion picture actress, Lan Ping, later known as Chiang Ching. He obtained a divorce from Ho Tzu-chen and married the actress. She appears with Mao in several photographs taken during the war years in Yenan.

Since Mao had four wives, two possibilities present themselves; either our hosts were lying to us about the matter or they were being as truthful as their own information would permit. The latter alternative seems more probable. While a Communist is no doubt as capable of lying as anyone else—and we know from history, to our sorrow, how everyone else lies—Communists are not stupid. It would certainly be stupid to deliberately lie about a question to a foreign investigator collecting information for a book and for television discussions about China. As regards the other possibility, however, there is ample evidence that China's government rigidly controls public information.

That Mao ate very well, to judge by his weight, and that he was normal enough to indulge in sexual pleasure will hardly be held against him in any Western nation. Chiang

Kai-shek and many Kuomintang leaders, it is said, kept concubines, a practice on which the Communists—like the Christians—frown.

The key question, again, is why such relatively innocuous information has been withheld from 800 million people. Is the reason perhaps that it would be considered embarrassing by the Chinese that their leader did not practice the sexual austerity recommended to the young people of China? The Communist Chinese consider it disgustingly typical of the powerful in pre-1949 China that they often had concubines. Adultery is punishable by law in modern China; if one is convicted of this offense he can be sent to jail. Perhaps it is against this puritanical background that the realities of Mao's personal life were considered to present something, as the Chinese put it, of a contradiction.

When I discussed the subject of what seems, to Western eyes, the incredible amount of public adulation of Chairman Mao, our friends almost, though not quite, conceded the point. "It is true," one woman said, "there are a great many pictures and statues of Chairman Mao. But he himself does not totally approve of this. He has said that he does not wish so much of this sort of thing to go on."

I did not press her for the source of the quotation, but if Mao were serious, he certainly had the authority to order that at least some of his likenesses be removed from public display. At the time we were there, one saw more pictures of Mao in Peking than can be seen of Christ in Rome.

Though every Chinese home has a picture of Chairman Mao, it may not logically be inferred that every inhabitant of China feels an equally fervent admiration for the leader. It may well be that only, say, 90 percent feel such an emotion. The other 10 percent will nevertheless display the portrait because it is viewed as obligatory. The absence of the picture could give rise to questions. Nevertheless, that Mao may have been favored by as many as 90 percent of the Chinese is remarkably impressive. With the possible exception of George Washington, there has never been an American leader who was as popular with the people he served. We generally refer to election victories

as "landslides" if the margin of victory is 60 percent for the victor, 40 percent for the loser.

One of the museum's displays is the stuffed off-white horse Mao rode when leaving Yenan. One assumes that there could have been no Nationalist troops in the immediate area since a white horse would have been a tempting target.

As of July, 1947, the Communist forces went on the offensive against the Nationalists.

One picture is captioned "Students in Peking protesting against atrocity." The crime referred to was the rape by American soldiers of a Chinese girl student.

In three great campaigns of 1948–1949, the display asserts, the Nationalists lost 1,546,000 men!

Museum posters give the Nationalist losses from 1946 to 1950 as 8,071,350!

P.L.A. troops occupied Chiang Kai-shek's presidential palace in Nanking on April 23, 1949.

Standing just to the left of Mao in a picture taken at the famous public victory ceremony in Tien An Men Square in October, 1949, is a Democrat named Hen Su-tung. Between them is Comrade Tung Pi-wu, the late chairman of the state.

When the Americans had to leave China in 1949, following the Nationalist collapse, they naturally viewed it as a national humiliation, but the satisfaction in China was far deeper than America's defeat alone, even Chiang Kai-shek's defeat could have produced. To China the important factor was that the American departure marked the end of over a century of foreign imperialist domination.

After leaving the museum we resumed our tour of the area.

When Mao first reached the region he lived in Yenan city, after which he moved to one of the cave dwellings in the Yang Chia Valley through which the Yen River flows. This was his residence from 1938 to 1943.

Most comfortable of his several houses was that located at the Date Garden, some three miles outside Yenan. There, from 1945

I reflect on the conversations Mao had at this stone table outside one of his homes, in the early 1940s, near Yenan.

through 1947, he lived in a house adjacent to his army's headquarters.

The houses are so remarkably similar that at first one wonders why he moved from one to the other. The reasons, of course, generally had to do with threats from Japanese or Nationalist forces at different times.

Mao's living quarters in the Date Garden— where we saw no dates—were like his others: simple, with the bare minimum of furniture, and whitewashed walls. On one of the tables we noticed a cigarette burn. What lout, I wondered, had made it? Had Mao been a heavy smoker or was one of his guests responsible?

On his writing table lay a small flat iron bar which, our guide explained, Mao had used to cool his hands after writing at feverish pace during hot weather. In a small alcove a low table was placed, on top of which there was a washbasin. Above the basin a towel hung over a thin line of twine. A standard Chinese metal cup with toothbrush was placed next to the basin. A large six-shelf bookcase against a wall

must have accommodated a fair-sized library, given the realities of the time and place. A large double bed and white canvas "beachchair" dominated the sleeping area.

In an adjoining sitting room eight comfortable chairs and a group of low tea tables, each holding a small white teapot with two matching cups, had obviously been used for meetings. Glass having been scarce in much of China during the 1930s and 1940s, the windows were covered with something like white cheesecloth and paper, which admitted a good deal of sunlight, although of course there was no view except through the opened door.

Yenan being decidedly a rural area, the sound of hacking, coughing and spitting here, too, followed us everywhere. This day a company of about eighty young P.L.A. men, making the same tour, could easily have been tracked by a blind man, so persistent, vigorous and unremitting was their bringing up of phlegm, coughing and spitting.

Undoubtedly the most charming moment of our visit came when one of the young guides, a sweet girl seemingly in her early teens, who was showing us through some of the historically important buildings in the Yenan complex, concluded her account with a song and dance titled "Support the Army." As an entertainer I know how difficult it is to perform a musical number with no accompaniment whatever, but here was this dedicated, feminine young girl smiling prettily, singing sweetly, and dancing, with Bill, Yeh Sing-ru and myself as her only audience. I smiled throughout the number, to encourage her, although she seemed to be not at all as ill at ease as I know I would have been in such a situation. When the last note of her song had died away Bill and I created as much applause as two people can.

NANIWAN VILLAGE

Our next stop—before we would fly to Peking, weather permitting—was to be the village of Naniwan, out in the countryside, where Mao had lived during part of the difficult years. We took off in a drenching downpour and had driven about an hour and a half out of Yenan when suddenly the car's engine made a most peculiar sound. The driver at once pulled over to the side of the road, got out and checked under the hood. Bill and I immediately assumed, from the sound, that the problem involved the transmission. The engine itself continued sound as a dollar but when we tried to move again terrible grinding noises ensued. Fortunately the car was able to roll. Bill, who is more mechanically gifted than I, thought the sound indicated a problem with the clutch plates.

The car moved ahead for another twenty minutes or so, during which the growling from the transmission became more and more alarming. Eventually we stopped. As we sat at the roadside wondering what the solution to the problem would be it suddenly occurred to me that I had earlier made a note that not once in China had we seen a car broken down. Now

we were seeing one from the inside. It was, of course, a Russian car.

The solution proved dramatic. Our driver flagged down a small blue Volkswagen-type bus going in the opposite direction, with a full load of passengers. After a few minutes' conversation, the decision was that our driver should take over the bus and move us forward to Naniwan. This was fine as far as our purposes were concerned but unfortunately it meant that the bus driver and his passengers—they turned out to number over a dozen—simply had to get out and stand in the rain to accommodate two visiting Americans and their guides. It seemed a very bourgeois thing to do. I bowed, smiled and looked as apologetic as possible to the poor souls, some of them children, now stranded, but the three Chinese members of our party seemed to give little thought to this aspect of the problem.

In a few minutes we came to a village where we turned off the road, immediately becoming almost mired down in the now thick muck of a clay courtyard. Within thirty seconds a large parked truck blocked our path so that we had to get back on the road and try to approach our destination by another route.

At this point Bill and I had visions of the afternoon plane leaving on time and our being unable to reach it. We pulled into another courtyard and went into an old building. It looked particularly gloomy in the dark rain. A cheerful gentleman in a P.L.A. cap and jacket, Mr. Ting, greeted us and ushered our party to a waiting room where welcome hot tea awaited.

Mr. Ting, it developed, was not the comrade scheduled to give us the briefing so our group simply smiled and drank tea for a few minutes. After a while I excused myself to go to the men's room, which in Chinese villages is always an outdoor latrine. Getting there proved a minor adventure in that the pathway was by now flooded.

Still waiting, Bill and I strolled out to the front steps of the building, built around a large courtyard in the ancient Chinese style, and looked through the gates and down a narrow mud path at the end of which a flight of worn steps led up a hill to the building that had been

Mao's home in this primitive mountain village. The doorway is marked with an identifying red-and-white plaque.

To our right, in the mud and water of the courtyard, stood a traditional ancient low stone Chinese table, slightly larger and lower than an American card table, surrounded by the usual four stone seats. Two disconsolate black chickens huddled beneath the table for protection against the rain.

Two small children and then a black-and-white mongrel dog made their way slowly up the clay street outside the gates. I had now been in China for five weeks and had seen perhaps a dozen dogs in all that time. Each one seemed to be the only canine inhabitant of its village, which raises an interesting question as to how this vanishing species in China manages to propagate itself at all.

Looking at the rain beginning to pile up in the rocky clay I had for the first time a grasp of the reasons why in such courtyards in China the level of the yard itself is about two feet below that of the walkway which rings the court.

After a delay of perhaps thirty minutes the man we were waiting for showed up. He was Liu Pao-tsai, formerly deputy company leader of the 359th Division of the People's Liberation Army. Mr. Liu was about eighty, short, very thin, and physically hard as nails. He looked only sixty-five in his rough peasant clothes, a white handkerchief turban wrapped around his head. His teeth were mostly gone, but in his capacity as deputy secretary of the party committee of Naniwan he was sent about to describe his former life to visitors such as Bill and myself. The story he had to tell was incredible. In 1941, during the anti-Japanese war, the 359th Division was ordered to withdraw to the rear to defend the Central Committee of the Communist Party. Thirteen thousand men retreated to Yenan, where for the next several years they served as farmers, road builders, carpenters, engineers, weavers and God knows what else. Naniwan in those days was a deserted, arid place. The unit had to dig wider paths and pave some roads even to reach it. There were no houses for them to move into. They set up quarters in caves but

there were not enough of them so new ones had to be dug. No furniture was available so they simply felled trees, produced lumber, and started to manufacture their own chairs, tables, beds and desks. Money was almost non-existent. It was as if they had been brought from another planet and to survive had to depend on their own resources. Fortunately they were able to establish a modest trade with peasants in the Yenan area to secure matches, salt and a few other essentials they could not produce themselves.

For digging caves they had no proper tools at all, merely small chisels and a few shovels. Only the fittest survived but the experience of being beleaguered created a lasting bond of unity and loyalty among such intrepid soldiers.

After thanking Mr. Liu profusely for his time and attention we traveled up a nearby hillside to Mao's old living quarters.

The young Chinese woman who showed us through the hillside dwelling Mao had occupied had a face full of freckles, the first we had seen in China. She, too, spoke with the same odd combination of artificiality and deep emotion characteristic of the young guides who conduct visitors to any of the chairman's former habitats or rostrums. Since they have to make the same speech hundreds of times, perhaps over a period of several years, they obviously cannot feel true full emotion at each repetition. Their performances therefore might be compared with those of an American or European actor who night after night, for many months, offers the same performance in a tragic drama. An added factor in the case of the young Chinese guides, however, is that there is a sameness to their recitations. Almost all the young women speak in the same reverential tone, whispering the more emotional passages, and in some cases sounding as if they are about to burst into tears. I do not make these remarks in a critical sense; the performances are appealing and most of the young women have a sweet, feminine quality, made even more doll-like in the case of those who speak in the peculiar, purposely unnatural style I have mentioned.

Although we finally got back to the hotel

early enough, it became increasingly obvious, from the vigor of the rainstorm, that our arriving plane would not be able either to get into Yenan or take off again if it did land. The scheduled departure time, 3:25, came and went. Bill and I hung around the hotel, did a bit of shopping at the lobby counter, read a great deal about China, played quite a bit of Ping-Pong, and after dinner saw two more films, one a documentary of the usual sort, extolling China's heavy industry, her oil fields and coal mines, the other a drama called *Pine Ridges.* It wasn't terribly good but was highly instructive in that it gave us a chance to see something of life in a mountain commune. The story would not have provided the basis for a motion picture anywhere else except possibly in the Soviet Union of the 1930s. A young girl wants to learn to manage a cart and team of three horses. A "bad element," who turns out to have been a former rich peasant, tries to sabotage the collective spirit by "taking the capitalist road." The film has no actual leading man but the one particularly heroic figure is the local party cadre, a former People's Liberation Army man. One encounters the same character in various Chinese films, short stories, plays and radio and television dramas. He is a type encountered in Western literature only in religious sagas in that his unselfish, spiritual and compassionate concern for the members of his commune would rival that of Jesus Christ or Francis of Assisi.

Bill and I retired that night with the unhappy knowledge that the rain was going to make us lose one of our precious days in Peking.

We slept late the following morning since we had already visited Yenan's main points of interest and the downpour made casual strolling out of the question. Actually the chance to spend a few extra hours in bed was welcome, particularly since I had by this time come down with an infection, with the classic symptoms of weakness, backache, loss of appetite and slight temperature, among others.

A couple of times during the day I felt a bit more energetic so Bill and I played a few games of Ping-Pong in the dining room. Much of the rest of the time the table was in use by young men who worked in the hotel. We saw perhaps a dozen of them play, all terrific. In fact, we had yet to see an inept table-tennis player in China. The state provides a great many tables, children get interested in the game at an early age, and it remains important to them. Choices of all kinds are limited in China, in comparison to the United States. This means there is more concentration on the limited available alternatives. In the case of table tennis the general proficiency is remarkable. On the level of international competition it isn't surprising that the Chinese are now the best in the world. The old small-school large-school factor, of course is operative. In the United States no small college can possibly have an outstanding football team because it has too small a student body to select from. In the case of China, with hundreds of millions of people, the chances are good that the best of them will be better than the best players in nations with much smaller populations.

Late in the day the weather cleared up and we were told that we would leave the following day at noon. But the next morning the sky was again gray and forbidding.

The day's adventure started when Bill, who had just entered my suite and walked into the bath, let out an oath.

"What happened?" I said.

"The biggest bug I ever saw in my *life* is here!" he said.

"It's probably one of those big beetles we saw out in the countryside the other day."

"No, it isn't. It's a hell of a lot bigger than that, and it's got long legs."

He got one of my shoes and tried to kill it; unfortunately it got away. For the next few minutes we kept a wary eye on the floor when walking around our quarters. Eventually the quarry was trapped and dispatched.

The weather finally cleared up and at one-fifteen we left the hotel for the airport, the sky partly cloudy, partly blue. Its runway is ringed with enormous sunflower plants about ten feet high.

After a round of warm farewells we piled into the waiting Ilyushin, for which we were by now grateful.

Because we flew out of Yenan at a fairly low

altitude, not far from the tops of the surrounding hills, we now saw something even more incredible than the sights that had greeted us on our flight in. Fields were being plowed and crops raised *on the tops of mountains*. This explained the peculiar impression I had gotten, on our way in, that tops of some of the mountains had been shaved off. They had indeed, so that they could be farmed.

Only in China.

11. Return to Peking

ABOUT half an hour before landing at Peking we were flying low enough to get a good view of the countryside. In contrast to the solid dreary tan of the preceding winter the fields were now lush and green, though here and there patches of brown showed through.

Closer to the city Bill's sharp eyes picked up three separate antiaircraft emplacements, each with several guns.

At this airport, too, in one of the great cities of the world, crops were growing close to the runway. As we taxied in after a smooth landing, I counted six giant four-jet passenger transports lined up off to the right.

When Bill and I emerged from the terminal building the first thing we saw was ten smart-looking new Toyota Corollas lined up to receive arriving passengers. We, however, were taken down a ramp to the right and to another of the old, comfortable Russian limousines.

As we pulled off the terminal lot and onto the road to town, the endless miles of rows of trees that stretched straight ahead—bare a few months ago—were now full and green. We drove at a good clip, honking all the way, of course. Incidentally, Ralph Nader would have his work cut out for him in China; with the exception of seat belts on airplanes little attention is paid to passenger safety. Motorcyclists never wear protective helmets—I doubt if they have heard of them—and there are no safety belts in automobiles. Dashboards, far from being padded, are hard as rocks.

In closer to the heart of town, we passed an open-air vegetable market. Large mirrors had been set behind racks of fruit at an angle so that people in the street could see over the heads of close-up shoppers and tell what was for sale. An excellent idea.

As we were hauling luggage out of the car at the hotel a blond woman who looked vaguely familiar—we later realized we had seen her as part of an American tour group in Nanking—said, "Mr. Allen, there's mail waiting for you at the desk." We thanked her and picked up two letters, one from Jayne and one from a young man who, in checking through letters waiting at the desk, had noticed my name and added a personal note himself.

The Peking Hotel had seemed pleasant enough, rather like an Oriental Hilton, when Jayne and I had first seen it in winter. Now, after weeks spent in "less presentable" cities and hotels, it seemed like a combination of the Plaza, the Dorchester and Buckingham Palace. On the winter trip I had not even been aware that our quarters were air-conditioned, for the obvious reason that mechanically cooled hotels are the norm in the United States. But now, entering our room on a hot day, we were bowled over by the cool, sweet draft of air from the quiet air conditioner.

We washed up, unpacked, relaxed for a short while, then once again went out to walk about the neighborhood.

On the busy corner just outside the hotel we found a long display case in which were exhibited captioned news photographs and whole pages of newspapers. The average Chinese does not subscribe to daily papers, nor can he buy them at a corner newsstand. They are simply opened and displayed, page by page, under glass at certain busy locations on the street. It is common to see a few dozen people standing close to the glass, moving slowly from one side to the other, reading the news of the day.

Papers and magazines are available, of course, at neighborhood and school libraries, and the famous political wall posters, China's free press, were—even in 1975—everywhere. Each citizen may write and display his own, if he likes. Chinese citizens, like Americans, also pick up news broadcasts on radio and, in rarer instances, from television. There were practically no privately owned sets in homes but they could be seen in public locations, hotels, meeting rooms. Television in China in 1975–1976 was in some respects like American television circa 1949–1950. By 1979 many more individuals owned sets.

In walking the streets of Peking we were impressed once more by the swarms of bicycles gliding by, blessedly quiet. Although one can be deafened at certain times of day, in certain neighborhoods, by the incessant honking from cars, buses and trucks, it's a relief to report that Chinese motorcycles run remarkably quietly. I wonder why our Japanese and American models do not do the same?

From time to time we passed old women with bound feet. By now we had learned that the practice was common in the northern part of China, where in the old days, incredibly, more than half the women had their feet bound, but not in the south, where women worked in the fields. In old China it was common for southern men to stay home, do the housework and take care of the children, while the women assumed what we would consider the more masculine duties.

A VISIT TO AN ARMY BASE

Sunday, July 27

Sunday morning we drove to visit the Yang Chun People's Liberation Army unit. The trip from Peking took almost two hours and brought us, I was eventually surprised to learn, to the outskirts of Tientsin. As we approached the base, the road, which wound past a canal, was clogged with hundreds of carts, trucks, bicycles, tractors and pedestrians, all in the same bustle and busyness we had seen in so many Chinese cities.

Our cars pulled off the crowded road and entered a well-paved concrete two-lane street, lined with trees, that farther ahead would lead into the base itself. On both sides rice paddies and patches of other crops stretched away into the distance. Working the fields is part of the P.L.A.'s responsibility. China is one of the first nations in history to come to the common-sense understanding that during peacetime military forces are very close to no earthly good whatsoever. They are like guns, bombers, tanks and missiles that—except for deterrent value—have actual use only in the context of war. But whereas most other military groups make busy-work to keep themselves active— "Police the area, soldier!"—once basic training is past in China the People's Liberation Army men and women also function as farmers, laborers, teachers and administrators, thus providing an important agency of social cohesiveness.

We stopped at the side of the road to let a busload of Americans catch up. After we had waited for perhaps half an hour one of the symptoms that had troubled me for several days returned so that I was forced, with some embarrassment, to make inquiries as to how long it might be before we reached the next men's room. Due no doubt to some peculiarity of my early conditioning I don't even like to discuss such matters with our family physician.

"Maybe quite a while," a guide said.

"How far away is it?"

"Not very close," was the answer, which entered my heart like an ice pick.

"Can you wait?" Yeh Sing-ru asked.

"Well," I said, squirming with embarrassment since I had by now become the object of group interest, "not a great deal longer."

Amid considerable merriment one of the gentlemen from the Travel Service inquired, in almost clinical detail, as to which of the two possible purposes of my requested visit to a toilet facility was dominant.

"The latter," I responded coldly.

This answer, too, seemed to amuse the other members of our party. It was decided that our three-car caravan should proceed to the base headquarters so that my acute problem could be dealt with promptly.

On the left of the road now were several new, brick three-story buildings, which proved to be barracks. A group working in the fields, wearing white shirts, waved and smiled as our cars passed. At the next corner a young soldier, red flag in one hand and a green in the other, signaled us to turn left. Driving through the camp, seeing the young men in their khaki pants and white shirts, was much like visiting a large boarding school or youth camp in a Western country. The typical young soldier looked about eighteen.

After passing through tall gates, we reached the military compound proper. It is modern, graced with trees, and consists of several well-constructed three-story brick buildings. The main administration center, like a number of other public structures in China, has architecture much like that of an American high school.

We were introduced to the political commissar for the base, Comrade Ting, a short, stocky, humorless, no-nonsense type whose totally blank exterior was in striking contrast to the warm, genial personalities of most of the Chinese we had met. After a latrine break for all hands, we were shown upstairs to the customary waiting room where welcome slices of bright red watermelon and dishes of wrapped candies awaited us. Chinese watermelons are round, about half the size of American melons but somewhat sweeter.

It turned out that the inconvenience I had caused our host was not such a serious matter after all in that the bus bringing another group of Americans had broken down, which meant that had we waited under the trees we would have had an awfully long stay there.

In most parts of the world military service is looked on as a serious imposition by the young. A percentage, hoping for adventure,

P.L.A. camp. Comrade Ting.

moved by patriotic impulse or dissatisfied with their civilian lives, will always enlist, but except in certain wars the majority ordinarily see military duty as something forced upon them. This is not the case in China today though it was in the pre-Revolutionary past. Service in the P.L.A. in most cases will offer a young man a better life than he has known in his home village, opportunities for travel, special education and important standing in his society. Chinese army life is often a stepping-stone to a position of greater responsibility.

Comrade Ting, we learned from a long chat, had been in military service for over thirty years. He saw action in the War of Resistance against Japan, "the War of Liberation against Chiang Kai-shek," and Korea, where he took part in four separate battles. He observed that the Chinese fought well in Korea because they had the sense of being in a just war. Their homeland was actually threatened by American forces crossing the Yalu River toward Chinese territory and they therefore fought with the same sense of purpose that Americans would have shown if they had thrown back a foreign invader approaching, say, Southern California and pursued him some distance down into Mexico.

Chinese officers and soldiers, Comrade Ting explained, do not come from a military caste separate from the people, as is the case in some nations, but are common citizens drawn from among the people themselves. Also the Chinese know that the sole purpose of their army is to serve the people. Much of the service now —it is hoped all of it—will take place in peacetime. But in either peace or war the people identify closely with the P.L.A., a state of affairs which has little precedent in military history.

I asked Ting if there had been any process in the military sphere similar to the partial revolt of the intellectuals during the early stages of the Cultural Revolution. In other words, had military men, too, "taken the wrong road," subsequently rethought their positions, repented of their sins, subjected themselves to public self-criticism and come back into the fold? (Some had, of course.) The question was stated in three different ways but the answer was difficult to come by. The final version was, "I cannot speak for other military units but I know that in our unit there were no such people."

After Ting spoke scathingly of Lin Piao for having tried to affect military policy, Bill raised the point that it did not seem to him a very great offense that Lin, who was head of the armed forces in China at the time, should have made a few suggestions about proper directions for military policy.

Although I was aware that women served in the P.L.A., there was nevertheless a momentary feeling of surprise when a pretty teenager in army uniform at one point opened a door for us.

Comrade Ting was kind enough to place me on his left when the formal meeting started after the American troupe—sponsored by *The Guardian*—arrived, their bus's problem having been resolved.

"Our 196th Division," Ting began officially, "was originally established in 1937, during the anti-Japanese war. At that time it consisted of small contingents of Red soldiers, divided into several guerrilla detachments. Gradually these detachments developed into the division. Under the guidance of Chairman Mao's thought our division has developed from small to large, from weak to strong. We have followed Chairman Mao's instructions that the P.L.A. should be not only military but also a big school. Therefore we have been following politics, cultural affairs and criticizing the bourgeoisie. We have also organized officers and men to carry on production labor with our own hands. During harvest time our men go to other nearby communes and brigades to help the lower and middle peasants in their harvest work.

"In addition to our farm fields we have set up medium and small-size factories. All of this enables us to keep good relations between the masses and the P.L.A. It is important that our officers take part in labor work with the men. They do not hold themselves as a special breed apart, better than their men; they work shoulder to shoulder with them. We agree with Chairman Mao that the sole purpose of our army is to stand ready to serve the Chinese people."

"Is the maintenance of discipline a simple matter?" I asked, several minutes later.

"Yes. Officers never hit the men. There is no corporal punishment in our army. Nor is there any difference between the officers' and men's uniforms. It is important to understand that in the old days, wherever the Kuomintang and warlords' troops went, the people were afraid and ran away from them because so often they looted and did other harm. The old armies oppressed the people. That is the real reason Chiang Kai-shek lost the war, because he had no broad support among the people. Our armies *did* have support among the peasants. That, in the long run, was the deciding factor. Even as regards prisoners of war the policy is *not* to beat them, insult them or search their pockets.

"We always say that the People's Army should not take so much as a needle or thread from the people. Anything we might have captured or borrowed we must always return. We have strict rules about this. One: While speaking to the people, be polite. Two: In selling or buying be certain that the prices are fair. Three: Anything borrowed from the masses must be returned. Four: If anything is damaged, the owner must be paid its value. Five: P.L.A. men must not beat or curse the people. Six: While carrying out military training or maneuvers the army must not damage crops. Seven: The P.L.A. must never take liberties with the local women. Eight: Never ill-treat prisoners.

"At present," Ting continued, "the international situation is excellent. This is most advantageous for the people. We must of course follow Chairman Mao's advice to keep vigilant and always be prepared to defend our motherland, but in the meantime we concentrate on doing everything possible for the people."

As he concluded his formal remarks Comrade Ting said, "Today we will see the troops, clubs and dormitories and how the officers and men live. After lunch we will visit a pharmaceutical plant set up by dependents of the soldiers. After that a show, with performances by the soldiers, then some military training exercises."

Our foot tour of the camp was enlightening, particularly to this old infantryman. The camp, with its green fields and smart brick buildings, is far more luxurious than California's Camp Roberts, where I underwent basic training in 1943. Our group's first stop was to the quarters of the 587th Regiment.

The building looks like a college dormitory, though on the inside the floors are plain cement and the walls have the rough, worn look of almost all public buildings in China except the most important. We were taken to a meeting room where for the first time in our experience the displayed picture of Chairman Mao showed him grinning so broadly he seemed to be chortling.

"In 1950," a new guide said, "the U.S. imperialists launched a war in Korea. Our company responded to Chairman Mao's call by being the first to join the People's Volunteers for service in Korea."

The company, one of those that broke

Rare poster of Mao smiling. People's Liberation Army Camp, near Tientsin.

through the 38th parallel into South Korea, won special honors for its service in Korean action. A visual display included maps, photographs, artwork and an array of rifles and other weapons used in Korea.

It occurred to me that, except for Ting and a few other old veterans, most of the youngsters now comprising the regiment had not even been born at the time of the Korean War.

As one might expect at a military base, the art posters were considerably more strident and militant than those generally seen. The downtrodden of the world were shown with raised rifles, and most of the faces had an expression of determination and vengeance.

One member of the American delegation stared particularly intently at the new rifles displayed, from which I assumed he had special knowledge of weapons.

"Were you in the service?" I asked.

"Marine Corps," he said.

"Then those rifles probably look familiar to you."

"Yes," the man said, with a slight smile. "You know, it's interesting that the whole unit volunteered for service in Korea."

"Well," I said, "in discussing Korea the word 'volunteer' is always used with quotation marks, even in some sympathetic literature."

"But they had to do it," he said, "when MacArthur got near the Yalu River. We would have done the same thing if they were threatening to cross our border."

The Korean War, incidentally, was of immense benefit to the Chinese Communist Party. To understand this the point must be considered within the context of the extremely difficult task that faced Mao and his associates in 1949, after the collapse of Chiang Kai-shek. Here was one of the world's largest nations, with the greatest population, after thousands of years of social chaos, poverty, degradation, hunger, drought, inflation, crime and corruption. Suddenly all the former administrators had left their posts and the country was in the hands of men whose primary experience was running military affairs and governing local, rural rebel regions.

But the Korean War, coming so early in the new Chinese administrative experiment, enabled the government to rally the entire nation to its support on patriotic grounds. The imperialist enemy—the United States, aided by other U.N. contingents from around the world —was once again at China's gates and seemingly threatening to shoot its way in. In any country in the world the immediate response would be a wave of patriotic fervor and a willingness to volunteer. Although the reason for skepticism about Chinese "volunteers" at that time is understandable, inasmuch as entire military units were assigned to Korean action, the fact is that the overwhelming majority of fighting men involved did enter the fray with a great deal of fervor. Many either volunteered or would have in any case; others no doubt went along, as soldiers down through history always have in certain numbers, simply because it seemed the thing to do.

We were next taken to a compound where enormous black hogs are raised. Each company keeps between thirty and forty pigs, which supply the unit with meat. All the ani-mals were asleep in the shaded part of their neat, well-built brick pens which, considering the heat, did not smell nearly as bad as hog communities around the world.

In a nearby house about the size of the average American living room two young soldiers using foot-pedal sewing machines were repairing military jackets. A third was fixing a pair of shoes. Every man in the regiment has a needle and thread and is encouraged to do simple repairs himself

The next room was a rice-processing workshop. A young soldier was feeding flat baskets of rough grain into a machine which divides the rice from the husk.

"By growing our own rice," the guide explained, "we reduce the burden on the people who otherwise would have to pay to provide our food. Also in raising our own grain we save our own money."

A third workroom processed bean paste, soy sauce and vinegar in large casks. The other half of the room housed machinery that grinds bean curd, a staple of the Chinese diet.

We were taken to lunch in a sizable dining hall, where food was served from large metal washbasins. The meal was quite good but unfortunately had acquired the overtaste of coal dust because of smoke drifting in through an open window adjacent to a chimney.

An extremely pretty young lady, a common P.L.A. soldier, sat with us at lunch. She wore her hair over her forehead in a loose bang and pigtails on both sides of her head. Although she was a medical worker she had no special rank.

For a young man to join the army, we were told during lunch, he must apply voluntarily and, oddly enough, his parents must approve. He also must come from a working-class background. An application must also be approved by both the neighborhood committee and his school committee. All those between eighteen and twenty-two have the obligation, as citizens, to serve in the army.

The P.L.A., however, can accommodate only a small portion of the many millions who are eligible. Therefore, among several hundred applying for entrance, only one or two may be selected. Because of this screening process those chosen for service are extremely happy and those, on the other hand, who are not selected are disappointed. Young men and women in the latter category can, of course, receive military training in the militia and in fact are likely to.

The periods of service are three years for the ground force, four for the air force and five for the navy, though if a man is involved with some especially sophisticated skill he may serve a longer term.

At one-thirty, after lunch, we drove to the pharmaceutical plant where dependents of the soldiers run a remarkably complex drug business, based on both traditional and modern medicine. In the pharmaceutical lab one of our guides brought my symptom to the attention of a young uniformed man who turned out to be a doctor. He asked me how many days the problem had troubled me, set up his black case on a nearby radiator, opened it, reached through a number of small jars of medicines and pills, shook several pills from a small bottle into a paper and presented them to me. The instructions: take two tablets three times a day. The medicine was described as an extract of Chinese herbs. I regret to report it had no effect.

Bill and one of the young ladies in the company tasted a sample of one of the digestive medicines, which looked like a little round chocolate ball, wrapped in transparent cellophane paper. At first, they thought, it tasted rather like a dried-fruit roll, but after that got less pleasant. The young lady described it as tasting like "apple mud."

We were taken though several workrooms where white-uniformed women were manufacturing and packaging medicines in glass ampules by the thousands. Then it was show time and we were ushered back into our cars. In the courtyard of the main building Mao stands, twenty feet high, in a hot white concrete overcoat, under the midsummer sun.

We were led into a theater where a couple of hundred seated soldiers applauded vigorously in the usual warm Chinese welcome. The entertainment started at once. A seventeen-piece orchestra and choir numbering about thirty-five sang and played wonderfully. The production included symphonic music, folksongs, ballet, excerpts from Peking opera, acrobatics and comedy. The level of the entertainment was as good as any we had seen in China, and remember, this was an army base. The girls were unusually pretty and talented and the boys, too, were an attractive bunch.

Comedian-writer-actor Buck Henry, who used to work on my TV show, saw one of these People's Liberation Army musicals when he was in China in 1975. The production started with a beautiful harvest moon projected on a backdrop and an army platoon standing under it singing. "Oh, look," Buck said. "Moon over my army."

Our next stop was a rifle range, more presentable than the one I remember from Camp Roberts. A company of young soldiers, suited up with full field pack, waved cheerfully to welcome us. The sun beat down on them unmercifully. We observers were shown to a comfortable hooded viewing stand, seated at tables with tea and orange pop, and treated first to a demonstration of excellent marksmanship by five infantrymen. A line of twenty-five targets with the outline of a human were set up. Firing in rotation, each man hit his target so that all twenty-five went down in just a few seconds. There were no misses.

We were enabled to see in close-up if we wished by the binoculars that had been provided. They were of German manufacture. Another ten targets were set up and a second detachment, of ten men, trotted out on the double to assume their firing positions. Each man put all ten shots on the mark, most near the bull's-eye.

A third demonstration involved three machine guns, each manned by three soldiers, shooting at a concrete pillbox and row of targets. The combined firepower and accuracy were awesome. Three men firing semiautomatic rifles aimed at the ten targets in a row. Nobody missed.

Next a squad of four, moving quickly across the field, attacked a pillbox. Antitank bazookas, mortars and hand-to-hand combat were also demonstrated, all with the same brisk efficiency.

At the end of our tour we thanked Comrade

Ting and his aides, took a few pictures, and climbed back into our cars.

I was not able to tell if the base was a special one where only superior personnel were stationed. If all Chinese units are so proficient the achievement is even more remarkable.

Let us hope the fine young people we saw performing will never have to see military action. Against today's weapons even such excellent soldiers are vulnerable.

Back in town Bill, Yeh Sing-ru and I stalked about again. Along Wang Fu Jing Street hundreds of watermelons were laid out in neat stacks on the sidewalk. They did not seem to be selling as briskly as their numbers required so I asked Mrs. Yeh if in a few days the price would drop to encourage their sale.

"Yes," she said, " when there is a bumper harvest of watermelons, tomatoes or some other item, the price is made very low so that none of the food will be wasted. When it is especially low people will buy in larger quantities. But to make sure that the individual commune does not lose money on the transaction, the government makes up the difference, paying the commune its regular price."

This is no doubt robbing Peter to pay Paul, but then Paul is the fellow who runs the communes and the whole structure depends on his good health.

Most of the Americans one meets in China are capitalists. In addition to the hundreds who are there to facilitate the export of Chinese goods one also meets, of course, Americans supervising the delivery or installation of American materials to China. On July 28, in the main dining room of the Peking Hotel, Bill and I talked to several of them, including one young man who had been in Peking for four months installing American data-processing equipment. Two other gentlemen were with an oil-products company based in Chicago. Although most travelers with a studious interest in China would consider themselves fortunate to be able to spend many weeks in one of the world's most fascinating capitals, most of the representatives of large American firms we talked to had become bored and frustrated by their long stays, partly they reported because

it was almost impossible to get the Chinese to give them permission to make trips to other cities. The Chinese themselves are so industrious that I suppose they expect the peoples of other nations to be the same in this regard, and they are frequently not. Life in Western nations, most particularly the United States, has a remarkable variety to it and when one is accustomed to such a wide range of experience it can be frustrating indeed to accustom oneself to the sort of social life common even in so interesting a city as Peking. Since our Chinese hosts kindly solicited our advice on dozens of occasions I include here the suggestion that they enlarge the social and travel possibilities open to Americans and others stationed for long periods of time in Peking or other Chinese cities.

By 1979 there had been improvement in this direction.

THE SUBWAY

The next item on our agenda was a visit to a May 7th Cadre School, something few American visitors to China have been able to see. The work, the very purpose of one of their countryside camps, is close to the heart of the modern Chinese experiment. Naturally we looked forward with curious anticipation to the next morning's journey, after which we would have lunch with George and Barbara Bush at the American liaison office.

It was raining when, with more difficulty than ever, I staggered out of bed and looked out at the dreary scene below from our twelfth-floor balcony. While eating a hasty breakfast (we had been told we'd have to leave the hotel at eight, half an hour earlier than usual) Bill and I chatted with a table of visiting American businessmen who told us they had been scheduled to leave a day earlier but that all flights have been canceled because of the heavy rains.

"The planes don't have landing instruments here, you know," one of the men said. "Just lights on the runway, and when those lights aren't visible from the right distance . . . that's it."

We went upstairs for a few minutes and promptly at eight came down in the elevator, accompanied by two Japanese businessmen who also occupied rooms on the twelfth floor. When we arrived at the lobby floor and the doors opened it became briefly impossible to get out because several athletes from a Third World country, apparently never having been taught that one group of passengers must get off an elevator before a second group can get on, simply rushed in upon us, effectively barring our exit.

At eight-fifteen, in the lobby, a change of plans was announced. Because of the heavy downpour the May 7th Cadre School grounds were extremely muddy. Therefore we would visit the Peking subway this morning. It was hoped that conditions would be improved enough for a visit to the school in the afternoon, after lunch with the Bushes.

The subway is less grand and ornate than its Moscow counterpart but, on the other hand, a great deal more esthetically attractive than New York's. The cost for a ride is 10 fen, or about a nickel. As in Moscow, there is lavish use of marble and mosaic tile in the stations. Illumination is by pairs of bare neon tubes overhead. Happily station platforms are well-lighted, which is not always the case in China's public facilities.

The station is spotlessly clean. As we stood waiting for a train a small group of perhaps forty people strolled about or lounged in chairs. A train passes through every ten minutes. While we waited, one came along going in the opposite direction. The bottom half of its cars were cream color, the top apple green. Windows are extra large so that passengers can easily see what stations have been reached. Our train came along and we hopped on. Inside, the car was clean and attractive. Two smiling young army men pointed out empty seats which had been vacated for us. Lighting inside the cars was too-dim neon.

Trips between stations take about a minute and a half. The cars move at a good clip, at about the same rate of speed, Bill and I thought, as the New York subway trains, although they started and stopped much more smoothly so that there was none of that staggering back and forth so common on American subways. The stations are nearly identical.

In some the supporting pillars are round, in others square. There are also slight differences of floor color. At the end of the line, because everyone got off the train, the platform suddenly had the crowded bustle that would make New York subway riders feel at home.

Construction on the Peking subway started in 1966. In 1969 the present section was completed and opened to traffic. As of mid-1975 there were twenty-three kilometers of track and sixteen stations. A separate new line, running around the city, was under construction.

The trains were manufactured in Changchun in northeast China. The escalators to and from the street level were not working in either the first or last station. They are made at the same factory that manufactures the elevators in the Peking Hotel.

In February, 1980, an expert on the subject matter, New York City's Mayor Edward I. Koch, visited the Peking subway and observed that it looked more like a movie set than the real thing.

"There's no graffiti," he marveled. "No littering. The floors of the cars are clean. People are very nice. Nobody was mugging anybody and the fare was only 7 cents."

After lunch—having changed our plans to meet the Bushes—we were told it would be possible to visit the local TV facility and, in particular, a comedian named Ma Chi.

A TELEVISION STUDIO VISIT

Bill and I eagerly looked forward to visiting with Ma Chi because, although we had seen two other comedians perform in Shanghai, we had not had the pleasure of meeting them. Our party arrived at the television station about 2:45 in the afternoon, in a pouring rain. Although we were at once introduced to several members of the station's staff we could have picked Ma out even if he had not been identified. He appeared to be almost forty, but had a childishly impish face that seemed to have been born with a grin. Even when his face was composed and placid, or seriously intent, his eyes seemed playful.

"Mr. Ma," I said, "my son and I have been waiting for quite some time to meet you since one of the purposes of my visit to China was to learn what I could about Chinese humor. Most Americans, I'm afraid, are not aware that there is such a thing as a Chinese comedian. Needless to say, I'll be happy to enlighten them when I return home."

Ma smiled and said he was glad to meet an American comedian.

"The first question I would like to ask," I said, "is do Chinese who as adults become professional comedians, or humorists, reveal their talent at an early age? In the United States this is usually the case. Most professional comedians in America were identified as funny by their friends or family when they were children."

"Yes," Ma said, "there are certain boys and girls who seem to have the ability to amuse their friends. Not all of them go on to entertain professionally, of course,"

"How old were you," I said, "when you began to realize that your particular gift was the ability to make people laugh?"

"Well." Ma chuckled. "I started to go in for *shingsun*—witty dialogue—at the age of twenty-two. Most professional actors, whether they are comedians or not, originally acquire experience as part-time actors. When we start to work with humorous material the routines are originally written and then, working on that basis, we can be spontaneous and create additions to the material."

"It's the same way some American comedians work," I said. "On another subject, some of our comedians work chiefly alone, doing monologues, while others prefer to work in sketches."

"Yes," Ma said, "we too have both monologues and scenes involving two or more people."

"Since I'm told you're a specialist in witty dialogue I wonder if you could tell us a bit about that particular form."

"Well," he said, "witty dialogue is also called 'live ammunition' or 'bayonet.' The point is it comes in lightning-quick thrusts. If the performer conceives a thought in his mind he must instantly reflect it. The dialogue actually goes back very far. It has a history of hundreds of years. In the beginning, we believe, there was only the monologue form, but the dialogue gradually developed. Witty dialogue—to be amusing—depends primarily on language rather than on behavior, on acting funny. Sometimes, of course, actions can enhance a point of view of the monologue or dialogue."

"One of the distinguishing characteristics of modern Chinese entertainment," I said, "seems to be the concentration on a limited number of songs, plays, operas, ballets and film stories. The entertainment itself is often of a high order of excellence, needless to say, perhaps for the reason that the performers are able to repeat again and again the same material. Now as regards witty dialogues, are the same ones repeated again and again or are new ones being created all the time?"

"Both," Ma said. "We do repeat routines that are popular, of course. For example, there is a particular monologue called 'Eulogy of Friendship.' We have noticed that if we perform this routine a few times for school audiences there are certain children who begin to memorize it. Then they imitate the monologue and amuse their classmates with it."

Parenthetically, while I was waiting for one of my longer questions to be translated, it suddenly occurred to me that the framed sketches of Marx, Lenin, Engels and Stalin on the wall were pictures of four *white* men. Whatever one might say critically of modern Chinese attitudes, antiwhitism would not seem to be involved. Do all the black Communists of the world, I wondered, proudly display the same four pictures of whitey on their walls?

"There are four separate skills involved in witty dialogue," Ma went on to explain. "Speaking, imitating, teasing to make audiences laugh, and singing. In the old days these four divisions were quite marked and a given comedy routine would involve only one or the other. But today a combination of any of the four may be used."

"Are there other well-known comedians in China besides yourself?" I asked.

"Oh, yes," Ma said. "We have a famous witty-dialogue man whose name is Ho Pao-lin. He works primarily as a singer. He makes audiences laugh by changing the notes of well-known songs, seeming to sing some notes wrong."

"There is an American comedian named Danny Kaye who does that," I said.

"Ho also does imitations of famous Peking opera actors," Ma said.

"Some of our comedians do the same sort of thing," I said. "They call it 'doing an impression' of whoever it is they are imitating."

One of the witty dialogues is titled "Sea Swallow." The routine opens with Mr. Ma singing about the seashore. The "Sea Swallow" is about the young women of the province of Shantung (Shandong) who were formerly not allowed to go boating. The women in the community decided, however, to break away from this restriction. Several finally succeeded in going boating, fishing and catching shrimp by themselves. The moral of the story is that times have changed; what men comrades can do, women can also accomplish.

"Since there is nothing inherently amusing about the story itself," I said, "is it perhaps the way it is told that makes audiences laugh?"

"Yes," Ma said, "but the story is humorous because we make fun of the older people who try to stop the younger ones from going boating. The speakers mimic them, their accents and their out-of-date attitudes."

Some Chinese comedians can imitate the dialects of all the Chinese provinces as well as those of some cities, such as Tientsin, whose residents have a unique accent. Often in a routine one performer will do a number of dialects, playing separate roles. He may speak properly in the Mandarin dialect and then also burlesque a local or regional accent.

Some monologues, oddly enough, are done in foreign languages, including Swahili. How do Chinese audiences understand what a man is saying when he speaks Swahili? A second performer does a translation every few lines.

Since the actors are speaking the actual language and not just double-talk the children who see these performances learn a few words. For example, they learn the Swahili word for *friend* and later call it out to the visiting Africans they see around Peking.

"Do 100 percent of today's witty dialogues carry a political, social moral," I said, "or is there perhaps an analogy with the delightful peasant paintings we saw a couple of weeks ago whereby *most* of the paintings carry a political message but a few were simply lovely representations of natural scenes?"

"No. Practically all shows have a political content now. Before the Cultural Revolution there were witty dialogues that did not have a political moral, but since that time all of them do." (By 1979 this was no longer the case.)

"Does this rule out all possibility of employing themes which have provided humorous material, in many parts of the world, for thousands of years?" I asked. "Routines about problems between husbands and wives, parents and children, comments on news of the day?"

Oddly enough, while I was posing the question it suddenly occurred to me, for the first time in my life, how much social and political philosophy is implicit in seemingly innocuous entertainment of the sort common in America. There are shows such as "All in the Family," "Maude," "Barney Miller," "M*A*S*H" and others in which important questions—birth control, divorce, women's lib, etc.—are dealt with in a straightforward fashion. But even in programs whose producers consciously reject reference to significant issues, it often happens that social biases—bourgeois prejudices, as the Marxists would say—are revealed.

"Well," Mr. Ma said, "in the past we too have given performances about gambling or drinking too much. But these performances had no particular thought content. They expressed no ideas important to society. If you do those old-fashioned forms, the people simply call you zany. Now that actors have political status in society we think it no longer necessary to perform these old-fashioned shows, because they are no longer in the mainstream of society's thought. Today there are many more important things that are to be portrayed in our life. Before Liberation, you see, those who performed witty dialogue were looked upon as low-class performers. In speaking unkindly about the physically handicapped, people would sometimes compare them to those who did witty dialogue."

"Since the Great Proletarian Cultural Revolution," said one of the television station's staff members, "a hundred flowers have blossomed in our artistic fields."

"I am a bit confused," I said, "by our friend's use of the phrase a 'Hundred Flowers.' When Chairman Mao used the phrase publicly in 1956, if I am reliably informed, he meant to indicate his willingness to listen to *criticism* from various sources. He used a poetic figure of speech, inasmuch as he is a gifted poet, to express this idea. But no criticism of government policy is now permitted on television. I am therefore confused by the use of this particular expression of Chairman Mao's."

Brows darkened briefly, replaced at once by patient smiles.

"Maybe," said one of our hosts, "you misunderstood the policy on literature and art. There is, of course, dross in artistic work, which should be swept out."

"Is the comrade using the phrase then in a sense of his own?"

"No, it is in line with Chairman Mao's directive." I did not pursue the point.

The next order of business was a tour of technical facilities.

The hallways of the television studio building were the dimmest, darkest we had encountered yet. Although there were overhead lights, some were not in use. The kind of power shortage the U.S. was facing in 1980 had long been common in China.

The equipment in the first control rooms we visited was of Chinese manufacture. Although there is much film projection, as in the United States, the studio also has videotape facilities. The viewing monitors in the control room were imported from West Germany. China manufactures its own sets but as of 1975 they were in the smaller screen sizes. I don't know the names of the large machines that are the nerve centers of TV studios in China any more than I understand the same equipment in the United States, but the Chinese equipment looked modern and appropriately complex.

The central control booth, where the directors work, boasted thirteen monitors and two control boards. Its equipment came from three different parts of China, except for one large West German monitor. The three videotaping

units were manufactured in Peking. The station has a separate central control room for black-and-white transmission. By 1979, when I would see it again, it had imported more foreign equipment. Each day's fare is 50 percent black-and-white, 50 percent color. Transmission is, however, simultaneous on different channels.

With the exception of Tibetan towns, every large city in China has its own television station, which operates independently but can be strung together with others in a network when the occasion arises.

A fascinating factor is that although each evening certain programming is sent out from Peking to the stations in the individual provinces, it is left to the decision of local authorities as to whether they wish to carry the network programming. It doesn't sound especially monolithic.

A great deal of floor space was taken up with motion picture projection equipment for television, which suggested that at the time not a great deal of the entertainment was live. "How much of your programming is in the present tense?"

"Approximately 10 percent."

After inspecting the technical equipment, we were taken to a studio, which looked exactly as it would in the United States. It had no audience facility, but neither do most American TV stations. Some of the cameras were made in Shanghai, others in Japan. The Chinese cameras use some Japanese lenses and other components. The camera carriages are of Chinese manufacture.

Scenery, of a modern Chinese village with a distant terraced hillside, was set up in one corner of the studio. It looked like scenery in any studio in the world. I checked out the piano. It seemed quite old, was reportedly of Chinese manufacture, and had a better tone than the two I had played earlier, although it was badly in need of tuning, from which I assumed it had not recently been much used.

Approximately 20 percent of TV fare, our hosts explained, consists of special programs such as sports, public health and children's shows. Perhaps 50 percent, we were told, involves entertainment, 20 percent telecasting motion pictures, including newsreels and documentaries. Believe it or not, there was then no such thing as a TV news program, in the Walter Cronkite sense, in China. That was left entirely to radio.

All the forms of entertainment one sees "live" in the major Chinese cities are, of course, also available on television: drama, dance—usually ballet—puppet shows, singing orchestral music, acrobatics and general vaudeville entertainment. Originally Chinese television simply put on the air what was already available in the theater, but in recent years there had been a tendency to develop artists and playwrights for the industry.

"Liu Shao-chi and his Revisionist line" were also blamed for earlier "ill effects" on Chinese television, until Liu was deposed during the Cultural Revolution.

At the end of the day we thanked Ma Chi and our other friends.

"I will share with my fellow Americans," I said, "the information you have been kind enough to provide us with today. My son and I have greatly enjoyed our visit to your studios."

TSINGHUA UNIVERSITY

Tuesday, July 29

The following day we were pleased to be able to visit Peking's famous Tsinghua University, where some of the most important battles of the Cultural Revolution had been fought in the late 1960s. The campus is in an outlying area of the city apparently occupied almost solely by universities and colleges. It is remarkably self-contained, partly for the reason that virtually all of its students live on campus, as do college students in other areas of China as well. Even if a school is located in a student's hometown it is unlikely that it would be near his home neighborhood. The few who do live close to their campuses, however, are permitted to go home Saturday nights, if they wish, and spend Sunday with their families.

The buildings one sees on driving through the main entrance are massive, understandable in that Tsinghua is China's most important

school of science and engineering. The campus occupies two hundred acres. As is the case with all Chinese universities, the appearance in college fields of crops rather than the usual lawn and forest areas at first strikes the Western visitor as odd. The students grow vegetables and fruits, thus playing their role in the all-important task of feeding the nation's over 800 million people.

A gentleman named Ma headed our reception committee, which ushered our group to a large, comfortable meeting room where it was explained that the university boasts eleven departments, divided into fifty-four areas of educational specialization, including electronics, automation, radio, mechanics, precision instruments, engineering physics and engineering mechanics.

Even in midsummer there were some 8,000 students on the campus, served by 3,000 teachers. When summer vacation was over, we were told, the number of students would rise to 11,000. This is a considerable increase over the 2,800 attending Tsinghua in 1971 when Socialist William Hinton visited the campus, in preparation for his dramatic study, *Hundred-Day War: The Cultural Revolution at Tsinghua University*. Even the anti-Socialist reader can learn a great deal from Hinton's painstaking report of the incredible events that took place on this Peking campus during the 1966–1969 period. One might say *especially* anti-Socialists, since Socialist scholars will already be familiar with Hinton's findings. Hinton's study is also valuable in that it gives ample exposition to what is now criticized as the Gang of Four line.

The library houses over a million and a half books, only two-thirds of which are in Chinese. As for foreign languages, English leads. In a separate wing of the building the liberal arts library is housed.

Periodical racks naturally featured a great many magazines, including one kind we had not expected, published by the various Chinese universities themselves. One rack included recent scientific works in English on solid state technology, radio electronics, scientific instruments, vacuums, etc. Copies of the American magazine *Science* were available, as well as the

Journal of the Franklin Institute, the *Journal of Strain Analysis* and other American and British publications. We also saw a copy of *Earthquake Engineering and Structural Dynamics,* published by the journal of the international Association for Earthquake Engineering, John Wiley and Sons. I cannot conceive of a better supplied library of science.

We were invited to walk behind the librarian's desk, and entered a fascinating inner sanctum, lighted from above and below, consisting chiefly of books on Marxism and Leninism in the various languages spoken in China. For our inspection a cover was removed from a box which enclosed about a dozen oracle bones many centuries old. Through a magnifying glass one could clearly make out the inscriptions. The bones had been found in the Anyang area.

A volume written in A.D. 1031, from the Sung dynasty, dealt with scientific matters. One page pointed out to us concerned the discovery of petroleum. We also saw a copy of the *Yung Lo Ta Tien,* the great encyclopedia compiled in the early fifteenth century. Emperor Cheng Tsu had decreed that a series of books of reference arranged according to subject matter be compiled. He conceived the project on a scale that would far surpass any previous work. The *Yung Lo Ta Tien* is the earliest and largest encyclopedia in the history of China, perhaps in the world. Its pages, needless to say, were all handwritten.

On a special display table were recent books on China, including Shirley MacLaine's *You Can Get There from Here.* An important work by William Hinton, *Fanshen: A Documentary of Revolution in a Chinese Village,* was next to Shirley's.

My observations in this chapter—and in the section describing our visit to Wuhan University—of course refer to the general state of Chinese college education as we found it in the early winter and summer of 1975. Even then there was no reason to assume that procedures and philosophies were firmly set for all time or even for the foreseeable future. The debate about educational philosophy continues in China, most significantly among members of the Communist Party. As of 1976 it could be

Baseball players on the Tsinghua University campus, Peking.

perceived that while apparently no one wished to return completely to the old educational policies, which tended to develop an intellectual elite and to favor the sons and daughters of the well-to-do, nevertheless some educators clearly felt that the better-Red-than-expert approach had erred at the other extreme.

The controversy about education that was such an essential part of the turmoil of the Cultural Revolution of 1966–1969 toppled from power the leaders of the great Chinese universities. Subsequently, however, many were quietly restored to their posts. As their confidence returned they began to criticize some, though not all, results of the modern procedure which had brought so many farmers, workers and soldiers into the universities. These last, perhaps correctly sensing that they were threatened if former views regain the ascendancy, were responding in late 1975 and early 1976 with the by-now traditional big-character posters, speeches and protests.

First Vice Premier Teng Hsiao-ping's faction supported those demanding that educational standards be raised. The theoretical justification for this, of course, cannot now in China be anything like education-for-its-own-sake or art-for-art's-sake, but that more competent scholarship will lead to increased industrial and agricultural production, a necessity if the Four Modernizations campaign is to succeed.

After the purge of Chiang Ching and other

Forbidden City, Peking.

radicals following Mao's death in 1976 one expected that in time educational philosophy would swing, however slightly, to the right. Entrance requirements would probably be tightened and pragmatism rather than politics alone would probably again become dominant.

By 1979 such a reversal of policy was in full swing. Hua and Teng recognized the need to encourage the best and brightest.

As we drove away from the campus I said to Yeh Sing-ru, "You know, I sometimes think that but for accidents of my early experience I might have been better fitted for life in the academic or intellectual community than for the fields in which I have worked. For some reason whenever I am in the company of scholars my own mind is tremendously stimulated so that ideas and insights occur to me that very probably would not have if the meeting had not taken place. I feel a pleasurable sense of being at home in the company of scholars."

"That," said Yeh Sing-ru, grinning more broadly than she ever had before, "is because you have the typical arrogance of the bourgeois intellectual. That is why you feel more at home at a university than you did in the factories and rural communes."

Beautiful! She had me. The two of us laughed our heads off.

We had spoken to George and Barbara Bush about the possibility of having dinner with them Tuesday, but Irene Tung called to say she and her teenage daughter Shiao-Chi could visit us that evening. I told her I'd see if the Bushes were able to confirm our appointment with them. After breakfast I called the American liaison office and reached George who, fortunately, as it happened, had already made a dinner appointment for that night. We agreed to get together for lunch at the embassy on Wednesday so Irene and I proceeded with plans to have dinner with Bill and Shiao-Chi, at our hotel.

By 8:45 that morning Bill and I had reached the Forbidden City, crossed over the famous gently curved white bridges and into the gates of this architectural Wonder-of-Wonders. Even in the rain it was beautiful. This time, in addition to showing Bill the fabulous main palaces, I took him to sections of the royal compound I had not visited the previous winter. The art treasures displayed are of incredible beauty.

LUNCH WITH THE BUSHES

Wednesday, July 30

On Wednesday Bill and I finally reported for lunch at the American "Embassy"—it was only a liaison office in the absence of full diplomatic relations between the U.S.A. and the

George and Barbara Bush, Bill, and I, Peking.

People's Republic of China. The Bushes, charming Texas people, made us welcome.

During lunch Barbara happened to mention that the liaison's office cook had just left, with no real advance warning, reportedly for personal reasons. He had not been replaced and so, Barbara said, "We're sort of ad-libbing the meal today." I later learned that although the Bushes had had a cordial relationship with the man they had heard no further word of him, nor had they been able to get the slightest information from the government about him, despite repeated inquiries.

Although the Chinese have special gifts at expressing warmth and cordiality, they nevertheless keep a Chinese wall, albeit an invisible one, between themselves and foreign visitors, as foreign visitors for several centuries have observed. In the diplomatic community in Peking one hears stories authenticating this point. A Western diplomat reported that one day as he was coming out of his apartment he ran into a Chinese official with whom he had had frequent and most cordial contact for the preceding two and a half years.

"Why, Mr. Wong," he said, "what are *you* doing here?"

"I live here," was the answer.

Mrs. Bush and I sat facing a wall with an enormous recessed niche in the center of which a beautiful needlepoint tapestry, done by Barbara Bush herself, was displayed. Since I had seen it in March, I drew it to Bill's attention.

"You know," Barbara said, "it really isn't the right size for that great big place on the wall. What is supposed to be there is a picture of Gerald Ford."

"Why is that?" I said.

"The Chinese," she explained, "built these things into all the embassies they've put up here in town. I guess they assume that if they would display a picture of Mao in such a place, citizens of every other country would want to hang a picture of their leader too. But . . . as much as we love Jerry . . ." She laughed.

The Bushes that day presumably had no way of knowing that several months later President Ford would nominate George to head the C.I.A. He held the post until the election of President Jimmy Carter.

Conversation during lunch was pleasant but slightly guarded. The servants, after all, are loyal Chinese, no doubt specially chosen for their posts. At one point, when no attendants were in the room, the subject of Chinese law came up.

The Chinese system of law-prisons-justice, I gathered from a comment by George Bush, is not concerned with the niceties of the Ango-American legal process. The same thing, of course, is true of much of the non-Communist world. In 1965 the Chinese were embarrassed when a Peking resident, having suddenly gone mad, attacked a Frenchwoman with a scythe and then ran into the Mali Embassy, where he injured several other persons and caused damage to property. An alarm having been given, the house was immediately surrounded by soldiers. The man was taken into custody, obviously in a severely disturbed state. The French Embassy received word four days later that he had been tried, found insane and promptly executed. The pro-death-penalty right wing in America would love quite a few facets of Chinese Communist practice. By summer of 1979 China was enlarging its freedoms by moving toward the rule of law, and thus away—at least slightly—from rule by party.

Bill and I thanked the Bushes, and members of their staff, for their cordiality (it was the second time I had been welcomed by them), took and posed for a few photographs at the front door and then got back on the tourist treadmill.

A MAY 7th CADRE SCHOOL

An American couple Bill and I had met in the dining room of the Nanking Hotel had said, "The most interesting thing we've seen in China was a May 7th Cadre School. If you can possibly arrange to visit one, by all means do."

I thereupon renewed this suggestion to Yeh Sing-ru and eventually we were able to visit such a school, although we had to drive a considerable distance from Peking to reach it. The controversial schools emerged as a result of the Cultural Revolution. Their name comes from Chairman Mao's directive of May 7, 1966, in which he said, "Going down to do manual labor gives vast numbers of cadres an excellent opportunity to study once again." After the overthrow of Chiang Ching and her

colleagues, many intellectuals and artists, among others, would complain of their experiences in such schools or camps.

Within half an hour after leaving the center of the city we were in a section so backward and rural that it was hard to believe we were still technically in the great world capital of Peking. Primitive huts, like those of centuries past, were on every hand, while roads were covered with hay spread out to dry in the sun. The peasants we passed looked like those of China's ancient ages. The roads were unpaved and in parts still muddy from the recent rain. The only factors that revealed the scene as modern at all were small telephone poles beside the road, a few bicycles, and our own cars.

At long last a small sign identified the turn-off to the Eastern City District Cadre School. We turned left, through a grove of trees, and onto an open area, where several smiling faces awaited us.

At the customary cigarettes and hot tea briefing we were told that the country boarding school had been established in 1968. Nearly 5,000 cadres had come to it for training by mid-1975. Present enrollment was 320, all of whom had started their training course in March, 1975. The normal term—we were told—was six months long, though I assume many were detained for longer periods.

After graduation the students returned to their original posts. They may have come from Revolutionary committees, the Bureau of Education, the Bureau of Public Health, the Bureau of Industry, from schools, hospitals, shops. A portion of the student body consisted of teachers from primary and middle schools. Although compliance was naturally not unanimous, cadres all over the country responded to Chairman Mao's 1966 call by expressing their willingness to go down to the countryside to remold their world outlook through physical labor, to learn "to repudiate and criticize the bourgeoisie," to do some "mass work" and engage in production.

The primary task of the cadre school was to instruct in Marxist ideology, not for its own sake but to enable the cadres to serve the people better. The aim of education: to organize the trainees to study Marxism-Leninism and

Mao Tse-tung thought. Linking theory with practice was stressed. An important object was to "criticize revisionism" and "to criticize the old ideas," though both terms would, by 1978, be otherwise defined. The class members first study alone, then join in groups to discuss what they have read.

At a third level teachers join the group and pass along the dominant line. Only part of the time is devoted to study, the rest to manual labor and learning from the lower and middle peasants. The primary purpose of the physical work is *to change the thinking* of the trainee, not merely to produce grain, or other crops. Always Chairman Mao's comment that cadres are *servants* of the people, not overlords sitting on the backs of the people, is stressed. Regardless of what high post a man or woman may hold once they attend the cadre school they will never forget that they are also common laborers, it was said.

We began to stroll about, still questioning our hosts. Some cadres, we were told, unaccustomed to physical labor, cooking and farming, at first feel uncomfortable. But that very fact, it is said, reveals to them the gap between themselves and the people and the necessity, therefore, of remolding their thinking. Eventually, it is said, the cadres are rather pleased with themselves in that they learn tasks at which they were formerly not much good— how to use tools, to cook, to do carpentry, painting, plumbing and farming. The trainees repair roads, raise pigs, farm crops, build their own living quarters, plant trees and reclaim land.

Individuals among groups of the cadres are encouraged to set their own standards and pace of work rather than simply being ordered from above. In the outer world people generally try to avoid hard work or, if they must do it, take the lighter tasks. But in the cadre schools they are encouraged to seek out the hardest work, the dirtiest job, the most demeaning activity. Catholic religious orders have preached the same. This "builds character."

From all of this the visitors finally grasp "the great truth that labor creates the world." If large numbers of the cadres learn this lesson

well, it was believed, revisionism, "taking the Capitalist road," could never really be dominant again. In the past, while reading Chairman Mao's instructions, party members have perhaps held a cigarette in one hand, a cup of tea in the other and occasionally used a fan as they sat in a comfortable office or lay on their beds studying the chairman's words. But now, in actually living out his instructions about the dignity of labor, the therapeutic benefits of hard work and the importance of the poor peasant and workingman, they grasp the abstract theory itself more clearly then ever before.

During their six months' course the cadres spend fifteen consecutive days living in a separate commune, like peasants. The farm workers, we were told, not only welcome them but hold certain classes of instruction for the cadres, rather than the other way around. In these classes the peasants, particularly the older among them, share their personal stories, and the histories of their families, with the visiting cadres, so that they will have an even clearer idea what life is like for the simple people of China. The cadres, in turn, help the peasants in their reading, studying, and analysis of current events.

The idea is to reduce the gap between the worker and the peasant, town and country, and intellectual and physical labor.

Contrary to common assumption, the school is not a place that produces cadres. The students are already cadres and simply go there for additional training.

After the introductory formalities, Bill and I visited a comfortable, clean small dormitory with room for nine beds. About a dozen friendly young people—in their twenties and thirties—sat about on the beds and stools, answering our questions. They told us that presently there were about 27 million party members in China. (By 1977 the figure was 30 million.) A party member is not automatically a cadre. Some cadres, in fact, are not members of the party. Party members and members of the Communist Youth League comprise over 80 percent of the student body. A young person becomes a cadre by special hard work, by achieving a high degree of Socialist consciousness, on being recommended by his colleagues, and finally approved by the proper offices.

The day at the school starts at 5:30 A.M. The students wash, dress, tidy up their quarters and exercise. Breakfast is from 7:00 to 7:30. The rest of the morning is devoted to work. From 11:30 to 3:00 is for lunch, napping and reading.

Studies and indoor labor may run from 3:00 to 7:00 P.M. Dinner is served from 7:00 to 7:30. Then the students are free until nine o'clock. All hands go to bed at 10:00 P.M.

Some of their books are brought from home, others are available from the library at the school. Our hosts did not know how many cadre schools there were throughout China but told us they existed in all provinces and major cities. Within the city district of Peking there were several.

By five-thirty, although we were tired and behind schedule in getting back to town, it became apparent that our hosts would be disappointed if we did not see a show that had been planned especially for the two of us. Once again eager, energetic young people proudly sang and danced for us. Bill and I applauded them heartily and smiled till our faces ached. Then, in a flurry of thanks, smiles and handshakes all around, we headed back for Peking in the late afternoon sunlight.

In early 1977 I made the following notation: "It will be interesting to see to what extent the antiradical shift of late-1976 affects the May 7th Cadre School program. Without Mao, without Chiang Ching, the movement's philosophical support may begin to evaporate. Time—not to coin a phrase—will tell."

It has. Hua Kuo-feng and Teng Hsiao-ping seem to be dismantling the "going down to the countryside" movement, though very gradually. It was not clear, as of early 1979, that they intended to do away with it totally.

TIBET

Thursday, July 31

The morning dawned bright, clear and sunny. The view from our twelfth-floor balcony was so impressive at seven o'clock that I took a picture of it and then awakened Bill. After a hearty American-style breakfast in the dining room, we left the hotel promptly at eight for what would be my son's first visit to the one supreme tourist attraction of China, the Great Wall.

For approximately an hour we wound through a hundred-and-one Peking boulevards, streets and byroads. At last, on such a trip, the countryside is reached; almost immediately, in the far distance, mountains leap into view. Within another half-hour the road lifts into the foothills and the climb begins in earnest. The preceding winter these rugged peaks had been bare and forbidding. Now they were lush and green to their very tips.

As we drove through the pleasant countryside, Yeh Sing-ru answered questions about Tibet, which was liberated—to use the Chinese word—in 1951. But in 1958, Mrs. Yeh explained, there had been a rebellion of serf-owners against the authority of the Chinese government. Her answers naturally stressed the degradation and servitude of the people of that mysterious land under the former regime. In Tibet, she told us, if a serf-owner wished to mount his horse one of his serfs was obliged instantly to kneel so that the master could step on his back to reach his saddle. Mrs. Yeh told us that she knew personally that the landlords and other wealthy Tibetans in former days would sometimes drink wine from cups made from the skulls of serfs.

"Sometimes the serfs would try to run away," she said, "but if they were captured they might be skinned alive and their skins used to make drums."

"Up to how late a point did such atrocities take place?" I asked, skeptical.

"Until the liberation of Tibet in the late 1950s. When our people went in there they discovered that beneath the one very beautiful palace, under the fountain, large numbers of serfs had been buried alive because of the superstitious belief that the building would enjoy good fortune if this were done."

"Which palace was this?"

"The Dalai Lama's house."

Since the Dalai Lama was a religious leader I took the occasion again to express the hope

Intersection of Chang An Boulevard and Wang Fu Jing Street on a day with somewhat less smog. Peking, 1979. Photograph by Michael Welch

that it might be possible to meet with representatives of the Religious Affairs Bureau while I was in Peking. Again I met with what I interpreted as polite evasions. The Polite Evasion, by the way, is a Chinese tradition, by no means specifically Communist.

Today's young Chinese would be honestly surprised if told that their government's takeover of Tibet—like Stalin's incursions into Eastern European countries outside Soviet borders—looked to others exactly like the sort of Western imperialism Chinese Communists *and Nationalists* understandably so vigorously condemn. The Communists feel that by going into Tibet they were rescuing helpless peasants from cruel feudal overlords.

A different view is provided by Dawa Norbu, whose *Red Star Over Tibet* comments on the modern relationship between China and Tibet from the viewpoint of an educated Tibetan. Dawa, editor of *Tibetan Review,* explains that when the Chinese invaded his country in 1950 thousands of specially selected young people were sent to China for training at the National Minorities University.

Apparently Chinese success in influencing the thinking of young Tibetans has been some-

what less than glowing magazine reports would suggest. Having found that in pre-Revolutionary Tibet only the aristocracy and the monks were given any education at all, the Chinese reasonably enough decided that the education of a broader stratum of young Tibetans was called for. But even though education has been thoroughly Marxist it has evidently not succeeded in eradicating nationalistic sentiment.

George Patterson's review of *Red Star Over Tibet* in the *China Quarterly* (June, 1976) reports:

Nearly 80,000 Tibetans have now had concentrated Chinese education, for 25 years. Yet, "In China's own sources," Dawa Norbu points out, "of the 56 office-bearers in the Committee for the Tibet Autonomous Region, established in August 1971, only three Tibetans are included. All three are secretaries, and two of these even had Chinese names.

This body is supposed to represent Tibetan "local government." On June 1, 1972, three sub-regional and one municipal Communist parties were set up in Tibet; but only six Tibetans were included out of a total of 293 office-bearers. The pressures which have been generated by the young Tibetans inside Tibet in the past three years have elicited some liberalization of the earlier oppressive policies; while, outside Tibet, young Tibetans exiled, educated in India and other countries, have also been demanding new policies from the Dalai Lama and his advisers which allowed them to return to work in and for Tibet.

If the Chinese authorities continue to be patient and understanding with the young Tibetans the future of Tibet is in good hands.

Among those Tibetans hardly reconciled to Chinese rule, whether Communist or not, are the Khamba tribesmen, guerrilla fighters who have been sniping at what they regard as the Chinese invader for thirty years.

The Communists, incidentally, happen to be perfectly right in a good many of their criticisms of the traditional mode of life in Tibet. There may be no particular reason to take their word—or my own—about the matter but I recommend to the reader *Seven Years in Tibet* by Heimrich Harrer, a book that is by no means Communist propaganda. It is, in fact, written in a sympathetic, friendly and pro-Tibetan tone, which is understandable inasmuch as Mr. Harrer for some years served as personal tutor to the Dalai Lama whom he met when that most august temporal and spiritual ruler of an enormous country was eleven years old.

Although most Americans think of Tibet as a tiny corner of the world, and would perhaps never have thought of it at all had they not seen the motion picture *Lost Horizon,* the country is larger than most of Europe. Harrer's book is a simple factual account of conditions of life in that vast territory. If Western readers would be horrified by much of what he reveals, they are only reacting as generations of earlier Christians have to the horrible poverty, superstition and general backwardness of Tibet. So primitive was the country in fact that until about the time of the Communist invasion few wheeled vehicles had been permitted there. The condition of the average inhabitant was that of the deepest poverty. Nobles and religious leaders, needless to say, were exempted from such destitution. Education, in the Western sense of the word, was practically nonexistent and almost all religious beliefs would be described by all devout Christians or Jews as incredibly superstitious if not bizarre. The Tibetans' religion was a form of Buddhism. They naturally therefore believed in reincarnation and specifically that their God-King was the literal reincarnation of the great Gautama Buddha himself. Belief in a whole list of demons and other spirits was also central to Tibetan religion. It has naturally been observed by the Tibetans over the thousands of years of their religious development that their individual God-Kings have died, the same as mortal men. This fact, however, has never affected the faith since they are of the opinion that when a supreme ruler dies his soul moves first to heaven and then, within a year or two, returns to earth entering into a newborn infant. This requires a search for and the identification of the new embodiment of Buddha. Toward this end the leading monks and seers throw themselves into trances to try to pierce the material veil.

Harrer explains that celibacy seems even more important to religious Tibetans than to Christians with the result that, at least before the Communist invasion, one-sixth of the male Tibetan population were celibate monks supported by the rest of the population. Harrer—again, be it remembered, a pro-Tibetan witness—reports that homosexuality was very common among the monks. In absorbing such information one recalls why the American Founding Fathers were so opposed to unions of church and state.

The Maoist leaders of China, being realists, were naturally aware that the Herculean task of turning around the consciousness of several million people who were steeped in long centuries of such superstition would not be easy. At first, apparently, they did not approach the problem of religion and superstition directly but simply took the land from the well-to-do nobles, built roads, power stations, schools, hospitals, etc., and began extracting the country's mineral resources. The record on the philosophical point is unclear. It seems probable that the Communists were content, generally speaking, to allow an older generation of Tibetans to simply pass away, feeling that it would be impossible to change their views, but instead concentrated on what they saw as the proper education of new generations being born. Since the invasion led to military confrontations in which the Communists had the benefit of superior numbers and modern weaponry the Tibetans who opposed them by force of arms were understandably defeated and partly wiped out. Since we Americans did exactly the same to the hordes of Indians who once inhabited our own continent we are, of course, in an awkward position if we pretend to oppose such historical processes on principle. Both we and the Chinese Communists were wrong to slaughter so many of these indigenous tribal populations, but on that point separate volumes can be written.

In any event both the United States and China can point to remarkable technical achievements and improvements in the areas in question. There is, of course, *the crucial difference that the Americans actually took for themselves the land belonging to the Indians* whereas the Chinese, as a general rule, are leaving the Tibetan inhabitants where they find them but simply trying to change their way of life by educating them, providing medical care, improving their economic lot, providing electric power, etc.

I had, at the moment, no way of knowing that in 1979 I would have two meetings with the Dalai Lama himself. They came about as follows.

When the Oriental leader visited the U.S., his travels took him to Los Angeles. During the two weeks before his arrival I received three separate invitations to attend social functions at which he would be present. Selecting one simply because the host's home was not far from our own, Jayne and I went, at the appointed late-afternoon hour, to the home of novelist John Ball, whose son had visited Tibet some years earlier.

We were ushered at once into the august presence; the Lama stood quietly against a fireplace answering questions. Fortunately, I had had the presence of mind to bring a copy of his newly republished autobiography, which he kindly autographed for me.

It was somehow difficult to get into focus, as I chatted with this simple, friendly forty-four-year-old gentleman, that in Tibet he is honored not only as the head of the national religion but also as head of state, though more like a king than president or prime minister. It is this political role that makes him important in the context of international relations.

At Ball's house I also met two young filmmakers, Philip Hensly and John Meza, who approached me about the possibility of appearing in a documentary film on the Lama on which, they said, they had been working for some three years.

The arrangements having been quickly made, I went, two days later, to the Beverly Wilshire Hotel, at 8:30 A.M. Hensly himself was waiting for me when I stepped off the elevator on the fourth floor. He ushered me at once to a suite at the end of a hall where cameras, lights, sound equipment and technical personnel were waiting. Two wine-red robed gentlemen were in attendance. As soon as I had been shown to a chair and fitted with a tie-clasp microphone, we were ready to proceed. One of the Buddhist monks stepped quickly out of the room, apparently to summon the Dalai Lama. The other approached me holding a white folded scarf. "You may present this to his holiness," he said, "holding it in this way, by one end, so that it folds open as you hand it, after you shake hands."

"Thank you," I said. "Oh, I have one question. Is it necessary to introduce every question with the phrase 'Your Holiness'?"

"No," he said, "it is not."

A moment later the spiritual and temporal head of the enormous, but thinly populated land of Tibet appeared and approached me. He had met so many hundreds of Americans in the preceding few days that I was not sure he could recall our earlier encounter. I opened his book, pointed to his signature and said, "Thank you again for your kindness in autographing a copy of your memoirs the other day."

"You are welcome," he said with a gentle smile.

"Your Holiness," I said, once the cameras had started to roll, "many Christians in the West today feel, as they look back over the

I meet the Dalai Lama.

past century, that the churches were perhaps too tolerant of the sufferings of the poor. They feel that it was a mistake to offer only prayer when the impoverished complained about hunger, sickness and illiteracy, whether in Europe or North and South America. As a result of this historic tendency—at least so goes the argument—the stage was therefore left open to the Communists who could say, 'You see, the churches do not really care about the disgraceful conditions of your lives, whereas we are truly concerned about your poverty, your ignorance, your hunger and so forth.' How does this line of reasoning sound as it falls on your ears?"

He paused briefly to reflect before answering. "Yes," he said, "everyone should do more for the poor. The religious, too, must make their contribution."

It was hardly an adequate answer but I did not press the point.

The Dalai Lama struck me as above all else a reasonable man. Neither his demeanor nor subsequent remarks gave the slightest indication of the sort of religious rigidity and fanaticism associated with, say, Ayatollah Ruhollah Khomeini. Buddhism, of course, is a more tolerant and peaceful religion than Islam.

Buddhists, however, are as firmly convinced that reincarnation is an actual process as

Christians are convinced that Jesus was either God or the personal Son of God. When a Dalai Lama dies, Buddhist officials—as mentioned earlier—travel about until they happen upon an infant who, in their opinion, embodies the same spirit as that of the late departed. Divinations and miraculous signs, it is said, confirm the hypothesis. Since Christians believe that true miracles can occur only within the context of Christianity, it follows that they do not accept as authentic reports of miraculous occurrences attributed to Buddhist experience.

The September, 1979, visit of the Dalai Lama to the U.S. was the first in history. His forty-nine-day stay was officially described as nonpolitical but in fact had political implications. The fervent outpouring of crowds, welcoming committees, dignitaries, and others was interesting in many respects and it is probable that it will take some time to understand all the factors associated with the visit. Five thousand of those who expressed their joy— and no doubt some curiosity—at "the Precious One's" presence were Catholics who gathered in New York's St. Patrick's Cathedral. Said Terence Cardinal Cooke, flanked by a Protestant minister and a rabbi, "This is one of the dramatic movements of the spirit in our time." The pronouncement itself was remarkable in that for at least two hundred years preceding it Catholic missionaries had tried to inculcate the same view shared by China's Communists, that Buddhism in practice was rife with superstitious nonsense.

One of the odd factors of timing in the overall drama was that the Dalai Lama arrived in the United States just when his elder brother Gyalo Thombup and other members of a Tibetan delegation were visiting China.

Since Mao had tried to make true believers of all Chinese he had naturally taken a stern line in dealing with the Tibetans. The Hua Kuo-feng–Teng Hsiao-ping government, by way of contrast, has tried to increase autonomy for Tibet.

As of year-end 1979, it was still too early to say whether the some three hundred Tibetan refugees in the U.S. would accompany their leader back to Tibet should such a return itself become possible. *Newsweek*'s researchers, working on a story published in the September 16, 1979, edition of that magazine, concluded that few would. It must seem strange to Christian churches, parenthetically, that although there are few Catholics and Protestants, if any, in Tibet, there are now some 200,000 Buddhists in the United States.

Well, to return to China and our conversation with Yeh Sing-ru, after discussing Tibet, I returned to my earlier question.

"The staff of the Religious Affairs Bureau," Mrs. Yeh said, "is either in the countryside working with the peasants or else out in the fields conducting investigations about religious practices." At the time, as it happens, such bureaucrats were regarded unsympathetically by the Gang of Four and their followers and were, presumably, "discouraged" from meeting with inquisitive foreigners.

"Do you suppose," I said, "that any staff members might return to Peking before I leave the city?"

"I don't think so."

"You know," I said, "I am obviously not familiar with Chinese bureaucratic practice, but in Western nations it would be a very unusual situation if every single member of a given staff were absent from the home office. It would be normal for a certain percentage of workers or administrative officers to be absent from the bureau's center, but, as I say, the idea that literally no one would be left behind falls oddly on Western ears."

"Oh," Yeh Sing-ru said, "there may be a few secretaries or security personnel in the building . . ."

"But no one I could interview?"

"I don't think so."

"Well," I said, "I do hope you will be able to find the time to convey to the ladies and gentlemen at the Religious Affairs Bureau that I would be very happy to communicate to the readers of the report I am preparing the government's side of the argument about an issue which, in the eyes of many Americans and Europeans, seems to involve the repression of religion. Surely there must be something identifiable as the government's case about all this and I find myself curious as to what it is. I also find myself curious as to why the present Chinese government, which obviously has such a well-developed sensitivity to the importance of propaganda, seems to have given little attention to this particular problem, one that is important to hundreds of millions of people in the West."

"Very well," Yeh Sing-ru said, "I will forward your message to the Religious Affairs Bureau, but I do not know what will happen." I would guess that during the four weeks Bill and I spent with Mrs. Yeh, we went over this same ground at least half a dozen times. No information was forthcoming, however.

I have since assumed that what Yeh Sing-ru either did not know, or what it might have been uncomfortable for her to bring to my attention, was that the Mao–Chiang Ching–Gang of Four faction had essentially closed up the Bureau of Religious Affairs. Consistent with this hypothesis was the news that on March 16, 1979, the Central Committee of the Chinese Communist Party announced that it was reinstating three departments: United Front Work, Nationalities and Religious Affairs.

This need not necessarily come as heartening news to religious believers outside China, since the newly rehabilitated bureau might decide, for example, to conduct an "antisuperstition campaign." *Renmin Ribao,* of the Chinese media, indicated that part of the new thrust would be to promote democratic reforms within religious institutions. To those faiths that already perceive democracy as appealing, this need not be dismaying news. But to those, such as the Catholic Church, which have essentially top-to-bottom authority structures such announcements do not necessarily come as good news. *China Talk,* published by the China liaison office of the World Division, Board of Global Ministries of the United Methodist Church, observes, in its March/ April 1979 edition, "Although in the past months religion has been gradually gaining more recognition the new announcement opened the way even wider for religious groups to assume a more official form of existence in China."

(I have lifted out of the manuscript of this book a chapter, numbering some one hundred pages, on the subject of religion. Enlarging on this base, I plan to issue a separate volume limited to this one subject.)

THE GREAT WALL IN SUMMER

Shortly after we passed the famous Chu Yun Kuan gate our driver pulled to the side of the road, lifted the hood of the car and inspected the engine. Bill and I got out for a few minutes, stretched our legs, and enjoyed the fresh mountain air and scenery, after which the drive to the top of the ridge was resumed. The stop at this point seems something of a tradition.

Bill felt the same thrill, when there began to come into view, fragments and sections of the wall that has been described by countless Chinese and foreign travelers over the centuries.

When a few minutes later we arrived at the fully restored portion of the wall upon which visitors are permitted to climb, I explained to Bill that I proposed to again tackle the steep side, this time to make it to the top, something

I had been unable to do the preceding winter, due largely to the bitter cold and icy winds that sweep down across the vast expanse of Manchuria during the winter season.

This time, unencumbered by heavy winter clothing and constantly refreshed by a pleasant summer breeze, I found the climb much easier. I felt considerably less bourgeois and weak on discovering, about two-thirds of the way to the top, that a young Chinese woman had collapsed in her tracks while ascending the Wall. She was lying on a step, attended by five or six men. We hurried past so as not to embarrass the group by our curious attentions. Climbing this portion of the Great Wall would be a somewhat difficult feat even at sea level but the mountains at this point are thousands of feet high so that one also must contend with a shortage of oxygen.

I explained to Bill that the wall is the only man-made structure visible from the moon.

The Great Wall is a wonder indeed. And perhaps one of the most wondrous things about it is that no one seems to know how long it is. Or was. My conclusion about the general ignorance on the point is based on the fact that I have read perhaps a dozen accounts of visits to the wall, each of which gives a certain amount of information about its general dimensions. To the best of my recollection no two of the accounts precisely agree. The shortest length, 1,700 miles, is given by Lisa Hobbs, whose *I Saw Red China,* published in 1966, is apparently the first account of a visit to China by an American since 1949. Other references fall within the 2,000-, 2,500- or 3,000-mile range.

Parenthetically, the same kind of confusion prevails about the distance of the famous Long March. The shortest and longest estimates I've read were an incredible 2,000 miles apart.

Later in the day, on the way back to Peking, we stopped at the famed sacred avenue leading to the nearby tombs of the Ming emperors. The roadway at that point is guarded by enormous stone horses, lions, elephants and camels as well as some mythical beasts. Colossal statues of warriors and officials also stand at the roadside, originally placed to defend the tombs against evil spirits. Bill and I unashamedly

Bill at the Great Wall.

climbed elephants, camels and griffins to pose for each other's snapshots.

That evening we dined at the Peking Hotel with Lily Wen's sister and her charming, shy teenaged daughter.

As I looked about the large, crowded dining room during dinner I had the impression that it was not customary for Chinese to dine with American or other foreign visitors in their hotels. But obviously it was not forbidden. Two years earlier, however, when Tung Kuo-ying had come to Shirley MacLaine's hotel to speak to her, she had been detained, and sharply questioned, by the authorities. While Shirley was in one room asking if anyone knew why Tung had not appeared, her would-be visitor was in the very next room, being interrogated.

At breakfast the next morning we again realized that most of the businessmen we met at the Peking Hotel, friendly, country-clubby, not quite scholarly types, were not nearly as fascinated by their stay in China as is the average American visitor. They found doing business with their Chinese counterparts frustrating to one degree or another and, because they sadly had little real interest in the history, political philosophy, military experience or culture of China, seemed to have become bored. They were obliged to keep their noses to the business grindstone six days out of seven—they told us—and for that reason, too, were not able to get as much out of their visit as would have been the case if they had been better programmed before arriving.

I would recommend that all American com-

Bill takes my picture near the Ming Tombs outside of Peking.

Bill atop one of the enormous stone animals guarding the road to the Ming Tombs.

panies assigning men to China duty require them to attend lectures, read certain books and view films before making the journey.

The night before Bill and I left for Japan, where I was scheduled to perform as vocalist for a week at a new seacoast resort hotel in the city of Atami, Mr. Yueh and Mr. Bi, executives of the Peking headquarters of the China Travel Service, kindly arranged a farewell banquet for us at the famous Peking Duck Restaurant. The meal this time was better and the company, as always, congenial. Toasts were drunk to friendship and understanding between the Chinese and American people. The Chinese—whether of the political Left or Right—are superb hosts.

In my then still persistent naïveté I did not fully grasp that Bill and I had been granted a private tour of China of a sort ordinarily accorded far more important personages. I recognized, of course, that in being permitted to remain for four weeks in the country, to visit so many cities and not to travel in the usual group we were being accorded unusual treatment. But I did not at the time appreciate just how unusual it was. Tour groups now sometimes number as many a hundred, although

so large a company may be divided into two or four subdivisions. My son and I are indebted to Irene Tung and the officials of the China Travel Service who made such a tour possible.

Hardly a day has passed since our two visits to China (this paragraph is written in December, 1976) without an echo of the experience. For example, at the end of September, 1975, I happened to spend three days in San Francisco. Stolling around Chinatown I noticed, plastered to various brick walls, yellow posters printed in Chinese and English that said, "Celebrate the 26th anniversary of the founding of the People's Republic of China. Sunday, September 28, 1975, 1:00–3:30 P.M. Portsmouth Square."

That such a poster could be publicly displayed where it was is a clear indication of how the climate of political opinion had changed in recent years, not only among the United States population generally but also the Chinese segment of it.

In the next block I came across more of the same posters. On some of these, however, someone had written, in Chinese, "We don't like Mao Tse-tung."

12. The Cultural Revolution

BEFORE giving an account of my two-week visit to China in February, 1979, I must pause here to "explain" an important social phenomenon, which must be at least to some extent grasped by anyone with even a moderately serious interest in understanding modern China: the Cultural Revolution, usually called in Communist Party language The Great Proletarian Cultural Revolution.

These last few chapters of *"Explaining China"* are directed chiefly toward the reader

whose interest in the subject is sufficient to lead him to wish to know more.

A considerable amount of information has been provided in the body of this book but, as suggested in the Introduction, China itself is such an enormous country, with such a large population and so ancient a history that no one volume, even by a qualified scholar, could do it justice. The material that follows, therefore, will merely enable the reader to understand better the account already rendered.

To American students of China, learning

about the Cultural Revolution is not merely something it might be interesting to do. It is a necessity, the absence of which makes modern China incomprehensible. The Cultural Revolution seemed, in the mid-1970s, almost as important in the context of modern Chinese history as, say, the Civil War in the history of the United States. In one sense it was even more important since—except for blacks—not a great deal happening in the United States in 1979 flows out of the events of the Civil War whereas in China literally everything has been profoundly affected by the Cultural Revolution.

The first thing to understand about this vast internal struggle is that it involved fundamentally a philosophical debate. This is often the case, of course, in political controversy but a too hasty examination could lead to the erroneous assumption that the conflict was merely "a power struggle," as if the competition were simply for the supremacy of Mao or Liu Shaochi and their respective cliques, all other things being more or less equal. A power struggle did indeed ensue but it came about because of a sharp philosophical cleavage.

On the one side stood Mao, supported by his wife, Chiang Ching, and other "radicals," not to mention millions of supporters in and out of the party. The Maoist camp consisted of True Believers with a fervent faith in Permanent Revolution, an almost Calvinist, semiparanoid sensitivity to the slightest tendency to "Revisionist" thinking, which would—by logic of the argument—lead to "taking the Capitalist road."

To assume that Mao and his radical supporters were speaking on essentially a top-to-bottom line—authoritarian Communist Party leaders preaching a spiritual revival to backsliding citizens—would be to miss the point of the Cultural Revolution. Mao's primary opponents were highly placed members of the Communist Party, not capitalist at all, not relatively uninformed peasants, and to no statistically important extent personally selfish or ambitious former members of the pre-1949 aristocracy lazily dreaming of a return to their old positions of eminence.

Actual capitalism, the flesh-and-blood Kuo-mintang, the Nationalists on Taiwan, distant American interests—none of these had any direct connection whatever with the Cultural Revolution. It was, at least as viewed from Mao's camp, a matter of the True Faith on the one side and an emerging heresy on the other.

It is a pity—parenthetically speaking—that the average American has no conscious interest in philosophy. Whether he knows it or not, philosophical considerations control almost his entire life. Philosophy dictates the form of his national, state, city and county governments. Philosophy controls the economic context in which he works, or is out of work. Philosophy molds the laws and customs of his society. There is, of course, intellectual debate on the philosophical level among representatives of the various American political divisions. But the underlying assumptions according to which all societies move are far too important to be left to specialists. It is odd that in a remarkably free democratic republic such as ours there is widespread popular disinterest in the most important questions whereas in a far more inhibited and controlled society—China—a great deal of philosophical debate presently takes place.

The discussion naturally occurs within a more limited area than it would in the West. There is little freedom for those who would advocate a return to a free-market economy in China, though a few of them put up "Democracy Wall" posters in 1979. Nevertheless, the Chinese people do involve themselves in discussion of fundamental questions.

The long-held American conservative view of world communism generally as monolithic, and each individual Communist government as even more so has, we now know, seriously misled us. For years conservatives assured us that the split between the Soviet Union and China was merely a public drama staged purely to confuse the West. Whatever disagreements were real, we were told, were decidedly minor. Russia and China were two mighty brothers combined in a strong union and dedicated to the physical destruction of the Western democracies. There were all along scholars—including a few on the Right—who knew this was nonsense but it is surprising how ineffectual experts can be in the United States when demagogues appeal to popular angers or fears.

The point bears repeating: it is impossible to understand the Cultural Revolution in China unless we grasp that it was based on a bitter philosophical argument between two separate camps within the Chinese Communist leadership. Since we have been taught to regard Mao Tse-tung as nothing more than a ruthless, Stalinesque tyrant with total control over the minds and fates of the Chinese people, as one with the dictatorial authority of a Hitler, we are naturally startled to learn that this peculiar impression does not fit the known facts.

In the early 1960s, as it happened, Mao's personal influence was at a surprisingly low ebb. He was by no means powerless. He was not in serious danger of being toppled. But Liu Shao-chi and others in high government posts who differed with Mao felt perfectly free to contradict him, to debate him, and to set up policies and programs in fundamental opposition to his own. Even the press in China— which we were then told was totally under Mao's control—repeatedly carried articles critical of his positions.

Now this is not as startling as it may sound. We have known more about freedom of the press in the Soviet Union and are correctly aware that there is little of it indeed. Oddly enough, there has been more in China. At a peak of Russian-Chinese animosity Chinese newspapers published several of the most vigorous *Soviet* attacks on Chinese policy. Although the Chinese taunted the Russians to do the same, Khrushchev did not do so, giving as his reason that he chose not to inflame popular feeling against the Chinese in the Soviet Union.

It is rarely possible to determine exactly at what point on the time-scale any large societal development began. A movement as broad and sweeping as the Cultural Revolution might be likened to a mighty river which also has no single point of birth but rather originates in scores of separate places as tiny rivulets that gradually combine into larger streams, repeating the process until the great river takes form.

While even Chinese authorities refer to 1966, or in some cases 1965, as the general starting period of the Cultural Revolution, my own hypothesis is that a more likely field for research on this question would be the "Let a hundred flowers bloom" experiment of the late 1950s.

Consider, for a moment, the following criticism of the Communist Party bureaucracy voiced by Mao in 1966:

The Rectification Movement is a movement in which Party members should get up from their sedan chairs. A number of Party members install themselves in sedan chairs, and set a distance between themselves and the masses. What kind of men have they shaped in the past eight years? The education they have dispensed has trained chair-carriers.

I confess to having played a trick on the reader. The speaker here has not been Mao but Yang Ya-chin, addressing the nation in 1959. But note how consistent the criticism is with Mao's general line of six and seven years later. Time and again he emphasizes that party functionaries, even in very high places, have no right whatsoever to consider themselves persons of great importance, to put on airs, and to treat the people rudely or impersonally.

Note this Hundred Flowers quotation from Ko Pei-chi, of the Physical and Chemical Research Center at the University of Peking:

At present, the Party and the people are a hundred miles away from each other . . .

There are some who say that the standard of living has risen. For whom has it risen? For those members and officials of the Party who used to drag about in down-at-the-heel shoes and who now go driving about and wear woolen uniforms.

Or consider the complaint of Teng Chu-min of the Democratic League:

There are some who, when they are promoted to official responsibilities, assume the air of Mandarins and adopt a bureaucratic style of work. Friends whom we treated as brothers and with whom we were on an equal footing before the Revolution have become distant and haughty since becoming officials ... if we do not take an interest in human beings, if we spoil human relationships, if there is neither friendship nor human feelings ... then of what good are Socialism and Communism?

Now it is clear that Mao and the other high party officials perceived clearly enough, in 1959, that where serious threats to party discipline were arising from the newfound voices of the academic intellectuals and other members of the *non*-Communist Left, the logic of Mao's position obligated him to withdraw his either naïve or Machiavellian Hundred Flowers invitation. But it well may be that, while he was willing to do nothing to weaken the party in 1959, *he nevertheless learned something from the chorus of antiparty complaints that floated up during the so-called thaw.* Perhaps consequently we find, several years later, Mao himself squaring off against a large segment of the party hierarchy. Mao and his allies, too, argued that too many party officials thought they were members of a privileged class and that rather than serving the people they actually looked down on them and manipulated them to suit their own ends.

Whether this hypothesis is valid is, I would guess, not something that can be determined solely by conjecture. Someone in the Maoist faction of the Cultural Revolution controversy should eventually be able to supply the definitive answer.

Again parenthetically, one party member told me in Peking in 1975 that what Mao had in mind in introducing his "Let a hundred flowers bloom" program was twofold. One object was to encourage "the good people" to speak their minds more freely, to make what might turn out to be helpful suggestions and criticisms. But the other objective was "to catch the bad people." It is precisely this last aspect which falls so harshly on American ears. Shirley MacLaine, among others, believes that Mao and Chiang Ching's radical faction really wanted to encourage debate. If indeed Mao's motives in this instance were totally well intentioned he must have been startled at the vigorous wave of criticism of

government policies that quickly developed. In any event he responded with a heavy hand and did not repeat the experiment.

Another point of high ground from which waters descended to help form the larger streams of the yet-to-emerge Cultural Revolution was the Socialist Education Movement of the 1960s.

Consequently, the S.E.M. must be grasped by anyone who would understand the C.R. Essentially the Socialist Education Movement involved a campaign from the highest level to urge young men and women to go to the countryside to serve the rural masses.

That this was beneficial to illiterate peasants, in greatly improving their education, no one denies. The only critical question ever raised concerned the degree of willingness of the urban students to serve their society in this way. Undoubtedly reactions among individual students ranged from bitter resentment to enthusiastic cooperation. With a population of some 800 million, in the early 1950s perhaps 80 percent illiterate, it is clear that anything like a normal educational process might have taken a century to do an effective job in the most backward areas of China. There were simply not enough professional teachers for the task, just as there are not enough professional psychiatrists in the world to serve all who are emotionally troubled. But the job could be accomplished, the Chinese authorities thought, if hundreds of thousands, eventually millions, of eager young students could be successfully imbued with the sort of patriotic fervor that would send them willingly out into the mountains, deserts, forests and farms of China to help their less fortunate brothers and sisters. A domestic Peace Corps combined with our Civilian Conservation Corps camps would be a workable analogy in U.S. terms. The bare idea would seem virtuous enough.

Mao had for years concerned himself with the question as to how China and its illiterate, teeming millions, for so long undernourished, ill, brutalized, ignorant, could be brought forward into the twentieth century and given a larger measure of social justice. In 1958 he had written something, the opening statement of which, if it had come from a Western source, would probably have been interpreted as insulting. "Apart from their other characteristics," he said, "the outstanding thing about China's people is that they are 'poor and blank.' This may seem a bad thing, but in reality it is a good thing. Poverty gives rise to the desire for change, the desire for action, and the desire for revolution. On a blank sheet of paper, free from any mark, the freshest and most beautiful characters can be written. The freshest and most beautiful pictures can be painted."

What Mao wished to write on that enormous blank page was his own version of Marxist philosophy.

Now let us return to the question: What was the basic argument between Mao and the forces of Liu Shao-chi, his apparent successor?

The Maoist position was this: it must be, and is, possible to keep alive the enthusiasm and personal involvement of the masses in the continuing reconstruction of their society. *The masses must not only actively participate as followers, they must provide leadership, suggest ideas, and be involved in the making of decisions. Otherwise the majority of people will sink back into their historic apathy, and will merely do what they are told by military leaders and Communist Party bureaucrats.*

Liu, while nominally praising the masses, and certainly not forbidding their participation in the administration of their affairs, nevertheless felt that such airy generalizations were not particularly helpful during the difficult years that China had faced and would continue to confront. The period from 1959 to 1962 had been extremely troublesome. Nature had been unkind, farm production had not equaled the need, and there was much dissatisfaction and confusion. Liu, like the later dominant Teng Hsiao-ping, felt therefore that the Chinese leadership should concentrate on questions of administration, of practical problem-solving. He believed it a waste of time to debate the question as to whether socialism or capitalism would win out in China. That question, he insisted, had already been solved; the Red Revolution had in fact been won. Now, he argued, the nation must simply roll up its sleeves and get about the difficult business of economic development.

As regards the question of which specific forms of development were best, he took a practical, pragmatic view. There was nothing wrong, he felt, with copying the Soviet model, at least in some of its aspects, such as the emphasis on technology and the training of specialists. He even saw nothing wrong with imitating some aspects of Western development. The important thing, he thought, was not to waste time and energy with endless debates about philosophical purity. The important thing was to place more and better food on Chinese tables, more and better clothing on Chinese backs, more and better consumer products into Chinese homes.

From our viewpoint of relative disinterest it is simple enough to see that this was by no means a black-or-white, right-or-wrong argument. There was something to say for both points of view.

Most Westerners will feel that they would have preferred to see the Liu Shao-chi forces win the argument. But—and the point is crucial—*this is exactly what Mao maintained.* He insisted that Liu was, perhaps inadvertently, "taking the Capitalist road." Mao could point to what had just happened in that, in the process of repairing the damage to the Chinese economic structure, the government had felt compelled to give a little, to become less dogmatic in its insistence on purely Marxist solutions to the serious problems of the 1959–1960 period.

The farmers had then been permitted to develop small private plots and to dispose of the crops grown on them in a relatively free market. There was some experimentation with the offering of material incentives to workers, to see if that would increase their productivity. Such developments are, obviously, viewed as hopeful signs through Western eyes. But to Mao they were a renunciation of the philosophical vision that had sustained him during so many difficult years. He knew enough of human nature to realize—as do Christians—that every man is prone to backslide if his faith is not kept lively. Anyone, he believed, might feel a tendency to enrich himself at the public expense, to increase not only his material holdings, but, even more dangerous to a Marxist society, his area of dominance and uncriticized authority. But, Mao believed, if ever any people on earth had suffered from centuries of ruthless domination, bureaucratic slowness and ineptitude, exploitation, it was China. The nation must not fall prey again to control by a small, selfish power elite, even one that was purely Communist.

Mao—again—far from being a total dictator, was in a remarkably weak position. He still enjoyed wide support among the people but between him and the masses there stood an enormous party structure. Party members and officials did indeed enjoy a privileged status. They felt no guilt about it whatever because, being dedicated Communists, they believed they were strong in the Marxist faith. Mao, however, refused to blame the people for their relative lack of participation. High party officials, he insisted, had set a bad example for lower-level cadres, who in turn had set a poor example for the people. But since *Mao was outmaneuvered in the party,* the only alternative available to him was an appeal, over the heads of the party, directly to the Chinese masses.

His task was made somewhat easier by the fact that Liu had stated that the fault of the situation lay with the people themselves. They had been almost totally illiterate, albeit through no fault of their own, as of 1949 when the Communists assumed power. A dozen or so years had simply not been enough in which to bring the people up to the level of sophistication and education necessary for the kind of participation Mao was demanding. Liu conceded that there was a problem. One of his solutions was to send groups of high party cadres into the rural areas to "cleanse and strengthen" the lower-level party members in the villages and communes.

Viewed from a great distance, from the United States for example, the difference between the positions of Mao and Liu may not have seemed very great. There was no important contradiction, for example, between the ultimate ideals of Liu and Mao, both equally loyal to Marxist principles as they understood them. The argument concerned the means toward the end, not the end itself. And even here —again, viewed from a distance—Liu's deviations did not seem so great as to merit the

torrent of abuse he subsequently suffered. Liu, like Teng, very much wanted China to march forward into the modern age. He wanted to build up industry, science, education. It seemed obvious to him that people genetically gifted with high intelligence should be able to place their special gifts at the disposal of the state. If they were true-blue Marxists so much the better, but even if they were not China could still benefit from their ability to build bridges, nuclear weapons, factories, and the other implements of a modern society.

Second, Liu realized that material incentives would spur factory and farm production in China as they always had in previous human experience. If a man sincerely thinks he can make only ten clay pots a day, it is usually the case that offering him an extra dollar or two for turning out eleven or twelve clay pots will produce the required number. What Liu seemed to be working toward was a sort of 99 percent Communist, 1 percent free-market approach to China's future. But Mao and his followers would have none of it. They argued that Redness—being a good Communist—was more important than expertness. They said that it did not *matter* if the nation lost the services of a handful of intellectually gifted people. What is far more important was that millions of poor peasants, workers and soldiers be given the opportunity for higher education, even if their I.Q.'s, to use a Western concept, were not as high as those of students raised in more fortunate social circumstances.

Mao was no doubt practical enough to have realized that material incentives would indeed have produced some improvement in production. But looking ahead, he saw this as an unnecessarily expensive way of achieving the desired result. Looking even farther down the road, we may assume, he saw that additional extensions of this practice, each slight in itself, could one day lead toward a general slide back toward the old order, toward a society of separate classes, toward corruption and personal ambition rather than the scrupulous honesty and selfless dedication to the nation's welfare which even in the West are regarded as virtuous ideals, however rarely they may there be encountered.

Liu, of course, was in any event not promulgating a new heresy. He was simply assuming that something could be learned from the Soviet experience. This point, however, particularly infuriated Mao, whose hatred of Soviet "revisionism," heretical deviation from the True Faith, as Mao viewed it, had led through stages of differences of opinion, moderate resentment, open grudge-bearing, increasingly violent argument, and finally to a bitter divorce between the two Communist cultures that, in the eyes of some Western anti-Communists, were pretending to argue merely to confuse the West. It occurs to me that such "experts" were quite confused enough without requiring any help from either China or Russia.

As for foreign policy, the differences between the camps of Liu and Mao were not terribly marked except in the foreign implications of the components of the domestic quarrel. If Liu, for example, was not only tolerant of Soviet deviations but actually wished to emulate some of them, it therefore seemed to follow that he could not really be a totally committed participant in Mao's attacks upon Khrushchev and the U.S.S.R. state apparatus.

In the light of Liu Shao-chi's eventual defeat, disgrace and disappearance, it seems remarkable, as one looks back, that in the early stages of the Cultural Revolution his position was quite strong. He dominated the Communist Party organization and a good deal of the organizational structure of the government as well. Also, of no small importance, he was influential in the press, radio and television because of his admirers in the media. The majority of intellectuals, some of whom had been at odds with Mao since the 1940s, naturally gravitated toward Liu's more relaxed philosophy of communism. Years earlier Mao had been forced to deal with the same insubordinate tendency when he convened the Yenan Forum on Literature and Art and, albeit in a cordial tone, nevertheless laid down the law to intellectuals and artists who, as the Marxist jargon has it, "had illusions."

Among Chiang Ching's allies were Wang Hung-wen, a bright, ambitious former factory worker from Shanghai, Chang Chun-chiao, a Communist Party secretary, also from Shanghai and an effective rabblerouser, and Yao Wen-yuan, one of the dominant heretichounders of the Cultural Revolution, who first came to prominence outside of China in November, 1965, when he wrote an article on behalf of Mao in the Shanghai newspaper *Wen Hui Pao,* criticizing the article "Hai Jui Dismissed from Office"—a veiled attack on Mao —and its author Wu Han. This was not the first time Mao had depended on Yao Wenyuan. In 1957 he had urged him to attack the same newspaper for publishing what Mao and the radicals viewed as "bourgeois rightist" criticism of Communist Party leaders.

In his 1965 attack Yao went so far as to assert that Wu Han, who was deputy mayor of Peking, because he had "distorted history" was therefore a dangerous class enemy. Indicted along with Wu Han were Tang To, secretary of Peking's Municipal Committee, and Liao Mo-sha, important member of the same committee. They too were accused of launching attacks on Mao in the guise of literary criticism.

It is important to realize that these charges were justified; the subsequent argument did not center on accuracy. The striking difference, of course, is in the treatment accorded those who criticize leadership in China, as contrasted with social critics of the Western nations. Yao's strength lay chiefly in his close connection with Mao's wife, Chiang Ching.

These literary maneuvers were, it ultimately turned out, the first shots in an extraordinary battle, not only dramatic within the context of modern China but in the larger setting of human history.

But where was Mao to turn for support in his confrontations with party and military leaders?

In 1966 when Mao, rightly or wrongly, thought he perceived a broad-scaled tendency to backslide he summoned a vast army of young Chinese, called Red Guards, to initiate what he called The Great Proletarian Cultural Revolution.

The Red Guards, practically all of whom had been trained from the cradle according to modern Chinese Communist methods of education and indoctrination, took to their task with such a will that even those who endorsed Mao's wisdom in initiating the purge now concede it to have been unfortunate in its extent. Its excesses—some of them stupid—inevitably produced an angry reaction.

The avowed task of the young people was to sweep out what were called the "Four Olds" —old habits, old customs, old ideas, and old culture generally. Unfortunately, certain members of the Red Guards defaced buildings of historical importance, attacked ancient treasures, and humiliated prominent intellectuals and professors on university faculties. Away from the cities thousands were killed or injured in clashes between—if one can believe it —rival factions of the Red Guards themselves! So fiery was the mood of the Cultural Revolution at this stage that whatever was construed as the slightest deviation from its aims was immediately seized upon as "revisionism" and soundly flailed. After two years of what still seems partly dangerous nonsense to many Western and Chinese observers, the army had to take a hand to restore order.

The Red Army, over the last thirty years, seems to have been in some ways a conservative or stabilizing influence.

Here is a particularly dramatic account, provided by Ross Terrill, in *Flowers on an Iron Tree,* of one aspect of the Cultural Revolution as acted out on the stage of Wuhan, the city where Jayne was born. The reader should be aware, in considering it, that there has been a long tradition of Wuhan's restlessness under the administrative control of the central government.

The events of 1967 proved, to Peking's great shock, that a tide of Wuhan rebelliousness is a potential fact of political life. What happened, in a nutshell, was the following:

The first stage of the Cultural Revolution had been a surge against "capitalist inroaders." Chairman Mao's weapon to humble these right-wingers was the Red Guard movement. But in some cities, including Wuhan, the left-wing Red Guards were not as popular as Mao wished or believed. Two forces in Wuhan resisted the young firebrands.

One was made up of military men, headed by the commander of the Wuhan Military Region, Ch'en Tsai-tao. Born and bred a Hupei man, Ch'en had been entrenched as Wuhan's number one soldier for thirteen years. He had no desire to see law and order undermined by a bunch of crusading kids.

The second force was an organization of rank-and-file workers, with the splendid name "One Million Heroic Warriors." These folk from Wuhan Steel and other factories were no more enthusiastic about the Red Guards than was the hard-boiled Commander Ch'en. During the early summer of 1967, Wuhan was tense with struggle between the Left (riding high in Peking), and these two strong, not very leftist forces that reflected local realities.

A great issue all over China at this time was how an intoxicated Left would relate to the solid rock of the military. The Cultural Revolution group, Mao's left hand in Peking, was starting to confront this problem. In such an atmosphere, the group sent two emissaries, Wang Li and Hsieh Fu-chih, to iron out the contention in Wuhan.

Wang and Hsieh almost got ironed out themselves. From Peking they brought a message of support for the local Red Guards. These leftists, organized under the apt title "Revolutionary Rebels," had a stronghold in Hankow, at the People's Cultural Park in Sun Yat-sen Road. They felt beleaguered in the face of Ch'en and the "One Million Heroic Warriors." Cried one Red Guard appeal on their behalf: "Wuhan is in critical danger! The Hill of the Tortoise and the Hill of the Snake are roaring. So are the Yangtze and the Han rivers. The tri-city of Wuhan is engulfed in white terror!"

White terror or not, it was enough to put Wang and Hsieh in virtual captivity. Force 8201, a Public Security unit based in Hanyang, arrested Wang, and berated Hsieh to the point where he fled to a college on Vantage Hill. The locals simply would not swallow the pill of "supporting the Left." Chou En-lai himself flew down from Peking to tackle what had become a rebellion by the city of Wuhan.

There was chaos, bloodshed, and alarm in Wuhan. So great was the confusion that at one point a mob of "Warriors," seeking to attack Wang at the East Lake Hotel where he was staying, set upon Commander Ch'en by mistake. Ch'en was then observed shouting out: "I am Ch'en Tsai-tao, not Wang Li."

On arrival, Premier Chou himself was nearly captured. But he diverted to a second airport when warned, by air force elements loyal to Peking, that Ch'en had sent twenty-eight trucks to nab him at the first. Chou succeeded, as he generally does, but not without the help of five ships of the East Sea Fleet, which steamed up the Yangtze to Wuhan. Wang and Hsieh were pried out of Ch'en's hands, brought back to a warm welcome in Peking. Ch'en himself fell from grace and from power. Wuhan returned, for the moment, to the fold of national policy.

I quote Terrill's description of this tense drama not because it was unusual but rather typical of the turmoil in China in the late 1960s.

One's evaluation of the Cultural Revolution may be founded first partly on prejudice either in favor of or against the Chinese Communist experiment generally, or second, on how "radical" or "moderate" a Marxist one might be. But all camps should be able to agree that Mao and his people did pay a price for the Revolution of the late 1960s, as the startling and dramatic events of 1976 would eventually make clear. There was in any event even more to the debate and physical confrontation than the clash between the Mao and Liu philosophical factions. Perhaps ultimately it will be learned that *Mao's fundamental opponents—as a decade earlier in 1957—were the academic intellectuals.* The universities were closed for three years. But Mao found that while simple people were relatively easy to mold, it was not so with informed intellectuals. He failed to persuade many by argument and education and had little better luck in attempting to reform some through obligatory manual labor. His solution to the dilemma posed by his "best and brightest" was certainly audacious. He more or less canceled out an entire class of educators, authors, scholars, administrators, and planned to replace them with children of the working class. From July 27, 1968, when peasants and workers forced their way into the universities, higher education was available to almost no one in China but the dutiful work-

ers, urban and rural. It has been interesting to see how dramatically this factor was modified as a result of the collapse of the radical faction in 1976 and the ascendance of Hua Kuo-feng and Teng Hsiao-ping.

It is odd that Mao viewed the pre-Cultural Revolution intellectuals, who were generally leftist, as natural reactionaries. Contrast this with the conservative attitude toward intellectuals in the United States, which is that they are natural radicals or revolutionaries.

The underlying unity of the two seemingly self-contradictory accusations is that intellectuals, in any and all cultures, since they can perceive more clearly than the average citizen what is faulty in the established order, are more likely not only to oppose it—as regards specifics—but to be articulate in their opposition.

Since it is easier to grasp an abstraction if we observe a concrete application of it, a student of the G.P.C.R., therefore, can profit by examining personal accounts of ways in which individuals were affected by the Cultural Revolution.

Joan Robinson, Professor Emeritus of Economics at the University of Cambridge, who by 1975 had visited China six times, quotes an insider's view of the Cultural Revolution in her informative paper "Economic Management in China, 1972," published by the Anglo-Chinese Educational Institute. The speaker, director of a textile factory, had been a Communist Party member since 1956. When the struggle broke to the surface in 1966, he confesses, he could not understand what was going on. His workers, who had formerly obeyed his orders, began to criticize him, publicly and to his face. Seizing control of the factory, they forced the director to go to work on the shop floor. This he did, functioning as a machine attendant from January to November of 1967.

"The workers criticized my methods of management; they said I was a boss. They linked me with Liu Shao-chi. I could not understand it but I lost my self-confidence. What was it all about? Hadn't I been a good party member? I was quite confused.

"There were two factions among the workers: *East is Red* and *Red Rebels*. A work team had been sent (as I realise now) by the Liu party and had set up a so-called Cultural Revolution Committee. The factions formed in disputing about it, but they very soon forgot all about criticising Revisionism; they were only interested in criticising each other. When it came to discussing the cadres in the factory, the East is Red group thought that I might still be useful, but the Red Rebels were 'down-with-everything' boys. They were against all cadres. 'Suspect all, depose all' was their watchword. I tagged along with East is Red. I just had to do as they did and keep quiet.

"I am glad to say that it did not come to blows with us as it did in many places, but the situation was really absurd. Both groups were working, but they would not speak to each other; one would not pass a tool to another. Each lot said to the others: We can carry on production without your help. There were two factions in every workshop. All the cadres were doing manual work, and the workers were carrying on as they pleased. All rules and regulations were defied. There were rival loud-speakers set up on the premises, blaring away at each other all the time. Some output was produced but of course it fell far below normal.

"Then in June, 1967, a group of Liberation Army men came in. They were really amazing; they were so calm and patient. They did not begin by shouting at anybody but settled down to study and investigate to find out what had caused the trouble. They came to the conclusion that both factions were good revolutionaries but that both had some faults. They set about to get them together. It was hard work. Neither gang would admit that the others were any good. The army men had had the greatest difficulty in persuading them to sit on the same bench.

"On September 14, 1967, came the Chairman's new instructions, saying that there was no fundamental cause for conflict within the working class. The P.L.A. men had it printed and distributed copies not only in the workshops but to the workers' homes as well. They kept on talking to the workers, in groups and one by one. Sometimes they would have 12 or 15 interviews with one man.

"On September 19 the army men got the two factions to unite formally, but they were still not agreed ideologically. The army men

held study courses on the theme of 'combat egoism.' They got each faction to make self-criticism. In November, the Revolutionary Committee was formed. There were wrangles till the last minute; it took three days to choose representatives. It was decided to have 15 members and one faction claimed the right to appoint 11. However, in the end it was settled at eight and seven."

Eventually, the manager recounted, he had had to present himself to the workers and announce that, as a result of study and rethinking his position, he was penitent.

"I took a portrait of Chairman Mao in my hands and a quotation about combatting egoism, and presented myself to one group of workers after another. I felt foolish at first and I was frightened at what they would say. I thought they would never forgive me. But, to my delight, they welcomed me. They said: 'It was a pity you did not start coming to us sooner.' They said: 'We only criticised you to make you one of the Left instead of the Right.' They hoped I would not lose touch with them again. It took me three days to go round all the workshops. In the end I was elected on the Revolutionary Committee and now I am chairman. Most of the high and middle cadres were also rehabilitated."

An especially interesting insight into the Cultural Revolution is that of Eric Gordon, a British Communist who lived in China from February, 1965 to October, 1969. In his report, *Freedom Is a Word,* Gordon, who had been hired by the Chinese to make their foreign propaganda more palatable to readers of the English language, tells of his adventures during this important period of modern Chinese history. On planning to leave in 1967 he was accused of smuggling out notes and papers dealing with the Cultural Revolution. That he had indeed made notes on the developments he observed goes without saying. What writer would not in a similar circumstance? But for all his loyalty to Marxist-Leninist philosophy, and his admitted enthrallment with the economic successes of the Chinese Communists, he was nevertheless detained for two full years. Inevitably his experience led to considerable disenchantment with certain aspects of the Chinese experiment. But he believes that the simple factor of having four years to study the situation firsthand would have in any case led him to question both the deification of Mao and the frightening excesses of the Red Guards.

It is important to appreciate that every war, every revolution, has its "excesses," committed by both, or all, sides. But the crucial question is: *"What percentage* of the total activity of a campaign consists of atrocities, cruelty, terror and irresponsible destruction? Inevitably anti-Communists will tend to exaggerate this element of the Cultural Revolution; Communists will minimize it. Since the Chinese themselves put such strong emphasis on social morality, it will be important for historians and scholars to try to determine the degree of barbarity in the Cultural Revolution.

I obviously cannot here fully outline the plot development of the Cultural Revolution. There are a number of valuable studies of this remarkable phenomenon; I advise the reader to inspect at least three or four since each has insights and factual information the others lack. Also, elsewhere in the present volume, in chapters and sections on communes, factories, hospitals and schools, I have related how profoundly all these institutions were affected by the philosophical upheaval of the Cultural Revolution.

As of 1979—thanks to Vice Premier Teng Hsiao-ping and Premier Hua Kuo-feng—the wave of the Cultural Revolution had been partly deflected, partly reversed. Liu Shao-chi, in a sense, had become at least the temporary winner of the philosophical debate. Mao, Chiang Ching and the Gang of Four had effectively lost the argument in China, though it continued at great heat in Marxist circles around the world.

In sum, the Great Proletarian Cultural Revolution was a Utopian experiment, not without certain aspects of nobility, which ultimately failed, I would think, because it was based on an unrealistic assessment of human nature, although the situation was, needless to say, incredibly complex. Another reason for the revolution's failure was that it was pushed with an unremitting harshness which must inevitably have produced widespread resentment.

That there was not even more resentment on the part of the millions sent down to the countryside may be attributed to the general perception on the part of those victimized that the campaign was, after all, intended for the benefit of the country and was not merely a matter of vindictive, punitive oppression.

One influential Chinese who had served his time, however unwillingly, in a rural commune, told me about his own surprise at the attitude of an extremely important general who had distinguished himself in the Korean War.

"I cannot mention the general's name," my informant said, "because he is back in town now and I would not wish to embarrass him. But I got to know him because we were in the same camp. I used to say to him, 'Doesn't it seem damned unjust to you that you would have to go through this, after your great military contributions to China?' "

" 'Well,' he said, 'I think maybe it is not so bad that we have to put up with something of this sort. Sure, it's tough, but maybe I did make some mistakes and have some wrong attitudes. It's all for the good of the country and we should, after all, know what life is like for the great majority of people—the villagers —who spend their whole lives in places like this.' "

Parenthetically, I assume, on the basis of other information, that the unidentified officer was General Peng Te-Huai.

Where Mao, Chiang Ching and the Gang of Four went wrong was in carrying to harsh extremes a program that might have succeeded had it been conducted on a more rational basis. Since there was a point, after all, to the argument that a Marxist society could hardly permit a return to the class divisions that were part of the old order, and since it was a good thing if the nation's fortunate few—the intellectuals, artists, bureaucrats, officials— knew precisely what life was like for the 90 percent of China's population living in rural areas, the people might have supported a program something like that of the Mormon

Church in which the faithful are required to give one year of their lives in full service to the church before turning to more personal pursuits. But to deliberately keep artists, scholars, administrators and others in the countryside for years was a combination of vindictiveness and stupidity which, not surprisingly, in time produced a reaction.

Well, this modest analysis can hardly hope to resolve an issue that has perplexed the minds of the best political scholars for fifteen years.

That Marxists are effective revolutionaries has been demonstrated, to the mixed sorrow and alarm of the West, in numerous instances. That as administrators of an equitable and rational economic system they are superior to their Western counterparts has by no means as yet been demonstrated.

COMMUNISM

If it were not already evident enough that this book is intended for the average American reader—the consumer of nonintellectual journalism, the sports pages, middle-brow television—this chapter would make the point clear. I offer here a few modest background notes on the complex subject of socialism-communism, the brevity and sketchiness of which will grate the teeth of scholars.

At least one of the reasons for the present troublesome international situation is that the hundreds of millions of human beings involved have a degree of knowledge and information servers from another universe would be thunderstruck by the disproportion. Think of it! Massive, mighty social forces, armed to the teeth, seething with suspicion, poised tensely in an attitude of mutual distrust and each surprisingly ignorant of the realities of existence in the other camp.

I am not naïve enough to imagine that one small effort at clarification, even assuming its competence, could itself relax the present tensions. But one does what one can.

It is not as though Communists are told nothing of the West or Americans told nothing about communism. The problem is that most of what we here are told is of a propagandistic nature, in which communism is sometimes portrayed in literally diabolical terms. (What Christian reader has not heard, for decades, that communism literally "is the work of the Devil"?) And on the other side the distortions are hardly less extreme.

Propaganda may be a necessary weapon in the context of war. Obviously if man is willing to kill, to bomb, to set afire, to exterminate, to smash in defense of what he views as his nation's interest, it can scarcely be supposed that he will draw the line at lying. Consequently, all governments immediately convert to organized teams of outrageous liars as soon as a war commences. Indeed they frequently do so if they feel threatened whether or not there is war, as Americans have seen by the two recent examples of the debacle in Southeast Asia and Watergate.

But the problem we address grows out of our responding to Cold War as we would to Hot War. It is true that in the 1970s China-U.S. tensions have finally been somewhat reduced, that locked borders have been opened, and a faltering step in the direction of sanity made. But let no one imagine that this has been done with the hearty cooperation of the total populations involved. Large masses and their leaders are demonstrably uncomfortable in the present thaw. They blink in the new light and shuffle warily back toward the cave. American conservatives today are like turtles with shells removed. They have had such a deep, emotional dependence on the Cold War, for so many years, that now they are uneasy, touchy, more suspicious than ever. Since they constitute only a minority, it might be thought that they should be left alone to make their own psychological adjustment to the new state of affairs. But they are not alone. They are on the same ship as the rest of us. And their fears, their animosities, communicated through scores of newspapers, magazines, radio and television programs and personal contacts, affect the common state of mind. They are not, after all, totally wrong.

The forces of Marxism do represent a challenge to the West. It is possible that Russian or Chinese arms could be turned against us, just as American arms could be turned against

China and/or the Soviet Union. Or Tanzanian arms could be turned against Switzerland. None of this is at all probable at present. But it is possible. And in today's volatile world rational considerations can be swept aside in a fraction of a second, given some dreadful mistake or provocation. An assassination, a nuclear accident, a terrorist outrage, a confrontation about Middle Eastern oil—who can say with confidence that full-scale war at present is impossible?

All possible efforts toward reason and understanding, therefore, must be encouraged. Americans ought to know a good deal more about socialism, in its various forms, than we observably do at present. Surely it must be possible to educate ourselves on this intricate subject without immediately cluttering our mental computers with emotional additives, without emphasis on pejorative adjectives and nouns—*vicious, evil, slavery, fiendish, tyranny, blind, savage.*

I do not suggest that emotional responses can be totally avoided. An atrocity is an atrocity. But to condemn a system—any system—in any and all of its parts before one studies it is absurd.

It is clear that the proper way to analyze any social phenomenon is to start by considering the factors that brought it about. Communism, after all, did not spring up on this planet entirely uncaused. Communism was caused by capitalism. Karl Marx and the other philosophers of the movement did not simply sit down at their desks and say, "Let us see now; what sort of dangerous nonsense can we dream up this morning that can be counted upon to cause a great deal of misery and bloodshed in the world?"

No, Marx and the others were driven to their writing tables because of their revulsion, their shock, their dismay at conditions they observed. *And any intelligent, compassionate person—not blinded by self-interest or personal greed—would react similarly.*

At sight of a starving child is one supposed to laugh, to turn away, to dismiss the matter from one's mind?

At seeing a small, decadent upper class living in luxury while hundreds of millions suffer in filthy poverty, should one merely shrug and say, "Well, that's life?"

At the spectacle of little children working for pennies in dangerous factories or mines, is one supposed to applaud their industry or the efficiency of the installation itself?

At witnessing thousands dying like flies from diseases that might be prevented if a government interested itself in shameful living and working conditions, is a reasonable man to walk away, never once looking back over his shoulder?

No, damn it. We must get this basic part of the drama clear in our minds. One is perfectly free to argue that the Chinese form of communism, let us say, is the wrong medicine for the disease. But to refuse to consider that disease, to turn one's back on those who suffer from it —as many in the West do—is monstrous.

The second step is to understand, and here the process becomes more painful, that ghastly, inhuman conditions—slavery, poverty, mass disease, hunger, ignorance—all of this came about *as part of our system.* Read this paragraph again. The point must be fundamentally grasped, otherwise everything that follows will be misunderstood.

I ask the reader to pause for a moment after studying the following few lines and give moral consideration to the information given. *As of 1927 the working day for factory laborers in large Chinese cities was twelve hours in length. There were no days off; the workers had to be present in their factories seven full days. No compensation whatever was paid for accidents, even those that were very serious. Children were not paid a single penny for the first five to seven years of their employment. They were, in other words, slaves, in the simple dictionary sense of that word.*

Where then were the American conservatives who now profess such a fascination with "slavery"?

One could go on almost for eternity cataloging the list of errors in American thinking about communism and the Soviet Union. Even some who have taken the trouble to study the matter suppose that until Khrushchev's speech of 1961 denouncing Stalin's crimes there was not the slightest hint from the Communist camp that the myth of Stalin's heroic greatness was about to be destroyed. Actually there had been dissension and debate among Communists for years on this issue. In *Notebook of an Agitator,* James P. Cannon took up the question.

Speaking of himself Cannon says, "I have been a friend and supporter of the Russian Revolution since 1917 and still am." Writing on July 30, 1951, he said:

The Stalinists didn't invent the art of lying, but they expanded it and developed it into a philosophy and a way of life . . . Betty Gannett, an American Communist, states categorically that Stalinist party members must believe in and explain the "profound and pervasive democracy in the Soviet Union . . . in order to give the lie to the charge of totalitarianism."

Just a moment, please. Let's have some detailed amplification on this point. I am interested in democracy, and profoundly believe in it as the mechanism by which the masses will organize the victorious struggle for their own emancipation from capitalism. . . . Just how is the participation of the ordinary man and woman in government manifested in the Soviet Union today? Do they have the right of free speech, free press and free assembly, the prerequisites of free democratic action? They do not. Betty Gannett knows what everybody else knows by this time, that all the talking in the Soviet Union is done by the ruling bureaucrats; and that all the newspapers and other mediums of information and communication are controlled by them. . . . No, *there is not a particle of free speech, free press or free assembly in the Soviet Union. Therefore there is no democracy,* "pervasive" or otherwise. Everybody knows this, and anybody who says otherwise is a liar by the clock. . . .

I have comrades in the Soviet Union who are formed into an opposition party—the Russian section of the Fourth International. It is an honest and revolutionary party, profoundly devoted to the October Revolution and the defender of its heritage. Soviet democracy was one of the first planks in the platform of their

long, heroic struggle. But these honest revolutionists are all in prision; that is, those who have not been murdered for demanding some of this pervasive democracy which Betty Gannett speaks of with such cynical falsity in her report to the Communist Party convention. . . .

The martyred victims of Stalin's "profound and pervasive democracy" number millions in the Soviet Union. . . . If you doubt the unanimous testimony of all who have escaped from Stalin's torture chambers and forced labor camps, just take a trip to the Soviet Union and see for yourself. . . . You will see all the democracy there is to see; all there is to see, that is, through the bars of prisons or over the gun towers of the forced labor camps, where at least 10 to 15 million work, suffer, starve and die without recourse, without attention to their cries. [Italics added.]

Just five years after Cannon's outcry, at the Twentieth Party Congress in 1956 Khrushchev himself—in a then secret speech—attacked Stalin's memory and was explicit in a recitation of his crimes. We can learn from such examples that it is absurd to think of communism as utterly monolithic. From the beginning there have been separate schools of thought within its ranks; there still are. Even the untutored can see that there are Yugoslavian communism, Cuban communism and Chinese communism, in addition to the Soviet and other brands. And even within the Marxist states there are various philosophical forces that contend for control.

As for China, most Americans seem to suppose that until 1949, when the Communists took control, the ancient Middle Kingdom was getting along reasonably well despite its problems and was somehow a valuable representative of the capitalist camp. Such a view is absurd. China's problems, before 1949, were—as they had been for centuries—enormous. Despair was more justified than optimism, except for the prosperous few. The nation was a vast chaotic laboratory providing a remarkable opportunity for the conduct of Marxist experiments.

Part III

The Third Journey
February, 1979

13. Tokyo to Peking

DURING the 1975–1979 period I busied myself chiefly with the PBS television series "Meeting of Minds," nightclub and concert appearances, a summer performing in my play *The Wake,* television comedy specials, guest appearances, including occasional fill-ins for vacationing Johnny Carson and Merv Griffin, and a good deal of writing, both books and music.

In 1979 we heard of the possibility of joining a group of film and TV people headed for China, applied, and were accepted. I knew the two-week tour would enable me to freshen up my observations about the People's Republic, so early in February off we went.

Monday, February 5

Jayne and I had decided to break the long, exhausting Los Angeles-to-Peking jump by leaving earlier than our TV-and-film tour group, so we could enjoy a two-day stopover in Tokyo. There we were very comfortably, if expensively, quartered at the Imperial Hotel, which is situated on what were once the private grounds of Japan's emperors. As always, it was exciting to wander the streets of Tokyo. The cabfare from the new Narita airport into town, however, had been a bit of a shock. The trip, which took an hour and a half, cost about $120.

Viewing once more the great number of taxis and private cars in Tokyo it struck me as remarkable that one sees there so few precisely similar in color. White is white, of course, and black is black, but the Oriental range of color far exceeds what one sees in the U.S. or Europe. Our Western languages do accommodate subdivisions of the primary colors. Under *red,* for example, we find such shades as crimson, scarlet, cardinal, maroon, etc. But a handful of such words are hardly equal to the richness of the theoretically infinite varieties of reds or greens or blues that flash upon your vision in the Japanese sunlight.

The night before departure to China, we went to the airport again, where we would join our group at the Narita Kikko Hotel. After checking out of the Imperial we went to the Hohozaki bus terminal where we were given a really thorough TV-detective-show frisking as an antiskyjacking measure. A sign explained that as "busjack" prevention a body check and inspection of carry-on luggage was required. "And also kindly limit the number of carry-on baggage to one piece," the printed instruction said. We, of course, were carrying our full complement of luggage consisting of 3 large bags and the usual 47,000 smaller pieces that always seem to be required when I travel with Jayne.

On the smaller bus that took us from the airport to the Narita Kikko Hotel the Muzak tape, strangely, played only one song, "Surrey with the Fringe on Top." Since the ride takes ten minutes we heard about thirty choruses of the number. The following morning, on the way back to the terminal, we were treated to a spritely arrangement of "On the Sunny Side of the Street," again with endless choruses.

The departure procedures at the terminal seemed, well, interminable, but I suppose they were all necessary. Then, at last, it was up, up and away, to China.

Our group consisted of Schuyler Chapin, Dean of the School of the Arts of Columbia University and popular New York man about town; Manya Starr, a TV and film writer with a Dorothy Parker sort of sense of humor; Irvin Yeaworth, producer; Arthur Zich, author and journalist; Ernest Kinoy, writer of some of the scripts of the television series "Roots," and his wife Barbara, a psychotherapist; James Devaney, TV and film producer and his publicist wife Susan; James Scott Cranna, writer-actor; Cheryl Downing, production assistant; Jeannie Myers, casting director; Mark Peterson, film documentarian; Edward Schumann, producer of *Same Time, Next Year* and other plays; Lila Shanley Finn, middle-aged stunt woman; Roz Bonerz, wife of Peter Bonerz, comedy actor of the Bob Newhart show; Ted Rhodes, stagehand and production aide; Tom Ackerman, cameraman; photographer Michael Welch, teenage son of travel-agency head Norvel Welch; Jayne and myself. Norvel accompanied us for the first leg of our journey but flew from Peking back to New York at the time we headed for Hangchow.

The day was great and clear, the temperature a brisk 40 degrees Fahrenheit when we landed at Shanghai, whether to reboard later or stay we could not at first determine. In this Terminal No. 2 we saw our first instance of the now-common large portraits of Mao and Hua Kuo-feng side by side, obviously intended to cast the mantle of Mao's authority over Hua's shoulders.

The Shanghai touchdown proved to be brief; our immediate destination was Peking. Our ignorance on the point is explainable; you don't know many details of your China tours until you arrive.

The weather was crisp and cold as we landed at the Peking airport, the main building of which will apparently soon be replaced by an attractive modern facility visibly under construction at the far end of the field. Almost as soon as our TV-film group entered the baggage area and met our hosts we started to hear about China's interest in U.S. films. An American woman who teaches English at Tsinghua University said, "The students here are very interested now in American movies."

"What films have they seen?" I said.

"*Julia* was shown at the International Club, also at local universities. Chaplin's *Modern Times,* and 16-mm. films of the television series, 'Roots.' The Chinese ideas about blacks in America date from the 1930s and *Gone With the Wind.* Consequently they were fascinated by the showings of 'Roots.' "

During the next hour or so of welcome-welcome and we-are-glad-to-be-here conversation, we learned that Sidney Poitier's film *In the Heat of the Night,* which deals with Southern racism, had also been well received in Peking, as had his *Guess Who's Coming to Dinner.* "Tickets to it," said Mr. Chang, one of our guides, "have been selling like hotcakes." The Chinese love to employ our American idioms since they are always rewarded by smiles for doing so.

Peking, we shortly learned, has some fifty motion picture theaters. Large factories and schools also have their own projection halls.

Among those who welcomed us was New Yorker Emile Chi, half-Chinese, a professor of mathematics teaching at Tsinghua.

Our China Travel Service guides also introduced themselves—a Mr. Liu Shen-ling, capable, intense, serious; goodlooking Mr. Chen, who wore a rather Western-looking gray-tweed cap, and Mr. Wang Chi-kang, quiet, bespectacled. Perhaps the word *guide* should be in quotation marks in the latter's case because although Mr. Wang did indeed accompany us and answer many of our questions, his

English was somewhat faulty and he was, in fact, not a regular agent of the Travel Service. A distinguished scientist, specializing in lasers at Tsinghua University, he would shortly be traveling—we were told—to the Massachusetts Institute of Technology, whether for a short visit or an extended period of study I did not learn. He also turned out to be something of a Ping-Pong champ.

It was good to see the Peking Hotel again; after the two earlier visits I felt rather at home there. The lobby seemed unchanged except that the lounge to the left, opposite the dining room, now accommodated many more tables and had become a much busier meeting place. Another difference became evident when we were shown to our rooms; every one had a color TV set.

Tuesday, February 6

Our team this first morning was, as I recall, off to the Great Wall and the Ming Tombs. Since I had seen them twice in 1975 I took the occasion to wander about.

As I came out of the hotel for a solo stroll about the neighborhood, I found myself walking beside a foreign visitor who looked like a cliché Hollywood version of a Latin American dictator-general. He wore a rakish visored cap and tailored gray uniform decorated with more gold braid and medals than one might see in a complete wing of the Pentagon.

Across Wang Fu Jing Street to the left, the well-known large signboard, bright red, which carried one of Mao's pleas for unity was, oddly, covered up to a height of about fifteen feet with new hand-lettered pink-paper wall posters, something that would have been a criminal offense a year or so earlier. A crowd of perhaps a hundred was reading them, although most briefly directed their attention to me as I began to dictate these observations.

To the left of the signboard stands a line of about thirty glass-enclosed cases, in which are displayed news photographs, with appropriate captions. Some show Mao, evidently in the last months of his life because he looks relatively thin, shaking hands with visitors from various parts of the world.

In an alley beside a small photography studio a street vendor was selling an item of food which looked like a series of cherry-sized dark red meatballs or fruits strung on kebab sticks.

To the left-front of a large department store, a few feet farther down the block, one sees more wall posters and a display attracting a large percentage of the attendant crowd, architectural sketches of a new building to be constructed either on the spot or—as seems more likely—in a nearby area.

A sign, *Xianhua Shudian,* identifies the next building as a bookstore. Book *(shu),* shop or store *(dian).*

I was surprised that some four years after my last visit I still attracted so much attention from passersby, whether dictating notes or not.

In one of the attractively decorated windows in a second department store there is the sign, "The third floor for foreign visitors and overseas Chinese only. Foreign Exchange."

In the shops now I noticed a greater variety of colors and patterns of women's suit jackets, dresses and sweaters than had been evident in 1975.

Farther down the street more wall posters were displayed, some apparently just put up, others old, to judge by their tattered condition, but all attracting interested readers. One message consisted of a dozen small pages of letter-sized paper, very neatly printed.

At 192 Wang Fu Jing Street I again visited a shop where well-tailored leather and fur coats are sold and this time purchased a handsome black coat with a fur collar. For the next few days the hipper members of our group and I exchanged German submarine-officer jokes.

A bit later, strolling about town, I saw four people—all very old—picking over a few low mounds of waste material. It was not "garbage" in that it contained no remnants of food, but consisted of bits of earth, glass, paper, metal and wood waste. Since there is no hunger in China now of the sort that was a curse to the country for so many centuries, I assume that such refuse is pored over because of the marketable value of scraps of metal, wood or paper. It is only the very aged who do this, by the way, no doubt continuing a behavior pattern learned in the old China.

PEKING FILM STUDIO

Wednesday, February 7

On this date, as we were on our way to the Peking Film Studio, Vice Premier Teng, speaking to Japanese leaders in Tokyo, was saying, "Vietnam ought to be taught a lesson," and "Aggressors must be punished." Within ten days the world would understand what he had in mind.

All of us were excited at the prospect of meeting our professional counterparts in the Chinese film industry. Shirley MacLaine had not been able to meet them, in 1974, and though I had chatted with a small film group in Shanghai in 1975, I had not been able to visit a motion picture studio.

Among those we met at the film center were: actor Chao Tsi-yueh, a "Godfather" sort of fellow, bald, middle-aged, with a marvelous half-evil, half-friendly face; Pu Ying, a pretty actress; Chen-chang, a comedy actor; Li Bai-wan; Ma Chang-yo; Lee Chao, a writer of comedies and also—oddly enough—a dancer; Chou Chao-yuen, actress and assistant director; and Yuan Wen-shu, director of the Film-workers' Association.

At the introductory meeting almost every member of our delegation announced that he or she had brought some technical equipment, scripts, recordings, textbooks, etc., to present to our hosts as a gift. When it came my turn to speak I said, "The rest of our group have brought things—lights, cameras, video and filming equipment—as gifts for our Chinese hosts and friends. I have brought my wife. But I am afraid I will have to take her back." At the translation the Chinese present reacted appropriately.

"Speaking as a comedian," I said, "I must say that it is an unusual experience to get bigger laughs in Chinese than in English."

After a general exchange of introductions we were divided into small groups—writers, cameramen, directors, actors—to exchange views with our peers. Ernest Kinoy, Manya Starr and I, as writers, put questions to our counterparts.

Film writers have the same fears the world over. "We are sometimes sad that we do not see the full effect of our work at the time we finish it," one of our hosts said, "as do poets and the writers of stories. In our case we must wait a long time, until the film is seen, before we can know of the judgment about our work. There is so much that is involved, in addition to our own contribution, that sometimes we think it is perhaps, after all, not such a terribly important thing to be a film writer."

Later we were taken down a hall to a comfortable projection room, remarkably like an American screening room except for a large blue Oriental antique rug on the floor before the screen.

In the first scene shown, a young Revolutionary of the 1930s was saying a tearful good-bye to his mother. In the next sequence, placed in a railroad loading area, ragged refugees milled about. In the background a sexy sign, showing a scantily clad woman, provided a not-subtle comment on the depravity of the pre-1949 society.

A cart held bodies of those who had just died from hunger. Some young children distracted the attention of Nationalist guards so that one of the film's heroes could climb aboard a freightcar and cut open a bag of grain with a bamboo pipe, out of which grain flowed into the children's baskets. The action was discovered, however, and two policemen attacked the hero. The children came to his rescue but in doing so left their precious stolen grain behind.

In a third scene, at nighttime, the children were making hot soup, a bowl of which they bring to the hero. Next we saw a little girl running beside her father, crying because she thought he was going to sell her. "No," he said, "who told you I was going to sell you? I am not." Richly dressed people pass by, ignoring the beggars who clutch at their sleeves. The story—of Wei Bok Ching, a Revolutionary martyr—was in production as of the time of our visit.

After the showing we joined a group of actors, directors and writers.

"The various forms of entertainment in films," I said, "are, of course, the same the world over. There are serious dramas, comedies, musicals. And in all countries audiences are provided with a combination of these various forms. Is there any particular form here that audiences prefer?"

"Yes. Comedies are most welcomed by our people. Before the Cultural Revolution we made more comedies. One was *The Adventures of a Magician.*"

"My wife and I went to Russia some years ago," I said, "and there seemed to be no comedy except for that provided by circus clowns. The people didn't laugh, practically nobody was funny. In China everybody laughs; you have a wonderful sense of humor. We have been to see your acrobatic shows—I have seen them several times—and they always have wonderful comedy. Comedy in America, too, is very popular. I think when people can laugh at themselves they are healthy."

"We agree. Lee Chao here, for example, is a very good comedy actor."

"He is a comedian?"

"Yes. Even in a serious role the audience would laugh at him. He wrote a comedy during the reign of the Gang of Four to express his opinion that there were too many meetings. Consequently, he was sent down to the country-side, where he had to spend almost all of his time attending meetings."

Much hearty laughter.

"When I had the pleasure of visiting your country a few years ago," I said, "I had the impression that every one of your films was political. Now that a freer period for the arts has been entered upon might we expect to see a certain number of films that have no particular political significance?"

"We do not divide films into political and nonpolitical categories," one of our hosts said, "as you do in your country."

I took this to mean that in China—at least as of 1979—there were literally no nonpolitical films. As I pointed out before, it would, of course, be a mistake for Americans to assume that all of our own pictures are nonpolitical. The word political in this context does not refer to films dealing primarily with senators, congressmen, voting fraud, etc. In addition to the other television programs, "Roots," for example, was a highly political television film.

Coming Home, Day of the Condor, Convoy, The China Syndrome, The Deer Hunter, The Godfather, and *Midnight Express*—among many other films that might be cited—are strongly political.

"Now that the Gang of Four has been overthrown," I said, "if I may return to the subject, do you expect to make any nonpolitical films?"

The future could apparently not be predicted easily.

BEI HAI PARK

After a stimulating morning, we were taken to a sumptuous luncheon at Bei Hai Park, which the present administration says was "Chiang Ching's private preserve" until her downfall in 1976. An enormous white Buddhist temple sits on top of a hill; the area is pure beauty and very "old China." One is reminded of the Summer Palace in that the same combination of man-made and natural beauty is encountered. It too was said to be the private playground of an empress. The park's small lake was frozen; ice skaters skimmed about its surface.

In the beautiful central dining room—the Fong Shan—we were introduced to a large number of dignitaries, including Wang Lan-sih and Shitu Waiman, vice-ministers of culture. One gentleman told us he had been in the U.S. forty years earlier.

"In what city?" I asked.

"New Haven."

"Did you go to Yale?"

"Yes." He smiled at my making the connection. "Yale Drama School."

One of our hosts was introduced as "the most famous film director in China." One of his pictures is *Early Spring.*

After lunch, on the way out of the park, I spied another instance of the by-now familiar temple roof-corner ceramic and took the occasion to ask—once more—if any of our guides knew the reason for the boy-on-the-chicken statuette seen on the upturned points of so many ancient buildings. Mr. Chen, one of our guides, said he thought it had some connection with a superstitious belief in fire prevention. An analogy might be made with the Catholic belief that statues of certain saints, or the veneration of the same saints, ward off particular disasters or diseases.

PEKING BALLET SCHOOL

Thursday, February 8

At the Peking Ballet School we were introduced to Madame Dai Ai-lian, whom I remembered having met at the airport at the time of our arrival. I later learned that she is a cousin of Jack Chen, well-known writer of books on China, including one on the Cultural Revolution.

She was married to a famous painter, from whom she was divorced in Peking in the early 1960s, at which time she married one of her students, which created something of a scandal in China, though such things are common enough in our part of the world. The student divorced her a few years later, during the Cultural Revolution. In the U.S. people may marry for money. In China there is no money to marry into, but one may marry for position. Or into a family with overseas Chinese connections, relations living in the Western world.

Madame Dai—small, energetic, ladylike—is still attractive though no longer young. I wish I could say the same for myself.

At the school, *Swan Lake* was being rehearsed for presentation "in several years." The ballet company was originally organized in 1963. At first many of the classic European ballets were performed. In 1964, under the influence of Chiang Ching, they were obliged to stage *The Red Detachment of Women* and *The White-Haired Woman.* After that the ballet deteriorated.

"We suffered, as if from Fascist dictatorship," Madame Dai said. "Chiang Ching didn't know anything at all about ballet but she made laws about what the ballet should do and what we shouldn't do. It destroyed the whole system of training so that the technique, the artistry, went very much down. Now it is only in the last two years that we are trying to return to the standard tradition of the ballet."

According to Martha Duffy, writing in *Time,* April 2, 1979, Chiang Ching insisted that ballet dancers were no longer to be permitted to do two of their most basic steps, the *entrechat* and the *pas de basque;* I have no idea why, although the rationalization advanced at the time was probably that the movements were "bourgeois." Being ultra-bourgeois myself, I naturally do not find the allegation shocking. If and when Marxist societies ever achieve their ideal they will discover that in doing so they have elevated everyone to the bourgeois level, in which case I suppose they will have to come up with a less pejorative term.

But back to Madame Dai. "Today," she said, "you will see, I think, the good parts and also the shortcomings of our company, which is the historical result of the tyrant that we had in China." The little woman spoke with great dignity and intensity.

"Our company, before the Cultural Revolution, had 250 people, with more than sixty dancers. We had an orchestra, we had shoemakers, everything needed for a ballet company. During the Cultural Revolution it grew to nearly six hundred people, which is too much for a ballet company. At present there are less than five hundred. So," she sighed, "we are trying now to heal the wounds of the Cultural Revolution, to make the ballet healthy, to serve the people and also to be compatible with all the peoples of the world, to promote friendship. Well," she said, "I wag my chin too much, because I think you would like to ask questions."

"Very well," one of our group said. "How do you find your prospective students?"

"It is harder to find boy dancers now because so many of the young fellows want to be scientists, because of the Four Modernizations. But our students get a complete middle-school education, not just instruction in the dance."

"Do they board here?" I asked.

"Yes," she said, "they are in residence at the school. It is particularly crowded during the holidays or festival days."

"You speak excellent English," one of our women said.

"Thank you. People say, 'Wow, you speak such good English, where did you learn your

Norvel Welch and I enjoying the wit of Madam Dai Ai-lian, Shanghai Ballet School.
Photograph by Michael Welch

English from?' Well, to tell you the truth I spoke English before studying Chinese because I was born in Trinidad. When I was fourteen I went to England to continue ballet training. I lived in England for nine years, then, in 1940—during the Second World War —I returned to China and have worked in China ever since."

"Did you dance with English companies?" I said.

"I couldn't get into a company"—she smiled—"because I am too short. I couldn't fit in even in the *corps de ballet,* but my teachers were always very good teachers. They were always very kind and friendly."

"As the head of this ballet school," I said, "are you the only such teacher trained outside of China, or would any of the other teachers have had training elsewhere?"

"We had one before. Before the Cultural Revolution there was another overseas Chinese. She had studied with the Royal Ballet and she taught in our academy for some time, but she left."

"Were there any, before the break with the Soviet Union, that might have been trained in Moscow or Leningrad?" I said.

"Yes. There was one such dancer. She was trained in Moscow."

"Gene Kelly," Jayne explained, "who is one of our fine American dancers, was very impressed with one of your dances that he intro-

duced on American television, the film of *The Red Detachment of Women.* He thought it was on a very fine level technically."

Madame Dai smiled and nodded but said nothing, perhaps because *The Red Detachment of Women* had been produced under Gang of Four influence.

The *Swan Lake* performance by her students was thrilling, touching. Our group applauded vigorously after each dance and spontaneously gave the dancers a standing ovation at the conclusion of their presentation.

The company hosts two ballerinas. One, who was twelve years old in 1954, graduated in 1959. A premiere ballerina, she had visited the United States in 1978. During the Cultural Revolution, Madame Dai said, "She was not allowed to dance." There was great emotion in the statement. Certain members of the dance troupe, we were told, did no dancing at all in the 1967–1976 period.

One of the young dancers asked if any one of our group who was an actress could tell them something about the life of an actress in the U.S. Since Jayne was the only one, she responded. We happened to have with us some photographs of her in the roles of Cleopatra, Marie Antoinette, Florence Nightingale and Susan B. Anthony, from our PBS-TV series "Meeting of Minds." As soon as the company of about forty dancers saw the pictures they broke ranks and clustered around Jayne's end

Members of the Shanghai Ballet performing Sleeping Beauty, *February, 1979.* Photograph by Tom Ackerman

of the table like eager smiling children, all anxious to see the famous women from history she had portrayed.

While I was quietly dictating a few observations I was suddenly surrounded by the eager chattering dancers, some of whom were applauding and smiling.

"What's up?" I asked one of our group.

"Jayne just told them that you're a pianist," she said. "They'd like you to play something."

I nodded, walked to a battered grand piano and played Jerome Kern's "The Song Is You." The interest shown by our hosts was polite. Then, on the spur of the moment, I started a vigorous boogie-woogie number, after briefly explaining that it was a musical form created in the 1920s by American black musicians.

The effect was electrifying! The dancers began to clap in rhythm and the next thing I knew Jayne and Manya Starr were up doing disco-rock steps, for which the applause and laughter were thunderous. Even some of the Chinese dancers got into the act.

A few minutes later one dancer said he would like to see an American ballet performance in Peking someday. There was hearty applause for this.

Madame Dai, we learned, had some years earlier been sent to a thought-reform farm until she suffered a nervous breakdown, after which she was placed in a sanatorium. "It was

there that I gradually got my health back," she explained. The harm done by the excesses of Mao's Cultural Revolution is brought into sharp focus when one meets its victims face to face.

PEKING CENTRAL MUSIC CONSERVATORY

Saturday, February 10

The weather was particularly cold the morning we visited the Peking Central Music Conservatory, the genial administrator of which, Mr. Chao Feng, turned out to be remarkably witty.

"When I say this is the main music institute in Peking," he said, in his introductory remarks, "I am not modest enough, but if I say that it is not then I am not honest enough.

"There are three beliefs that are common," he added, a moment later, in discussing China's composers. "The mother-in-law always praises the son-in-law, the wives of other men are good, and one's own musical compositions are good." Then he turned serious. "Our music school was closed for almost ten years during the Cultural Revolution.

"We have here at the conservatory," he continued, "eight hundred students and six hundred teachers and staff people. In other words we are bureaucratically inefficient. In any event, the chief project facing us at the moment is the study of our cultural heritage, the music of ancient China."

The professor interrupted his remarks two or three times not only to light up himself but to offer cigarettes to his visitors. After his third urging I said, "It occurs to me that the professor may soon be invited to the United States, not so much to tell of the music of China but to speak on behalf of our American tobacco companies."

After laughing at the translation of my remark, our host said with a smile, "I would be very happy to do so, if they would pay me."

Topped again.

As we strolled about the grounds, several buildings of which were beautifully constructed in the ancient imperial style, we were told that Pu-yi, the last Ching emperor, had been born on the premises.

After a reference to the fact that the Chinese would welcome being able to hear more Western music I said, "Your young people now have their own radios, and more and more people are acquiring television sets. Do many have recording equipment so that they can listen to record albums?"

The professor said, "As yet only a small number have such equipment because it is expensive. The recordings also are rather expensive; therefore they chiefly hear records at their schools or music academies."

Our group was taken to a projection room where we enjoyed a color film showing several students in concert. Each was highly gifted. The average number of hours devoted to daily practice, we were told, was eight!

PEKING TV STUDIOS

After lunch we went to the Peking TV studios, where—just as on my visit four years earlier—an armed guard stands at the front door. A far greater number of guards, of course, now defend the NBC, ABC and CBS studios in New York and Los Angeles.

At the end of a hallway was the by-now common tall white statue of Mao. On the walls of the meeting room to which we were taken to be officially welcomed and instructed there

were, surprisingly, *no* political photos or posters, only artistic pictures.

We were introduced not only to executives, producers and directors but also to a camerawoman, a director of the cultural department, a designer and scenic painter, a sound man, an editor from the news department and a technical engineer, among others. I don't believe I met any of the same people in 1975. The head of the studio was Ms. Mong Chyu.

The studio, we were told, had opened in 1969. Color television started in 1973. "Because of sabotage by the Gang of Four we still have quite a few shortcomings in our work."

"How many hours a day are you on the air now?" I asked.

"About nine. Educational television, music, drama and news are presented in the evening. The 'University of the Air' started yesterday."

"How many channels do you have?"

"Two. One, by microwave, for the whole country. The other is for local programming."

Between seven hundred and eight hundred people are employed at the station. There are "betweeen one and two million sets in all of China" as of 1979 though no one seems to know the exact figures. The number of those who can see a show, of course, is much larger because many sets are located in schools, universities, public agencies, apartment complexes or communes.

After the question-and-answer briefing we toured the premises. One of the engineering rooms was provided with Ampex brand videotape equipment, which the Chinese had ordered directly from the company. Ampex, in fact, dispatched its engineers to Peking to make the installation. In an adjoining room were film-editing tables. The main control rooms did not seem to have changed appreciably since my earlier visit.

While hurrying through the hotel lobby late one afternoon I ran into Ralph Nader and his sister, who had just arrived in town. When he asked how I happened to be in the People's Republic I told him I was doing research for a book, in which, come to think of it, I had already mentioned his name. "They're so busy here catching up with the pace of Western industrial progress," I said, "that they haven't as yet gotten around to the factor of consumer safety." The United States, of course, had been, to some extent, similarly remiss until Nader himself forced the issue into the public consciousness by his courageous work.

I look forward to reading Ralph's comments on what he observed in the People's Republic.

Riding to one place or another on a bus, one has good opportunity for putting questions to the accompanying members of the China Travel Service.

"When I was here in 1975," I said, "we heard daily, even hourly, reference to Liu Shao-chi. Since it has never come to my attention that his death was officially announced I wonder if he might still be alive."

"I do not think so," our guide said, "because on January 29, at a public celebration of Chinese New Year, his wife was introduced as Liu Shao-chi's widow."

The fact that Madame Liu was introduced at all I take to be politically significant inasmuch as she had stood shoulder to shoulder with her much-maligned husband during the days when he was saying so many things that it is now possible to perceive as remarkably similar to the views of Teng Hsiao-ping.

PUBLIC BATHHOUSE

One cold night Art Zich and Irvin Yeaworth said that they were planning to go to a public bathhouse.

"How do you know about such a place?" I asked.

"I read about it," Zich said, "in Ross Terrill's *Flowers on an Iron Tree.*

"Mind if I tag along?"

"No, we'd like you to."

So off we went, by cab, to a bathhouse called Great Fragrant Garden. It was not many blocks from the Imperial Palace and the great public square before it.

At the side of the building a horizontal chimney poured out thick clouds of smoke. Inside you pay the fee—very little—and are given a small bamboo stick with a number on it, which corresponds to the number of a

locker inside the changing room. Its set-up is much like that in bathhouses around the world, lockers and a series of cots to sit on while removing your clothing as well as to flop on after coming out of the hot-bath room.

The lockers were equipped with small locks which a smiling attendant snapped shut while we were in the tub room.

Zich seemed puzzled by the presence of lockers.

"Terrill said that this place had a system where an attendant takes your clothes, puts them up with a long pole to a railing of hooks near the ceiling."

"There seems to be room up there for that kind of storage," I said. "Maybe they've changed the system since Terrill was here last."

Though the place was crowded with males from eight to eighty we were not the object of as much open staring in these close quarters as would have been the case on the street or in a large store, perhaps on the unspoken theory that whatever his color a man naked, or clad only in a towel, has somehow more a right to privacy than one fully clothed.

To the right of the steaming tubs was a line of showers, the water of which turns on only when you step on a wooden platform, thus preventing waste. The tubs were long, narrow, white-tiled troughs about three and a half feet high, each accommodating three or four men and a steaming hot liquid I can only describe as People Soup. Since remaining too long in either a sauna, steam room or hot tub can be quite enervating I sloshed in the water like a lazy hippopotamus for only about five minutes. Art and Irvin soaked a bit longer.

Climbing out of the tub, I cooled off with another shower, wrapped a towel around my waist and returned to my bunk, where I stretched out, feet high up on the wall, and rested for a few minutes. I'm so accustomed to reclining in this position that it no longer seems unusual to me but it seemed to strike a number of the neighborhood gentry as amusing. I explained to one of them who spoke English that I assumed such a position as a way of getting an extra supply of blood to my brain and thus refreshing myself after having had the starch taken out of me by the steamy water.

Art, Irvin and I felt so invigorated after leaving the bathhouse that we decided to walk back to the Peking Hotel, through the chilly night, rather than take a cab.

The day before we left Peking, Jayne and I went out for a late-afternoon stroll, our ultimate destination a Friendship Store about two miles down Chang An Boulevard to the left. Crossing Wang Fu Jing Street and its crowds still reading outspoken big-character posters, we noted first, against a stone wall, an old woman sitting on a low stool, at what looked like an American shoeshine boy's box; but she was repairing the shoes of passersby, not shining them.

About two blocks from the Peking Hotel there is a large one-story building which from the outside looks as if it might be a garage. It looks like a garage on the inside too, come to think of it, but it is a neighborhood food market and an exciting one through which to stroll.

On one wall meats are displayed. Even though this is a no-tourists-see-type market, the fruits and vegetables are nevertheless arranged in an artistic and creative fashion, rather than simply piled up in the way we are familiar with. One large, slanted case contained perhaps a thousand eggs—half-white, half-tan—laid out in a beautiful geometric pattern. Very Chinese.

Outside the grocery, at a clean white van-truck, from which two young women were selling pastries, we bought what looked like croissants but were greasier, though quite satisfying.

In the next block we ran into some of our group: Jim Cranna, Mike Welch, Cheryl Downing and Mark Peterson, who were joking with a group of local teenagers and taking their pictures.

A few blocks closer to the Friendship Store Jayne and I encountered an old street vendor selling little toy windmills made by hand out of thin bamboo. Propeller blades of paper, alternately red and green, were set into a delicate wheel of bamboo straw. When one waved the thing into a breeze the blades turned a small spindle which encountered two tiny drumsticks that beat upon a tomtom about the size of a small sink-stopper. A colorful triangular lavender paper pendant adorned the top of the toy, which I bought for about a dime. For the next few minutes, as we strolled along, passersby smiled or laughed aloud at the sight of an American freak playing with a Chinese child's toy.

We came next to a sort of "freeway interchange," a crossing of one new roadway over another, construction on which had just started when I last passed the spot in 1975.

Wishing to study the situation at the city's Democracy Wall at close quarters I drove there, with Tom Ackerman. Although there were walls in various parts of the city on which big-character posters were then being displayed, the main center of activity was several blocks to the right of the Peking Hotel along Chang An Boulevard. As expected, several thousand people—the majority young men in their twenties and thirties—were gathered in loose clusters, individuals moving slowly along the wall as they read what were for the most part remarkably outspoken statements. Although I speak just a little Mandarin Chinese I do not read it at all and therefore was obliged to take close-up photographs of some of the posters so that later I might have them translated. The one on page 274 is typical enough. Displaying it publicly would require considerable social courage even in New York, Philadelphia, Chicago or San Diego. The fact that such political protests could be displayed in February, 1979, in the People's Republic of China is remarkable. Within two months the administration, in fact, would begin to discourage what they viewed as the more irresponsible of such angry expressions of sentiment, although they were not, at that time, forbidden altogether, whereas during the Gang of Four period the situation was quite otherwise.

The following example is interesting on a number of scores, one being that it refers to the ongoing debate about the whole issue of public protest itself.

Protest—The Shuen-Wu District Police Station's Provocation of the People's Democracy

On January 18th at 4 A.M., a young girl named Fu Yue-hua, who had previously joined the present democracy movement, the organization of January 8th's *"The Civilians to Central government's debate group,"* and the *demonstration against starvation,* was illegally arrested by the Shuen-Wu District Police Station.

The police had failed to show any warrant of arrest, nor had they given any reason for the act.

When Fu Yue-hua's family went to the station to inquire about the matter, the police stubbornly refused to answer any questions.

We charge that this kind of behavior is directly against the spirit of our constitution, rule number 7. It is also an act of ruthless put-down of the law. Furthermore, it is a diabolical provocation directed toward the present movement for democracy.

A view of Chang An Boulevard and the south entrance of Wang Fu Jing Street. The large buildings at the right are the Ministry of Foreign Trade. The apartment buildings behind these large ones are the dormitories of the officers who work for the ministry.

The building behind these apartments is the Peking Hospital, where Premier Chou En-lai died on January 8, 1976.

In the foreground are two huge red signboards made for Chairman Mao's quotations. Civilians are now allowed to paste posters here, a remarkable change, made after Teng Hsiao-ping took over. During the Cultural Revolution anyone covering the chairman's words would be arrested immediately. The crime, "Insulting Chairman Mao."

← *Part of a larger poster. The complaint is made by a group from Honan Province who, dissatisfied with certain decisions by their local authorities, came to Peking to present their grievances to the central government. They were, however, advised to return to their local authorities. The poster was written to complain about the Peking central government, saying, "How can a fair judgment and decision be made from the accused instead of a third party?"*

Apparently some in the group who had defied their local Honan authorities were arrested on dubious charges.

From the above grievances, we strongly protest to the Beijing Bureau of Police, and the Shuen-Wu District Police Station. We demand the answers to the following questions:

1. Announce to the public whether Fu Yue-hua's arrest was approved by her own work organization beforehand, and the location of her prison.
2. Announce to the public the reason for Fu Yue-hua's arrest and the reason for the illegal procedure directed toward arresting civilians.
3. Request the court for an open public hearing on the case, and to allow a defender for the accused.
4. The Senate of Investigation should start an immediate probe into the entire matter, which has seriously broken the law and the body of democracy. We demand the result to be announced to the entire country.
5. We demand the punishment of the offending individuals by the court and the Senate of Investigation.

If the Beijing City Hall refuse to answer these questions, the "Detect" editorial department will take united action with the people's newspaper [not government's], and the organizational group's magazines.

We hope the people of this entire country will support our fight for the protection of the constitution and our fundamental human rights.

Justice Will Prevail!

"Detect" Editorial Dept.
2/7/79

For a farewell dinner on the night of February 10, our party was taken to the Hsin Ciao Hotel. Exiting from the elevator on the sixth floor we entered the old luxurious, pre-Revolutionary billiards rooms, complete with bar, and were ushered down a narrow hallway to a dining room furnished with about a dozen tables and large enough to accommodate a party of two hundred.

Various dignitaries of the Ministry of Culture, films, television and the theater were introduced, many smiles exchanged and toasts offered during the serving of the banquet, which was, needless to say, a superb meal. The printed menu read:

Cold Dishes
Pigeon Egg with White Fungus Soup
Shark's Fin with Mixed Stuffs
Two Tastes of Prawns
Crisp Fried Boneless Duck
Roast Turbot in Chili Sauce
Mixed Sea-Food in Steamed Casserole
Cauliflower with Mushrooms
Chinese Cakes
Cold Fruits

During the meal there was the usual flurry of toasts, with many a hearty *Gom Bei*. At one point Chao Feng of the Music Conservatory approached our table, Mao-Tai glass raised high, and offered to toast me personally, to which I was, of course, required to respond. I made a pass at tasting the bitter liquid, at which there was general laughter. I later learned that Chao's glass was full of Laoshan water, not Mao-Tai. Now why hadn't I thought of that?

During the dinner Schuyler Chapin thanked one of the important visitors for showing up to give our party such a pleasant farewell.

"Not at all," the man said with a smile. "I had to."

Also present was Chou Shao-yen, a charming soprano, actress and director of the Peking Film Studio, who told me she had been born in Jayne's birthplace of Wuchang.

I later learned that at the dinner one of the women in our group said to the Chinese woman on her right, "I have with me some long, thermal underwear that I will not be needing anymore. I purchased it just for use in Peking and since the weather is warmer in Shanghai and Canton, and inasmuch as I won't be using it in Southern California, I would be happy to present it to any of your friends who might be able to use it."

"That is very kind of you," the Chinese woman said.

"Could you yourself use the underwear?"

"Yes, I suppose I could."

Whereupon the American woman explained that she happened to be wearing it at the moment and that since the two would not

I entertain at Hsin Ciao Hotel banquet, Peking. Photograph by Michael Welch

be meeting in the morning, because of the early hour of our departure, perhaps the best thing to do was to take the underwear off then and there. At which the two repaired to the nearby ladies' room where the garment was removed and turned over.

After dinner, when Schuyler Chapin introduced me as "the floor show," I said to our hosts, "On the way from my chair to this microphone I recalled the first time—years ago—that I ever entertained a Chinese audience. It happened in one of our American provinces, or states, called Arizona. There was, just outside the city, an airfield where Chinese flying cadets were trained to come back and take part in the war against the Japanese. This was in 1943. My then partner and I were invited to perform our comedy act at the class's graduation dinner, and when I made an entrance I was greeted with a great roar of laughter, due entirely to the fact that I was attired in a funny costume. That, sad to say, was the last time anyone laughed at us that evening. We later were advised that the reason was that no one in our audience spoke a word of English.

"But, in all seriousness, I am happy to have the opportunity to say that I have long had a particular fondness for China and its people. One of the reasons, I'm sure, is that my wife was born in your country, in the city of Wuchang. A number of our Chinese friends have told me that she seems to them, in many ways, very Chinese. And I am sure that this is one of the reasons that she was from the first, and remains, attractive to me. She is, for example, a remarkably creative and inventive person, particularly when confronted with difficulties, and this trait has always been typical of Chinese behavior.

"A thought occurred to me a moment ago, as I was enjoying this wonderful banquet, and that is that Chinese food is distinguished not only by its variety but by the creativity of its preparation. It is no accident, to my mind, that the three best cuisines of the world are the Chinese, the French and the Italian, because these are the most artistic cultures known to history.

"In perhaps belated conclusion, and speaking for my friends here tonight, we express our gratitude for the emotional warmth of the welcome that has been extended to us. We have come among our counterparts in film and television not to inform you but chiefly to learn from you, which is hardly surprising when China has a history of some five thousand years upon which to draw and my country can boast of only two hundred. It is also true, of course, that we can learn from each other.

"You have been kind enough to refer to me as a humorist but there was a far more gifted American humorist, whom I'm sure you would have liked very much if you had had the opportunity to know him. His name was Will Rogers, and he was a man of the people, a simple cowhand from our Western plains. He once said that we are all ignorant, only on different subjects. China and the United States have for too long been ignorant of each other, perhaps even dangerously so. It is good that our mutual ignorance is finally being dispelled, and our personal contacts strengthened, by cultural exchanges such as this."

Producer Ed Schumann, of our group, a few minutes later, introduced an Australian TV film he had brought, a ninety-minute ballet of *Don Quixote* featuring Nureyev. It had been a long, tiring day. After a quarter of an hour, fearing the ballet might run its full length, I took advantage of the darkness in the dining room to tiptoe out to the elevator.

Leaving the Hsin Ciao Hotel at five minutes past nine, I strolled alone through the chilly China night, along I knew not what streets, enjoying every minute of it. Behind high wooden gates to my right I heard the sound of two men energetically shoveling coal. A young father passed carrying a warmly bundled infant. A moment later a young woman crossed the street in front of me.

In the middle of the next block, from a comfortable looking club to my left, came dance music and the sound of carefree laughter.

Shortly I reached Chang An Boulevard and turned left toward the Peking Hotel, where Jayne, who had a bad cold, was waiting.

14. Shanghai in Winter

Sunday, February 11

 THE weather in Shanghai, at least when we arrived, was a good deal warmer, though it soon became chilly. But in contrast to the dry air of Peking, the sprawling port city was humid to a pleasant degree.

We were quartered this time in the Ching Chiang (Jinjiang) Hotel, 59 Mowming Lu, South, where President Nixon stayed during his 1972 visit, and in which the historic Shanghai Communiqué was signed.

After the Maoist victory in 1949, the hotel had been given the new name Ching Chiang by the mayor of Shanghai, Ching Yi, who later became Minister of Foreign Affairs and attended the Geneva Conference. In 1950 he said, "Now we need a place that is safe and protected, for the security of the high officials and also for peace delegations from the foreign countries." According to official policy the government could not then simply commandeer such properties so it was decided that someone in an unofficial position should communicate with representatives of the Sassoon interests, British owners of the establishment.

At the first stage the new government greatly increased the taxes on property owned by foreigners. The Sassoon people consequently owed China about one billion yuan. Irene and Lily Tung's mother, then a successful restaurant operator, said, "All right, I will talk to them." It was felt that the hotel's regular staff—the cooks, the workers—because they were connected with the old regime, could not be trusted to take care of the Communist leaders and the foreign delegations. Madame Tung, therefore, placed at the new administration's disposal the staff from her own restaurant and teahouse, people she knew could be trusted because they had worked for her since 1925.

Before the Nationalists left, Chiang Kai-shek's son, Chiang-kuo, later president of the Taiwan government, is said to have created a policy that every citizen who had gold must sell it to the government. The government was, of course, the Nationalists who by such means acquired a good deal of the nation's gold, which they then took to Taiwan.

"We have machines that can detect the metal," they said, "so do not try to withhold it. We have ways of finding out where you have it hidden."

A few people were shot on the streets of Shanghai to dramatize the policy.

The gold was thereafter sold at very low prices. Payment was in a paper currency which after the Nationalists left the country no longer had the slightest value. In the view of many who lost all their holdings, the gold was in effect stolen.

Many merchants, shopowners, and business people—by no means Communist—were bankrupted overnight by the policy.

The mother's own teahouse was at the back of the former French concession park, her restaurant in the British concession, beside the Big World amusement park. But her employees were not enthusiastic when she told them she was expanding. "This is a crazy thing to do," they said, "there's nobody on the street at night now. Business is bad. Why do you want to have us work in a hotel? The place is very big. Where will its customers come from? This venture is sure to fail."

Madame Tung was not at that point able to tell them that the building was going to be taken over by the new government.

In 1954, when a policy involving the National capitalists was instituted, one party spokesman said to the employees of the hotel, "Now we can tell you that Madame Tung will-ingly gave up her holdings to China, to the party, to the people. You are therefore now permitted free medical care and benefits because the hotel was already nationalized four years ago, although you did not know it then." The employees were therefore the first in China to enjoy benefits that later became available to all.

The beautiful floor of the Art-Deco lobby was described by one member of our party as "parquet marble," a good description in that its squares consist of neatly striped rather than randomly veined marble, set in alternating horizontal-vertical patterns.

The establishment, which originally housed luxury apartments, divided them into separate smaller suites and rooms, which are quite comfortable. And, since the hotel is not situated on the waterfront, its grounds are blessedly quiet.

"The hotel gardens," green-thumbed Jayne noted at once, "are even neater and more beautiful than those we saw in Japan." Tree branches were thinned out, earth loosened. The planning of the gardens is artistic indeed. The hedges are neatly clipped. "Everything is the way I wish mine were at home."

As quickly as possible I went downstairs to stroll about; one sees so much more afoot than on a bus. Just across the street outside the hotel compound there is a pre-1949 building—well, come to think of it, almost everything one sees in Shanghai is that old—anyway, there is a theater which as of the day of our arrival featured a Chinese stage production of *Much Ado About Nothing*. A poster on the side of the building carried a sketch of William Shakespeare. Chiang Ching had permitted nothing of the sort.

A beautiful pale green building opposite the hotel's main gate had been, in the old days, a swank club for the French. Because of the generally European architecture of the neighborhood, in fact, one has the impression, walking down the street, that hundreds of Chinese extras have been bused to a provincial French town for the filming of a picture.

In a grocery window at the end of the block, canned mushrooms were for sale, Narcisa brand. Some of the labels were printed in English, others in French.

I stopped into a store and bought, for 3 cents, a doughnutlike pastry encrusted with caraway seeds. At an adjacent shop window, opened to the street at counter level, people were purchasing what looked like dry, limp noodles in small baskets. I was suddenly the object of much curious attention here, as had been the case in Tientsin on my first visit four years earlier.

A middle-aged man passed, his face sadly deformed by I know not what disease or injury. I thought of the word leprosy but it would be unlikely that he would be walking the streets in such a condition. On the corner two young men were playing badminton, from one side of the street to the other.

Farther down the block hundreds of rough baskets were stacked in random piles. Near them an evil-looking liquid filled several enormous clay pots. The faint odor of fish floated from the area. Several flat fish lay drying on nearby basket tops. From a truck which suddenly pulled up about thirty similar baskets, full of iced fish, were quickly unloaded. As the baskets were slid down a metal ramp, two workers threw grappling hooks into them and quickly worked them into place. Under an overhanging roof, hundreds of animal skins, perhaps pig, were drying.

I turned right again and entered a narrow alley about ten feet across. Except for bicycles, and the suddenly distant sound of truck and auto horns, I might have been in the China of fifty years earlier. Overhead, from bamboo poles, there hung an assortment of clothes, some unfortunately ragged. One is reminded again and again—and quite properly so—that China is a poor country and that its people, separately and individually, still suffer from this so far inescapable fact. Reaching the end of the alley, I found myself back on the street on which I had begun my walk.

Stopping to stare into the window of a small store, I was immediately surrounded by several beautiful children, five or six years old, who were as curious about me as I was about the objects in the window: toothbrushes for sale at about 11 cents each and badminton shuttlecocks costing 12 cents.

On the nearby corner two men, apparently in their thirties, were playing a card game at a low table, watched by about a dozen old-timers. Obviously at least some people in China have the time to goof off, as we do at home.

The children near me looked so curious as I dictated these notes that I stopped to let them speak into the tape recorder. When they heard their voices back they laughed, heartily, which little drama itself attracted a larger crowd.

I passed two small windowed rooms, outside which about a dozen pairs of shoes and sandals were lined up against the wall, obviously placed without fear of theft. Having made a wrong turn into an alley, I was suddenly lost and retraced my steps. Three men, squatting down beside another who was making a chair out of wood scraps, looked up and smiled.

Some of the buildings along the street have balconies typical of French architecture. So many shirts, jackets, blankets, sheets and tablecloths hang from the balconies, windows and tree branches of such streets that one is reminded of the device scenic designers employ when they wish to reproduce colorful tenement or slum quarters.

Some of the faces I passed justified the Occidental cliché about Oriental inscrutability. Needless to say, the same wide variety of facial types and expressions are encountered that one might see anywhere in the world.

At the end of my thirty-minute stroll I was once again in the bourgeois security and luxury of our hotel. On the way back into the hotel grounds I met Irvin Yeaworth coming out, and explained to him that I had just taken a walk around the neighborhood.

"How was it?" he asked.

"I found a lot more staring here than in Peking."

"Well," he said, with a grin, "have you *seen* yourself today?"

Three members of our party who took separate strolls the next morning arrived independently at the impression that the faces on the street were a bit less friendly than those in Peking.

At two, after lunch, our group was taken by bus to an antique shop, every object in which was incredibly beautiful and—at least to those not sophisticated about antiques—incredibly expensive.

One of our guides told us more or less off the record that antique prices had gone up almost 50 percent since the preceding December. He did not argue with our contention that they had gotten prohibitively high. It is a good question as to why the government decision-makers have raised prices to such a degree. The only certain effect of it, I suppose, is to slow down the buying and selling. There could be some wisdom to this since the increasing hordes of American and other tourists might otherwise clean China out of its few remaining antiques in fairly short time.

Leaving Jayne to make decisions about such matters, I wandered outside where two little boys sat atop a large stone Fu dog at the store's entrance. At the curb, a three-wheeled street-sweeping machine, obviously effective to judge by the lack of litter, sat with its motor idling, befouling the atmosphere and wasting fuel. I stepped across the street to a small odds-and-ends store where a smiling, middle-aged woman returned my Chinese greeting. From her I purchased—out of curiosity—a tube of local toothpaste, White Jade brand.

Across the street another brisk card game was in progress, four young men sitting around a low wooden table, again with several older kibitzers looking on.

On a piece of twine outside the door of a dwelling some fish was drying. As I passed a small grocery store an old woman was walking out with an open piece of paper filled with dry spaghetti-like noodles. One strand fell to the ground; she retrieved it, putting it back into the pile.

At the end of the day Jayne and I felt too tired to attend a local lantern festival at Yu Gardens Park so we retired early.

TELEVISION STUDIOS

Monday, February 12

A dictated note:

As we come out of the hotel at eight-thirty on a gray, cooler, Monday morning, two chimneys from a nearby apartment building are belching out thick clouds of ugly smoke. Suddenly Jayne and I are recognized by a traveling group of friendly, middle-aged Americans. After shouting our names, one says to their puzzled Chinese guides, "These people are movie stars." The Chinese do not appear to be unduly impressed by the allegation.

Piling into our own bus our group was then taken to the Shanghai television headquarters, where we were welcomed by Mr. Chen Ku-hwa and his associates. (Another source spelled the name Chen Kuo-jo; even many Chinese are not sure how to spell their names in English.)

The most physically memorable detail of our visit to the Shanghai television station was its skyscraper transmission tower, to the tip of which one ascends in a small elevator. The view from the top is—inevitably—breathtaking. Two hundred and ninety feet below us the massive city stretched as far as the eye could see, which, considering the pollution problem, wasn't all that far. But even with limited vision the view was impressive.

Back down on the ground I noticed that construction of a nearby building was being accomplished by a combination of modern and ancient methods. There were pile drivers, steel girders and other twentieth-century details, but bamboo poles and straw mats were also in evidence.

"Our studios," one of our hosts said, "were constructed in 1958, although the building you are now in was not erected until 1973, which was the year we began working with color television."

"We would like to know about the equipment you use," one of our group said. "How much of it is Chinese?"

"Most of it is still made here," came the answer, "though we have some American equipment. Later we will show you a video recorder from the United States. We also, of course, have some Japanese and West German equipment, as well as some things from other countries. On the whole, however, our equipment is not as good as that of the advanced countries. In some instances, in fact, it is quite backward, as you will see for yourselves."

"What kinds of programming do you offer?" one of our people said.

"We have three kinds. One is educational, including material at the secondary, technical-school and university level. We even have a course in physics, which is being telecast at present. We also naturally have entertainment programs. In this second category we sometimes relay, for local telecast, programs that were originally produced, videotaped, in the central studios of Peking. Also there are news and documentaries."

"How many people work here?"

"Something less than three hundred."

"How many channels do you have in Shanghai?"

"We have two, although the programs for them both are telecast by our one station."

"Does anybody know how many television sets there are in your city?"

"Not really. It is estimated that there are some three hundred thousand sets here, although there are no precise statistics, partially because some people may purchase their television sets in other cities and then bring them here. We do know that the supply of TV sets at present cannot meet the demand. Even though the sets are rather expensive a surprising number of families can afford them because if there are several members of the family, each one can pay part of the cost."

"Do you have much dramatic material written directly for television?" Ernest Kinoy asked.

"At present there are only a few plays written for television. Most of the dramatic shows we carry are either films that already exist or else remote telecasts that we pick up by sending cameras out to local theaters."

The building's one large studio was approximately the size of an American equivalent except that the physical set-up enables shooting on three sides of the rectangular room. At one end was the sort of scenery we associate with a musical production number. At the opposite end a raised platform with table and chairs seemed suitable for the delivery of news features or interviews. On a third wall was a sort of Western parlor interior with piano, that looked as if it would be well suited to a presentation of a talk show, a form which, as it happens, has not as yet been introduced in China. One of our party, during a meeting there, identified me as creator of the talk show but the term did not seem to communicate anything of interest to our hosts.

FILM STUDIOS

After a sumptuous lunch we were taken to meet our peers in the Shanghai film production center, the exterior grounds of which looked more like a college campus than like M-G-M or Warner Brothers.

Since Shanghai, not Peking, was in the old days the "Hollywood of China," it's not surprising that its studios are still the largest in the People's Republic. Some 1,600 people were employed at the time of our visit. The Cultural Revolution–Gang of Four period naturally had led to a sharp curtailment of production but by 1977 the studio was gearing up again for full operation and turned out eight films. The number of pictures projected for 1979 was seventeen.

In the portraits of Mao and Hua in the meeting room of the studio the photograph of Hua had been taken from a slightly closer position, the effect of which was to make his face and head somewhat larger than Mao's. Whether this is purely a matter of accident or represents a subtle attempt to emphasize the new premier's importance I am not able to say.

Among those who welcomed us were Ching Yi, a famous actress; Mr. Cheng Chin-chiang, playwright and assistant director of the Film Bureau, who studied in England and the United States; Wong Yin, film director; and Sun Shi-lin, cameraman.

After the introductory meeting we saw some silent "rushes" showing peasants attacking a rich estate, after which a well-dressed man in Chinese gown and Western fedora leads them out from a temple, or mansion. A portion of a second film concerned a princess —being sent away to marry a Mongolian ruler

—who expressed her sadness at leaving her home and dear friends.

A few minutes later, as we strolled about the grounds, I noticed on a second-floor balcony a little boy, perhaps eight years old, looking out over the courtyard, a fairly typical encounter in China in that one sees children in places where, in the United States, they would not be found.

We were then taken to a soundproof audio-dubbing studio. Except for handsome Oriental rugs it looked like such a facility anywhere. A wooden staircase-to-nowhere along one wall was for the purpose of making sound effects.

Meeting a group of actors and actresses, we immediately made friends with a woman who was Jayne's counterpart, a pretty film star named Yu Ping.

The studio's music recording stage seemed as well equipped as anything in our part of the world. For the musicians there were comfortable folding chrome-and-padded-leather chairs. They are made, we were told, in Peking.

Audio speakers were made in Nanking, the microphones were all German Telefunkens. Recording and tape equipment was of Swiss manufacture. The instruction words such as *play, stop, record, edit,* etc., on the equipment were, however, in English, not Chinese, French or German.

We were next directed to a set where we found actors in costumes and full makeup. The lead actor in the scene being filmed was playing the part of Premier Chou En-lai. The film is titled *Newspaper Boy.* The scene: a cave in Chungking after World War II.

Everything visible was as it would be in an American or European studio except that there was no microphone over the action; most sound is dubbed in at a later stage. After posing for pictures with our hosts we were taken to view a filming of a new comedy. The scene was a neat, white-bricked two-room apartment. A young man, fanning himself, sat working at a desk, writing a book. A pretty young woman in bright red-and-tan-checked blouse entered and spoke to him.

The comedy, which deals with birth control, tells the story of a woman who has only daughters. She keeps having children because she says she will not stop till she has a son. One daughter decides that the way to solve the problem is for her to get married and bring a son-in-law into the house.

On the next stage, a remarkably realistic re-creation of a village of the 1930s was erected. The locale was Chungking (Chong-qing). Because the village was scaled for perspective, the actors could not stand close to some of the more distant portions of it because doing so would make them look ten feet tall.

During an open discussion with a group of actors, actresses, writers and directors I again thought of the question as to whether the new, freer creative climate might make it possible to produce an occasional nonpolitical film.

"At the time of the Gang of Four the topic commission strictly forbade such films. However, the audience is now very much interested in pictures about how the family lives, their social lives, personal feelings and so forth. For instance, the Chinese filmmakers did a picture entitled *Five Golden Flowers,* which depicts a story about little commune members, who share the name Golden Flower. It is a comedy and there are some truthful lines which won great applause from the audience. Nowadays we are trying to produce more films of that kind, to meet the needs of the mass audience, to produce more entertaining films."

"Is there anything you would like to ask us?" Jayne said.

"I know so little about your American film industry," one of our hosts said, "that I do not really know what questions to ask. China has been locked away from the world for the last ten years or more. We did not even know much about our side of the wall, much less yours."

"But with respect to your hope," a director said, returning to the subject of nonpolitical films, "it will be taken into consideration. We may do so in the near future. Such developments take time."

"There was an earlier precedent," I said, "regarding motion pictures from the Soviet Union, going back about twenty or thirty years. A few of the early Russian films were recognized in the West as very good, very artistic, but much of the Russian production created a negative effect in the West because it was totally political. Too much propaganda and not enough art. Therefore, that kind of mistake should be avoided, by all cultures, simply because audiences, generally speaking, do not care about it. But American audiences, whether of the Right or the Left politically, *would* be fascinated and enlightened by any film from China that showed the past history of those problems in China that created the possibility of a Mao, created the need for radical social change. If Americans are shown in what ways the old order was destructive they will be open to the information, I believe."

"We hope so. But the minds of all people still need to be emancipated. It takes time to emancipate the minds of the people here, too, because for over ten years our minds have been abused by the Gang of Four. In the near future we will try our best to produce much better films.

"When you were in China, last time, Mr. Allen, I understand that you explained that you are a gentleman who introduces actors or actresses on TV and since we don't have such a profession we would like to know something about that subject."

"Perhaps you mean masters of ceremonies or what we call talk-show hosts," I said. "It is a profession that does not require any talent at all, except on the part of those being introduced. It is rather like the young ladies who introduce your vaudeville acts."

Our hosts next wanted to know what American actors or actresses do when they are not in a film or play.

"In the old days," I said, "they starved. Now they can get payments from the state to sustain them till they find work."

"And the ones who do not work a lot," Jayne said, "if they are ambitious, may go to class. Or they work as waiters in restaurants, as taxi drivers. They work in hotels carrying bags, they work at other jobs, especially the young ones. Unfortunately some of them never can study and that's why they don't do well."

"I see."

"Are there many good women's parts in Chinese films?" Jayne asked.

"In the past the main starring roles were always played by women. But now men play the leading roles."

"That is the exact opposite of America."

"Well, you see, it's because in China, during the Japanese war, the men played the great part in the war. They fought against the enemy very bravely. And also in the Revolution men played a great part. So we have given the men the most important parts in the films because they played such roles in life."

"I see," Jayne said. "But, in the old days, why were the women's roles more important in films when women certainly weren't important in Chinese society?"

The answer to this seemed evasive or vague, perhaps because Jayne's question had not been properly understood.

"Would you ask them," she said to the interpreter, "if they think it could be that the pictures today deal with reality whereas the old movies were fantasy and the woman, too, was fantasy—an imaginary, beautiful, romantic figure—rather than realistic."

"Yes," came the answer. "In our society, before Liberation, the bosses of the film studios wanted to make more money so they tried to seek more beautiful persons to play in the pictures. This was so they could attract audiences and so make more profit."

"That's what I wanted to hear him say," a second Chinese actor added, "because I believe it also."

"Do your actors ever get stuck in one kind of role?" Jayne said. "It's what we call typecasting."

"It all depends. Sometimes they are the main actors of the film and sometimes they are the supporting actors."

"So they play many different kinds of roles?"

"Yes. In China we do not have too many main star actresses in films, so we do not have such competition for good parts. For instance, these three are film stars in China so they have always played the main parts in films, and although they do not now play the leading roles [because they were over fifty years old] they play supporting roles. They are still very popular, though."

"How many days in a month might they work in a film?"

"It all depends. Maybe the actors and actresses will work every day. Their job can last one month or several months."

"Do they ever come in and read the part to the director? Do they do as we do in America, audition? Is there competition for a role?"

"No. No competition. The director just picks them."

"How much freedom does the actor have in creating the role?"

"He can always discuss it with the director and maybe improve it."

"Who generally wins?" At this they smiled and laughed, but gave no other answer.

"Do children in China want to be actors and actresses as so many do in America?"

"We receive lots of pictures and letters from different parts of the country. They say they want to be actors and actresses."

Jayne next asked an unusual question. "The universal feeling of being sensitive—in sympathy—to fellow actors all over the world, do you feel the same thing?"

Our counterparts' faces lighted when the question was translated.

"Yes. They agree," the interpreter said, smiling.

"It's wonderful," Jayne said. "I'm glad they do."

"Although our language is different," the first actor—a handsome young man—said, "I can feel from your eyes and judge what you mean."

"I feel the same way," Jayne said, returning his warm smile. "Do they want to ask us any questions?"

The first actor leaned forward and said, "An actress in your country, do they have certain schools to train them? If so, at what age do the children become actors and actresses?"

They also asked about American actors and actresses studying their craft, and they knew the word Stanislavski. They were interested in the actor's preparation for his roles and explained their own experience on this point.

"What do you do when you are not working on a picture?" Jayne said.

"If we are not actively playing in a film then we do some plays, do performances for the workers and soldiers. And sometimes we go to the factories and the countryside to put on shows."

"That's wonderful. So if you play the part of a worker then you have the feeling of being a worker?"

"That's right. That is very important to us."

"Do people here like to go to the theater?"

"Oh, yes. Very much."

They told us of large and small theaters.

"The theaters and the studios are owned by the government, and actors themselves belong to the government. So the system is different from the United States. If people have spare time they do go to the theaters, according to their interests. Also, at the rural people's communes we have performer schools and the people organize themselves to be their own actors and actresses."

"In America," Jayne said, "the accent is on youth. The good parts today are mostly for young actors and actresses. Is the same thing true in China?"

"Not to the same extent. In China, it's more the medium age."

"What do you mean, medium?"

"Middle age. Thirty-five to fifty."

"Isn't that interesting? In the U.S. most of our stars today, on television and in films, are much younger."

"You know," one of the Shanghai directors said, gesturing to his friends, "when the Gang of Four was in power these veteran actors and actresses were put away. They were banished."

"To where?"

"Some of them were in prison."

"In prison?"

"Yes. And some worked in the fields as farmhands. During these ten years the actors and actresses did not have a chance to train so there is now a gap in the ages of our film actors. All these famous actors and actresses," the interpreter said, "became helpless."

The most popular American film, in Chinese theaters, as of the time of our visit, was

Convoy, starring Kris Kristofferson and Ali MacGraw. In case the reader has not seen it I should explain that it is a picture directed by Sam Peckinpah and is therefore characterized by what even many Americans would describe as a certain vulgarity and excessive reliance on violence.

"I find it somewhat surprising," I said, "that the authorities here would put this particular American motion picture into so many of your theaters since your culture presently is, compared to our own, quite puritanical. Is it perhaps the case that you are intrigued by the fact that the film's hero is an antiestablishment figure, that some of its villains are Southern American Fascist police types, and that the picture also makes a statement about American political corruption?"

One of our hosts smiled but did not directly respond to my question.

"Perhaps," he said, "it is that the Chinese identify with trucks and also like films with very vigorous action. For example there is a film called *The Milestone of the Winds and the Waves* made by the P.L.A. movie studio."

"You mean," Jayne said, "the army has its own film production unit?"

"Yes. It is called the August the First Film Studio."

"Why is it named August the First?"

"That is the day on which our army was founded, August 1, 1927."

"The army films are mostly documentary?"

"No, they might do any kind of film."

"How interesting," Jayne said. "Are there women in the army as actresses, or would they get actresses from you?"

"They have their own."

"Was Chiang Ching really an actress before she married?"

"She was. Oh, yes."

"Boy," Jayne said, shaking her head, "did she treat her fellow actors badly."

The host group laughed heartily, then returned in seriousness to the grim subject. "By suppressing the veteran actresses and actors Chiang Ching meant to use them to reach party power. And there were many more reasons."

"What do you mean?"

"The veteran actors were suppressed by Chiang Ching because they knew more about her history in the early days."

At the end of our visit our hosts bid us a warm and emotional farewell.

Our driver took us to the Bund area (Zhongshan Road) in the little time left before dinner.

A poster on one of the waterfront buildings said "Unity and Stability." We next drove close to the river and stopped in the area of the Cathay or Peace Hotel, and the "Big Sign." It was agreed that we would be back on the bus in twenty minutes. A snappy-looking Chinese gunboat lay at anchor off to the right. On the left was a barge, its deck loaded high with Chinese cabbage.

The stream of humanity along the Whangpoo was dense, the crowds like those we see at home going into or out of a football stadium. Two very pretty Chinese girls, one wearing a bright blue and the other a red sweater, sat perched on the stone wall at the river's edge. As the various Europeans and Americans stopped to gawk or to take pictures they were at once surrounded by crowds of mostly young people. Some good-natured but somewhat loud Americans, having recognized me, stopped to take my picture. They were not the usual sort of politically oriented travelers— Right or Left—who visited China during the first few years after the Nixon-Kissinger opening up, but were connected with a round-the-world ship tour group. This has become more common, nor is there anything wrong with it, but one does not perhaps learn a great deal about any one place on such short stops.

The crowds were even thicker now; as Jayne and I made our way back toward our bus we saw that it was surrounded by a sea of humanity, three or four hundred of whom suddenly boomed out—in thunderous unison—"Hey, Steve Allen!"

Schuyler Chapin, in his own record of the incident, reports it as follows:

Manya Starr's Polaroid color camera causes a sensation and within moments the crowd has tripled. They laugh with delight and crush forward to see the prints. Presently it's time for us to move on and we reboard the bus. Once

Jayne and I on the waterfront, Shanghai, February, 1979. Photograph by Tom Ackerman

on we notice that Steve and Jayne Allen are missing. I see them about twenty yards away looking at the Whangpoo River but it is hopeless to catch their attention. Mark Peterson calls out to the crowd and they turn to listen to him. He explains, in Chinese, that two of our group are missing and we must call to them. He explains that on the count of three they must call out the name of Steve Allen. He counts: "Yi, er, san (one, two, three) and they yell to a man and woman: S-T-E-V-E A-L-L-E-N!" I see Steve and Jayne turn, not quite sure what they heard. "Again!" says Mark. "Yi, er, san—S-T-E-V-E A-L-L-E-N!" And this time the Allens hear and burst out laughing and wave. I beckon to them to come to the bus and Mark points in their direction and suddenly the crowd parts, like Moses and the Red Sea, and the Allens approach to vast applause. We leave the Bund in triumph.

Above is a picture of Jayne and me snapped a moment later by Tom Ackerman.

Once back on the bus we waved our thanks to the smiling mob that had surrounded us. When Mark told them that Jayne had been born in China, they let out another gleeful roar.

As our driver pulled back into traffic, it occurred to me the moment might be appropriate for learning why posters and signs had been put up about the city—by the authorities —asking that traffic not be blocked by demonstrations.

"We have heard," I said to one of our guides, "that there have been recent street disturbances here." This led to a brief series of discussions, from which two possible explanations emerged.

1. Some of the educated youths who were sent to the countryside had grown tired of life in the villages and wished to return to their former lives, or 2. Gang of Four sympathizers were behind the unrest.

A solid crowd of perhaps five hundred people—all seemingly eighteen years old—surrounded us as we got off the bus at a bookstore. "Hell-o, how do you do?" some called in cheerful English. We returned their greetings in Chinese, at which they smiled and laughed.

In all bookstores, being hooked on books, I am like a child in a candy store. A twenty-minute visit here was not nearly long enough, though I picked up some interesting items, one of which gave China's side of its dispute with Vietnam. We did not at that moment know that troops of the People's Republic would shortly invade the nation that had, during the U.S. involvement in Indochina, seemed a staunch ally of the Chinese. Marx would not only turn over in his grave; if he were let out he would jump right back in.

As we drove away from the bookstore, again surrounded by eager, smiling, utterly friendly faces, we unanimously withdrew our earlier feeling of being less than ideally welcome on the streets of Shanghai.

Forcing our way through the crowds inside the Shanghai No. 1 Department Store was a dizzying experience. Actually "forcing" is the incorrect verb. The sea of humanity melts away at the merest approximation of contact. There is no pushing or shoving.

PEKING OPERA

That night several members of our group were taken to a local theater—bustling crowds, every seat taken—to see an example of a famous and ancient Chinese art form, the Peking opera.

The individual performances were fascinating although after several minutes the fact that the foreign visitor could understand nothing said or sung introduced an element of monotony. But the individual components were most interesting. There was no scenery in the conventional sense, merely blazingly red banners and imperial chairs. The costumes of the few characters were—is it necessary to say?—beautiful, typical of the ancient Chinese ability to create art by stitching patterns on silks of exquisite colors. The actors and actresses wore makeup reminiscent of the Japanese Kabuki in that they were not realistic but somewhat exaggerated and masklike. The most striking element of the performance was that neither the singing nor the speaking was done in anything remotely resembling the normal Chinese manner of speech. Every line was delivered in a freakishly high-pitched, twanging falsetto, as if the human actors were providing voices of tiny animals for an animated cartoon. This lent to every speech what seemed, at least to my naïve American ears, a comic coloration. It made the women characters—a wife, a maid—seem "cute" and doll-like, an illusion enhanced by their funny little chop-chop, dancing, prancing movements, some like those associated with *tai chi chuan* exercises. For the next several days I spoke to Jayne and other members of our company, at least at certain times, in the high-whining Chinese double-talk style of the Peking opera. One would have to consult my companions to see if they were amused.

Another interesting aspect of the separate dramas shown was that the women dominated the men, who were weak and the butt of derisive laughter.

One more fascinating aspect of Peking opera is that it is done to what, to Western ears, seems a peculiar sort of musical accompaniment, consisting mostly of small drums, clackers, gongs and cymbals, although certain passages were played by string instruments or flutes. But the primarily rhythm-instruments sound, which often punctuates dramatic or comic lines, is strongly reminiscent of the rim-shot accompaniment that in American show business accents the jokes of schlock small nightclub or Las Vegas lounge comedians.

SHANGHAI MUSIC CONSERVATORY

The following morning, at the Shanghai Music Conservatory, not far from our hotel, we were welcomed by, among others, director and violinist Tan Shu Zheng; Shu Chen-tan, vice-director and professor of voice, who had studied in the United States, at Juilliard, in the late 1940s, under Edith Piper; and Ms. Lois Woo. The two women, it turned out, knew our friends the Tung sisters, and asked us to convey their warm good wishes to them.

In the hallway of the conservatory, I saw a piano—brand name Petroff—which I took to be Russian. In the spacious, attractively appointed meeting room to which we were ushered we saw our first instance of the Marx-Engels-Lenin-Stalin portraits during this trip.

"What was this building in the old days?" I asked.

"It was then the Shanghai Jewish Club."

"Wouldn't you know it?" Jayne said. "It's the nicest looking place we've been to."

The conservatory was founded in 1927, though it has moved to a number of different locations over the years. Before 1949 there were relatively few students but the school expanded greatly thereafter. During the years of the Cultural Revolution, we were told, Western music had been banned. Even more surprisingly, ancient Chinese classical music was forbidden. As if that were not enough, some of the school's ancient instruments were smashed during that period.

We were treated to a concert, first by a young pianist who played Chopin, a young woman who sang "How Magnificent Is Our Motherland," finally by Pao Di-tang, an eighteen-year-old girl who played the violin brilliantly, doing a scherzo by Bach and tarantella by Wienowsky.

A few minutes later we heard, from down the hall, Lee Zou-ling, a man with a glorious baritone voice. He was practicing in a room with two grand pianos, one a pre-World War II Bechstein.

The conservatory also has a department where violins are made and another where old pianos are repaired and restored. In an adjoining room stood a beautiful, perfectly professional harp, which had been made on the premises. The artistic motif on the top of the harp's column is a very good bas-relief of the Nanking Bridge.

We were shown a recently invented instrument, a Chinese version of the European bass-viola, with a larger than usual sounding compartment.

The strings of a Chinese dulcimer were—astoundingly enough to this Occidental pianist—voiced in whole-tone scales. Inasmuch as Europe did not use the whole-tone scale until after centuries of experimentation, and considering the age of the Chinese instrument, the implications are exciting.

We learned—at about ten-fifteen in the morning—that the institute would be without electric power for a few hours that day because of shortage of coal. The more important needs of industry—factories and private dwellings—have priority.

Outside the building, on the usual blackboard, was written, in English:

Dear Student:
The new term begins. Starting from this year the focus of the entire party's work is shifted to the modernization of the country. Let us join hands and work together for this glorious goal. We wish everybody keep fit, study well and work hard in the new term.

The word *keep* was spelled ke-ep, the word *term* te-rm.

A WORKERS' RESIDENTIAL AREA

Tuesday, February 13

After lunch we were taken to inspect a workers' residential area (as I was on my first visit to Shanghai), a large neighborhood unit under one administrative office, where our group was greeted by smiles and applause from children and adults standing about or coming out of shops along the busy street.

The area was established—on farmland—in 1952. Its apartments are occupied by 61,000 people, most of whom work in nearby steel, iron, machinery and textile plants. The complex boasts four high schools, eight primary schools, twelve nurseries and kindergartens, fifteen medical-care centers, department stores and swimming pools, as well as numerous small shops.

Some 1,600 retired workers live in the housing project. Men must retire at sixty, women at age fifty, though they may work a few years longer at white-collar jobs. After retirement they get a pension of 75 percent of their previous wage and still enjoy free medical care.

There are about seven hundred separate buildings to the complex. At one of them, a few of us were taken to a neat two-room apartment where we were welcomed by Mrs. Chang, a retired worker. Framed certificates of retirement were proudly displayed on her walls. The apartment is occupied by six people. In 1960, monthly rent for such quarters was 9 yuan. In 1979, only 7 yuan, about $4.

We noted Mrs. Chang's small TV set and asked about it. There are four TV sets in the immediate area, she says.

Mr. and Mrs. Chang draw 140 yuan per month for their pension. Their son and daughter-in-law earn 225 yuan each month. We are told the small TV cost 225 yuan, which is very inexpensive.

Two families share the kitchen and bath facilities. There is no central heating, something possible only in a relatively southern city such as Shanghai.

Even so competent and fair-minded a China specialist as Linda Mathews of the *Los Angeles Times* misperceived some of the realities upon which she comments. "To an American," she wrote in the February 9, 1979, *Times,* "the Canton apartments would qualify as slum living."

The small plain apartments in China's urban centers are like American slum quarters in one regard, that they may be occupied by several people. As one who inhabited American slum quarters in my childhood I am aware that they are almost universally filthy, whereas the typical small Chinese apartment is clean and neat. In the most depressing room in which I lived in my youth, in Chicago's Hyde Park neighborhood in the 1930s, enormous rats almost nightly tore holes in the baseboards, hundreds of bedbugs infested the mattress, and the wallpaper was smudged and gray. None of the scores of Americans who have reported to me on their visits to Chinese living quarters have observed anything of the kind.

On a wall calendar the picture for the month of February showed a small blond, blue-eyed child, clutching a panda doll. He looked very much like my son Brian when he was about four years old.

Some of the children we saw in the area—boys about nine or ten years old—were wearing the khaki jackets and bright red neckerchiefs that identify them as members of the Young Pioneers.

One always is taken to schools, whether in cities or in the countryside. In the first classroom we entered, eight tiny children were standing with Ping-Pong paddles in their hands, four facing four. The balls were suspended on strings from two lines overhead. Thus the training of the necessary eye-hand coordination starts at an early age. No wonder China has millions of superb table-tennis players.

After visiting several classes we were directed to a music room where some of the little darlings put on a show for us, and very ably too. It almost seems that at kindergarten age the Chinese curriculum includes instruction in cuteness, adorableness, warmth and sweetness.

At the close of the day, I hopped off our bus and wandered about again, alone. Shanghai's Democracy Wall, just down the street from our hotel, was attracting even denser crowds than we had seen greeting the bold new posters in Peking. In a nearby shop display, next to a barbershop, I was surprised to see an arrangement of attractive white, blue and pink brassieres. Practically every sweater, skirt, scarf, shirt and pair of gloves in these windows, in fact, was of a strikingly bright color. Perhaps their vividness represented a reaction against the long dark winter.

In a nearby shoe-store window, attractive black, Western-style dress moccasins, costing about $9, were on display. The other shoes were much lower in price.

One of the more surprising displays, in the window next to the department store, was that of an enormous wedding cake, of the sort one might see in any American city. Of three smaller cakes in the window one carried the message "Merry Christmas" and the other "Happy New Year," both in English.

I strolled into the bake-shop, hoping to buy some sweet rolls to take back to our gang at the hotel, but there were so many people at the counter I could not get through to be served.

I next stopped into a store selling scarves and bought a handsome, thick and very wide

Democracy Wall, Shanghai, February, 1979. Photograph by Ted Rhodes

one—in gray wool—for about $5. It would cost perhaps $25 back home.

I turned back down the block in the opposite direction but now had to walk in the street because there were such large crowds reading the posters there was room only for them and their parked bicycles.

Some of the posters had what would appear to be angry retorts or editorial comments writ-

ten across them, or in their margins. A few were in various stages of disarray, having been ripped or scratched, suggesting that lively debate on important questions continued to that date.

At the point where the posters end and the wall is blank, an old man stood doing *tai chi chuan* exercises so slowly that I was reminded of a slow-motion film sequence.

15. Hangchow

Wednesday, February 14

 OUR next stop, dreamy, romantic Hangchow in Chekiang Province is one of those beauty spots of which one automatically says, "What an ideal place for a honeymoon." Its situation in nature—by the Chientang (Qian Tang) River at the southern end of the ancient Grand Canal—is one of overpowering charm combining, as do so many of China's attractions, a perfect blend of scenic and man-made elements.

By 1979 the population of this 2,000-year-old city—once the capital of the empire—passed the one million mark, though the area retains its somewhat sleepy, picturesque appeal. It has seven universities and colleges, seventy-two high schools and twenty-three hospitals.

As early as the Tang dynasty (A.D. 618–906) the city's West Lake had become famous for its beauty. Crossed by two causeways, the Su and the Bai, the lake boasts three small man-made islands, the very names of which are poetic, Three Ponds Reflecting the Moon, The Mid-Lake Pavilion, and Ruan Gong Islet.

Sites of interest which also sound as if they were named by a poet are Orioles Singing in the Willows, Autumn Moon on the Calm Lake, and Flower Harbor Park. In the surrounding hillsides are springs, the best known of which are the Tiger Spring, the Dragon Well, and the Jade Fountain. The area is also famed for two striking structures, the Pagoda of the Six Harmonies and the Bao Shu Pagoda. We viewed these attractions from a boat, open-decked, equipped with dining table.

It is amazing to think that seven hundred years ago Marco Polo wrote of precisely the same sort of pleasure-boat tour, on this same lake, giving quite a complete description of "one of these barges which are always to be found furnished with tables and chairs and all the other apparatus for a feast. . . ."

One of the wonders of which Hangchow may rightly boast—though none of its residents do so—is the enormous Ling Yin Temple (Temple of the Forest of the Clouds) which lies at the base of a low mountain. Built in A.D. 326, the first year of the Hsien Ho period of the Eastern Ching dynasty, it has been pillaged or allowed to fall into disrepair and was rebuilt frequently over the centuries. It consists of the Hall of the Four Major Protectors and the even larger Great Buddha Hall.

In early 1949, a guide told us, the enormous crossbeam of the latter hall collapsed, unfortunately destroying a number of priceless and irreplaceable sculptures. The giant gold-painted Maitreya Buddha which sits in splendor inside the front hall is two centuries old.

The wooden pillars in the Temple of the Big Buddha are made from California redwood, according to our guide. The buddha—the largest we had ever seen—appears to be about twenty feet high and is a truly dazzling sight. It was finished, oddly enough, in 1956. Yes, by the Communist government. Our guide said that this fact in itself demonstrates "that we have religious freedom in China." Not quite; the situation is complex. Religious freedom itself, the reader should be aware, has been an extremely rare commodity down through the centuries. The norm in Judeo-Christian history, God help us, has been precisely the opposite.

The temple had been closed from 1966 to 1972 due, of course, to the Red Guard disturbance. During the Cultural Revolution the middle-school students, we were told, did not want the Red Guards to disturb the temple. The university students too thought it should be preserved. The case was handed up to higher courts until it reached Premier Chou En-lai himself, who ruled that the cultural treasure should be preserved, not as a monument to superstition but because it had been built by the people.

In a back area, behind the buddha, there is an incredible panorama stretching from a few feet above the floor almost to the high ceiling. Giant carved figures and others of life-size people the stage.

As some of our group were about to leave the area, a very old woman, a Buddhist religious believer, suddenly appeared and kowtowed to the statue of a goddess on the back panel. A young Chinese who spoke English quite well said he did not know why she bowed to this particular figure except perhaps in the hope of ensuring that her daughter-in-law would bear a son.

Nearby is a wooded hill called Peak Flying from Afar, famous for its stone caves and 330 carvings from the tenth to the thirteenth centuries.

SILK BROCADE FACTORY

The balcony view from our upper-floor room the morning of February 15 was bleak, gray and drizzling. The water and low hills below seemed shrouded in a magical mist, like a panorama in an ancient Oriental painting.

The introductory briefing at the Hangchow Silk Brocade Factory repeated information provided by a pamphlet given to us the previous day.

In the designing room one young woman was working on a special order on which the words *Aloha Waikiki* were printed. She was copying the picture from a photograph of a cheap Honolulu ashtray. The tray sat to her left.

The picture was then copied on large rolls of paper about eight feet wide, reproduced on a much larger scale, almost in the way newspaper pictures are, which is to say by a series of tiny dots and lines. When the sketches are completed they are passed along to large worktables on the other side of the room, where three men sit adding colors. Here again the coloring is not simply a matter of painting an automobile blue, a horse brown or a fence green. Rather, every individual leaf, twig, or stone is colored, by the use of sharp pencils dipped into little saucers containing the various paints. It is as if one colored a 9-by-12 rug with a ballpoint pen.

A third stage involves making punch cards by means of which copies in infinite quantities can be run off.

The mill, built in 1922, produces dazzlingly beautiful satin, brocade and silk art pieces such as silk-woven pictures, tablecloths, bedspreads and cushion covers. Before Liberation, we were told, the factory employed some forty workers operating seventeen handlooms. No more than seventy kinds of silk fabrics were produced. Today there is a labor force of 1,800, 53 percent of whom are women. Equipped with 330 power looms, it produces almost 2 million meters of silk products every year. The number of products has passed the thousand mark.

The next day we were taken through a "garment center" processing plant where the most beautiful robes, dressing gowns and women's jackets in brightly colored patterned silk are produced.

We buy such garments casually, hang them in the closet, and scarcely ever give thought to the painstaking work of the millions of gifted hands that have created them stitch by stitch.

One woman at the end of a worktable was taking scraps and remnants of various colors and shapes and making placemats or fans with them. In a thousand-and-one ways one is reminded that in China nothing is wasted.

All of the production for this particular plant is for export, of course. Much of it is sent to Hong Kong, a small portion to the Friendship Stores where foreigners buy.

Our local guides being bright and personable I took every opportunity to learn from them. "One hears," I said, "about the troubles in Peking, Shanghai, Canton and other major cities during the struggle between the Gang of Four forces and their more moderate opponents. But did the Cultural Revolution have any considerable effect here?"

"Yes, indeed. There was more trouble in Hangchow than in many cities in China."

"Trouble of what sort?"

"We have here in our city the famous silk and satin factory you have seen, the biggest in China. There was a young worker, Wen Senho. In 1974, during the campaign to criticize Lin Piao and Confucius, he was suddenly rushed to the top, to positions of influence, by a process which we call 'helicoptering.' That means he did not proceed in an orderly and fair way but was simply lifted up—helicoptered—ahead of others who were more deserving."

"What did Wen Sen-ho do that was so terrible?"

"He sabotaged production."

"How?"

"I will give you an example. He went to the printing shop one day and asked for a large supply of the paste which is needed in the manufacturing process. He wanted the paste, he said, to put up some big-character posters. The workers who needed the paste argued with him and told him that it was necessary for them to complete their assigned tasks to keep up production. But he denounced them and said revolution was much more important than production. Finally he grabbed the pot of paste and in the struggle threw it over one of the workers. The next day most of the workers refused to do their work, as a protest against this man."

"And you feel the Gang of Four was behind such people?"

"Oh, yes. The Gang of Four was worse than Hitler. They gave such people their power."

I later learned that after the arrest of Chiang Ching and her associates Wen Sen-ho too was arrested.

"Since you are in the arts you will be interested in this. During the Gang of Four period only eight operas were permitted. No doubt you have heard the names of them, *Taking Tiger Mountain by Storm, The Red Detachment of Women,* and so forth. It was not that these eight shows were so bad in themselves— there was often good singing, good dancing, good music—but that we were not allowed to see anything else. We had a saying at the time which referred to an ancient delicacy called beggar's chicken. Beggar's chicken is, as I say, delicious but everyone would be very angry if they were told all they could have to eat for the rest of their lives was beggar's chicken."

"And I imagine you interpreters and guides must have been particularly annoyed," I said, "in that you had to sit through the same productions again and again."

He smiled but said nothing.

"Do you think," I said, "now that Teng Hsiao-ping is so influential, that this will lead to more real democracy, in the traditional sense of the term?"

He thought for a moment then said, "Democracy has never really taken root in China, not in the old days either, but I believe it will. Our leadership now favors freedom although we are really just making a beginning in this direction."

The conversation then turned to marriage and love.

"How do people go about getting a divorce in China?" Manya Starr asked.

"As of 1979 if you want a divorce in China you first have to ask the person you work for, your bureau chief, who would discuss the problem with you. If he believes it reasonable then you might go to a judge."

"Do people who are in love here ever just live together?" one of our group asked.

"Not to the degree that is common in your country, where such things can be done openly. Here it must be done in secret, which in some ways is more amusing."

16. Canton

Friday, February 16

AS I have earlier noted, each city in China has its own character, customs and color, just as is the case in the United States. As for almost-tropical Canton, which bestrides the Pearl (Zhu Jiang) River some forty miles from the South China Sea, one senses a hard-to-define looseness and somewhat lower efficiency than in Peking or Shanghai. Some of the clues were very small. The ashtrays in the reception room at the Pearl River Film Studio, for example, were already filled when our group entered the room; this sort of thing would never happen in the other major cities.

Later, as I shall explain, we noted that the level of efficiency at the Tung Fang Hotel (Dong Fang), the largest in Canton, was much lower than one might expect, given the current Chinese emphasis on service and attention to detail. Our film studio hosts gave us, however, the usual warm welcome. All of them—some sixteen in number—were men, mostly middle-aged. The windows of the comfortable reception room were wide open, revealing a pleasant blue sky, tall pine trees and other greenery on this beautiful, cool, sunny, spring day.

As we listened to the opening remarks, the moisture in the humid Canton air made condensation circles on the glass tabletops under our cups of steaming hot tea. On the wall was a picture of Chou En-lai with Mao, a fact that

I took to be politically significant since in 1975 —as earlier reported—one saw practically no pictures of Chou.

A Chinese friend, a leftist, has said to me, "You must understand the difference in attitude that the people had toward Mao and Chou. Mao was respected, in some cases feared, admired, but from a distance. He seemed powerful, remote, like a traditional emperor. He did not have the personal touch. Chou, on the other hand, was a man of great grace and charm. By those who had the good fortune to know him he was sincerely loved. He conducted himself in a simple, human manner and never played the role of the great man."

A Chinese woman, who was in her home country during the ten hard Cultural Revolution years, has said, "Chou protected many of his friends during the bad times. I don't suppose anyone will ever know how many. He could not oppose Mao openly but within the limits set by the situation he tried to help as many people as possible."

The general trend of the main conversation and subsidiary discussions by separate groups —writers with writers, actors with actors, etc. —was much the same as at the Peking and Shanghai studios. Most of those with whom we spoke had personally been sent down to the countryside during the Cultural Revolution and had suffered in other ways, including the lack of opportunity to practice their professions.

As at Shanghai there was considerable interest, on the part of the older spokesmen, in the present fate of U.S. film stars of the 1920s and 1930s. What, they asked eagerly, had happened to John Gilbert, Fredric March, Charles Laughton, Ramon Novarro, Sylvia Sydney, Gary Cooper, Greta Garbo, John and Lionel Barrymore, Wallace Beery, Norma Shearer, Katharine Hepburn, Charles Boyer? Upon being told that almost all of these were dead their faces grew solemn.

One of the gentlemen—Tao King—had been a major star before 1949, appearing in some two hundred films, primarily out of Hong Kong, and earning hundreds of thousands of Hong Kong dollars per year. Despite

Right, Tao-King, a graduate of the National Dramatic Institute, a famous school during the 1930s and 1940s. At first a stage performer, during the Japanese occupation Tao became a movie actor. Canton, 1979.

Before Liberation he'd gone to Hong Kong and worked in films. In 1951 he returned to the mainland working first in Shanghai, then in Canton at the Pearl River Film Studio. In 1979 he had become one of the executive officers of the studio.

his fame and prosperity he had voluntarily returned to China in the 1950s to make what contribution he could to the rebuilding of his nation.

The studio, we were told, had turned out four feature films for 1978 but—and this struck all of us as odd—there were no films in production as of the time of our visit.

After a tour of the Pearl River facilities, much like those one might see anywhere in the world, we were shown portions of films for perhaps half an hour. Oddly, one was old black-and-white footage from a 1950s picture, *Searching Wave.* The most unusual film was a documentary about the sea cow, in which one of the enormous beasts, having been trapped and killed, was surgically opened, after which its internal organs were displayed in close detail and full color.

Even now, three long years after the overthrow of Chiang Ching, the studio still faced a number of difficulties, one of which was a shortage of electric power. Also some of the film stock on hand, which had not been stored at a low-enough temperature, was beginning to lose its sensitivity.

From the hilltop perch of the brick-red, five-story Chen Hai Tower (Zhen Hai Lou) which houses the displays of the Guangzhou Museum one sees in the immediate lower foreground a good-sized football (soccer) stadium, with a sizable expanse of the city slanting away before it. Although English-speaking and other foreign visitors are commonly taken to the museum, not a word of the printed text that accompanies photographs, statues, maps and other displays is printed in any language other than Chinese. It is therefore virtually impossible for visitors who do not read Mandarin or Cantonese to make much sense of the exhibited material, an oversight I assume the authorities may be disposed to make up for and one I did not see committed anywhere else in China.

Several members of our group were struck by the presence in the tower museum crowds of a score or so of young hotshots from Hong Kong, teenagers who stood out in contrast to local young people as glaringly as did any of us with white skins. Their hair was styled in rather mod fashion, their clothing tight, tailored and somewhat garish, and their attitude unattractively hip as compared to the dignified and composed manner of the mainland young people. Art Zich, of our tour group, very far indeed from a Communist sympathizer (he did intelligence work for the American military during the Korean War), seemed to take a dim view of the young visitors, who are apparently in the habit of coming on strong with girls from Canton, flashing money about and all in all not making many friends for themselves among either the local Chinese or foreign tourists.

Canton in general, however, seemed less under Peking's dominance than do other cities major and minor.

According to a report in *Newsweek,* on January 16, 1978, a few professional prostitutes were then active in Canton though such behavior was totally uncharacteristic of China generally. And, reminds *Newsweek,* "The People's Republic is light-years behind the rampant sensuality of pre-Revolutionary China when Shanghai had a brothel on every corner and Mandarins retained stables of concubines."

That afternoon Arthur Zich, Jeannie Myers, Jayne and I took a long, delightful and fascinating walk through the streets of Canton, entirely on our own. The day was pleasantly hot, skies clear, the city alive, electric, as we strolled through spotlessly clean back alleys, peered over fences and into courtyards, spoke to people sitting outside their homes and apartments, window-shopped, bought a few odds and ends, and at last came to the famed Sha Mian Island, the old Europeans-only enclave with its once fashionable homes inhabited by the wealthy foreigners who conducted their various businesses in this bustling port city. The late afternoon sunlight glistened on the Pearl River as we sat for a while resting on a stone bench, looking out at the busy water traffic of tugs, junks, sampans, ferries and freighters.

Canton does not have the rich charm of Peking or Shanghai, nor the beauty of certain smaller cities in China, but its river prospect pleases the eye and its people were, to us, uniformly friendly.

The city also has its share of artists, craftsmen and other creative souls (needless to say, on this score China never disappoints), including practitioners of the dazzling techniques of carving ivory into the most detailed and intricate shapes and patterns.

In Pearl Buck's *The Three Daughters of Madame Liang* she describes the beauty encountered in a small ivory factory in Canton:

. . . the show pieces she remembered, the ivory balls, one carved within another until there were as many as twenty-six, each perfect and free of every other, but this was not what caught her gaze. Art, so she reasoned, does not boast of what it is, but, like a misty landscape, its meaning steals into the perception. She saw such a landscape carved in ivory which breathed of spring in its blossoms and weeping willows. She saw galleons with sails set full, pennants waving and tiny figures bent to the wind. She saw an ivory fisherman casting his ivory net, every mesh perfected by a fine electric drill.

"A drill?" she inquired of the carver. "And what if the point slips and your art is destroyed?"

The man smiled, a bronze-faced old man. "It never slips," he said.

She wandered among the ivory pieces, examining each in its perfection. She saw ivory junks with twisted ropes of ivory; she saw dancing girls of ivory, their ivory scarves whirling in the dance; she saw old men and women with ivory wrinkles, and laughing Buddhas all of ivory. Such were for export, through the gate of Hong Kong, to the Western world, but certain ones were too rare for export. She saw a pagoda, within its tusk confining thirteen stories, each corner tipped with a freely swinging bell. She saw palace gardens with every tree and flower perfected, and she saw wild rocky mountains in a landscape and such varied sights that she was awed by all she saw.

The Communist administrators of post-1949 China have had the wisdom to perceive that the art of fashioning ivory is one best left undisturbed by political fiat in its choice of subjects. Though the ivory craftsmen have produced some "political" art there would seem to be a certain artistic stupidity in making ivory statuettes of, say, Chairman Mao. The Chinese have never been a stupid people.

A PRODUCTIVE COMMUNE

Saturday, February 17

At Tali (Great Strength) People's Commune, quite a long bus ride outside the city, we were taken to a spacious, second-floor meeting room, whose ceiling and roof were supported by four enormous Chinese-red pillars. Its architects have had, thank God, the wisdom to incorporate traditional features into the commune's new administrative buildings.

Laborers in the countryside, we learned during the introductory lecture, are not on a fixed salary but are paid in relation to their production. A worker may earn 350 yuan per year. After the welcoming remarks we were taken for a stroll about the premises and at once first entertained by a group of about forty five- and six-year-olds, who did an intricate song-and-dance routine, something that fifteen-year-old children in other parts of the world would have had a difficult time performing so well.

We then were invited into an adjacent building, a kindergarten, where a class of three- and four-year-old cuties hailed us with more dance and songs. There seemed to be no shortage of teachers—all young women. A good many laborers and farm workers were active in the area outside the school.

In America there is a saying, "Throwing money at problems," which does, in fact, sometimes help solve them. In China I have the impression that the equivalent is "throwing people at problems."

Like the communes described in earlier chapters, this one seemed richly productive and well administered. After visiting some of its workshops and a machine-tool factory, we repaired to a central hall where a delicious lunch awaited us, including duck raised on the premises.

As regards eating duck in China, by the way, while it is true that Peking-style duck—with the sizzly, crackly baconlike skins—is delicious, Chinese duck generally is no great shakes. The reason, it seems to me, is that unlike American ducks and chickens which when raised for eating are kept in small pens that ensure soft muscles by limiting their movements, most Chinese ducks wander about the countryside, the backyard or the rice paddy and are therefore generally quite tough.

Another problem factor is that, for some unknown reason, Chinese chefs separate a duck by use of a meat cleaver, which means almost every piece of duck meat the diner picks up will have sharp bone fragments in it.

The lunch was nevertheless quite good, particularly the dessert of small, very sweet and juicy oranges grown in the commune's groves.

After the meal we were taken to the commune's main hospital which is primitive by Western standards, but far better than no hospital at all, which was the norm in rural areas of China in the old days. The complex of two-story buildings, which includes an operating room, a dental clinic, a laboratory and an acupuncture department, has a staff of two hundred, sixty of them doctors. It is always saddening to see bedded patients, in the best

Workers' apartment building in a productive commune.

hospital in the world, but those we saw at the commune can be grateful for the conscientious care they receive. A very old woman lay in one room dying, I would think. I smiled at her and nodded, a pitifully inadequate gesture. In another room, an elderly man, seemingly emotionally confused, walked about aimlessly, helped by an attendant. The saddest sight of all was that of a young father sitting beside his fatally ill son, perhaps six years old.

At an area of peasants' living quarters we were encouraged to visit anyone we wished and to ask whatever questions might occur to us. Some of us selected what turned out to be the home of Mrs. Ts'en, forty-seven, who looked rather like a Mexican Shirley Mac-Laine.

Unlike a commune dwelling I had visited four years earlier, the floor of this one was not of pressed earth but was set with one-foot-square paving stones. On one wall was another instance of the paired Mao Tse-tung–Hua Kuo-feng portraits in which Hua's face loomed slightly larger. Against one wall stood a serviceable sewing machine, covered and used as a table.

Our group being seven in number there were not enough chairs, a lack which Mrs. Ts'en

cheerfully hustled about to make up for. Her absent husband was a team leader. Elections for such offices are held every two years.

"How many are there in your family?" I asked.

"Seven."

"What is your total income for the year?"

"One thousand, seven hundred yuan for the whole family," our guide said. "In addition they also receive an allotment of firewood, cooking oil and other basic needs."

They occupy four rooms. Mrs. Ts'en was born in this area.

"How often are you troubled by tourists such as ourselves?"

She smiles at the verb I have chosen. "Three or four times a year. It is no trouble."

"What happens to this house when you and your husband die?"

"It remains in the family," the interpreter explained, "to be passed along to their children." We returned again to the question of earnings.

"The workers," our translator said, after conferring with Mrs. Ts'en, "are divided into three categories. They get a mark of ten, which is equivalent to a hundred percent. The mark is given in advance every month. They are then

reassessed and their rating added to, or sub-
tracted from, depending on the kind of work
they've done. Then their mark for the month
is multiplied by twelve. The grading is done by
their coworkers, who decide whether they
should be graded first, second or third class.
Depending upon what class they are in they
share in the commune's profits."

There are 68,000 people and 19,000 houses
in the commune. It has 19 production brigades, under which are 243 work teams. Rice
is the main crop. Each year the farmers also
raise some 90,000 pigs, 400,000 chickens and
ducks. There are about 1,800 water buffaloes
and many ponds for raising fish. The commune has 32 reservoirs, 47 pumping stations
and facilities for stored water.

We note—on a table—a handsome red banner, which is unrolled for our inspection. The
whole production team was given this honor
because they had the best work record last
year. They were presented with the banner in
front of 3,000 people. Specifically the team not
only increased the output of rice but developed
a better kind of rice.

Before Liberation, Mrs. Ts'en told us, her
family had a very small house, and were so
poor they had to tear down other people's
walls to steal bricks. Now, she proudly said,
after Liberation they built this house honestly
and own it outright.

Water conservation is important and is related to the work-point system. A flag is given
to the best improved camper in the group.

Mrs. Ts'en has never gone to school. The
one daughter who works in another city comes
back home once a month.

"If one of Mrs. Ts'en's children got married," Jayne said, "where would he or she go
to live?"

"A daughter would go to live with her husband's family. If the family gets too large to
live under one roof a new house is built."

"It seems odd to us," a woman in our group
said after one of our hosts offered us cigarettes,
"that you so often urge your visitors to smoke
cigarettes. Back home our government tries to
discourage smoking."

"I know what you mean," was the response.
"During the Gang of Four period our young

people, for some reason or other, took up
smoking, which they hadn't done much before. Now the young people coming along are
cutting it down more."

"We are smoking less," Jayne said, "because we've learned it causes lung cancer."

"The most common kinds of the disease in
China are liver and abdominal cancer," one of
our hosts answered. "The cause of these must
be dietary."

Oddly enough there is more cancer of the
stomach and liver in the northern part of
China than in the central or southern areas.

"What do you think is to blame?" Jayne
said.

"We do not know. Perhaps it has to do with
salt because our people salt their vegetables
over the winter to preserve them."

The name of Mrs. Ts'en's husband's work-
team is Hero and Beautiful Production Team.

"The Gang of Four—one readily accepts—
did much harm in the cities," I said, "with
educators, intellectuals, artists, hospital personnel, government bureaucracies. But, as
scores of travelers have reported, the communes of China seem remarkably successful,
the fields richly productive. Is it possible that
the Gang of Four did more harm in the cities
than in the countryside?" The question required an extra bit of discussion.

"Mrs. Ts'en says there were troubles on the
communes, too," our translator said.

"So I understand," I responded. "I was referring to the question of comparative degree."

"Her husband," the guide said, "has been a
cadre since 1963 but during the time of the
Gang of Four he did not like to be a cadre. Too
many orders came down from upper levels as
to what percentages of crops should be grown.
The local people felt such decisions should be
left to them. There was not enough democratic
participation." Oddly enough, in 1975 the
dominant group had made the same criticism
about its opponents.

I did not pursue the subject.

"Four years ago," I said, "everywhere I
went I met a 'chairman of the Revolutionary
Committee.' If I went to the men's room I met
a chairman of the Revolutionary Committee.
But this time—very few."

The answers to my questions as to where all the former Revolutionary Committee chairmen are now turned out to be evasive, with considerable chuckling, smiling and clearing of throats. This almost certainly means that either the situation was unclear to our immediate hosts or there was something about the present state of affairs that it embarrassed them to discuss.

We were put back aboard our bus and driven to the far west area of the commune; the length of the ride gave us a good idea of its enormous size. When the bus stopped, our group climbed, happily by means of concrete steps, to the top of a nearby hill. From the summit one could see for miles in all directions. The commune's aqueduct and irrigation system was truly impressive, having converted, as it did, an area that formerly produced relatively little, into a rich farming resource.

On the way back to the city—as we passed over the bridges that crossed the two wide rivers—we noticed something remarkable: hundreds of people lugging sometimes quite heavy loads of one sort or another on the backs of bicycles. Some carried what appeared to be bags of grain, others baskets of vegetables, some large plastic containers that contained liquids. Many transported goods that could not be identified because they were in cardboard or wooden boxes. When I asked one of our guides whether the cyclists were carrying things in from the countryside for their personal use or for delivery to stores he said, quite openly, "This is the produce from private plots. The people are taking it into the city, to the various street markets, to sell it. Sometimes they drive a hard bargain but in any event they get whatever price they can and they may keep the money."

During the last thirty years, I would think, there must always have been a certain amount of what might be called "garage sale" marketing in China.

By April, 1979, free enterprise marketing had come almost to account for an incredible 20 percent of retail sales in some parts of the country. When Mao and the Communist Party took control of China in 1949 it was

Part of irrigation project—a dam, Linhsien, 1975.

naturally not possible for them to initiate an entirely new social program the following morning. Changes, both small and large, were made gradually, in increments. As regards the establishment of the commune system almost ten years later, China had the poor luck almost immediately to run into the "three bad years," 1960, 1961, 1962, when nature itself was uncooperative.

While the resulting food shortages were certainly not primarily the fault of the new system, as its subsequent successes demonstrated, there were nevertheless at the time many complaints. Obviously something else had to be done. That something turned out to be a partial return to a free rural market operation, not replacing the communes but in addition to them.

With the coming of the Cultural Revolution and its characteristic doctrinal rigidity, the peasants' freedom to make extra money outside the basic system was again greatly restricted by Mao.

It remains to be seen how permanent an institution the enormous farming commune will be. A long-time critic such as Chang Kuosin, writing in the *Hong Kong Standard* of February 21, 1979, takes the view that it is a mistake to credit Mao personally with conceiving the commune program. He should be credited—or blamed, as the case may be—for initiating the agricultural cooperative movement which started in 1951, and continued for seven years. "But then," says Chang, "a new development in 1958 . . . persuaded Mao to change course. While still plotting new agricultural cooperatives in his office in Peking's Chungmanhai, Mao heard that some of his cooperatives in Hopei, Honan and Shantung had merged themselves into larger combines called 'People's Communes,' 'Communist Communes,' 'Great Communes' and 'State Farms.'

"Intrigued, Mao went out to take a look and was said to have become immediately fascinated. He decided then and there to . . . abandon the agricultural cooperative movement. He decided on the name 'People's Commune' and it is by that name that they became the new basic structure of the Chinese society."

Chang concludes his case by saying "The People's Communes . . . have become a hated monstrosity, *targeted for eventual dissolution by his successors.*" (Italics added.) This, the pro-Taiwan view, represents a prediction that most China scholars consider unlikely, though the commune system under Hua Kuo-feng and Teng Hsiao-ping may well grant increased freedom to farmers with particular initiative.

Canton's Tung Fang Hotel is enormous— 2,000 guest rooms—and its new wing cannot be many years old. Its spacious interior garden and lawn area is attractive with its right-angled covered walkways, small pools and flowers. But it has neither the old-time charm of the Hsin Ciao Hotel in Peking nor that of the newer Peking Hotel itself, with its delightful and modern accommodations. It is, in fact, to put the matter plainly, very poorly run, or at least was as of the time of our visit.

On Saturday afternoon about five minutes to four o'clock, Art Zich and I came outside to get a cab. There were, happily, about six lined up. But the guide explained we were not permitted to simply jump into one of them and take off. We had to walk down about a hundred yards to the right where there was a taxi dispatcher station. When we got there we discovered that there were about ten people lined up waiting but no cabs available. Eventually one showed up.

But a more serious problem about the hotel is that its food is, in a word, the worst. This is not merely one man's opinion; all twenty of our team concurred about three minutes after our first meal had been served. We thereafter avoided the hotel's main floor dining room like the plague and fortunately as a result enjoyed some superb meals in other Canton restaurants such as the Bei Yuan at 318 Dengfang Beilu, North, as beautiful an establishment as one will ever see. Even the men's room has stained-glass windows. The Ban Xi at Liwan Lake Park is another marvelous eating place. When we ordered lunch there Art Zich referred to the ancient Chinese custom of tapping the table with two knuckles, meaning, "I would like more, please." It grows, according to Zich, from an incident involving one of China's ancient emperors who, with two advisers, stopped—incognito—at a small restaurant. He poured tea for his aides, at which custom required them to bow to the floor. But to have done so in the public inn would have blown the emperor's cover. The two therefore made a sign with their fingers as if kneeling.

As for the Tung Fang, I hasten to explain to our gracious hosts that my comments about the hotel are not merely an instance, however minor, of Ugly Americanism. Everyone in our party was crazy about Chinese food and was enthusiastic about practically every other meal we had while in the Celestial Kingdom.

Not only was the fare at the Tung Fang third-rate—by both Chinese and American standards—but room service was either deplorable or nonexistent; we couldn't quite determine which. Jayne and I are both slow starters in the morning and therefore, when traveling, prefer to have breakfast served in our rooms, if possible. Although there had been no trouble with the necessary arrangements in Peking, Shanghai and Hangchow, where service was uniformly excellent, complex negotiations seemed to be required to even make our simplest wishes clear to the seventeenth-floor hotel staff, whose command of English was minimal. The first morning our scrambled eggs arrived ice cold. The second day they did not arrive at all until Jayne had thrown a bit of a fit, after which the eggs were delivered—again cold—just as she was rushing out of the hotel, already five minutes late, to join the rest of our party downstairs.

Then there was the matter of the mouse. Or rat. Or small grizzly bear, or whatever it was that ate one of my socks in the night.

At the end of our first day, in room 1742, I collapsed, or retired for the night, as the case may be, at about nine o'clock, wearily dropping my heavy woolen Norwegian skiing socks atop my shoes on the floor beside the bed. I was asleep a moment later.

Jayne was up for the next hour, doing some unpacking and straightening up. About 9:45 she stepped down to the service desk on our floor and spent perhaps twenty minutes chatting with other members of our party. When she returned she noticed that one of my socks was lying next to the bathtub but gave the matter no particular attention.

In the middle of the night I got up to go to the bathroom and observed that the sock had been stuffed about halfway into a small hole in the tile base of the tub. I assumed that Jayne had perhaps feared that the hole might be the front door of a family of unwelcome insect pests and had stuck the sock into the hole simply to close it up.

The next morning I said to her, "Why did you stick one of my thick woolen socks into that hole under the bathtub?"

"I don't know what you're talking about," she said.

"You mean that you did *not* shove my sock under the tub?"

"That's right."

At that I marched into the bathroom. The sock was now even deeper into the hole. I leaned down, pulled it out, and discovered that the front third of it no longer existed.

The hotel is overrun by rats, something I doubt can be blamed on the Gang of Four, though you never know.

When we complained to the young floor attendants about the matter they just laughed, perhaps in embarrassment.

Traps and poisons apparently having proved ineffectual, the hotel's management might want to consider ordering a dozen or so of a device called a Sonic 2000, manufactured by Invento Products, New York, New York. The Sonic 2000 is an "ultrasonic rodent controller" invented by accident when the owner of a shop that sold musical instruments found dead mice on his floor in the morning every time he accidentally left an electric guitar amplifier turned on overnight. It's gotten rid of field mice in our own house and would probably clear out the Tung Fang in short order.

Many foreign visitors to China are even now going only to the city of Canton, to attend the world-famous Export Commodities Fair, or to do a bit of sightseeing and shopping. Since this is the city that will give many new visitors their chief impression of "what China is like," the Peking government, and the city of Canton itself, might concentrate more resources on improving at least its major hostelry.

One gets quite a lot of exercise while on tour of China. Not only do the guides run you ragged seeing various sites of importance but there are unanticipated physical requirements. Jayne, for example, had had the foresight to provide herself with a pair of tan plastic, fleece-lined cold-weather boots which came in very handy in the chilly weather of Peking and Shanghai. But she has an unusual arch so that it was difficult for her to get the boots on and off. So difficult, in fact, that she had to be assisted in this chore. Each evening, as I was near the point of collapse from the day's exertions, I had to further extend myself yanking and tugging until I pulled Jayne's boots off. One day in a Friendship Store when the weather was warmer, she decided to buy a pair of Chinese "Mary Janes," the low soft comfortable slipper worn by most Chinese women. This required her to remove her boots, for the purpose of trying on the shoes for size. Since I was on another floor she asked one of the young store employees to assist her. The woman seemed to know the proper position for boot removal, which involves the remover straddling the wearer's leg and trying to run straight ahead, which was all very well except that the floors of some Chinese Friendship Stores are made of smooth marble. Jayne estimates that it took about thirty yards of slipping and sliding for each boot to be removed, the sight of which occasioned general hysteria from the other employees.

Speaking of Friendship Stores, it is still remarkable how much misinformation about China one can pick up. That this would be the case with off-the-cuff comments of casual visitors to the mainland, or for that matter people who have never been there at all, is not surprising. But even Usually Reliable Sources can mislead. For example, I have read perhaps half a dozen guidebooks, newspaper features and general accounts that the honeymoon is over in China as far as finding bargains is concerned.

"The country has already been picked clean by the Japanese," was how one expert put it. Or, "Inflation has done its dirty work in China as it has everywhere else." Or, "The Chinese have gotten hip to what Americans are willing to pay and their prices have gone through the roof."

There is a degree of truth to such statements in that prices in 1979 were indeed higher than those I had found four years earlier, although the raises were nowhere near as dramatic as those in the U.S. over the same four-year period. But there are still plenty of bargains in China, some of them quite dramatic.

Hong Kong is a place famed for its low prices, at least compared to such other world capitals as New York, Tokyo, Los Angeles, Paris. But Jayne happened to see a petit-point bag with a jade bracelet handle in a Hong Kong shop and—just out of curiosity—went in to see what it was selling for. The price: $42. She had bought the identical bag in Shanghai

a few days earlier for $13. It would cost perhaps $100 in New York. She got an even more dramatic bargain in a lovely lavender jade ring which a Hong Kong jeweler appraised at about five times what she had paid for it in China.

All of our tour group, especially those who were knowledgeable about China, sensed hopeful signs of the enlargement of freedom.

One member, young Mark Peterson, who speaks Chinese well, got into a chat with a Canton bus driver who told him that things were much freer now in 1979, that in years past it would not have been so easy for foreign visitors to wander the streets at will, to take photographs, etc.

Until fairly recently, the driver said, "Our spokesmen, tour guides, would sometimes exaggerate the truth, painting a rosier picture than the social realities justified. But now," he said, "it is not necessary to do that. Foreigners are permitted to see what is really the case, partly because of the newly enlarged freedoms and partly because China is confident that things are truly improving and that in the near future they will be even better. The fact that you and I are talking like this," the man said, "would have seemed terrifying to people just a few years ago."

The night before our group left Canton, some of our party had a relaxed chat with our hard-working main guide, Mr. Lu, in the hotel's bar-coffee shop, during which he revealed that he himself had spent over three years—1969 to 1972—in the countryside during the Cultural Revolution. Having been sent to a May 7th Cadre School in Hunan Province, he was forbidden to speak English. When in 1972 he was finally permitted to return to Peking he felt tongue-tied when he began to speak the language again.

Sunday, February 18

The morning we left Canton, and China, we were told that war had broken out with Vietnam. The news was a sobering conclusion to an otherwise pleasurable and stimulating visit, suddenly bringing into sharper focus the ugly realities behind the pleasantries we had enjoyed. As of that morning only the Chinese high command was aware that a limited incursion into Vietnam's territory was planned, "to teach the Vietnamese a lesson." Our immediate hosts had no certainty that a full-scale military confrontation had not broken out, which might even escalate to involve the Soviet Union.

The two-hour Sunday morning train ride from Canton down to Hong Kong was pleasant. The sky was a dusty blue, the railroad bed smooth, the scenery—as always in China—fascinating. On both sides endless miles of fields, some flooded, some not, in dozens of separate shades of green.

The landscape eventually becomes hilly, in the near distance, mountainous. But almost every inch of soil not devoted to reforestation is plowed, furrowed, planted, irrigated.

The border-crossing station is a madhouse, although an orderly one. Ellis Island a century ago must have been something like it with hundreds of people milling about.

No sooner had we crossed the border to the free world side than we were dramatically reminded of one of the relevant differences. A member of our party pointed his camera at a working woman—as we had done hundreds of times in China—but in this instance the woman looked the man straight in the eye and made the unmistakable gesture that says, "You may take my picture but only if you pay for the privilege."

Our new train's first stop thereafter was Sheungshue, a small Tijuana-like town about ten miles past the border. In another twenty minutes or so we stopped at Taipo Market, a more prosperous-looking community.

DEPARTURE FROM HONG KONG

Hong Kong itself seemed another planet after the scarcity and plain living of China proper. The old British crown colony, which is only leased from China, is sort of a Disneyland of capitalism, a crowded center of luxury hotels, jewelry stores, camera and audio equipment shops, expensive restaurants, glamorous

Chinese workman studying while on the job, Canton, 1979. Photograph by Michael Welch

Chinese workmen in large truck play cards while en route to make a delivery, Canton. Photograph by Michael Welch

women, skyscrapers, Rolls-Royces, diamonds, minks, models, prostitutes—all the benefits, or moral scandals, as the case may be—of the free enterprise system. When our exhausted and dusty group landed in the swank waterfront Peninsula Hotel we were, for the first few minutes, overwhelmed by its opulence, its perfume, its tinkling glasses, soft cocktail music. It was a case of true culture-shock.

There is more to the city, of course, than beauty, glamour, commerce. One sees pathetic beggars, lost souls who somehow do not fit into the large machinery of success. One sees thousands of the poor, many of them refugees from the mainland.

Walking from the Peninsula Hotel down to the Star Ferry dock—where we would shortly board the S.S. *Rotterdam*—I passed a middle-aged woman, clad in black, moving along the ground like a sort of grotesque four-legged spider, sliding in a seated position across the street, up over the curb, and behind me.

What does one do? Give money? Stare? Pray? The tragedy of such a creature's predicament somehow splashes about her, staining the shoes, the eyes, the hearts of those who see her.

During the next few weeks, as Jayne and I visited Thailand, Singapore, Sri Lanka, Bombay, our thoughts frequently returned to China, to which our subsequent stops were now inevitably compared. And, of course, a visit to a place that is, from our point of view, so unusual as China provides the unexpected bonus that the traveler returns to his native land blessed with a somewhat foreign eye. I presently perceive American institutions and customs in a more unusual light. Our motorcars, our hotels, restaurants, universities, hospitals, roller skates and toothbrushes are not simply taken for granted, as is usually the case, but looked at in a fresh way.

A French thinker once said that every so often a man ought to take a chair, put it on top of his kitchen table, get up and sit in it, since doing so would give him a fresh angle of vision on long-familiar objects.

My three trips to China have put me in a chair on my kitchen table.

Part IV

Thoughts on China
and America

17. The U.S. and People's Republic Compared

UP to this point the present study has, understandably, concerned itself with China; there have therefore been only passing references to American or other Western comparisons, purely by way of clarifying practices observed in China. But I propose now something far more painful, for at least certain American readers, than any complimentary references to modern Chinese practice in the preceding pages, for this chapter will deal with a partial point-by-point comparison between China and the United States.

I have been specifically warned not to include such a chapter in this book. In a conversation with several editors of the *Los Angeles Times* I was advised that, while one might now safely tell the truth about praiseworthy developments in today's China, some readers would be made uncomfortable if faced with comparisons in which the Chinese factor was superior to the American.

My advisers assumed such comparison would be perfectly accurate and valid. Their point was that the very truth of such assertions could be counted upon to infuriate a certain segment of the American audience.

If it is indeed the case that some of us are so insecure in our roles as citizens of the world's most powerful society that we literally cannot emotionally tolerate the suggestion that anywhere outside of our boundaries there are instances, categories, within which the United States is simply something less than the champion, the record holder, the winner, then I do not see why speaking honestly on such an important matter as China–U.S. relations must be inhibited by the neuroses of a segment, however sizable, of the American population. Let that segment attempt to recover from its disease, rather than have the disease inhibit responsible reporting.

I am not running for office and have more regard for accuracy than popularity. God knows our political "leaders" are inhibited enough by such considerations. They often get elected by playing to popular passions and fad-interests, however unedifying, rather than encouraging civic virtue. A corrupt society may not wish to entertain exhortations to decency and honesty, but for the very reason that political figures, and even the media—often beholden to advertisers, who are beholden to customers—sometimes carefully modify reports, there is all the more need for frankness about matters of life and death.

Among the factors working against a rational resolution of U.S.–China tensions at present is a sometimes unconscious, other times witting sense of superiority, on the part of both the Chinese and Americans. While every person, every people, is entitled to that sense of confidence and courage which grows out of accurate perception of his, her or its virtue, an exaggerated, distorted sense of self-importance is harmful to both individuals and societies.

So, having hopefully clarified, in a thousand and one ways, that I personally, selfishly speaking, would prefer to live in Los Angeles rather than Canton, prefer the free enterprise system to the Maoist economic structure, prefer our freedoms of speech, of assembly, of faith, of the press, to their relative lack on the Chinese mainland, I am nevertheless forced, by the inexorable weight of tangible evidence, to spell out a list of comparisons according to which it will be seen that spokesmen for the American cause should diminish belligerence and conceit and enlarge that combination of humility and wisdom which befits the just individual. Arthur Zich, Irvin Yeaworth and I were impressed by the comments of our guide in Hangchow, a Mr. Qian Wei (I depend on Zich's notes here).

"The Chinese today enjoy a democracy we never enjoyed in the past. We need more: free elections, freedom of speech, a binding legal system—because without these, the nation could turn Fascist again. Premier Teng has promised them, and I believe that we will get them. What is important is that our system will be a Chinese one. Our historical experience is different from yours; the system that grows out of it will be different, too. We want to modernize, and we have much to learn from America. But we intend to achieve what Mao envisaged back in 1956: democracy and centralism, freedom and discipline, personal ease of mind and unity." And then he made what may be the most important point of all: "It is crucial to Chinese-American friendship that your people understand this."

American critics of Chinese Communist economic practice for the most part make an invalid comparison in contrasting China-1980 with the U.S.A.-1980. Obviously, as regards the majority of factors considered, such a comparison must be to China's disadvantage. One could make out a long list of specifics and decide on such a basis that the United States has the preferable system. Salaries, for example, both actual and relative, are higher in the United States. There are more TV sets, telephones, bathtubs, automobiles, power mowers, refrigerators, hair dryers, trash compactors and record players per capita in the United States. There is a greater variety of artistic and cultural materials available in America, more books, magazines, libraries.

On the scale of the freedoms that most Americans actually and a few only allegedly hold dear, there is, again, practically no comparison.

It should not be assumed, however, that China rates second to the U.S. in all categories. Consider:

1. We have a drug-abuse crisis. China has none.

2. The United States faces an increasingly severe problem of political and financial corruption. (See my 1979 report, *RipOff,* published by Lyle Stuart.) The problem has almost totally disappeared in China, though it was common before 1949.

3. Millions of Americans face either long-continued or permanent unemployment; there is no serious unemployment problem in China, though obviously some individuals are not working.

4. In the United States the streets and alleys of even our leading cities are frequently disgracefully filthy, blighted by garbage, rats, insects, and rubble. In China cleanliness and neatness are national watchwords.

5. National debt in the United States is of monumental proportions. Nor is this a difficulty unique to capitalist states; the Soviet Union also carries a heavy national debt. China, on the other hand, did not—as of late 1978—owe a penny either to other nations or to banks. It began to borrow in 1979 but on a relatively modest basis.

6. In the United States, as countless journalists, theologians, and other scholars have observed, there is a growing malaise of the spirit. In China the majority is willingly dedicated to the task of rebuilding the nation.

Jayne, Bill and I—like thousands of other foreign visitors—became aware in China of a sense of dedication and purpose that we Americans are able to capture now only in the limited contexts of commitment to our churches, schools, to a charity drive, to some more or less localized concern to which we can contribute energy and commitment. Arthur Zich—certainly no Communist—has written that today's Chinese are "purposeful people . . . contented people . . . they are not zealots, zombies or xenophobes. They seem—I'm almost embarrassed to use the term—one, big, happy family—" (*Signature,* July, 1979).

7. Jayne said to me recently, "Do you realize that almost all of the reforms that Christian missionaries like my parents prayed for—for three hundred years in China—and never lived to see realized, have been produced, in less than thirty years, by the Communists? The society that was perhaps the most degenerate on earth has become the most puritanical. And our society, originally puritanical, is now among the most degenerate, with venereal disease, prostitution, pornography, illegal gambling, organized crime, narcotics, violent gangs, street crime and family breakdown."

The U.S. indeed faces a serious moral problem as regards sexual excess, illegitimate births, divorce, and pornography. I do not refer to new or long-developing attitudes emphasizing sexual freedom, some of which are beneficial enough improvements over certain earlier forms of Victorian repression and denial. But surely no unbiased observer can deny that the most degraded forms of sexual pathology are now being paraded, or marketed, in the hope that the umbrella of sexual freedom will somehow either legitimize them, or at least permit their public practice unimpeded by legal restriction or the criticism of an offended majority. In the United States at present teenage children are giving birth to over 600,000 unwanted babies a year. In China, on the other hand, there is clearly none of the sexual obsession which psychologists, American and otherwise, have long considered a clue to our immaturity.

8. Another yardstick of comparison concerns a problem extremely grave in the United States but practically unknown in China— vandalism, particularly against schools. There is not a major city in our country which is not perplexed by the sometimes horrendous damage wrought by angry young people, frequently against the schools they themselves attend, damage of a kind the media invariably describe as "senseless." It is rarely accompanied by theft which, though immoral and illegal, has a certain sense to it. What is involved is destruction for destruction's sake. Windows are smashed, obscene or violent language scrawled on walls, typewriters, television sets, teaching machines and files smashed, ink and paint thrown about and fires set. The total of damages runs into uncounted millions each year. The perpetrators are rarely apprehended. Nor is it true that the damage is confined only to lower-income and ghetto neighborhoods. Middle-class areas, too, are attacked.

At the Evanston Township High School, in a wealthy suburban area near Chicago, thefts and crimes of violence have become such a serious problem that in 1975 the school was forced to hire eight security officers and to ask Evanston authorities to assign a greater number of city police to the area. Among the crimes that led to this state of siege: a freshman girl was raped, a school accountant robbed, thirteen typewriters and calculators stolen, arson and vandalism committed. As of the late 1975 period there were *more than 70,- 000 assaults on teachers* in American public schools each year, as well as over a hundred murders! Cost of vandalism and crime in American schools is now approximately equal to that spent on textbooks, about *$500 million a year!*

In China, by way of contrast, students are so eager to get an education that when they hear of such crimes in America they assume that at least a portion of our young population has gone insane. The sharp difference is, of course, by no means entirely a matter of Communist indoctrination. There is apparently no school vandalism on Taiwan either.

9. It is a cliché to observe that freedom places on those who enjoy it a counterbalancing set of responsibilities and obligations. Per-

haps the reason the statement is so often repeated is that it does not seem to have penetrated the American consciousness. Increasingly our society looks bad in regard to certain important areas of social concern. Consider, for example, the problems of the aged in the United States. To grow old in America today, unless one is wealthy, is to enter a separate, strange, frightening subculture. The problem starts from the fact that because millions of American families no longer have geographical roots they are simply not equipped to care for the aged in the way common when ours was chiefly a rural nation.

Poverty is a serious handicap to anyone, regardless of age, but to the very old it is far worse. Some 5 million of the aged in our country have incomes of under $2,000 a year, decidedly below the poverty line specified by government economists. *Fully a third of the old in America are poor.* Many thousands have no alternative but to live in nursing homes; some of these are disgraceful, in some cases criminal, institutions that treat their residents like cattle, in some instances even worse in that cattle are at least well fed, fattened up.

In both the New York City and Southern California areas—where one might think nursing-home care would be superior simply because both communities are under the noses of officialdom and the communications media— recent investigations have produced evidence of exploitation and abuse of helpless patients. Unannounced visits to nursing homes have revealed old men and women lying in their own excrement, doped to keep them quiet, ignored, insulted and in some cases in fear of punishment by attendants or hospital authorities if they complain publicly.

In China now no old person falls through the screen of public concern. Everyone is attended to. Old people are well cared for.

Again, there is no question but that freedom is more attractive than tyranny. But the modern debate does not concern itself only with verbal and philosophical abstractions. What is of interest is what actually happens. I don't give a good goddamn how embarrassing or annoying it is to be confronted with such reality. The important question is: What are we

going to do *in response* to the reality? When we merely respond, "Oh, sure, old people are well-treated in China but freedom is still preferable to tyranny," we make ourselves look like the most incredible sort of asses.

10. In the United States litter is a national disgrace. Clean-up of public areas costs an estimated $500 million annually. Adding the cost of litter removal from private property, the annual national litter bill approaches $1 billion! Every year American motorists throw 16 million pieces of trash on each mile of primary highway, according to a study by the Highway Research Board of the National Academy of Sciences. An estimated 130 persons lose their lives in litter-fed fires annually. Every twelve minutes a home is destroyed or damaged by a fire starting in trash. In one state, foreign matter on the roadway contributed to 21 fatal and 1,068 nonfatal accidents in one year. Litter provides a breeding ground for disease-carrying insects and rodents.

In China the littering problem does not exist.

11. Our family is just one among the millions in America but consider what we have suffered at the hands of thieves. My business offices have been burglarized, my home has been burglarized, a $300 camera belonging to my son Bill was stolen out of our house, not by strangers but by one of his friends, and the office of my wife's travel agency has been illegally entered twice. One time her safe was broken into and almost $2,000 taken; on the other occasion a large supply of airplane ticket-stock was stolen.

Recently I had the pleasure of staying at the Hilton Hotel in New York. A brightly colored card placed on the dresser in my suite said, "Please remember to bolt and chain your door before retiring to ensure your privacy and security." On the door itself, pasted next to a chain lock, was the admonition, "Protect your privacy. Chain and bolt door. Under New York State law the hotel has no liability for loss of money, jewelry and other valuables unless they are placed in the free safe deposit boxes in the lobby." Both signs are rendered in several languages, including Chinese.

China has no national problem of street crime or breaking-and-entering, merely isolated incidents.

But none of these comparisons—oddly enough—have primary relevance to the Chinese themselves. They will not bring them up in conversation with Western visitors. The basic comparison that is valid to today's Chinese is that between conditions of the Chinese present and those that prevailed in the past. Once this is grasped it becomes easier to measure what the Communists have accomplished in modern China.

Consider:

1. The nation—and not terribly many years ago—was notorious for prostitution, which almost invariably grows out of widespread poverty. Now prostitution and its degradation of woman are a thing of the past, despite scattered instances.

2. Before 1949 addiction to opium and other drugs was a serious social problem in China. It is no more.

3. Visitors to the mainland, even from nations not famed for high ideals of personal cleanliness, used to be appalled by the dirt and squalor in most parts of the nation. Today perhaps the Chinese might say that cleanliness is next to un-Godliness.

4. Political and economic corruption, once seemingly characteristic of the Chinese—and which did much to weaken respect for the Kuomintang—are gone, replaced by a system which does not accommodate bribery, kickbacks or even tipping. There must be individual exceptions among 800 million people but the improvement has been dramatic nevertheless.

5. Death from disease and starvation was once as common in Chinese life as it is to animal populations which, since they are unable to plan, are frequently the victims of nature's blindness. Today vigorous programs emphasizing health care and sanitation have reversed the situation.

Parenthetically, there has sometimes been an ugly and unedifying tone to certain American journalistic reports of crop failures or near-famines in parts of China during the last thirty years. Famine has not occurred in China since 1949, but that is irrelevant. The point is the journalists, who assumed their pessimistic reports were accurate, rarely expressed sympathy for the Chinese people who, God knows, had suffered enough real famines before 1949. It would be understandable that some Westerners might resent Chinese Communist successes and relish their failures. But to express this contempt without at the same time drawing a careful distinction between rulers and ruled is unpardonable.

6. In the old China, woman was an inferior, often abused, creature whose feet were bound. Girl babies were often simply discarded, like unwanted dogs. Today Chinese women have a new stature, importance and freedom.

7. Another respect in which modern China differs from that of pre-Communist days is that where once there were hordes of beggars in the streets, as there still are in India, Africa, Latin America and elsewhere, the mainland Chinese would not think of begging now. The utter collapse of the Communist economic structure—which many Americans would welcome—would, of course, immediately plunge hundreds of millions back into that system of poverty and starvation which produces beggars. To stop the practice, apparently only two things were necessary: (a) providing the former beggars with enough food and other basic necessities; (b) instilling self-respect in them.

If China ever goes capitalist again, by the way, we should of course at once prepare for demands for an enormous volume of loans and foreign aid.

8. Old China was largely illiterate and ignorant. Modern China has many new schools. Education from nursery to university level is at last open to poor peasants and their families.

9. Old China had little or no large industry of its own, except for that run by Westerners for their own profit. New China is becoming industrialized.

10. So serious was the problem of both petty and serious thievery in pre-Communist China that even in the Episcopal Mission and school run by Jayne's mother and father it was found necessary to keep sugar, flour, lard,

canned goods and other kitchen provisions under lock and key. Mrs. Cotter would personally open a locked cabinet when it was necessary to use or distribute the contents.

I have learned, since our first two trips to China, that some Americans are so poorly informed as to believe that the present all-pervasive Chinese honesty is explained by nothing more than fear of the consequences of getting caught stealing. A Los Angeles policeman, for example, said, "Sure, they're honest. Because they know if they're not they'll get a bullet in the head!"

On the contrary, the primary explanation is that *the reasons for the former corruption and thievery have been removed.* Once the disease of *more-more-more* is cured, once greed becomes socially irrelevant, once everyone has enough to eat and to wear, there is no longer much point to thievery, petty or otherwise. (The only kind of stealing not caused by poverty or greed is kleptomania, a mental illness. There must be a few kleptomaniacs in China.)

This chapter—no doubt painful reading for some—has a simple purpose, which is certainly not to recommend Marxist solutions for all the world's ills. *Its purpose is to diminish that thoughtless, unexamined American attitude of superiority by sketching for U.S. readers the scene of international confrontation as it might look through Chinese eyes.*

18. Western Precedent for Chinese Communist Practices

ANOTHER of the means I shall employ, for the purpose of explaining modern China to Americans, is the reference to facets of the present Chinese experience which either now have, or have in the past had, their counterparts in American or other Western practice.

Consider, for example, the sense of sleeves-rolled-up dedication, the boundless energy, the willingness to accept hardships, which all observers, pro and con, agree characterizes the new China. It is sometimes said that, by contrast, Americans are now lethargic, committed only to their own selfish interest, unwilling to make sacrifices. But historically the accusation is unjust. While most of us at the present moment have little to boast of on this particular scale, it has by no means always been so. In World War II, for example, there was widespread popular willingness to pitch in and make an extra effort, to work overtime, to accept less than satisfactory working and living conditions, to sacrifice certain consumer goods and services on the home front in order that additional support could be given to men in the armed forces. The almost unanimous agreement on the philosophical aims of the war was, of course, the dominant factor explaining the national sense of commitment and unity at that time.

This is not absolutely all there is to present conditions in China, of course; hard work and thrift have traditionally been important in Chinese culture and practice, although in times past, for millions of the poorer peasants, conditions were so degrading that these natural tendencies were sometimes blotted out by suffering. But Americans can and still do feel these same emotions of cooperation and dedication when they can be made to perceive a large social purpose that logically calls forth such effort.

Something else characteristic of today's China—the new puritanism—clearly cannot be thought of as a factor foreign to Western experience, but rather as entirely consistent with a strong influence on American behavior. The word *Puritan,* obviously, is not Eastern. The emphasis on thrift, hard work, waste-not-want-not, simple living, simple food, agreement on the vulgarity of ostentatious displays of wealth—all of this was once considered important and virtuous to many Americans. While it is generally considered as part of the Puritan-Protestant-Quaker ethic it was by no means entirely foreign to American Catholic experience, if not perhaps as dominant in the Catholic culture as in the Protestant. But generations of hard-working Irish, Poles, Italians and others who lived simply, saved their money, educated their children, and lifted themselves out of the slums give testimony to the appreciation of *the very attitudes that today are dominant in China.* It must be conceded, therefore, that the Communist Chinese rulers have done something wise in calling their people to a renewed respect for such traditional human virtues.

But, if there are reasonable and productive factors in present-day Chinese experience that are by no means foreign to American history and practice, *negative or questionable practices and attitudes also have their counterpart in Western practice and history.*

Though it is true that relatively little political or philosophical heresy is tolerated in China now, it rarely was in the past either; and Western man has little to be proud of, and much to regret, as regards the historic record of the ideal of freedom in practice and in theory. The 2,000 years of Christian history in particular are almost entirely devoid of that spirit of tolerance which some modern American Christians erroneously assume is as much part of their religious as of their political tradition. One does not have to be a scholar of religious history to know that, from the very first, followers of Christ, sad to say, have freely criticized and slaughtered each other in presumed defense of one version of the faith or another. Neither Protestants nor Catholics can take a superior attitude as regards this issue. What we are discussing here, of course, is not a specifically Christian failing but rather

one that seems invariably to follow commitment to *any* large philosophical entity, whether in the realm of religion or politics. Believers and nonbelievers have for thousands of years been willing to resort to the sword when it was felt that the boundaries of persuasion had been reached. So, while the present limitations on freedom in China are lamentable, American Christians ought not to becloud their vision by hypocrisy in considering this part of the large question. As descendants of the American Founding Fathers we do have laws and customs of which our nation can be proud, although we should not blind ourselves to recent disturbing findings suggesting that some specifics of our Bill of Rights would be swept away were they put presently to the test of popular vote.

Even now, in whatever are the least restricted portions of planet earth, the freedom men care about most passionately is *their own,* not freedom as an abstract idea and not the freedom of others. But of course it is precisely in regard to the freedom of *others* that one reveals one's true feelings on this all-important question. The worst tyrants who ever lived were jealous of their own freedom and intensely angered by infringement of it.

It must also be appreciated that the Chinese Communists did not invent the practice of placing art in the service of the dominant social philosophy. We are unlikely ever to know precisely who the creators of such a policy were. It is sufficient for the present purpose to note that for long centuries in Europe the artist was expected to glorify—not criticize—the state, the church and the reigning philosophy generally.

Another illustration of a questionable factor characteristic of modern China, but not foreign to American experience, is the Maoist emphasis on achieving basic education and political or social indoctrination simultaneously. The Chinese feel it is wasteful to teach a child to read a sentence with no philosophical content, such as "See the ball bounce." They believe it more effective to teach a sentence, such as "See how the people love Chairman Mao," or "See the little boy helping his neighbor." The reading factor is the same in both cases but the latter examples add the element of indoctrination. It is interesting that American conservatives forcefully support a philosophy of the teaching of reading that is in general perfectly consistent with Maoist theory. What they want to inculcate, of course, is Americanism: respect for the home, the church, the flag, the free enterprise system, and such. I take no exception to emphasis on these ideals but merely underline that in advocating such a *technique,* conservatives are not differing with Mao but agreeing with him.

One Communist Chinese political practice I find objectionable is the forcing of officials or others to publicly apologize—frequently in the most self-abasing and exaggerated terms—for actual or alleged philosophical errors or acts contrary to the public welfare, as determined by the dominant Communist authorities of the moment. But even in considering this practice, two points, at least, must be borne in mind. First, such a thing was not unusual in China long before communism was introduced. Second, Americans might ask themselves if they would really consider such treatment irredeemably cruel if the suffering parties were members of whatever political camp the reader abhors.

Assume, for example, that the offender is an American Nazi who glorifies the atrocities of Hitler and his pathologically criminal supporters. Naturally all right-thinking Americans thoroughly detest nazism. So the question is: Would we really consider it cruel or unreasonable if monstrous Nazis were made to publicly confess the error of their ways and to ask public pardon for past transgressions?

Or let those Americans who morally equate communism with nazism raise the same question with a Communist in the dock. Suppose we heard tomorrow that, by some magical process, Chiang Kai-shek's followers had been able to regain control of China. Suppose we heard that captured Communist leaders were being "given a dose of their own medicine," that Communist authorities, brought to account before—let us arbitrarily assume—an angry public, were now forced to recite a list of their former offenses, to ask the public's

forgiveness, to swear not to repeat their transgressions. Would the American majority really be shocked at such practices?

Walter Gordon wrote an interesting series of articles for the *Toronto Star* and other Canadian newspapers in June, 1959, subsequently published as *China—1959* in paperback form by The American Friends Service Committee, in which he made the same point about the Chinese Communist emphasis on slogans, catch phrases, posters, displays, songs, and other forms of what Westerners consider "public brainwashing." Gordon observes that in America we resort to precisely the same devices and methods, far more insistently, the only difference being that we only occasionally employ them for political purpose. Most of the time we use them for commercial purposes, to pound home the merits of a popular face cream, a soft drink, a make of automobile or some other product.

In depending heavily on music as a means of indoctrination the Communists have simply employed a custom that was known in China long before they came to power. In the 1920s the Christian general of Shensi, Feng Yu-hsiang, regularly taught important lessons to his troops by means of song.

Among the morals so taught were "We must not gamble or visit whores," "We must not drink or smoke," "Save your ammunition," "Be honest in business," and "Plow land, weave cloth, read books."

Some Americans criticize China as well as other Communist countries because of their practice of capital punishment. As an opponent of the death penalty I agree with such criticisms, but it is by no means the case that capital punishment has become exclusively a Communist practice. For the most part, as it happens, it is Americans of the Right, most highly critical of their Eastern counterparts, who are the staunchest defenders of the death penalty.

Present entirely understandable Catholic lamentation about the interference of the Communist state into church affairs to the point of the seeming outright attempt to bind the church in China to the state is understandably objectionable within the *American* tradition of separation of the two. Yet over a greater span of history it is entirely consistent with Catholic and Protestant experience. Historically, the idea of a *separation* of church and state was viewed by Christians as a radical and dangerous notion. It was *union* of church and state that Christians preferred.

When individual nobles and princes began to realize the selfish advantages that accrued from manipulating the church in the seventeenth and eighteenth centuries, what gradually resulted was a situation in which the clergy became hired agents of the individual princes and the church became an arm of the state. The situation observable in modern Spain, where many Catholics have felt that church-state union is perfectly reasonable, was common in other Catholic nations as well, and we are painfully aware of the unhappy results.

The point, again, is that in one more instance the Chinese are making no startling departure from tradition but rather acting in a fashion consistent with long periods of European experience.

These observations are not a defense of China's policy on church and state; I view such situations as deplorable, in any historic context. I am merely concerned to show that the Chinese have introduced nothing unusual in this regard.

COMMUNES IN THE U.S.

As it happens I have, for the past several years, been studying the remarkable phenomenon of the Jesus communes that have sprung up in various parts of the United States, in preparation for writing a book on the subject. While there are inevitable differences of style, belief and practice among the separate sects, they have in common a general renunciation of American capitalist attitudes, a communal, tribal-family structure, an emphasis on simplicity, neatness and order in daily living, and a tendency to ignore purely rational conclusions in favor of the spiritual, the mythological, the emotional and in some cases the

fanatical. The variety of human custom around the world makes it clear that man is able to derive social satisfaction in a great many different ways. But the one factor that seems to distinguish the new communal movement is that of Instantaneous Conversion. Some sect members are rather slow-thinking, simple folk, others are high-energy, high-I.Q. types. But all report essentially the same process leading to their affiliation—a sudden, wrenching change in world-view followed by an immediate fanatical confidence in the new belief. There may be some common factor between this social phenomenon and that of conversion to communism, or to any other rigidly structured political belief. This is not to ignore the fact that some people come to communism by a long, slow process of study and speculation. But the end product of total, unquestioning faith, the fiery insistence on dogma, the wholehearted dedication to a way of life, seem similar in both camps.

There can, for better or worse, be no similar adherence to Western democratic ideas and practices. We in the West can feel the emotional pull of a marching band, a flag waving in the breeze, a stirring speech, but what we are sensing in such instances is the age-old appeal to the primitive patriotic impulse, apparently much the same the world over, and organically plugged into nationalistic or tribal, not economic circuits. But freedom, even when it is decidedly relative, is a matter of the absence rather than the presence of things. We may find the writings of, say, John Stuart Mill, Adam Smith and Thomas Jefferson appealing and reasonable. But few in the West are likely to feel the kind of fervor about Smith, Jefferson and Mill that Communists feel about Marx, Engels and Lenin. It is in the field of religion that one finds similar processes and patterns.

In China, Mao occupied a position analogous to that of Marx or Christ, in terms of emotional dynamics.

Another point of comparison between modern Chinese and traditional Western experience is that of the Christian monasteries in Europe. Although they eventually were touched by corruption and fanaticism they were, at their best, admirable and heroic institutions without which the lamp of Christian scholarship might have been extinguished during the darker centuries of European history. The important point here is that *a monastery is a collective commune.*

The individual monks and priests lived purposely in poverty, were economically self-sufficient in that they raised their own grain, tended their own herds, baked their own bread, etc., and concentrated on stamping out selfish individualism, which they sought to replace, through conformity with the highest Christian ideals, with an interest in the well-being of one's brothers in the commune, in the church, and among humanity generally.

Conservatives like Ayn Rand are perfectly free to argue that this Catholic behavior was all psychological nonsense and that man's selfishness is not a sin, as Christians argue, but a high virtue. I am concerned here only to demonstrate what is perhaps obvious enough, which is that in basic structure there is a remarkable, if by no means total, similarity between the Catholic monasteries and the Chinese communes. Residents of both hear a one-sided version of social reality, live very simple, frugal lives, devote themselves to consideration for others, and are strongly critical of the usurious, robber-baron, capitalist mentality. Commune and monastery alike emphasize the important social and therapeutic effects of physical labor, the avoidance of luxury, the serious moral danger of sexual excess, and the natural tendency of man to revert to sinfulness, selfishness and depravity unless he is guided by an ethical-moral code.

Though the monks and scholastics start from a belief in God whereas the Chinese Communists do not, what is remarkable is the degree of similarity in their conclusions. Both camps are repelled by corruption, thievery, prostitution and materialistic worldliness generally. While few Americans, even few Christians, would personally choose to live in either a commune or a monastery, they are nevertheless hardly in a philosophical position to convincingly argue that the communal structure is *inherently* sinful.

Yet another practice for which Chinese Communists are criticized in the West is that form of social punishment in which an individual's name is erased from the public records so that he becomes, in a sense, a nonperson. But again, Mao and his followers have created nothing new. For some 2,000 years before 1949 it was commonly recognized that the most severe punishment the head of a family could inflict upon a troublesome member was to literally erase his name from the tablets on the family altar—found in almost every Chinese home—the place where the ceremonies of ancestor worship were performed. Such erasure banished the luckless individual not only from the family but from the clan and, according to Christian scholar William Hung, "from Chinese civilization."

Next, consider the deplorable Red Guard excesses of the Cultural Revolution, often criticized as if the West had known nothing of street riots, picketing, violence and public boorishness.

As an example of especially beastly Red Guard behavior I submit the information in the following quotation:

Whenever there is a sufficient unity among students on a given issue it is generally expressed in a plan of action which serves to extend it both upward into official circles and downward to the masses. The students have frequently marched in a body upon the officials, demanding certain changes in government policies. When their demands have been refused, they have gone so far as to beat officials and wreck offices, thus creating a sensation throughout the country and focusing public attention on issues which corrupt officials have been eager to keep hidden from the people. Often the students send deputations to lecture in the streets of cities and villages to the merchants, laborers and farmers. Through organized efforts such as these, public opinion on certain national issues is being crystalized.

I confess to have played one more trick on the reader. The description above could not possibly refer to the Red Guards of the Cultural Revolution because it comes from an American book published in 1932 edited by William Hung. The section in question was written by Hung, professor of history at Yen Ching University in Peking and Harvard. He and all his coauthors were young Christians sympathetic to the West, desirous of changing China for the better, but in this instance simply describing *how Christian and other Western-educated young Chinese dared, in certain instances, to resort to physical assaults and destruction of state property by way of emphasizing their demands.* One is perfectly free to criticize such behavior—whether perpetrated by Christians or Communists—but it is clear that there was nothing whatever novel about Red Guard behavior.

19. The Hardest Question

I HAVE left to this late point a consideration of the most painful question of all about post-1949 China. It is by no means addressed personally to the scores of likable and gracious people we met during our visits. None was a high government official; all were kind and helpful. They would be welcome in our home should any of them have occasion to visit the U.S. in the future. Nor am I deluded that the question should be addressed only to the Communist rulers of China. It is an ageless question, equally properly addressed to the Israelite tribes of the Old Testament, who believed that God personally instructed them to slaughter their enemies by the thousands to the last man, woman and child, on scores of occasions.

The Chinese Communists have never been guilty of that specific degree of savagery. But the painful question about mass violence must nevertheless be squarely, if quietly, addressed, no matter how one might wish, for reasons of concord and good will, to turn away from it.

Those who defend Chinese or Soviet communism, either totally or selectively, fall into two quite distinct categories in considering the question of violence. The first consists of people who do not at all object to the entirely truthful assertion that they personally are hard, ruthless and quite prepared to kill for The Cause. Far from rejecting the description, they revel in it. We live in a tough, dangerous world, they say; the dream of the tame, sensitive Socialists, that power in every country can be acquired by peaceful, parliamentary methods, is absurd. The superrich, the antipoor, the reactionaries, the Fascists, the robber barons, the royalists never have and never will give up power voluntarily. It must be taken from them, by force.

The second category consists of those who pursue the dream of communism-with-a-human-face. Yes, they sadly concede, violence does take place in revolutionary situations. It certainly did in the American Revolution. The people do have to oppose the guns of status quo armies and police with weapons of their own. And, after all, *every* state employs violence in defense of its interests.

The primary difference between the two groups is that the former argues that violence is admirable, even heroic, that it separates men from boys. Those in the latter category see bloodshed as a profoundly tragic, if unavoidable consequence of rebellion.

Of the two, sad to say, it is the former that has the clearer vision of revolutionary reality. Morally they may be wrong, but as for describing objective reality, they have a sharply focused view of what takes place.

Peasant violence in China, of course, did not originate in 1949 after Chiang's defeat. It is centuries old. In 1926 Mao wrote of the peasant uprising that so alarmed my wife's family and the thousands of other foreigners in central China at the time:

In recent months there occurred a great insurrection in the Shanpei area of [Tz'u Hsi

County]. The peasants of this Shanpei area are violent by nature, and frequently indulge in armed combat. On top of this, in recent years the officials and police have been unreasonably oppressive and the bad landlords have stepped up their exploitation. So the accumulated exasperation of the peasants was already deep. By chance the climate this year was unstable, and as a result the rice and cotton crops failed, but the landlords refused to make any reduction whatever in their harsh rents. The peasants' insurrection against famine thereupon exploded. . . .

They burned down the police station, and distributed the arms of the police among themselves. They then turned to go to the homes of the village gentry landlords to "eat up powerful families." After eating them up, and out of anger at the evils of the village gentry landlords, they destroyed the landlords' screens, paintings, and sculptured ancient doors and windows. They did this every day; they did not listen much to others' exhortation, but let off their steam in this manner.

The following year, in his now-classic *Report on an Investigation of the Peasant Movement in Hunan,* Mao predicted,

Within a very short time, several hundred million peasants from the provinces of China's central, southern and northern sections will rise up, and their power will be like a blasting wind and cloudburst, so extraordinarily swift and violent that no force, however large, will be able to suppress it. They will burst through all trammels that restrain them, and rush toward the road of liberation.

Clearly what is involved in such historic dramas is part of a social pattern ages old. The elements are simple enough: long-continued exploitation, cruelty and brutalization by a small dominant class, leading inevitably to resentment and hatred on the part of the oppressed. When such passions reach an utterly intolerable stage, an explosion occurs which, if leaders are present to channel energies, becomes a formal revolution which, in turn, may either fail or succeed. What I am concerned to demonstrate is that *the revolutionary leaders who appear at such moments in history are by no means merely evil plotters stirring up otherwise peaceful and contented peasants.*

But now, in surveying the turbulent drama of a revolution, we come to the precise point at which the obviously unavoidable killing that results from military confrontation is separated by an enormous moral gulf from one type of the slaughter that begins *after hostilities have ceased.*

Even at this point, to be entirely fair, common sense requires the concession that, after the losing force has surrendered and the people have, for the most part, gone back to their daily business, there may be a few war criminals, perpetrators of atrocities against the people so heinous that capital punishment is popularly thought to be called for. I am personally opposed to the death penalty, as I've said, but am aware that when political passions are aroused the popular will generally support the execution of those guilty of serious offenses.

There was, for example, no popular outcry in Western nations against the executions of the German monsters who had administered the hellish concentration camps and execution chambers. So let us concede that the popular mind, everywhere, will support a second stage of reprisal against those specific members of the defeated force whose conduct in power was so cruel as to render them likely targets for vengeance. The world has recently seen the same tragic situation in Iran.

Although it is impossible to be even remotely precise about such matters, let us assume that a few hundred individuals might be justifiably killed in this stage—perhaps, in states with enormous populations, several thousand. But at this point then, *the deep moral gulf can no longer be avoided. Those who build a bridge across it and proceed on to the slaughter of not additional hundreds or thousands, but of millions, can find no possible moral defense.*

An important difference, affecting the morality of the equation, operative at this last stage, is that the violence now is perpetrated no longer by *the people* but merely by *the state.* The people may no longer have a voice in the matter. The individual citizen, in fact, who protests too loudly against the massive exterminations knows that he runs a serious risk of being added to the list of victims.

Nor should anyone—whether pro- or anti-Communist—waste a moment in thinking that such organized programs of slaughter might rightly be compared to the Crusades, the Inquisition or the wars of religions in which Christians and their churches were the ruthless executioners. For in the case of slaughter by Christians, what was involved was obviously an inexcusable crime that flew in the face of the essence of Christianity itself. In the case of Marxism, however, the messiah has written, in the revolutionary year of 1848, "There is only one means of shortening, simplifying, concentrating the murderous death-pangs of the old society, and the bloody birth-pangs of the new, only one means—revolutionary terror."

Marx did *not* intend that the weapon of terror should be set aside at the precise moment that the Old Guard surrendered. Trotsky, Lenin, Stalin, Mao, Castro, Guevara repeatedly proclaimed the advisability of ruthless, totalitarian methods of continuing to hold power *after* it has been won.

In trying to arrive at a rational conclusion as witnesses to the East-West debate, perhaps the most important in all history, it is necessary that we remind ourselves, again and again, of the moral components of the equations by which we are perplexed. Consider, for example, the revulsion that automatically wells up in the hearts of all but the most depraved at consideration of the reality of the concentration camps exposed to world-view at the end of World War II. All atrocities are by definition hideous, but even among such crimes there are degrees of ugliness. The gas chambers, the ovens, the vicious medical experiments, the sadistic rapes, the beatings, the starvation—it is all of such monumental horror that in the face of it, even considered as an abstraction, one's confidence in the inevitability of human salvation or progress is severely shaken.

But if all this is so, and there is no escaping it, then it follows that a concentration camp is, *in any and all circumstances,* a vile and shameful place where unspeakable crimes are com-

mitted. If Hitler is a monster for having slaughtered some 9 million men, women and children, there can be no defense for Stalin, who deliberately put to death over 20 million human beings, almost all of them not foreign enemies but residents of the territories Stalin controlled!

Nor was it necessary to await the end of a world war to know the truth of the Russian concentration camps. The Soviet terror began in 1918 and has not stopped to the present moment. It is no defense of any of this that a good many horses' asses have over the years become vocal members of the anti-Communist legions. Communists, of course, derive enormous satisfaction, as well as propaganda capital, from being able to point to the millions of Nazis, Fascists, Ku Klux Klanners, John Birchers, anti-Blacks, anti-Semites, and reactionaries of various sorts in the ranks of their enemies.

State executions for largely political motives are by no means limited to Communist nations. The United States after the Spanish Civil War remained a firm ally of Spain's Franco, but in *the first five years of his regime alone, approximately 200,000 Republicans were either executed or did not survive a prison sentence.*

Chiang Kai-shek—on several occasions—conducted "annihilation campaigns" the purpose of which was to *kill all Communists. Had he been able he would have slaughtered them by the millions;* before, during and after formal hostilities. We must grasp this.

But to what—precisely—does one appeal, now, in making such observations? To a collective human conscience? Perhaps. But I am not as certain as I once was that such a thing exists. Everywhere, among Communists and anti-Communists, there is the attempt to clothe violence—which is really a matter of agonizingly sliced flesh, smashed teeth, torn breasts, stomped genitals, blasted skulls, bleeding stumps, ripped-out bowels—there is the attempt to clothe all this bloody savagery in the mantle of philosophical justification.

It does not work, goddamn it! Cruelty is *not* justified. Philosophy becomes stained by blood. And who *listens* to the pitiful screams of the victims, the wail of the burned, maimed or abandoned children, the sobbing of widows, the whimpering of orphans? Where *is* the collective human conscience? Why does it speak not at all or mainly in a whisper, the general silence broken only by the occasional shout of a Solzhenitsyn, the painstaking work of organizations such as Amnesty International or the concern of a few of the clergy?

I can find no forgiveness in my heart for the Germans who massacred Jews like cattle during World War II, nor for Stalin, who slaughtered scores of millions of his own people, nor —it must be said—for Mao Tse-tung, who personally authorized the execution of millions of Chinese. Though the exact number can never be known, the moral element of the crime is the same whether the number is 5 million, 10 or 20. This is by no means simply a matter of being personally opposed to capital punishment. I quite understand that those who do not share my view on the death penalty feel that there are certain crimes so heinous that they are punishable only by death.

But simply being a capitalist is not one of those crimes. Simply having been a supporter of the Kuomintang is not one of those crimes. Simply being a landlord is not one of those crimes.

Against this it may, perfectly legitimately, be argued that in China a landlord is by no means merely a man who had accumulated a certain amount of real estate. Had the case been so simple, fewer landlords would have been executed. In reality the landlords ruled the vast countryside of China; the formal officials were subservient to them rather than the other way round. This need not, of course, fall strangely on American ears since there are in our political experience more than enough instances of congressmen, senators and governors who were merely minor local figures until wealthy businessmen urged them to run for office and subsequently supervised and paid for their campaigns, naturally expecting favors in due course.

So great has been the suffering of the Chinese people over the centuries that even such massive tragedies are not without precedent. Consider the period of the Taiping Rebellion, 1850–1864. Under the self-deluded Christian schoolmaster Hung Hsiu-chuan, the Taiping rebels stimulated widespread popular opposition to the Manchu government. During the course of the many battles that resulted, well over 20 million lives were lost and countless millions of others suffered misery and deprivation. Li Ung-bing in his *Outline of Chinese History* states that "more than 600 cities and towns were laid in ruins and trade, art, literature, and civilization all received a setback" during the period of the Taiping chaos.

If life on this dangerous planet can ever achieve a plateau of at least relative civilization, of at least comparative moral decency, it will come to pass only when men whose hands are on the levers of governmental power inhibit their lust to slaughter their philosophical enemies. The alleged—even actual—justice of the cause which seeks vengeance is utterly, totally irrelevant. The greatest, most honorable, most efficient, most admirable government that ever existed would have no more right to slaughter millions of people than did the moral monster Adolf Hitler.

But why the strange insensitivity to brutality on such a massive scale? Perhaps because our emotional receptors have not been prepared by the evolutionary process to deal adequately with shocking phenomena in such enormous volume.

Close, personal tragedy we respond to in some approximately reasonable proportion. A friend is killed; we weep. A total of twenty-seven tears may be shed. We may sob for fourteen minutes, feel depressed for nine days. But at the news of 20 million deaths, how can we possibly respond proportionately? We cannot shed a million tears, cannot howl out our grief for a century. Our circuits become flooded, we become numb and may even seem calloused. We are like the doctors who, because they could not save lives if they were racked by grief at the spectacle of every wound, inure themselves and become stoic, at least in regard to the sufferings of others.

I have once before experienced an instance of ongoing insensitivity to the possibility—as distinguished from reality—of mass destruction and that is in the context of attempting to awaken people to the dangers of nuclear holocaust, a campaign I joined in 1959. Smaller, more localized threats they could understand, but the possibility of 100 million deaths, or more, was too much to grasp; many simply turned away from what was and continues to be a very real danger.

TERROR, 1950–1951

During much of the first year after their 1949 victory, the Communists apparently concentrated chiefly on halting inflation, restoring law and order and conducting a campaign of public instruction and education, explaining their views and plans, as quickly as possible, to the world's most massive population. As a result of those efforts conditions for most people began to improve in many particulars and there was a general sense of hopefulness.

In 1950, however, Prime Minister Chou En-lai signaled a crackdown to come in a speech about the people's judiciary system. His remarks were largely complimentary but he observed that certain errors had been made, chiefly that a number of judicial workers "had misinterpreted the policy of clemency with regard to the suppression of counterrevolutionary elements. They have only shown clemency to the counterrevolutionary elements, without suppressing them, so that the masses of people blamed them for their 'boundless clemency.' The masses of people are right in blaming them, for the principles set up by Chairman Mao Tse-tung for the treatment of counter-revolutionary elements were to 'punish the ringleaders, leave their misguided followers alone, and reward those who render assistance and service in the struggle.' "

By February, 1951, Peking was ready to announce formal Regulations for the Punishment of Counterrevolutionaries. For certain crimes against the state the death penalty was specified. This in itself could not structurally have come as a shock since it had been Chiang Kai-shek's program as well—practiced, too, on Taiwan—and for that matter perfectly in accord, not only with custom in most Communist and Fascist states but the thinking of the American right wing.

In March, 1951, two dramatic develop-ments occurred. Of primary importance were massive public trials, in many parts of the country, conducted by Communist mayors, which led to conviction of hundreds of thousands of Chinese identified, in most cases correctly enough, as counterrevolutionaries. The most dramatic factor in these strange demonstrations was the participation of large crowds of citizens, either peasants or city dwellers. They were not only permitted to view the proceedings, but were encouraged to play a role in them, to step forth to make personal charges, to give evidence against the accused and, perhaps more significantly, to demand the punishment of death for the worst offenders. The same crowds would then also attend the executions, which one assumes took place shortly after the trials.

It is important for American anti-Communists to understand that their impression as to how Communist executions are customarily carried out might conform, in some instances, to proceedings in the Soviet Union but have generally not been applicable in the Chinese context. In other words, the Chinese Communist cadres did *not* simply seek out, Nazi-like, individual anti-Communists and shoot them in their beds in the dead of night, against the wishes of neighbors. Rather the first appeal was made *to the neighbors themselves* and, because of the oppression and cruelty to which the Chinese masses had undoubtedly been subjected, it did not prove difficult to arouse popular hatred not only of the former landlords, policemen, merchants and other bullies, but to use the emotion so stimulated to actually provide energy for the entire judicial process. What actually happened therefore was—God help us—popular, in the simple sense of the word. To say as much is not to argue that the entire process was justified but rather to clarify that what was done was in accordance with the wishes of many, perhaps the majority.

Denis Warner, in *Hurricane from China,* explains:

The cadres coaxed, urged, directed, and the people of China, intoxicated by the bloodletting and the chance to vent old resentments, did the rest. In city streets, in public squares, in the villages, towns and cities, counterrevolutionaries and suspects were accused, stoned, spat upon, shot. Along with the campaign against the counterrevolutionaries and sometimes confused with it, went the land-reform campaign. Mao had laid down that the peaceful redistribution of land was part of a Marxist theory of social revolution, that the landlord class would not disintegrate by itself but had to be knocked out, and that the more violent the land reform the more successful it would be. . . .

Land reform, like the campaign against the counterrevolutionaries, was at once a systematically applied terror, a form of thought-changing (or brain-washing) and a social revolution. By eliminating the landlord class, by class war, it aimed to make a major break with the past.

It is interesting that in 1954, when the outside world knew close to nothing about the mass trials taking place in China, and when I personally was unaware of their existence, I wrote a short story called "The Public Hating" which has had an odd history.

Perhaps I should explain that I have written a number of short stories over the years, two volumes of which—*The Girls on the Tenth Floor* and *The Public Hating*—have been published and republished. Several originally appeared in magazines and attracted no particular attention. But *The Public Hating* has subsequently been published in Sweden, Germany, Japan, in anthologies of science fiction, of short stories and in two college texts.

It concerns an execution, in New York's Yankee Stadium, at some point in the not-distant future. The condemned, a political criminal whose crime is deliberately not specified, is neither hanged, electrocuted, shot nor gassed because capital punishment in these forms has been outlawed. He is, instead, literally hated to death in a frightening scene of mass fury.

While there probably now can be no precise information as to the number of executions by the Chinese Communist government, it is important nevertheless to obtain as much accurate information as possible. If the Communists made no pretense of morality, if they were merely uniformed savages such as Hit-

ler's Gestapo and SS, there would be no sensible purpose in studying the matter. The world verdict has long been that the worst of the Nazis were beasts that walked on their hind legs. But the Chinese Communists assign themselves a very different role in history.

On February 21, 1951, the central Chinese government issued its sternly worded decree dealing with the "Punishment of Counterrevolutionary Offenses." This did not announce a crackdown; one was already under way in the countryside and in certain cities. The February 21 pronouncement therefore was in part an attempt to legitimatize the wave of vengeful trials and executions that had begun more or less spontaneously, though with the Communists obviously doing nothing whatever to inhibit them. There was, again, little terror of the specifically Nazi or Stalinist types. The Communists professed to view this sort of behavior with horror although they were more prone to criticize German or Japanese perpetrators than Russians. But they were at least on record as critical of such procedures. The Kuomintang officials, heartless landlords, corrupt businessmen and citizens known to be violently anti-Communist were at least accorded trials. They would hardly pass for fair legal procedure in Western Europe or the United States, but they were trials nevertheless, conducted publicly. Some percentage of the unfortunate victims no doubt would have been judged guilty by Western courts of law. Many had indeed committed serious offenses against the Chinese masses. But only the most fanatical Communist could possibly argue that all of the victims were so vicious and depraved.

The popular antirightist hysteria of the moment served to facilitate and speed up the whole grisly process. The Korean War had broken out, China was literally threatened by invasion and the people reacted just as Americans or members of any other nationality would have, with fear, gossip, rumors, suspicion and vengeful denunciation. Reports Seymour Topping in *Journey Between Two Chinas:*

The Communists never disclosed the total number of those executed in the nationwide purge which continued into 1952. In October, 1951, it was announced that the People's Courts alone had tried 800,000 counterrevolutionaries during the first half of 1951. In a speech on June 6, 1957, Chou En-lai stated that 16.8 percent of the counterrevolutionaries put on trial had been sentenced to death, most of them before 1952.

This would mean that at least 134,400 had been executed in the first six months of the purge. Jacques Guillerma, the distinguished Sinologist who served as French military attaché in Nanking during the Civil War and later in Peking, estimated in his *La Chine Populaire,* published in 1964, that a total of one to three million were executed. Other independent experts have made estimates ranging from hundreds of thousands to several million. The claim put forward by Nationalist officials on Taiwan that the figure was in excess of 10 million has been dismissed by most scholars as propagandistic.

As regards the nonmilitary killings, they seem to have been common even during the 1946–1949 period, when thousands of landlords who had abused and exploited the peasants over the course of many years were publicly tried and executed. While such mass slaughter cannot be justified, it bears repetition that there is a clear distinction between the two processes that lead to killing in revolutionary situations. In one the chief executioner is the *people.* In the other it is the *state,* as party, army or secret police.

For example, the German Nazi Party, some branches of the military and the Gestapo were responsible for the shattering atrocities in the 1930s and 1940s, although the German people, it has been argued, shared the moral guilt for not having spoken out against such outrages. But the general view of history has involved a far more understanding attitude toward killings by masses of common people who execute their former tormentors as part of the essential process of a violent revolutionary uprising. The same number of executions, cold-bloodedly ordered by the state, however, has in almost all historic contexts been perceived as far more evil. As for the people, it might be said, "Forgive them, Father, for they

know not what they do." They act out of an animal lust for revenge, perhaps goaded by personal suffering at the hands of their exploiters. In that collective madness known to students of mob psychology they lash out like a blind colony of creatures defending their center against whatever force is perceived as The Enemy.

The idea of public executions, while abhorrent to most—unfortunately not all—Americans, is of course not unusual in the context of thousands of years of Chinese experience. Seymour Topping of the *New York Times* was in China in the 1940s. In *Journey,* he describes an instance of public execution:

One hot afternoon in 1947 I went outside of the city [Nanking] to a large dusty field and watched, without being able to feel pity, as several of the Japanese generals who had entered Nanking in 1937 were hauled roughly from the back of a truck, their hands tied behind their backs. They were forced to their knees and executed, each with a simple pistol shot to the back of his shaven head, while a Chinese mob jostled and jeered behind a cordon of Nationalist soldiers.

Since such methods had been used for centuries by the emperors, and as this example shows were also common to the experience of Chiang Kai-shek's troops, it can hardly be argued that the Communists, in continuing the ancient practice, were introducing something new. Military forces down through history have executed prisoners, by no means always following a trial. What is significant in this case is Topping's description of the approval of the mob gathered to witness the killings.

For much the same reasons as those behind their hatred of the Japanese oppressors, thousands of Chinese peasants and workers gathered in countless unknown fields, mountainsides and streets across the face of China during the first years after the defeat of Chiang Kai-shek to cheer and applaud the execution of how many landlords, agents of Chiang's secret police, narcotics peddlers, gangsters and other enemies of the people we shall never know.

There is still a degree of mystery to this chapter of Chinese history. We should seek to clear up such mysteries, to understand what may be partially justifiable or pardonable. But we must never sweep under the rug of history large accumulations of ugly, unpalatable fact.

There is a degree, obviously, to which such matters may be described as China's business. But humankind itself is more important than any one people. Whether there is a God or not, moral standards are still important. This must never be forgotten.

20. Looking Back on the Chinese-American Debate

IT is interesting now—and instructive—to look back at American speculation on China since 1949. Anyone who assumes that the problem was nothing more than a flat matter of black and white, right or wrong is, to state the point charitably, something less than a student of the situation.

There were a number of factors that had to be borne in mind. China is the third largest nation on earth, with the largest population of all. Each year its population increases so greatly that within another thirty years half the people on earth may be Chinese. The present Communist regime has been in control of the mainland for thirty years, and though most Americans would have been pleased to see the Nationalist forces once again take control, there has not been the slightest prospect during the past three decades that they could have done so, nor is there any indication in the foreseeable future that they will be able to.

When one has a firm grasp of such basic realities one begins to understand why a November 11, 1959, report of the Senate Foreign Relations Committee stated that: "Communist China presents the most complicated and serious problem faced by the United States in Asia. It is also a problem more likely to grow than to diminish, and one for which there are no easy answers."

In trying to pick out threads that led to the present tangle I believe it will help if one realizes that, as Hans J. Morgenthau observed in *The Purpose of American Politics,*

The issue that the United States had to face in China was from the outset genuine revolution and civil war, inextricably intertwined with Russian power and Communist expansion. Such an issue provided very limited opportunities for successful outside intervention. The Chinese themselves would settle it one way or the other; outside intervention might at best facilitate and accelerate, but could not *determine* the nature of that settlement.

This much almost any casual student of the Chinese situation can understand, but Morgenthau introduced a more remarkable point:

A foreign power faced with so essentially intractable an issue would have been well advised not to commit itself too deeply on either side, to keep an avenue of retreat open in case things should go wrong, and to safeguard in advance its freedom of movement in a situation both uncertain and uncontrollable. The Soviet Union by and large followed this course of action, *giving moderate and provisional support to the Nationalists* as long as they had the upper hand and switching that support gradually to the Communists as their chances improved. The United States, on the other hand, viewed—and hence misjudged—the issue of China from the perspective of its historic experience. (Italics added.)

Conservative intellectuals know that reactionary attempts to suggest that Chiang would have won the Chinese civil war if it had not been for "traitors in the American State Department" are false. In the New York *Herald Tribune* of September 8, 1949, Walter Lippmann wrote:

On the prospects of Chiang and his government the judgment of all the generals was the same. None thought that Chiang would win, all were convinced that Chiang was losing the civil war. Marshall's estimate supported Stilwell's and Wedemeyer's supported Marshall's and Barr's reconfirmed the estimate.

Despite all this the American Right responded to Chiang's defeat by the search for scapegoats. To criticize Chiang Kai-shek was viewed as subversive. But consider: in 1947 the United States had sent an observer to China for the purpose of making a study and report. In due time the American observer returned with, among other things, a denunciation of the incompetence, corruption and weakness of the Kuomintang–Chiang Kai-shek regime. The conservative response would be, of course: "Well, what could you expect? Wasn't our State Department honeycombed with Communists? Who made this report? Have we checked his political background?"

It happens that the report was returned by a man prominent in various right-wing organizations, Major General Albert C. Wedemeyer, who was not only vigorously anti-Communist but personally friendly to Chiang Kai-shek.

In 1945, when Japan was preparing to surrender, Wedemeyer wrote the following description of the plight of many of Chiang's soldiers:

A Chinese conscript's pay can be pocketed (by his officer) and his ration sold. That makes him a valuable member of the Chinese Army. . . . As they march along they turn into skeletons, they develop signs of beriberi, their legs swell and their bellies protrude, their arms and thighs get thin. Scabies and ulcers turn their skin into a shabby cover of an emaciated body which has no other value than to turn rice into dung and to register the sharp pains of an existence as a conscript in the Chinese Army. . . . Many of those who run away run off during the first few days. Later they are too weak to run away. Those who are caught are cruelly beaten. They will be carried along with broken limbs and with wounds in maimed flesh in which infection turns quickly into blood poisoning and blood poisoning into death.

"Millions of such conscripts," says Oscar Gass, Far Eastern expert, in *Commentary,* November, 1962, "went over to the Communists without fighting."

The same summer—1945—the Military Intelligence Division of the U.S. War Department issued a *Report on the Chinese Communist Movement,* which said that

. . . the Chinese Communist Regular Army is a young, well-fed, well-clothed, battle-hardened volunteer force in excellent physical condition, with a high level of general intelligence, and very high morale. Training . . . may be rated as fair . . . even though it is woefully inadequate by American standards. Military intelligence, for their purposes, is good. The most serious lack . . . is in equipment.

But, naïve Americans might ask, Why were there any Chinese Communists to begin with? Why didn't all Chinese remain loyal to Chiang? The answers should be pondered by every concerned American. There was the poverty and oppression under which the Chinese people had suffered for centuries. Though Chiang at first, in the early 1920s, was sympathetic to the working class, and was even considered a Red by some conservatives, he changed his position in 1927 and began to repress the workers. He instituted purges in which thousands were killed. His political opponents were beheaded or shot in the streets. In his prisons mutilations and torture were common. In the rural areas peasants were burned to death, buried alive or cut to pieces.

This is one of the reasons Chiang's troops could be pushed off the mainland.

Chiang was no saint. It was, therefore, absurd to assume that he was above criticism. His subjugation of the native inhabitants of the island of Taiwan, comprising over 80 percent of the population, engendered considerable resentment there which still smolders.

In the 1950s and 1960s, since we had no way of knowing with certainty whether the Chinese had grand *territorial* designs on the rest of Asia, it was reasonable to support a Nationalist counterforce just in case. It may be said the Chinese Marxists had *ideological* designs upon at least Southeast Asia, but that does not establish that the total Asian triumph of communism, it if occurs, will have been accomplished by the force of Chinese arms, any more than Communist victories in China or Cuba were won by Russian troops.

In any event, Chiang's Taiwan armies could be effective only against the open military threat and only partially at that. Certainly they could never have been expected to attack the mainland. *Nor did his forces have anything to do with attempts to crush Communist movements in Vietnam, Laos and Cambodia.*

The one sort of force, indeed, which could have dealt with such threats was a really strong United Nations army, but rightists around the world have been alert to prevent the formation of any such power. They are not the only ones to blame, of course. The Soviet Union learned its lesson in Korea. It is probable that man generally is still not civilized enough to perceive the wisdom of, indeed the ultimate necessity for, a strong central world peace force. We seem to prefer monstrous tragedies like World War II, in which some 40 million were killed.

Conservative critics are entitled to disapprove of American handling of the Chinese situation at the time of the war between Mao and Chiang. Certainly those China experts who believed that the Chinese Communists were chiefly agrarian reformers were completely mistaken. But Chiang himself, in fact, was among those who made the mistake of calling his rivals "just agrarian reformers." With one or two exceptions, however, no critics of the administration publicly advocated the use of American fighting forces in China, which—as Hans Morgenthau and others have observed—would have been the only means of preserving part of mainland China for Chiang, if, indeed, any action by the U.S. could have achieved such a result. Vietnam would certainly cast doubt on the hypothesis.

We presumably learned in Southeast Asia that providing rightist generals with guns in not enough. There are far more important factors that determine the success or failure of specific national Communist revolutions. The most crucially important is the matter of popular sympathy. Another is the degree of local Communist Party strength and determination. We suffer from the delusion of omnipotence if we assume that it was solely in our power to "win" China, Vietnam, Laos, Cuba or other trouble spots.

So: Americans may not like the present situation in China, but it exists. We cannot deny its reality and hope to keep our political sanity.

The American public, of course, may be forgiven for deluding itself about China because it was very poorly informed about the matter. What should have been the subject for the most impartial and scholarly analysis was dealt with rather on the basis of one-sided political propaganda. I saw nothing wrong in publicity to support Chiang as against Mao Tse-tung—I supported him myself—but when such press-agentry was almost all the American people had to go on it is obvious that the results would be less than satisfactory.

On this point read *A Curtain of Ignorance,* by Felix Greene, subtitled *How the American Public Has Been Misinformed about China.*

If Mr. Greene is even one-third correct, I do not see that the best interests of either the Chinese or the American people are defended by the incredible boobism—and worse—that characterized American reporting and speculation about China for a full quarter-century.

There has been, unfortunately, a great deal of unclear thinking about almost every aspect of this complicated situation. For example, Generalissimo Chiang himself, in a letter published in the early 1960s, said, "I hope you will bring home to your audiences the truth that a free world cannot coexist with Communism, just as Our Lord cannot coexist with Satan."

The generalissimo's statement is logically absurd within the context of Christian theology. Within such a context, Christ and Satan *do* coexist. The important question to put to those who make such statements, of course, is, "How do you propose to put an *end* to the present fact of coexistence?" If the answer is "by war," then the air, at the least, will have been cleared.

If the answer is simply a call for anti-Communist efforts short of war, the response must be that this is nothing but a description of the situation as it has prevailed for half a century and as such is premised on the undeniable fact of coexistence between communism and the West. This too may be a painful reality but again nothing is to be gained by lying to *ourselves* about it.

One aspect of the problem, so far as I have observed, has attracted no public attention but I think it deserves investigation nevertheless. Why have some Americans manifested more hatred toward *Chinese* Communists than toward *Russian* Communists? This may be explained on racial lines. Think back to World War II. We were the enemies of both the Germans and the Japanese. The Germans, we now know, were guilty of far worse atrocities than the Japanese. There were no gas chambers or ovens for humans in Japan. But the Germans, after all, were white, as well as nominally Catholic or Protestant, and the Japanese were not, and so before many years had passed we had contrived to propagandize ourselves into the belief that the Japanese were subhuman savages and not the same sort of enemy at all as the blond, Nordic Germans. Cruel the Germans might be, but the Japanese were savage barbarians of a lesser race, we came to think. We had no "relocation" camps for German-Americans, only for Japanese-Americans. Because our vision of this situation is not, in the year 1980, blurred by passion and prejudice we can now perceive the rationale behind all of it as largely nonsense, but the problem faces us again when we regard the Chinese Commu-

nists. In the 1960s one heard the view that we could do business with the Russians but that there was far less hope of a meaningful exchange of views with the Chinese because they were of another kind.

If there is value to this hypothesis it may be of great significance in that it points out a pitfall which could plunge us into war. In my view, we would never have dropped atomic bombs on such enemy cities as Berlin, Hamburg or Rome, but we were able to drop them on Hiroshima and Nagasaki partly because of our hysterical belief that the Japanese were somehow creatures of a different breed. Projecting these attitudes into possible future East-West confrontations one can envision fearful consequences.

The thaw following the Nixon-Kissinger initiatives did away with this sort of racial and political madness; we once again have the Chinese in focus and recognizable as human beings, but the future is notoriously difficult to predict. One hopes that during the 1980s, at least, there will be no reversion to the former sort of delusion.

In *Letter to a Conservative,* published in 1965, I ventured a prediction:

An interesting possibility is that the generally Republican American business community will eventually become so enamored of the idea of Chinese trade—excepting, of course, war materiels—that it will exert a moderating influence on the American right wing, to which it is now the chief financial contributor. Certainly trade with Red China could become attractive to American industrialists since they could almost certainly undersell the Soviet Union and other Iron Curtain countries. Just as conservative American wheat farmers and our conservative U.S. Chamber of Commerce enthusiastically endorsed the sale of wheat to the Soviet Union so might American farmers and businessmen one day come to have the same reaction to the prospect of general trade with the Red Chinese. Some may view such an eventuality as a capitulation of principle on the part of our people. Others see trade as a civilizing, peaceful influence that may tend to make the Chinese Communists more amenable to reasonable negotiation about various knotty political matters.

By the mid-1960s we could see that our allies the British, Canadians and French were not nearly so horrified by contact with the Chinese as we were; they were growing indications that the rigid American policy of *Never* was undergoing reexamination, even by anti-Communists who originally insisted on its validity. Conservative Clare Boothe Luce, for example, long an outspoken foe of communism, knowledgeable about China and certainly no respecter of liberal sensitivities, suggested in June, 1964, that the United States should at last begin to consider the question as to how to relax tensions vis-à-vis Red China. The alternative, as Mrs. Luce saw it, was endless war in the Orient. Aid and trade with the Communist Chinese might be advisable, she suggested, and we might reap the same sort of benefits that accrued from the wheat deal with the Soviet Union. The sale of wheat to Red China, she said, could help feed "far hungrier and more desperate people than the Russians."

Events of 1976–1977 in China seemed to suggest that the edifice Mao carefully, painstakingly built was being to some extent modified, if by no means dismantled.

That the ruling triumvirate—Chairman Hua Kuo-feng, Vice Premier Teng Hsiao-ping and Defense Minister Yeh Chien-ying (Ye Jianying)—had clearly moved out into non-Maoist or even to some extent anti-Maoist policy directions was clear by late 1977. Maoist insistence on self-reliance to the relative lack of interest in foreign trade had definitely been reversed, as had the Mao–Chiang Ching stimulation of constant ideological fervor, which stressed that it was more important to be Red than expert or—shall we say—better to be Red than ahead.

The shifting emphasis, which by late 1977 was accelerating, reopened the fundamental ideological debates of the Cultural Revolution and, more surprisingly, actually indicated a move toward the policy of the long-derided Liu Shao-chi. Since Liu had been treated as a devil figure by the Chiang Ching faction, and

hence by most of the Chinese people (because Maoists controlled the media) whatever the private wishes of the present leaders might be they could scarcely rush Liu back from the political dead, as was twice done with Teng Hsiao-ping. This is not to say that such a revision of attitudes might not eventually occur but it would presumably have to be done slowly.

Linda Mathews of the *Los Angeles Times* revealed in the October 3, 1979, edition that three pictures of Liu appeared in the photographic exhibit that had just opened at Peking's National Museum of History. While the resuscitation of his reputation may have brought satisfaction to his supporters it can bring none to Liu since, it has been reported, he died of pneumonia in 1969.

By the end of 1978 there were angry demonstrations in Peking. "Long live democracy!" leaders shouted. For the first time in twenty years Chinese citizens were being permitted to speak the unspeakable. "How can the United States, a capitalist country only two hundred years old, be the most developed in the world?" one asked publicly.

By July, 1979, the Chinese legislature was able to endorse "the rule of law" by enacting the first legal codes in Communist China's history. The legislature also approved a system of direct popular elections for local offices. Shortly thereafter China published its first law since the Communist Revolution permitting foreign companies to invest capital and take profits out of the country.

In late August, 1979, a crowd of approximately two hundred poverty-stricken protesters staged a sit-in in front of the Forbidden City demanding jobs and economic justice.

By late February, 1980, there was again a swing back toward the repressive side. Vice-premier Teng Hsiao-ping had called for a constitutional amendment to abolish certain freedoms, among them the right to put up wall posters. While not denying the appeal of such activities, Teng said that their constitutional guarantee should be deleted because the practice "has consistently been abused by troublemakers and anarchists."

By October there were reports of beggars in

Gansu Province having become desperate enough to invade restaurants and snatch food from the tables of foreign tourists. Food shortages in the region were attributable not to breakdowns in Socialist production methods but to the ancient factor of drought. But the troubles, despite their cause, placed additional strain on the Chinese economy. By year's end there were additional numbers of footloose young people in China's major cities, having returned from rural communes with or without permission.

By late 1979 there was also an increase in instances of juvenile delinquency and street crime. Not surprisingly the perpetrators were the runaways and jobless youths driven by their social predicament to acts of desperation. It was clear then, by the beginning of 1980, that China's new leaders had concluded that their nation needed outside assistance if they were to solve the many problems that still troubled the Chinese economy. The nation's per capita income, after thirty years of dedicated effort, was only $13 a month. The average wage of a city worker was $30 a month. The bare figure will be misleading to all but scholars since China provides at little or no cost many services that are quite expensive in Western nations. And money buys a great deal more in China than in the U.S. It might be helpful for Americans in considering such arithmetic to recall that in the 1920s American salaries too were quite low. I worked one summer at a clothing store for $15 a week. But even when all such considerations are taken into account the per capita income in China is still very low and China is still a poor nation.

By 1980 it was clear that Mao was being downplayed. The Chinese—in the mid-1970s —gave credit to Mao for practically everything. There is a degree to which this was reasonable but another sense in which it was absurd. Mao indeed succeeded in summoning up and sustaining the collectivized energies of hundreds of millions of people, something that had never happened before, in China or anywhere else.

His theories and personal qualities of leadership obviously made their contribution. But the Chinese people have done the work themselves.

To deny this hypothesis, the Chinese, it follows, would have to argue that as a people they are no better than any other. My own view is that they are, in the most factual, literal sense, a superior people with a historically unprecedented combination of strength, patience, creativity, intelligence and determination. Five thousand years of history do not count for nothing when considering such questions. My own ancestry is Irish and German, but if anyone tells me that either of my people could have built the Red Flag Canal—in the way it was built—I must assume that his knowledge of either the Irish, the Germans or the Chinese is deficient.

To argue that the Chinese are superior does not, of course, mean that they are superior in all possible respects. This cannot possibly be the case of either a people or an individual. There are, let us say, 10,000 kinds of human activity; a person is accounted remarkable if he excels at so much as a dozen of them. That the Chinese can be shown to be inferior to the Japanese in one respect, to the Italians in another, to the French in another, and to the Jews in yet one more, is obvious. I still consider them an unusually great people.

Mao made the same mistake as Calvin and the Jacobins—if mistake it was—in believing that the state was justified in concerning itself with practically every facet and element of human experience. Most Western scholars and philosophers, including some Socialists, would argue that the state is justified in acting only in regard to matters concerning which individuals are powerless.

An individual, for example, cannot wage war against another nation or people. One man cannot tax another or he is called a robber. But it is the essence of Maoism, as it was of Calvinism, that a well-intentioned ruler, himself incorruptible and self-sacrificing, knows best what is good for his people and that if left totally to their own devices millions of individuals will create varying degrees of social chaos by following their selfish pursuits, "taking the capitalist road."

Surely it is part of wisdom to recognize that such large questions cannot be meaningfully dealt with on an either/or basis. There are very few adherents of either total anarchy or total dictatorship. But toward the center from these two extremes a reasoned case can be made for large increments of law and order on one hand or large increments of freedom on the other. Nor should those who ponder this fundamentally important question handicap themselves by supposing that, because a given solution seems preferable—in the context of its alternatives—for one nation or people, at one time, it is therefore necessarily, in the same form, the best available solution for all other cultures at all times. So while the relative freedom and prosperity of a Western capitalist nation such as the United States in the 1980s is such that only a small percentage of its people will have any serious interest in prescribing Marxist tonics for their social ills, history may ultimately decide that some such solution is called for in instances where the vast majority of a society is living in the most degrading poverty, squalor, sickness and ignorance, free-market or capitalist methods having been tried and obviously seen to fail.

Whatever the ultimate verdict of history, it will no doubt come as something of a surprise to both camps.

In the meantime rational communication is essential, even for the most selfish of motives. No one defends poverty, sickness, illiteracy. Everyone would like more freedom. We agree on that much, at least. No doubt we can learn to agree on even more.

The Soviet invasion of Afghanistan in January, 1980, led, almost immediately, to an even closer relationship between the People's Republic of China and the United States.

In February, 1980, the Western world learned, to the astonishment even of scholars, that Communist party chairman Hua Kuo-feng was in danger of being forced to relinquish the post of premier. He appeared in no danger of being banished, but there was a growing objection, among other Chinese officials, to Hua's serving simultaneously as premier and party chairman, something Mao Tse-tung had never done. The rumored move was part of a nationwide campaign to detach party political influence from the conduct of administrative and business affairs. An un-

identified Chinese source quoted by Linda Mathews of the *Los Angeles Times* said that the replacement of Hua by Szechwan Province party chief Zhao Zivang was in accordance with the wishes of vice premier Teng Hsiao-ping.

But the most dramatic turn of events, considering the longtime abuse to which Liu Shao-chi had been subjected, came on February 29, 1980, when the ruling 342-member Central Committee of the Communist Party formally contradicted Liu's Maoist critics, thus restoring in full the reputation of Teng Hsiao-ping's patron. This was apparently the ultimate repudiation of the Cultural Revolution, taking place fourteen years after that massive social upheaval had been launched.

Lest there be any misunderstanding of the Communist Party's intentions, the official announcement referred to the banishment of Liu as "the biggest frame-up" in party history.

By the summer of 1980, there were reports of growing unrest among millions of thoughtful young Chinese, not just troublemakers or shirkers. Older citizens who remembered the pre-1949 suffering could appreciate the progress made. But the young, who have known nothing but sacrifice and repeated calls for renewed revolutionary zeal were reportedly becoming restless and in some cases disillusioned.

At the present moment in history, then, two great peoples—the Chinese and the American —look at each other in some confusion and wonderment. Each lives in a troubled society. On our side of the Pacific we are dismayed by the collapse of the family, an epidemic of drug abuse, widespread financial corruption, pornography, street crime, vandalism, organized crime, pollution, radiation, poverty, deteriorating services and standards. For their part the Chinese want freedom and a higher standard of living.

The world awaits developments of this strange half-alliance, half-opposition.

These were two more surprising turns of events in the always fascinating history of U.S.–China relations. We shall see if the near future brings an acceleration of this trend.

In the meantime this volume is respectfully

submitted as a most modest contribution toward achievement of the universal ideal of peace, political sanity, social justice and human brotherhood.

Well, having visited China three times, studied it for some eighteen years, having spent four years, on and off, in writing this book, from the overly long manuscript of which perhaps another three hundred typescript pages have been eliminated, only now do I begin to get the hazy impression that I am approaching the merest possibility of understanding China, much less being able to explain it to others.

Selected Bibliography

Alley, Rewi. *China After the Cultural Revolution.* New York: Vintage Books, 1970.

————. *Fruition—The Story of George Alwin Hogg.* Christ Church, New Zealand: Caxton Press, 1967.

————. *Over China's Hills of Blue.* Christ Church, New Zealand: Caxton Press, 1974.

————. *Prisoners Shanghai 1936.* Christ Church, New Zealand: Caxton Press, 1973.

————. *Selected Stories of Lu Hsun.* Peking: Foreign Languages Press, 1972.

————. *Travels in China 1966–1971.* Peking: New World Press, 1973.

Alsop, J. W., Jr.; Bissell, R. M.; Cheever, F. S.; Childs, R. S.; Corning, Erastus II; Cross, H. P.; Hill, A. D., Jr.; Macy, H. R.; Morrow, D. W., Jr.; Pulling, T. J. E.; Schieffelin, Cooper. *That Untravell'd World.* Concord, N.H.: Rumford Press, 1928.

An Amnesty International Report. *Political Imprisonment in the People's Republic of China.* London: An Amnesty International Publication, 1978.

Ando, Hikotaro. *Peking.* Tokyo: Kodansha International, Ltd., 1968.

Belden, Jack. *China Shakes the World.* New York, London: Monthly Review Press, 1949. Introduction, 1970.

Bloodworth, Dennis. *The Chinese Looking Glass.* New York: Farrar, Straus & Giroux, 1967.

Boone, Muriel. *New Archaeological Finds in China.* Peking: Foreign Languages Press, 1973.

————. *The Seed of the Church of China.* Philadelphia: United Church Press, 1973.

Buck, Pearl S. *The Three Daughters of Madame Liang.* New York: John Day Company, 1969.

Bynner, Witter. *The Way of Life According to Lao-tzu.* New York: John Day Company, 1944.

Candlin, A. H. Stanton. *Psycho-Chemical Warfare.* New Rochelle, N.Y.: Arlington House, 1974.

Chapin, Schuyler, and Brown, Miriam L., and Leggett, John. *Arts of China.* New York: Horizon magazine, August, 1979.

————. *The Breach in the Wall.* New York: Macmillan, 1973.

Cannon, James B. *Notebook of an Agitator.* New York: Pioneer Publishers, 1958.

Chai, Winberg. *The Search for a New China.* New York: Capricorn Books, 1975.

Chaplin, Dorothea. *Chinese Literature.* Peking: Foreign Languages Press.

————. *Mythological Bonds Between East and West.* Copenhagen: Einar Munksgaard, 1938.

Chen, Jack. *Inside the Cultural Revolution.* New York: Macmillan, 1975.

Cohen, Joan L., and Cohen, Jerome A. *China Today.* New York: Harry N. Abrams, 1949.

Committee of Concerned Asian Scholars.

China, Inside the People's Republic. New York: Bantam Books, 1972.

Cotter, Rev. Francis. "Notes on Chinese Sociology." Wuchang. Not a published work.

Craighill, Marian G. *The Craighills of China.* Ambler, Pa.: Trinity Press, 1972.

Crankshaw, Edward. *The New Cold War: Moscow vs. Pekin.* Harmondsworth, England: Penguin Books, 1963.

Creel, H. G. *The Birth of China.* New York: Reynal, 1937.

Crozier, Brian; Chou, Eric. *The Man Who Lost China.* Charles Scribner's Sons, 1976.

Dedmon, Emmett. *China Journal.* Chicago: Rand McNally, 1973.

Duncan, James S. *A Businessman Looks at Red China.* Princeton: D. Van Nostrand, 1965.

Dunne, G. H., S.J. *Generation of Giants.* Notre Dame, Ind.: University of Notre Dame Press, 1962.

Fairbank, John King. *The United States and China.* New York: Viking Press, 1962.

Fessler, Loren, and Editors of *Life. China.* New York: Time, Inc., 1963.

Galbraith, J. Kenneth. *A China Passage.* Boston: Houghton Mifflin, 1973.

Glahn, Twitchett, et al. *Half the World.* New York: Holt, Rinehart and Winston, 1973.

Gordon, Eric. *Freedom Is a Word.* New York: William Morrow, 1972.

Gordon, Walter. *China—1959.* Philadelphia: American Friends Service Committee, 1959.

Greene, Felix. *China.* New York: Ballantine Books, 1961.

———. *A Curtain of Ignorance.* Garden City, N.Y.: Doubleday, 1964.

Guillain, Robert. *When China Wakes.* New York: Walker and Company, 1965.

Hardin, Harry, Jr. *China, the Uncertain Future.* New York: Foreign Policy Association, 1974.

Harrer, Heinrich. *Seven Years in Tibet.* New York: Dutton, 1953.

Hersey, John. *A Single Pebble.* New York: Bantam Books, 1956.

Higgins, Mary Tyng. *Up in Kuling and Down.* Pinehurst, N.C.: Higgins, 1968.

Hinton, William. *Fanshen: A Documentary of Revolution in a Chinese Village.* New York: Vantage Books, 1966.

———. *Hundred-Day War: The Cultural Revolution at Tsinghua University.* New York, London: Monthly Review Press, 1972.

Hobbs, Lisa. *I Saw Red China.* New York: McGraw-Hill, 1966.

Hsin, Chi. *Teng Hsiao-ping: A Political Biography.* Hong Kong: Chung Hwa Book Company, 1978.

Kahn, E. J., Jr. *The China Hands.* New York: Viking Press, 1972.

Kan, Michael M. *One Heart Full of China.* New York: Carlton Press, 1968.

Karol, K. E. *China: The Other Communism.* New York: Hill and Wang, 1967, 1968.

Koen, Ross Y. *The China Lobby in American Politics.* New York: Harper & Row, 1974.

Kubek, Anthony. *The Red China Papers.* New Rochelle, N.Y.: Arlington House, 1975.

Lacy, Creighton. *Coming Home—to China.* Philadelphia: Westminster Press, 1978.

Lacy, Walter M. *A Hundred Years of China Methodism.* Nashville, Tenn.: Abingdon Cokesbury, 1948.

Lindquist, Sven. *China in Crisis.* New York: Thomas Y. Crowell, 1963.

Lowe, E. H. *The Chinese in Hawaii: A Bibliographic Survey.* Taipei, Taiwan: China Printing, 1972.

Macciocchi, Maria Antoinetta. *Daily Life in Revolutionary China.* New York: Monthly Review Press, 1972.

MacInnis, Donald. *Religious Policy and Practice in Communist China.* New York: Macmillan, 1972.

MacLaine, Shirley. *You Can Get There from Here.* New York: W. W. Norton, 1975.

Mao Tse-tung. *Selected Works.* Vols. I, II, III, IV. Peking: Foreign Languages Press, 1967.

Maxwell, Neville. *India's China War.* New York: Pantheon Books, 1970.

Mehnert, Klaus. *China Returns.* New York: Signet Books, 1972.

Milton, Daniel, and Clifford, William, Eds. *The President's Trip to China.* New York: Bantam Books, 1972.

———. *A Treasury of Modern Asian Stories.* New American Library, 1961.

Milton, David, Milton, Nancy, and Schurmann, Franz. *The China Reader People's China*. New York: Vintage Books, 1974.

Min, Lin. *Red Flag Canal*. Peking: Foreign Languages Press, 1974.

Morgenthau, Hans J. *The Purpose of American Politics*. New York: Knopf, 1960.

Norbu, Dawa. *Red Star Over Tibet*. London: William Collins, 1976.

Nossal, Frederick. *Dateline—Peking*. London: MacDonald & Company, 1962.

Pein, Chai. *A Glance at China's Culture*. Peking: Foreign Languages Press, 1975.

Ping, Ti-ho. *The Cradle of the East*. Chicago: University of Chicago Press, 1975.

Powell, John B. *My 25 Years in China*. New York: Macmillan, 1945.

Ricket, Allyn, and Ricket, Adele. *Documents of the First Session of the Fourth National People's Congress of the People's Republic of China*. Peking: Foreign Languages Press, 1975.

———. *Prisoners of Liberation*. Garden City, N.Y.: Doubleday, 1973.

Robinson, Joan. *China—A Geographical Sketch*. Peking: Foreign Languages Press, 1974.

———. *The Constitution of the People's Republic of China*. Peking: Foreign Languages Press, 1975.

———. *The Cultural Revolution in China*. Harmondsworth, England: Penguin Books, 1969, 1970.

———. "Economic Management in China, 1972." Anglo-Chinese Educational Institute.

Ruo-Wang, Bao, and Chelminski, Rudolph. *Prisoner of Mao*. New York: Coward, McCann & Geoghegan, 1973.

Schurmann, Franz, and Schell, Orville. *The China Reader: Communist China*. New York: Vintage Books, 1967.

Selmon, Bertha L. *They Do Meet*. New York: Froben Press, 1942.

Service, John S. *Lost Chance in China*. New York: Random House, 1974.

Smith, Lloyd. *Hong Kong*. Hong Kong: Yat Sun Printing Company, 1962.

Snow, Edgar. *China, Russia and the U.S.A.* New York: Marzani and Munsell, 1961.

———. *The Other Side of the River: Red China Today*. New York: Random House, 1962.

Solomon, Richard E. *Mao's Revolution and the Chinese Political Culture*. Berkeley, Calif.: University of California Press, 1972.

Suyin, Han. *The Morning Deluge*. Boston: Little, Brown, 1972.

Suzuki, D. T. *A Brief History of Chinese Philosophy*. London: Probsthain & Company, 1914.

Tai, Dwan L. *Chiang Ch'ing: The Emergence of a Revolutionary Political Leader*. Hicksville, N.Y.: Exposition Press, 1974.

Taylor, Harry, M.D. *My Cup Runneth Over*. Ambler, Pa.: Trinity Press, 1968.

Terrill, Ross. *Flowers on an Iron Tree*. Boston: Little, Brown, 1975.

Topping, Seymour. *Journey Between Two Chinas*. New York: Harper & Row, 1972.

Tsu, Rev. Andrew Y. Y. *Friend of Fisherman*. Ambler, Pa.: Trinity Press, 1953.

Tuchman, Barbara W. *Stilwell and the American Experience in China, 1911–1945*. New York: Bantam Books, 1971.

Tyng, Ethel A. *Chinese Literature*. Vols. 5 and 6. Pinehurst, N.C.: Village Printers, 1967.

———. *The Gate of the Moon*. Pinehurst, N.C.: Village Printers, 1967.

Warner, Denis. *Hurricane from China*. New York: Macmillan, 1961.

Watanabe, Masahiro, and Rogers, Bruce. *Instant Japan*. Tokyo: Yohan Publications, 1970.

Wells, Henry W. *Traditional Chinese Humor: A Study of Art and Literature*. Indianapolis: University of Indiana Press, 1971.

White, Theodore, and Jacoby, Annalee. *Thunder Out of China*. New York: William Sloane Associates, 1946.

Yutang, Lin, Ed. *The Wisdom of China and India*. New York: Random House, 1942.

Zagoria, Donald S. *The Sino-Soviet Conflict*. Princeton: Princeton University Press, 1962.

Index

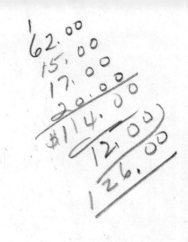

62.00
15.00
17.00
20.00
$114.00
12.00
126.00